GOD WILLS IT!

AN ILLUSTRATED HISTORY OF
THE CRUSADES

W.B. BARTLETT

SUTTON PUBLISHING

First published in the United Kingdom in 1999 by
Sutton Publishing Limited · Phoenix Mill
Thrupp · Stroud · Gloucestershire · GL5 2BU

Paperback edition first published in 2000

British Library Cataloguing in Publication Data
A catalogue record for this book is available from the British Library

ISBN 0-7509-2558-2

Cover illustrations: battle between crusaders and Muslims from Romans de Godefroy
de Buillon .et de Salehadin, *fourteenth century (Bibliotheque Nationale,
Paris/Bridgeman Art Library, London); the dome of the Rock, Jerusalem (Sonia
Halliday Photographs).*

Typeset in 11/12pt Ehrhardt.
Typesetting and origination by
Sutton Publishing Limited.
Printed in Great Britain by
Butler & Tanner Ltd, Frome, Somerset.

Jerusalem is the navel of the world, a land which is fruitful above all others, like another paradise of delights. The redeemer of the race illumined this land by his coming, graced it by his living there, made it holy by his suffering, redeemed it by his death, distinguished it by his burial. This royal city, set in the centre of the world, is now held captive by its enemies and is enslaved in heathen rite by people who do not know God. Therefore, the city demands and desires to be set free, and calls upon you without ceasing to come to its assistance.

Robert The Monk – The call to arms of the First Crusade

To Angela and Deyna

Contents

List of Illustrations and Maps

MAPS

List of Colour Plates

Picture Credits

The author and publisher wish to thank the following for permission to reproduce pictures:

Black and white (numbers given are page references):

The City of Bayeux: 9 (top and bottom), 47; Bibliotheca Lawrenziana: 241; Bibliothèque Nationale, Paris: 55, 66, 78, 93, 119, 211; Bridgeman Art Library: 31, 37, 53, 68, 71, 101, 124, 141, 147, 189, 209, 242, 247, 255, 262; British Library: 28, 76, 233; The Master and Fellows of Corpus Christi College, Cambridge: 40 (photo: Conway Library, Courtauld Institute of Art), 133, 164, 171, 226, 231, 238 (photo: Conway Library, Courtauld Institute of Art); E.T. Archive: 73, 178; Katz Picture Agency: 13, 194, 202, 206; A.F. Kersting: 15, 61, 79, 105, 112, 150 (top), 155, 157, 170, 174, 197, 203, 215 (top and bottom), 260; Mary Evans Picture Library: 27, 150 (bottom), 173, 183, 245; Monte Cassino: 42; Sonia Halliday Photographs: 84; Sonia Halliday Photographs/F.H.C. Birch (photographer): 57; Sonia Halliday Photographs/Jane Taylor (photographer): 107.

Maps drawn by Mike Komarnyckji.

Colour plates (numbers given are plate numbers):

Bodleian Library, Oxford: 6; Bridgeman Art Library: 7, 9, 11, 12, 19; British Library: 1; Burgerbibliothek, Bern: 17, 20; E.T. Archive: 2; A.F. Kersting: 10, 15, 21; Graham Lawrence: 4; Mary Evans Picture Library: 13, 18; Sonia Halliday Photographs: 5, 8, 16; Sonia Halliday Photographs/Laura Lushington (photographer): 3; The V&A Picture Library: 14.

Introduction

The story of the Crusades is one of history's richest dramas. Historians have argued for years about the significance of the Crusading movement, and continue to do so, but few would challenge the assertion that it represents one of the most colourful pageants of the Medieval world. For the student of human nature, there is everything that could be wished for and more: gallantry and cowardice; brutality and honour; wisdom and foolishness; greed and self-sacrifice. And, above all else, contradiction.

Fate also played its part, as it so often does in history. The Crusades were launched at a uniquely propitious time. Although the Byzantine Emperor, Alexius, would surely have seen an opportunity for profit in the divisions of the Turks at the time that the Crusades were launched, he would have been surprised at the extent of the success of the Christian counter-attack in the East. If the First Crusade had not been launched when the Muslim world was at its most divided, the whole concept might have died shortly after its conception. Because, by miraculous chance, it succeeded, an awesome sequence of events was launched. The emotions released were red-raw, the fanaticism of Western Christendom helping to create, or perhaps to perpetuate, a violent counter-reaction in the Muslim world.

Throughout this book, for the sake of continuity I have talked of Franks and Muslims as two discrete entities. However, these classifications, although convenient in narrative terms, are a generalisation because neither group ever represented a unified spiritual or political entity; at no time was either grouping a coherent whole. Over decades the inhabitants of Outremer, as the Christian enclave in the East became known, were described as 'Franks'. This is derived from the name given to the invaders by the Muslim world, that is the *Franj*. The French were undoubtedly dominant, and occasionally predominant, in the advancement of the Crusading ideal, but they were far from the only element to become embroiled in the affairs of the Levant. A vast array of Normans, Flemish, Germans, Italians, English, Scandinavians and Hungarians, amongst others, all played their part and in some of the Crusades launched against the Muslim East nationals from these lands took a more active role than the French.

Similarly with the Muslims, there was never one entity alone involved. There was often pretty infighting between minor Muslim principalities and, as history moves on, between the large power blocs based on Damascus and Cairo. Religiously – and we cannot underplay the role of religion in the inception of the

Crusading movement and the formulation of the Muslim response to it – at least three different main strands of Islam were involved: Sunni, Shiite, and Ismaili. Sometimes the hatred between these branches of the same spiritual tree was far greater than that evidenced between Christian and Muslim.

I have attempted to portray in this book an interpretation of the development of the Crusades in the East. History is not an exact science. Historians can often say where and when events took place, but as far as the 'why' is concerned there is room for a great deal of debate. If commentators cannot accurately ascribe motives to current affairs, then it is little wonder that the events of a millennium ago can cause intense discussion, particularly given the sketchiness and inconsistency of many of the records available.

The chronicles on which our knowledge of the Crusades is based – and there are a number of them – often contradict each other. This makes it difficult to have total confidence in our understanding of events. To quote just two examples, historians have long disagreed over the events leading up to the Battle of Hattin and the inception of the Fourth Crusade. In the case of the former, was Raymond of Tripoli a traitor, as some of his contemporaries alleged, or was he merely astute enough to realise that Muslims and Christians in the East needed to make an attempt to co-exist? And did the Fourth Crusade plan to sack Constantinople from an early stage, or did it happen through a series of accidents? In both cases, there is enough evidence in the chronicles to justify either conclusion, and to do them justice, both topics deserve a book of their own.

Herein lies one crucial factor that the reader must, from the outset, understand. The evidence on which our knowledge of the Crusades is based is sometimes limited, and often hides a hidden agenda. The chroniclers of the time, whose accounts document the story of the Crusades for us, were rarely impartial observers. Most of them were closely allied to a particular party, and as such were far from unbiased. It was in their interest to ingratiate themselves with those who led the party to which they 'belonged'. Consequently, they often overplayed the roles of the men whom they supported, while at the same time frequently diminishing the part played by other men in events.

This makes for exciting reading on occasion, but it is rarely conducive to easy historical analysis. Given this, and the frequent scarcity of corroborative evidence, my analysis represents an interpretation of events. Many of my views may be subject to an alternative perspective. Where major difficulties arise, I will attempt to make this clear in the text. However, the reader should be aware of the evidential problems that exist with any given perception.

Despite their partiality, we are fortunate in the number of chronicles that survive, often written by active participants in the Crusading movement. Fulcher of Chartres, for example, was a participant in the First Crusade and wrote graphically of it. Villehardouin, the author of a chronicle of the Fourth Crusade on which many of our perceptions are based, was an important figure in the political goings-on that shaped events. And William of Tyre, who wrote a great chronicle towards the end of the twelfth century describing the development of Outremer, was a man who lived much of his life in the region. According to some chroniclers, he also died because of its politics. The narratives of these men may be biased but nevertheless they provide the backbone for our understanding of the Crusades, and as their authors were eyewitnesses to the events described, these accounts are invaluable if treated with due caution.

What follows in this book is a description of a sequence of events that, I hope, forms a consistent narrative. Undoubtedly, not everyone will agree with all the interpretations offered. However, if I stimulate the interest of readers to the extent that they wish to read more about this fascinating and dramatic chapter in history, then my objectives will have been achieved.

CHAPTER 1

The Catalyst

In the spring of 1071 Romanus Diogenes, Emperor of Byzantium, left the relative safety of the huge walled city of Constantinople at the head of a great army. Leader of the world's oldest and longest-lived empire at that time, the Emperor, backed by thousands of troops, must have presented an impressive display. Ahead of Romanus, after the short sea crossing over the Bosphorus, lay a long march east, to the very extremities of Asia Minor itself. His mission was to protect his empire from the increasingly persistent raids of Turkish marauders. The battle that followed would mark the end of Romanus' reign. More importantly for history, it would act as one of the catalysts of the Crusading movement.

To a casual observer, the empire over which Romanus ruled may have seemed vibrant and powerful. It held dominion over Greece, Bulgaria and Asia Minor, including even some of the cities on the Syrian shores of the Mediterranean. However, even the slightest investigation into the history and present circumstances of the empire would soon correct this misguided perspective. In recent decades, the throne of Byzantium had passed through a succession of inferior emperors who, with the odd exception, had proved incapable of arresting an ever-increasing decline in Imperial affairs. Within Constantinople itself, there was a variety of factions and no emperor could rely on the loyalty of his subjects.

Romanus, albeit a man of some virtue, would, like so many of his predecessors and successors, prove to be out of his depth. Although a brave man, he lacked judgement, as events would show. And his enemies were close at hand. Among the leaders of his army were several men whose devotion to Romanus was, to say the least, questionable. The role of one of them, Andronicus Ducas, in the campaign that lay ahead would prove crucial and disastrous.

Many soldiers in this army were mercenaries. Although half of the force consisted of native troops, these were poorly armed and equipped, meaning that Byzantium's reliance on its mercenaries was disproportionately heavy. The elite of the latter was the Norman heavy cavalry, irresistible in the charge. At its head was a man named Roussel of Bailleul, a powerful and charismatic leader. Many of the Norman mercenaries had in the past proved extremely unreliable. They would serve under no one except one of their own countrymen and their loyalty to the empire was questionable in the extreme. Romanus' concerns about their reliability would not have been helped by one of the last items of news to reach him before he left his capital. For years, the Byzantine Empire had been fighting a losing battle to retain the last of its possessions on the Italian mainland. As he left

Constantinople, Romanus heard that the port of Bari had fallen, the last Italian town of importance held by the empire. It had been captured by Normans, kinsmen of the very mercenaries upon whom Romanus was now forced to rely.

The Muslim Turkish enemy whom Romanus must now face was under the command of Alp Arslan, an experienced warlord. He had been concerned that the Byzantines had been forging closer links with the Egyptians in recent years, and an alliance between these two powers could push the Turks out of the region. Alp Arslan had launched his raids into Asia Minor partly to drive a wedge between Egypt and Byzantium. He was at Aleppo when he heard that Romanus was on his way to confront him and, answering the challenge, set out to meet the Byzantines with a large force of his own. Romanus played straight into his hands.

As the two armies approached each other, Romanus made two fundamental mistakes. Individually, they were both serious but the combined effect of them was fatal. Firstly, the Emperor neglected to send out adequate scouting parties with the result that he was unaware of the movements of the Turks. Secondly, he compounded this by splitting his force in two – the troops led by Romanus made their way to the fortress-town of Manzikert while the remainder besieged the nearby fortress of Akhlat.

Romanus was not aware of the approach of Alp Arslan until the Turkish force was almost upon him. He sent out desperate orders for the troops at Akhlat to rejoin him but the enemy was already dangerously near. On 19 August 1071 the Turks prepared for the attack. Alp Arslan was apparently taken aback at the size of his opponent's army, even if it was split into two, and tried to bargain for peace. However, Romanus offered harsh terms that proved unacceptable to Alp Arslan.

The diplomatic manoeuvrings having proved ineffectual, battle was joined. It began badly for the Byzantines. When a small Turkish reconnaissance force was recklessly attacked, the Byzantine force sent to intercept it rode straight into an ambush – a favourite Turkish battle tactic. Within minutes, this force was fighting for survival. Another force was despatched to retrieve the situation, but by the time it arrived it found nothing but corpses.

The Turks then began their attack in earnest, adopting another time-honoured tactic. They circled the Byzantine army with hordes of horsemen, armed with their most popular weapon, the bow. Large groups of these horse-archers probed constantly for an opening. Where it could, the Byzantine cavalry struck back but with very limited success as the Turks simply withdrew whenever they were attacked. Their greater mobility made it easy to avoid the Byzantine counter-attacks. By early afternoon, the frustration of the Byzantines was unbearable. The pressure to strike back was overwhelming. Natural as such a desire might seem, it should have been strongly resisted. However, the rash nature of Romanus convinced him that he must attack.

Accordingly, the order was given to advance. The Turks retreated slowly before Romanus, and his troops made little impression. By nightfall, tired and hungry, the Byzantines faced about and prepared to return to camp. Although the situation was dangerous, it was not yet disastrous. But it would soon become so. Unknown to Romanus, the Norman mercenaries refused to return to help. Worse still, in the Byzantine army were many Turkish mercenaries. Fuelled partly by blood-ties, but more by the fact that they were unpaid, these Turks decided to join the forces of their countryman Alp Arslan.

The Byzantine retreat was not orderly. Gaps appeared in the ranks, which the Turks quickly sought to exploit. Romanus turned about again to face the enemy. Andronicus Ducas, however, who led a significant part of the army, would not join him. Probably motivated by his personal ambition and his disliking of Romanus, he continued to retreat. This move consigned the Byzantine army to catastrophic defeat.

A widening gap materialised between the troops of Romanus and the retreating forces of Andronicus that was quickly prised further apart by the Turks. The front line of Romanus separated into ever-decreasing pockets of resistance. His right wing broke and fled, and his left, now split apart from the centre, joined in the rout. As darkness fell, the centre collapsed. Its disintegration was followed by slaughter. Not a man of the centre escaped death or capture. Romanus had his horse killed under him, and was wounded before being made a prisoner. It was a defeat of enormous proportions.

Few battles are decisive. In Western European history, Manzikert barely merits a mention, yet its results were immense. Although it survived for several centuries more, from this day forward the Byzantine Empire began to slip ever closer to the edge of an abyss. It is not in the loss of men or material that the battle's significance lies, important though this is. It lies rather in the psychological and spiritual effects of the battle. For at Manzikert, the major casualty was the soul of an empire itself. From this epic reverse, a dramatic chain of events was set in motion.

The defeat heralded the beginning of an apocalyptic age for Asia Minor. The country, once fertile, became a wasteland, and its people were ruthlessly exploited. Villages were reduced to rubble and the native population fled the marauding Turks so quickly that often they did not even take their flocks with them. Large numbers of Turks, led by a man named Suleiman ibn Kutulmish, moved in to take over significant tracts of Asia Minor. However, the Turkish forces lacked discipline or co-ordination. Most of them were little more than packs of bandits, ambitious to take over their own territories and each with their own leader – men such as Danishmend, Menguchek and Chaka. Alp Arslan died and was replaced as overlord by Malik Shah but allegiance to him was at best nominal.

The Byzantines sought desperately for an effective response. Romanus was deposed in his absence, and when he was subsequently released and returned by the Turks it was only to die a brutal death soon after. His successor, the Emperor Michael, despatched an expedition into Asia Minor to try and restore some of the empire's lost prestige. One of the leaders of this force was Roussel of Bailleul, whose mercenaries had abandoned Romanus at Manzikert. Shortly into the venture, Roussel threw off all vestigial pretence of loyalty and cynically joined forces with the Turks. The mission failed totally.

Any residue of control over most of Asia Minor quickly slipped from the grasp of Byzantium. In Constantinople a succession of usurper emperors wheedled their way to power, and usually lost it again shortly thereafter. They were not above using Turkish mercenaries to help them in their schemes. Some of the cities in Asia Minor still held by the Byzantines were given over to these mercenaries to garrison – few reverted to Byzantine control again. Within ten years of Manzikert, the Turks had established one of their major cities at Nicaea, a holy and ancient Christian city, and only a few days journey from Constantinople.

Within Asia Minor, a few cities defied all odds and survived as nominal vassals of the Emperor, although communications became virtually non-existent. Antioch, second only in importance to Jerusalem as a Christian city in the Levant, survived until 1085 but was then lost. The Turks inexorably swept across Asia Minor to the shores of the Aegean itself. As they did so, they also pushed south into Syria and Palestine. Here, they came into conflict with the Fatimid Egyptians, who ruled Palestine at that time. Although they were also Muslims, their strand of Islam was different from that of the Turks and the two parties had great enmity for each other. Open confrontation was not long in coming. In the same year as Manzikert, the Turks took Jerusalem itself from the Egyptians.

Constantinople teetered on the edge of oblivion. However, in this hour of great need and imminent catastrophe, Byzantium at last found a leader of true worth who would give it new life and hope. Inevitably a usurper emperor, his name was Alexius Comnenus. His major rival for the throne was his brother, Isaac, who

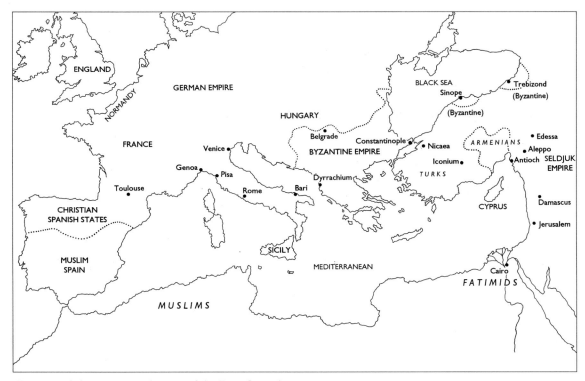

Europe and the Levant at the time of the First Crusade.

fortunately – from the viewpoint of stability – was content to take a supporting role in Byzantine politics.

Alexius quickly reviewed the situation when he took the throne in 1081. It was frankly awful. The Empire was being attacked from all sides. Apart from the chaos in Asia Minor, the Normans of Italy were attacking the Adriatic coast, while to the north Slavic tribes were pushing at the borders of Byzantium and Petcheneg Turks raided into Imperial territory with impunity. The army with which Byzantium attempted to fight back was manifestly inadequate for the purpose.

Alexius, an outstanding statesman as well as a good military tactician, was a man who employed a variety of strategies to further his goals. He knew when he should use force and when he must employ cunning, when to be magnanimous and when to be ruthless, when to forgive and when to punish. He attempted to rebuild relationships with the West which, as we shall see, had been difficult for some time. He also adopted a series of revenue-raising measures with which he financed the rebuilding of his army. Fines were imposed to the limits of extortion, and taxes introduced at exorbitant levels. Favours were sold to the highest bidder. Classical economic policy it was not, but it proved effective. The army, benefiting from its increased funding, started to recover. Important victories were won against the Normans on the Adriatic coast, and the Patzinak Turks, dangerous insurgents in the north, were overwhelmingly defeated.

However, more progress was needed in Asia Minor, crucial to the well-being of the Empire. By the combination of diplomacy and arms, a few small victories had been won even there but they were insignificant in the wider scheme of things. In the course of time it became apparent that the chances of a major and lasting success were small without outside help. Coldly analysing his options, Alexius believed that the best hope for help came from the West. Western mercenaries, such as Roussel of Bailleul, had proved untrustworthy in the past, but such men could be magnificent warriors. Tentative steps to aid Byzantium had been taken in the West by Pope Gregory VII shortly after Manzikert, but they had come to nothing. Alexius decided to resurrect the idea.

Accordingly, in 1095 a letter was composed to the current pontiff, Pope Urban II (Pope from 1088–99). Alexius 'humbly begged the lord Pope and all the faithful of Christ to send some help to him for the defence of the Holy Church against the pagans. For these pagans . . . had conquered almost all the lands up to the walls of Constantinople.' Alexius was far from simple and made few mistakes in his career, rarely misjudging situations or people. Yet even he cannot have predicted how vast would be the response to his plea, or the nature that this response would take. A tidal wave of humanity was about to sweep into the Middle East and it was Alexius' letter that unleashed it. The Crusading movement was born.

CHAPTER 2

The Christian World

To understand the incredible events that resulted from Alexius' appeal for help, it is necessary to consider the state of the world at the close of the eleventh century. Europe and the Middle East at this time could be sub-divided simplistically into three power blocs. At the eastern extreme was the world of Islam. In the west, bordering the Atlantic, were the feudal states of Western Europe, emerging, as if from a chrysalis, from the shadowy period known suggestively to historians as the Dark Ages. And, between the two, at the centre of the world, was Byzantium.

Following the death of the Roman Empire in the west, the mantle of Christian civilisation had moved to Constantinople. Constantinople – the largest city in the Christian world, bigger by far than any city in the west. Bedecked with sumptuous treasures, and cloaked in an aura of religious splendour by its magnificent churches, it could – and would – amaze travellers from the west with its opulence and majesty. Its survival had not always been assured, and it had been forced to fight off some very serious challenges from its enemies. Despite all this, more than six centuries after the sacking of Rome, Constantinople lived on.

Indeed, parts of the tenth and the early eleventh centuries can be considered a golden age for Byzantium. A great and warlike emperor, John Tzimisces, had reconquered many cities long lost to the Byzantine Empire, cities such as Antioch and Aleppo, which would play distinguished parts in the Crusades that were to come. The Empire stretched from the Adriatic, including parts of Italy, in the west to the Syrian coast and the extremities of Asia Minor in the east. However, as the Byzantines were about to retake Jerusalem – a city they had lost at the beginning of the seventh century – events elsewhere intervened, Tzimisces turned back and Jerusalem remained in Muslim hands. Nevertheless, during the early part of the eleventh century many independent Armenian states in Asia Minor were annexed and added to the Empire.

Asia Minor played an important role both in the strategy of the Byzantine Empire and in the course of the early Crusades. It was hugely important to Byzantium. Firstly, it provided a strategic buffer zone between the troublesome tribes to the east of the Empire and Constantinople itself. While it was well garrisoned and the roads across the hinterland were maintained it served in this role extremely effectively. The country also offered other major advantages. It was rich in manpower, and many of its inhabitants would serve as soldiers in the Byzantine army. Additionally, where it could be cultivated the country was very fertile and provided crucial agricultural supplies to the Empire. Its importance, as both a source of men and as the granary of the Empire, is difficult to understate.

Asia Minor and the East Mediterranean at the time of the First Crusade.

Partly because of the trauma in Asia Minor, the use of mercenaries became an integral part of the defensive strategy of the Byzantine Empire. War was treated by the Byzantines as a science, and a large number of manuals existed to guide the would-be commander. But despite this there was still something of a stigma about warfare. Byzantium's native forces suffered a high degree of attrition. Its borders were widely spread and most of its neighbours at one time or another were involved in conflict with the Empire. Not enough native troops could be raised to man the army adequately. Seriously stretched in defence of its borders, the Empire routinely turned to mercenaries for help – with, as we have already seen, limited success. This need for men was one of the motivations behind the plea for help from Alexius that prompted the First Crusade.

Throughout Byzantine history, violence could be – and often was – used as a way of furthering the aims of the state. There were frequent coups and counter-coups, which often ended with the eyes of the deposed emperor being gouged out.

However, there were other weapons in the Byzantine armoury as well as those of such an obviously military nature. War was not glorified for its own sake, and more peaceful methods were also employed, often with success. The Byzantines thought nothing of turning to diplomacy as an instrument of policy. Craft and guile were respected as much as, if not more so, than military might – a contrast to the state of affairs normally pertaining in the West, whose warriors would not readily understand the use of diplomacy as a weapon of state.

There was plenty to admire in the Byzantine world. The Byzantine mind was sophisticated. Culture was at the heart of much of the empire. This was hardly surprising as, although Byzantium theoretically existed as the continuation of the old Roman Empire, its outlook and culture were greatly effected by its Hellenistic roots. The Byzantines were a proud people, conscious of their traditions, their wealth and their standing in the world. They looked out at the newly emerging nations of Western Europe and saw only barbarians. Yet the West was vibrant and vital, with many changes taking place that would lead to its place of prominence in later times. In contrast, tired from centuries of defensive exertions, its borders seriously overstretched and short of manpower, and with economic difficulties besides, Byzantium was approaching exhaustion.

Thus, despite its long-established traditions and superficial revival in the tenth and eleventh centuries, Byzantium was an empire in a state of irrevocable decline. The Imperial throne passed through the hands of a string of usurpers, many of whom met their deaths in suspicious circumstances. Local governors in the Byzantine administrative districts (known as 'themes') became increasingly independent and the ability of the Emperor to maintain centralised control over his widely dispersed dominions was seriously eroded. And the necessity of hiring large numbers of mercenaries to protect the infrastructure of the Empire served both to highlight its integral weakness, and to exacerbate such frailties further. The renaissance epitomised by the reconquests made by Tzimisces in the tenth century was in fact the deceptive flickering of a dying flame. The Byzantine Empire was terminally ill, its end still centuries away but, even at this stage, pre-ordained.

In theory, Byzantium and Western Europe shared a Christian faith that should have brought the two cultures together. The reality was somewhat different. Western Europe provided a number of contrasts to the Byzantine Empire. Many of its nations were newly formed and peopled by men who prized military prowess above most other virtues. Only a few generations earlier, some of the leading races of Western Europe had been pagan marauders who had primarily converted to Christianity because of the respectability that acceptance of the Christian faith appeared to confer. This is not to say that the descendants of these men now held no deep Christian conviction of their own. Indeed, the opposite was the case. The eleventh century in Western Europe was a time of great religious change. Driven on by a renaissance in monastic institutions, of which the most famous but by no means the only example was that of Cluny in the east of France, an intense religious feeling was abroad in Europe. It could be witnessed in the large number of itinerant preachers present in society, who often acted independently and beyond the control of the official Church and who were to be instrumental in the evolution of the First Crusade. Equally, it was present among the laity, who experienced sometimes enormous hardship and deprivation on the pilgrimages they made to the places that were of especial importance to their faith.

The Christianity of Western Europe was one that, judged by modern standards, might appear to be full of contradictions. Today perhaps we equate Christianity with pacifism, but violence was rife within eleventh-century society. One reason for this can be traced back to the beginning of the ninth century, at which time the Emperor Charlemagne had imposed a significant

The state of military architecture in the West at the start of the Crusades – a motte and bailey castle being erected in England. (The Bayeux Tapestry – 11th century. By special permission of the City of Bayeux)

This famous section of the Bayeux Tapestry illustrates well the state of arms and armour in the period immediately before the Crusades. (The Bayeux Tapestry – 11th century. By special permission of the City of Bayeux)

degree of order over his lords. Subsequent to Charlemagne's death, however, centralised control had been eroded. In place of this centralisation, local lords began to exercise more autonomy in their actions. This was the beginning of feudalism in Western Europe, when each man had his lord in a hierarchical society. The rule of order was seriously stretched as the local lords began to assert their power more aggressively, and they did not hesitate to use violent means both to protect their own rights and to interfere with the rights of others. Tangible evidence of the aggressive nature of Western Europe at this time can be seen in the gaunt stone donjons of the lords, which appeared with ever-increasing frequency during the period leading up to the Crusades; places of refuge in times of trouble, certainly, but equally a blunt and all too visible statement of dominance. It is easy to perceive why the Byzantines regarded the West as the home of barbarians.

Writing in *c.* 1015, the Archbishop Adalbero divided society in Western Europe into three classes: those who prayed (the clergy), those who fought (the lords), and those who worked (the laity). According to Adalbero, the clergy were at the top of this hierarchy because they interceded with God. They were followed by the lords, and finally the laity. Despite this formalised approach, each class had to be dependent upon the others if society were to thrive. However, there were grave frictions within this hierarchy that helped to shape the environment within which the Crusades evolved. The oppression of the lords, and the harmful effects of their violence on both the clergy and the laity, led to the development of so-called peace movements, which attempted to impose 'the Peace of God' on the world.

The peace movements were coalitions between some elements of the Church and the laity. Their formation was a well-intentioned attempt to impose some order on the military aggression of the lords. It is perhaps understandable that self-interest lay at the root of this, the establishment of such movements representing a desire to protect the property of the Church and the well-being of the laity. Lords were asked to pledge peace towards both the possessions of the Church and unarmed clerics. Various truce days were set aside on which men could not fight; only a few at first, but over the course of the eleventh century their scope broadened until eventually the days that warfare was not allowed exceeded those when it was permitted. Inevitably, these injunctions were frequently ignored – the Battle of Hastings, for example, was fought on a truce day despite the fact that William the Conqueror had sailed to England with the blessing of the Pope.

Not everyone who was a member of the clergy agreed with the peace movements. To some, the ideas propounded seemed dangerously radical. Ultimately, the movement would fail in many of its objectives; in one famous example at Benecy in France, a League of Peace was crushed in battle when it attempted to impose its non-violent objectives by force. Seven hundred clerics reportedly died in the fight. In many areas, where objectives were not achieved outright, they were at least modified to meet local realities and, instead of rejection of violence in toto, regulation became the goal – an important precedent for the Crusades. Unable to ban war, the Church would seek to control it.

The attitude of the Christian Church towards violence is a complex one with a long history. Whether Christians could shed blood with a clear conscience or not had been the subject of intense debate for centuries. St Augustine, the late Roman writer who was still an important theological source in the Medieval period, espoused the 'Just War' whereby wars could be waged 'by command of God'. Augustine felt that war-like acts by Christians were admissible either in self-defence or to recover lost possessions; the second criterion in particular gave wide latitude to interpretation. There were later attempts by some pontiffs to further justify violence in defence of the Church. One, Pope Leo IV, in the ninth century, declared that if a man were killed in battle while defending the Church then he would receive a reward in heaven. Later still, others stated that those dying for such a cause should have their sins remitted – an important consideration to Medieval man. However, not everyone agreed with this stance, and some theologians were particularly incensed by wars fought against fellow Christians.

During the eleventh century, the Church engaged in a policy of directing aggression towards non-Christian enemies. It was a short step from allowing Christians to commit violence in certain circumstances to actually encouraging them to do so. Significantly, there were several major confrontations between Muslim and Christian forces in Western Europe during the century before the First Crusade was called. One was in Spain, where Muslims had ruled large parts of the country for hundreds of years. A great Christian counter-offensive was launched that, in a process known as the *Reconquista*, began to win back the country from Islamic forces. Pope Alexander II endorsed the warfare by giving it his explicit blessing, while ten years later, in 1073, Pope Gregory VII encouraged the leaders of Western Europe to join the conflict. These were significant events in the creation of the climate within which the Crusades evolved. The idea that a Christian might receive endorsement from his spiritual peers for waging war on non-Christians was an important one.

The period also saw some dramatic events affecting the position of the Papacy, so much so that one historian, R.W. Southern, describes the changes that occurred as 'the most remarkable fact in Medieval history'. At the turn of the millennium, bishoprics were the gift of princes, who often used them as a source of income or a means of gaining influence. The Papacy was equally under the control of lay authority, in the form of the Holy Roman Emperor, and most Popes were at this time secular appointees.

However, from the middle of the eleventh century onwards several pontiffs challenged this process. One of them, Nicholas II, in his Election Decree (1059), outlined what amounted to a Declaration of Independence; he stated that from now on only a small group of clerics would elect the Pope. This was an overt statement of a radical concept – that the Pope was independent of secular authority and indeed that the authority of the Church was superior to lay authority. It was an important development. The monasteries, then enjoying a strong revival in their position in society, were inward-looking, 'Noah's arks' as one writer has described them, where those who sought God could take shelter from a troubled world in their attempts to find fulfilment. In contrast, the Papacy chose not to set itself apart from the world but rather to shape it in a more acceptable way. Because of its attempts to challenge the status quo of the secular world, and its efforts to address its internal problems, the institution at this period is known to historians as 'The Reform Papacy'.

Following this threat to the Imperial prerogative, an explosive confrontation occurred during the primacy of Pope Gregory VII (Pope from 1073 to 1085). The Holy Roman Emperor, Henry IV, attempted to assert his right to appoint his own bishops but Gregory chastised him. Henry IV ignored Gregory's protests, whereupon Gregory launched a spiritual thunderbolt in his direction in the form of a sentence of excommunication. This was a bold move on his part; Henry was the most powerful man in Western Europe and would not acquiesce to such threats with impunity.

However, support for Henry fell away and he was forced to seek pardon from Gregory. In what must be one of the most dramatic moments in the history of the Medieval Church, the Emperor of the Holy Roman Empire was forced to stay outside the gates of the town in which Gregory was resident for three days, barefoot and dressed in humble woollen garments. Eventually, Gregory let him in and a reconciliation was affected although, unsurprisingly, it did not last. Henry appeared to win this particular contest when Gregory was eventually forced to flee from Rome and died in exile. However, all this is a striking example of the conflict for supremacy that was being fought, and would continue to be fought, between the secular authorities and the clerics. It was also a powerful statement of a much more confident and independent Papacy – one that would feel empowered to launch a Crusade. The Papacy would not reach the zenith of its power for some time after the primacy of Urban II, and for years pontiffs such as him would act in opposition to an Imperially nominated Anti-Pope, but its authority and self-belief expanded dramatically during this period of confrontation, which would be called the 'Investiture Conflict' by later historians. Without this change in mood, the Crusades would not have developed as and when they did.

Such lofty power struggles would have been lost on many of the laity. Everyday existence for ordinary folk provided more than enough challenge to occupy their minds. The threat posed to their well-being from the growth of feudalism and the increasing power of local lords was frightening enough in itself. Living a hard life of poverty and struggle, their suffering was not helped as the land available to them for cultivation decreased as population and usage grew. An increasing number were forced to look for itinerant work in small towns or the countryside. To add to their trials, the eleventh century saw more than its share of famine and pestilence. In *c.* 1032 the chronicler Glaber wrote in horrific terms, describing how children were kidnapped and eaten because no other food was available. Even allowing for exaggeration, this suggests a society that was suffering appalling deprivation. As a result of these pressures, a large number of migrants existed, moving listlessly across the face of the land. It meant that many men had few ties to land or property and, according to one contemporary writer, when the call to go on Crusade came they would be easily persuaded to abandon their lands as these had been 'plagued for some years by discord among the people, famine and many deaths'.

Perhaps the immediacy of these terrors was the impetus behind the piety that characterises this period in history. Men were genuinely devout in their attitude to Christianity. It was a religious ethos that relied more on action than contemplation; indeed, outside of the monasteries few men could read. Nevertheless, Man was acutely aware of the existence of sin in the world. 'Life on earth' was seen as a proving ground for life in the hereafter. Doomed as he was to sin against God, Man must do something to achieve forgiveness for those sins. Only then could he hope to be spared the horrors of hell when this life ended, and the next began. The inner thoughts of these people were probably rarely motivated by complicated theological discussions, but were driven by these very fundamental and uncomplicated beliefs. The vision of divine punishment was a terrifyingly real one to the people of the era. Its most obvious manifestation was the fear that the world was about to end, both in the year 1000 and also as the thousandth anniversary of the death of Christ approached. These millenarian manifestations are the more extreme demonstrations of the fear of retribution that haunted the minds of many at that time, but they give us invaluable insights into the psyche of the age.

As a result of these beliefs, men would often go to considerable lengths to earn forgiveness. The most obvious example of this was that of the pilgrimage. The

For medieval man, the horrors of hell were a reality. Here, heaven and hell are depicted in a thirteenth-century mosaic on the ceiling of the Baptistery in Florence.

desire to stand on the very ground where prophets have stood is found among most of the world's leading religions. The Muslim *hajj* – the pilgrimage to Mecca – is still an integral part of Islam. Christianity was no exception in this respect. As early as the fourth century, pilgrims visited the Holy Land to see the sites that had played a fundamental part in the history of their religion. From that point on, pilgrimage was an important aspect of the Christian's devotions. Not everyone accepted its merits – Augustine for one felt that it did little good – and it would be more popular at some stages of history than others. However, in time it became established as a hugely popular way of expressing religious devotion.

Partly, of course, the attraction of pilgrimage was vicarious – a hope that by visiting a spot where a holy person had once stood, something of their influence would remain with the pilgrim. There would also be many relics at the sites visited by the pilgrim. The remains of the prophets and saints of Christianity were deemed to be imbued with great power. Pilgrims hoped that by visiting them great benefits might accrue; saints were deemed to be able to make barren marriages fertile, or to restore failing health. People would go to extraordinary lengths to visit these relics, and would often try to bring them back home if they had power or money enough to affect this. There are examples extant of relics being stolen from one church and carried to another, so efficacious was their power believed to be. They were at the heart of Medieval Christianity, leading one historian, Luchaire, to state that 'the true religion of the Middle Ages, to be frank, is the study of relics'. Relics were an integral part of the faith of the Medieval Christian, and the extent to which belief in their effectiveness could motivate the devout was considerable.

Pilgrimage also had another important facet – it required sacrifice on the part of the pilgrim. It was expensive for the pilgrim to travel, and it also involved danger. Contemporary chroniclers describe how on occasion pilgrims were attacked and killed while on their journeys. Partly because of these sacrifices, pilgrimage was regarded as a penitential act. Pilgrims believed that God could be moved by their actions and would be more inclined to forgive their sins as a result of participation in a pilgrimage. Even the great of society would go to extraordinary lengths to redeem themselves in the eyes of God through such a journey. One such example was Swein Godwinnson, a leading noble in England, who was involved in a murder. In contrition, he set out on a pilgrimage to Jerusalem in 1051. He died in the mountains of Anatolia – in an attempt to make his penance even greater he was walking barefoot through them when he expired from exposure.

During the tenth and eleventh centuries, there were two elements in particular that encouraged the growth of pilgrimage. The monastic revival, emanating from the Abbey at Cluny, approved of such journeys, and therefore men were encouraged to take part in them. In addition, the resurgence of the Byzantine Empire in the tenth century opened up the land routes across Asia Minor and improved access to the Holy Land. Before this, journeys had tended to be made by sea – relatively safe and quick, but expensive. Travel overland was slower but cheaper, enabling many more to make the journey.

Centres of pilgrimage became thriving communities, the greatest of which were Santiago de Compostela in Spain, Rome and – *primus inter pares* – Jerusalem itself.

The Muslim rulers of Jerusalem welcomed the pilgrims as they brought some economic benefit to the city. Occasional problems arose, such as when the Church of the Holy Sepulchre, the greatest church in Christendom, was destroyed by the Muslim ruler al-Hakim in 1009, but they were decidedly the exception. The pilgrimage cult would exaggerate the status of the holy places in the eyes of the believer. Of nowhere was this more true than Jerusalem, to many Christian travellers truly God's city on earth. This image was developed by many of the itinerant preachers, who spoke in biblical imagery so vivid that some simple people tended to confuse the earthly and the heavenly Jerusalem. As a result, Jerusalem itself had a strong symbolic appeal to the Christian. Its loss to a perceived enemy of the Christian religion was likely to result in a powerful reaction. In the context of the Crusades, it is significant that there were some very large pilgrimages to Jerusalem during the course of the eleventh century.

The east end of the Greek Church in the Church of the Holy Sepulchre, Jerusalem.

The growth of pilgrimage and the importance of Jerusalem as a religious centre provided strong spiritual reasons to make a Crusading call attractive. There were other, less altruistic motivations why men might be encouraged to join a Crusade. There was a vitality and a quest for growth within Western society at this time that manifested itself in increasingly expansionist ways. Expansionism was not a new feature in the West, and neither did this period see its climax, but many examples of it can be found. Some expansionism was directed from one West European power towards another, such as the conquest of England by William the Conqueror. However, expansionism was also directed outside of the boundaries of Christendom. An example of this that has already been touched upon is the *Reconquista* in Spain. In such conflicts, religious reasons underpinned the actions of the participants – it is significant that many of the warriors who took part in the Spanish campaigns were attempting to re-open the pilgrim roads to Compostela – but there were other considerations as well.

For example, various social factors nurtured the phenomenon. Primogeniture became an increasingly common feature in northern France during the tenth century, and in southern France and Germany in the eleventh. This restricted the amount of land available to younger sons for their inheritance, facing many with a choice between either a career in the Church or adventures abroad to win territory for themselves (the career of Baldwin, younger brother of Godfrey of Bouillon during the First Crusade provides a good example of this). The lure of plunder in the form of more portable goods also attracted many to the Crusades – as it attracted men throughout the Medieval age and, of course, in most other periods of history. This is not to say that these material motives were the primary factor in the reasons for the Crusades' popularity. There are many instances of Crusaders, both lord and commoner, suffering great deprivations during their journeys; the rate of attrition during the First Crusade was appalling and for every successful pilgrim completing his passage to Jerusalem, many more would die en route. Such self-sacrifice suggests deeply held convictions among the Crusaders. However, the expansionism of the age created an environment conducive to the development of the Crusading movement, and material motives were an important, if often secondary, impetus for many of those taking part in it.

It would be wrong to consider the increasingly outward-looking nature of Western Europe purely in terms of military expansionism, important though that was. It can also be witnessed in the economic opportunism of some of the developing states in the West, who had been building trading links with both the Byzantine and the Islamic worlds for many years before the Crusades. Many Italian cities, such as Amalfi, benefited from this. Another city, Venice, had, by the turn of the millennium, secured for itself significant advantages over its rivals with the Emperor in Byzantium. The existence of these trading links means that the Orient was far from unknown to the West before the Crusades began. Equally, the process was a two-way one; the Islamic writer Ibn Hawqal writes knowledgeably of Amalfi in 977, demonstrating that parts of the West at least were well known to the Muslim world. These links, and the knowledge that came from them, stimulated the commercial interest of the West in the Eastern world. In the midst of the militarism of the Crusades, it is easy to overlook the economic aspects of the movement, which also played an important role. As we shall see, the leading Italian city-states, especially Venice, Genoa and Pisa, played a prominent and sometimes decisive role in the Crusading movement.

Contacts between the West and Byzantium had been encouraged considerably by the growth of pilgrim traffic in the tenth century. The land routes across Asia Minor were very popular, as the roads across the country were relatively safe to travel at that time. Byzantium generally welcomed these visits as they were financially beneficial. Many of the pilgrims were drawn to Constantinople as, among other things, it possessed a vast stock of relics. There were occasional problems – for example, the decision of the Byzantine Emperor to impose taxes on the pilgrim traffic in the eleventh century caused understandable resentment.

Despite the civility between Byzantium and the pilgrims who journeyed there, in the second half of the eleventh century relations between Eastern Christendom and the West – or, to be more specific here, the Normans – deteriorated markedly. A major flashpoint was Italy. The Normans were an opportunistic race, who had first made an impression in Italy when small groups of adventurers had made their way to the region in the years immediately following the millennium. It was not long before they seized the opportunities given by the condition of the country at that time to build and expand their own territories. When this expansionism began, the Byzantines still held significant territories in Italy and they were among the first to suffer from the Norman threat. The country gradually slipped completely from the grasp of the Byzantines with, as we have already seen, Bari being the last bastion to fall on the eve of Manzikert. The aggression of the Normans in Italy naturally enough created a strong counter-reaction in Byzantium with the result that, for a time during the middle years of the century, the pilgrim traffic experienced some difficulty. The Normans' Italian campaigns also brought them into conflict with the Papacy.

Neither was the disposition of Byzantium towards the Normans improved by the actions of the latter in the years after Manzikert. Once the Norman territories in the south of Italy and Sicily (at that time in Muslim hands) had been secured, the adventurers then turned their attentions to the lands across the Adriatic. The disaster at Manzikert, and the ensuing chaos in Imperial affairs, made the lure of the Byzantine lands on the shores of the Adriatic an irresistible one to the Normans. Accordingly, they launched a raid in 1081 when a great Norman leader, Robert Guiscard, sent his son Bohemond to conquer Corfu and then move on to the vital Byzantine port of Dyracchium. Ultimately, the expansionist movements of the Normans into the Byzantine domains would be repulsed by the advent of Alexius Comnenus. However, such actions of course could not fail to arouse the deep distrust of the Byzantines. It is not difficult to imagine the thoughts of Alexius when he was informed that one of the leaders of the First Crusade who had responded to his plea for help was that same Bohemond who had been so prominent an enemy in these confrontations between the Normans and the Byzantines.

At the secular level then, there was much distrust of the West and its armies – particularly the Normans – before the Crusades began. A recognition of this will help to explain some of the subsequent dealings between Eastern and Western Christendom. Neither was there consensus at a spiritual level. Particularly, the claims of the Papacy to supremacy were not acceptable to Byzantium, where the Emperor was regarded to be supreme in spiritual as well as secular affairs, even by the leading Greek (Byzantine) churchman, the Patriarch of Constantinople. The idea of the Patriarch humiliating the Emperor, in the manner that Pope Gregory had humbled the German Emperor Henry IV, would have been unthinkable. The Pope was acknowledged as holding a special place in the Church, and would have even been deemed to be a 'first among equals', but that was held by the Byzantines to be the limit of the Papacy's unique status.

There were also doctrinal differences between the Byzantine Church (also known as the 'Orthodox' Church) and the Roman (or Latin) Church, led by the Pope. In the context of the times, these differences assumed serious proportions. Some Greek emperors were inclined more towards accommodation with the Latin Church than was deemed desirable by the leading Greek Churchmen. A crisis point was reached in 1053. The need for an alliance between the Papacy and the Byzantines against the aggression of the Normans in Italy was widely acknowledged, and discussions were held to explore the possibility of affecting this. However, there was opposition from the Patriarch at that time, Michael Cerularius. He was deeply opposed to closer ties with the Latin Church. The Pope, Leo IX, sent delegates to Byzantium to try to advance negotiations, which were proving difficult. Leo then had the misfortune to fall into the hands of his Norman enemies before the negotiations were concluded. He was subsequently held as a prisoner for nine months. Cerularius decided that this made further negotiation pointless. Leo's delegates attempted to carry on regardless, but without success. Finally, incensed by the intractability of the Patriarch, they resolved to leave Constantinople. Before they did so, they strode down the aisle of St Sophia, the greatest church in Constantinople, and flung a bill of excommunication on the High Altar.

This was a dramatic and symbolic statement, though it should be remembered that Cerularius was the target of the excommunication and not the Byzantium Empire in totality. However, it highlighted the different views regarding the status of the Papacy held in East and West. Neither would the situation improve significantly in subsequent decades. The Papacy attempted to interfere in the affairs of the Eastern Emperor as well as the Western, and when the Byzantine Emperor Michael VII was deposed his successor, Nicephorus, was excommunicated. When Alexius Comnenus in his turn replaced Nicephorus, he was also excommunicated. Indeed, for a time following this the Latin churches in Constantinople were forced to close (as they were following the dispute with Cerularius) – a state of affairs that led the modern historian Sir Steven Runciman to declare that, at this time, 'relations between eastern and western Christendom had never before been so cold'.

Urban II attempted to rebuild bridges with Alexius, and the excommunication on the latter was removed. However, these symbolic gestures, significant in their own way as they were, were not enough on their own to change the fundamental attitudes held by the different societies of Christendom. Unfortunately, when the Crusades brought East and West into closer contact, there came to light crucial and potentially irreconcilable differences in approach between the two halves of the Christian world. Alexius had asked for mercenaries, men who would be accountable to him and who would meekly restore lost Byzantine lands when they reconquered them. The men from the West did not see things in this light at all. They did not understand the diplomacy often employed by the Byzantines in their dealings with the Muslims. Sadly, events would demonstrate that East and West were so different in the views that they held of the world in general, and of the reasons for the Crusades in particular, that difficulties between the two were not only probable, they were virtually inevitable.

CHAPTER 3

Islam and the East

In the year 622, in the city of Mecca, a preacher named Mohammed gathered around him a small group of followers. He taught a new religion, one influenced by Judaism and Christianity, but possessing its own unique beliefs. His teachings were not instantly accepted, so much so that he had to flee from the city, but they struck a chord deep in the psyche of at least some of his listeners. A band of supporters gathered around him, who fought on behalf of the new creed. By the time he died in 632, Mohammed was lord of much of Arabia. Many legends grew around him, not least of which was the tale that, in a dream, he had been transported into heaven from Jerusalem. Thus Jerusalem, already a sacred place to both the Jews and the Christians, also became sanctified in the eyes of the followers of Mohammed.

The rise of Mohammed and his successors was truly meteoric. It might have seemed miraculous that the Prophet had managed to win much of the Arabian Peninsula for himself but this achievement pales in comparison with what followed. Buoyed by their success, his followers sought to widen their sphere of influence. The Persians, a significant power in the Middle East, were ejected from Bahrain. Small raids were then launched by the adherents of the new religion, known as Islam, into Palestine. These grew in intensity. The city of Gaza on the shores of the Eastern Mediterranean was captured. At the time, Palestine was part of the Byzantine Empire. A confrontation between the fresh and triumphant forces of Islam and the Byzantines was inevitable.

On 20 August 636 the Byzantine army was routed on the banks of the River Yarmuk, a defeat rich in symbolism, denoting as it did the escalating might of Islam and an enormous threat to the existing balance of power. Then in 638 Jerusalem itself fell. A year later, Egypt was invaded. By the end of the eighth century, North Africa was in the hands of the Islamic forces, to be followed soon after by Spain. The advance continued into France and was only halted at Poitiers. However, even this latter victory did not seriously threaten the vast Empire of Islam, which remained securely ensconced in Spain for another three centuries. Within one hundred years of the death of its founding prophet, the dominions of the new faith stretched from the shores of the Atlantic in the west to India. Even Constantinople itself was attacked, although the lack of experience in siege warfare of the Islamic forces would, for the time, prove conclusive.

The new faith held certain fundamental beliefs. It did not experience any philosophical difficulty in expanding its aims by force. The concept of Holy War, the *jihad*, was embraced enthusiastically by the followers of the creed of Mohammed, the Muslims. By the sword, much of the known world was won for the Prophet. However, in victory Islam proved a tolerant religion. Mohammed had taught that the 'People of the Book', the Jews and the Christians, should be respected. Largely, his teachings were followed. With occasional exceptions, neither Jew nor Christian was persecuted in the lands captured by the Islamic forces. They were allowed to keep their faith and their places of worship, although there were some restrictions placed on them and they had to pay a special tax, known as the *jizya*. There were no attempts to convert them to Islam, and they were treated generally fairly.

Indeed, many Christians still lived within the Islamic Empire in Syria and Palestine. Many of them did not share the Orthodox beliefs of the Greek Emperor but had their own way of practising Christianity, neither Greek nor Roman. Differences in ritual and belief had, on occasion, led to them being regarded as heretics by the Greeks, and consequently there was a mutual antipathy between the Syrian and the Orthodox Greek Christians. The Syrians benefited from the tolerance of their new Muslim masters, enjoying a greater degree of freedom than had ever been the case when they were under Byzantine control. Many of them owed little loyalty to their former Christian Emperor, and presumably had little desire to be ruled by him again.

However, Islam had its own problems. With the benefit of hindsight, it is perhaps transparent that the Islamic Empire was too widely dispersed, and contained too many different cultures, to continue as it did in its initial glorious decades of conquest. The first great dynasty of Islam, the Omayyad, was replaced after a bitter civil war by a new dynasty, the Abbasid, in the eighth century. The status of chief city of the Muslim world, which had already been moved from Medina to Damascus, was then transferred to Baghdad. Here a magnificent culture flourished, endowed liberally with artists, scientists and poets. However, the scientific and artistic creativity of Baghdad could not disguise the fact that Islam was divided, its power base too widely spread to survive unchanged. Over the next three centuries, the Islamic Empire began to unravel. Spain, in the far west, asserted its independence early on and other regions followed suit. There were numerous rebellions in most parts of the empire as the centralised control nominally focused on Baghdad became ever less a reality. By the time the eleventh century approached its close, it was apparent that the unity of Islam was a mirage. And in the discord of the Muslim world lay Christendom's greatest hope of success in any Crusade that might be launched.

Some of the disputes within Islam were political in nature. Local governors, aware of the weakness of central government in Baghdad, were not slow to attempt to profit from this for selfish reasons. However, there were also serious and fundamental doctrinal differences within Islam. Two distinct sects had developed, known as the Shiites and the Sunnis. The Shiites believed that spiritual authority was held by the holy men who claimed their descent from Ali, the son-in-law of Mohammed. The Sunnis disagreed with this view. Their spiritual leader was the Caliph, resident in Baghdad. Over time, the real power of the Caliph would be eroded as the Abbasid dynasty, on which he depended, declined but the symbolism of his position would remain significant. Increasingly, differences between these two sects became more exaggerated and bitter. Fragmentation within Islam thrived on the disputes between these two branches of the faith (and indeed continues to do so in the modern era). Two distinct power blocs developed within the Muslim world. Beneath them, a multiplicity of individual cities and small states asserted independence or at best were only prepared to pay lip service to supporting one or the other party. The situation became acute, especially in the Muslim lands of the Levant.

The Shiite branch of Islam found its strongest support in the shape of the leader of Egypt, the head of the Fatimid dynasty. As the strength of the Caliph in Baghdad weakened, the influence of Egypt grew. By the end of the tenth century, not only was the Fatimid ruler in control of Egypt but he also held southern Syria, including Palestine. At one point the major Greek city of Antioch was attacked, and this at a time when the Byzantine Empire was in the ascendancy once more. The Egyptians took dramatic steps towards opening up trade, which

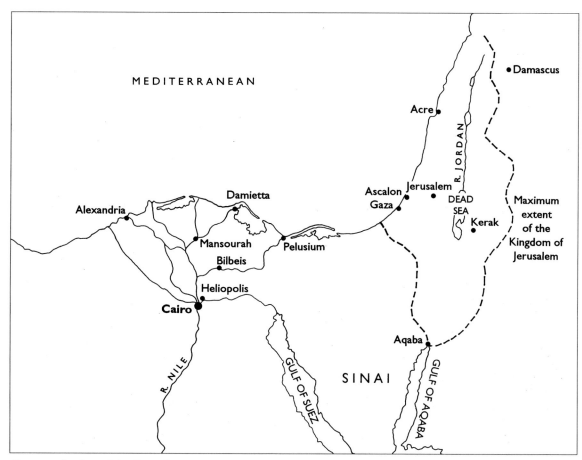

Egypt at the time of the Crusades.

had a significant impact on the west. They were helped by the increasing pressure on trade routes across the Middle East, as a result of which the Red Sea became an increasingly important conduit for commerce between West and East. The Fatimids were quick to exploit the opportunities for trade offered by the Mediterranean. Commercial links developed, particularly in the first instance with the merchants of Amalfi in Italy. So strong were these links that by the 1030s Italian vocabulary could be found in the Muslim language. Indeed, in the year 1070, merchants from Amalfi built a hospital in Jerusalem. This was to become the Hospital of St John, the guardians of which were to play a major role in later Crusader history as the Knights Hospitaller.

However, momentous changes were about to take place in the Middle East, resulting in a serious disturbance to the political equilibrium of the region. These would alter the situation in the area dramatically, and would both lead directly to the calling of the First Crusade and explain its ultimate progress. A new Muslim power was about to play a major role in Middle Eastern politics, in the shape of the Turks.

The Turks were a nomadic people from the steppes of central Asia. To speak of them as one coherent racial grouping would be misleading; there were many different clans of Turks, who were often at odds with each other. They were in broad terms a people who had strong migratory tendencies and who were not slow to exploit any opportunity for gain that presented itself. In the tenth century they were ruled by the Persian Samanid dynasty. Through this ruling caste, they were converted to Islam. Although they might have been late to accept the teachings of the Prophet, and although there were still strong paganistic tendencies within some of the Turkish clans, all the same they became staunch defenders of their faith, which was of the Sunni persuasion.

The Turks had long been raiders, even into Asia Minor. During the tenth century, their raids into the region became so irritating that they acted as the catalyst for a period of reconquest in the region, initiated by the Greek Emperor Basil II. However, their greatest expansion took place in the eleventh century. The Samanids were ejected, and the Turks assumed self-rule. A large empire in central Asia was quickly built. Turkish influence spread throughout the Muslim world, often as a result of the many mercenaries of Turkish extraction who were employed by a number of Islamic armies. Ironically enough, they also frequently found themselves in the employ of the Byzantines.

One of the Turkish clans was known as the Seldjuks. They became increasingly aggressive and powerful and in 1050, under their leader Tughril Bey, they launched a devastating incursion into Persia, conquering much of the country. However, this dramatic turn of events was soon to be overshadowed by something of even greater import. The Caliph in Baghdad had become an increasingly powerless figurehead. Alarmed particularly by the threat posed from the heretic Shiite Fatimid dynasty in Egypt, he desperately needed a protector. Accordingly, in 1055, he invited Tughril Bey into his city to assume this role. The Turks accepted his offer eagerly. They were Sunni Muslims, and as such they had respect for the position of the Caliph as a spiritual leader. Of course, it was also a great opportunity to increase their power base, and to assume a degree of legitimacy from such an important symbol within the world of Islam.

Their impressive advance did not stop there. Seldjuk raids into Asia Minor increased in intensity and penetrated far into the heartlands of the country. Although they were relatively inexperienced in siege warfare, as a result of which many towns were beyond their reach, nevertheless, the frequency and scale of their raids inevitably led to a number of successes, and they were a source of great anxiety to the Byzantines. The Byzantine army suffered reverses in several significant engagements, culminating in the arrival of Turkish raiders on the shores of the Aegean in 1070. The threat could not be ignored by the Byzantine Emperor and led to a major response that culminated, as we have seen, in the catastrophe at Manzikert in 1071.

It appeared to be impossible to stop the Turkish tide. As well as the successes in Asia Minor, the Turks also advanced into Syria and Palestine. Here they came into conflict with the Fatimids, whom they despised as heretics. Once again, they were the victors. Jerusalem was captured (in the same year as their victory at Manzikert), as was Damascus (the latter city was lost again soon after but was recovered by the Turks). The region was in ferment.

After Manzikert, one group within the confines of Asia Minor took advantage of the ensuing confusion to assert its independence. These were the Christian Armenians. For centuries they had existed as a proud and independent people. However, the tenth-century expansion of Byzantium, and the recognition by its emperors that a buffer zone was needed to protect its dominions, had led to a change in this situation. The Armenian territories within Asia Minor were taken over by the Byzantines and assimilated into the Empire. The Armenians suffered further during the incursions of the Turks in the early part of the eleventh century and many had migrated from their homelands in the east of Asia Minor to find more secure territory elsewhere in the region.

Many had settled behind the protective barrier of the Taurus mountains and, following the decline of Byzantine power, various small Armenian city-states seized the initiative and reasserted their independence. Some still held nominal allegiance to the Emperor in Constantinople but it was impossible for him to impose his authority, and as a consequence the governors of these cities had virtual autonomy. Other Armenian leaders sought peace with the Turks, and held on to their cities as a result. However, they were essentially a Christian people and, further, a group who looked towards Rome for spiritual guidance; during the early Crusading period they would often be well disposed towards the West, a situation that was to benefit the warriors of the Western armies greatly.

Despite this Armenian revival, the fact cannot be ignored that at this stage the area appears to have been on the verge of Turkish domination. Then the Turkish advance suffered a serious interruption. Unsurprisingly, given the lessons of history, the Turks themselves were their own worst enemy. They were composed of many clans. Nominally, the head of each clan owed allegiance to one supreme overlord, known as the Sultan. It was always difficult for the overlord to keep the adventurous and opportunistic clans under control. Tughril Bey had been succeeded by several strong leaders, first by Alp Arslan (who led the assault at Manzikert) and then by Malik Shah. While men of their calibre were Sultan, there was a possibility of some order being imposed over the Turks, although even then there was occasional trouble. In 1084, for example, when Malik Shah was Sultan, the leader of the Seldjuks in Anatolia (part of Asia Minor), Suleiman ibn Kutulmish, invaded Syria. Suleiman fought Tutush, the brother of Malik Shah, and was killed. Complete chaos ensued.

A number of different Turkish clans dwelt in Asia Minor, such as the Danishmends or the clan led by Chaka, who set up his capital at Smyrna, on the Aegean coast, and in truth they needed little encouragement to fall out among one another. Alexius Comnenus, by now Emperor of Byzantium, did his best to obtain maximum benefit from the situation by playing off one Turkish leader against the other, with some success. In 1092 Malik Shah appointed Kilij Arslan as the ruler of Nicaea. Kilij Arslan solved the problem of the territorial ambitions of Chaka in the region by inviting him to a banquet at Nicaea and then having him murdered. The fact that Chaka was his father-in-law did not seem to weigh unduly on his conscience.

Troubles escalated when Malik Shah died in November 1092. Without his firm control, the fragile unity of the Turks in the region dissolved completely. Tutush, his brother, did not recognise Malik Shah's son as the new Sultan and a bitter civil war broke out. Even when Tutush was killed in battle, the Syrian possessions of the Turks were threatened by the internecine rivalry of the sons of Malik Shah, Ridwan of Aleppo and Duqaq of Damascus. Preoccupied as they were with their struggle against each other, they failed to notice that other threatening forces were developing in the region. Turkish leaders such as Kerbogha, in the city of Mosul, were establishing power bases of their own that would further break down the cohesiveness of the Turks.

The Fatimids attempted to take advantage of this dissension to recover some of their lost ground in Syria and Palestine; indeed, in 1098 they retook Jerusalem itself from the Turks. A number of semi-independent Islamic city-states in the region, including Tripoli and Beirut, did manage to preserve some degree of autonomy by negotiating with the Turks or the Fatimids in an attempt to avoid conquest, and many of these were still independent when the First Crusade was launched. They further confused the situation as, even if they owed nominal allegiance to one lord or another, those ties were often forged of necessity and would soon disintegrate under pressure.

The fragmentation of the region bordering the Mediterranean cannot be overemphasised. At this point, there appeared to be no two cities in the hands of the same ruler. The chaos that inevitably ensued had several repercussions. The confusion and breakdown of order made pilgrimage a much more hazardous undertaking than previously it had been. We know that pilgrims still made their way to the East, and still managed to reach their ultimate destination in Jerusalem, but we also know that the dangers of travelling in the region were enormously increased. Asia Minor was in turmoil, and the overland crossing of that region had been the mainspring of the pilgrim revival in the tenth century. The Syrian and Palestinian coastal region was no better. The increased hazards of the journey seem to have touched a chord in the West. It is interesting to note that one of the leaders of the First Crusade, Peter the Hermit, is reputed to have experienced difficulties in travelling to Jerusalem in the period leading up to the Crusades.

However, the most significant repercussion was that the Muslims in the region were too busy fighting each other to notice danger from any incursion from the West. There was constant conflict within Islam, with the Sunni Turks engaged in confrontation with the Fatimid Egyptians as well as with each other. And the Turks, more than capable of repulsing any attack from Western Europe if they united their forces, were so embroiled in their internal affairs that they would not recognise any threat from that direction until it was too late.

The conditions could not have been better to launch a Crusade. There was a strong religious feeling abroad in Europe, led by a confident and assertive Papacy. The cult of relics and the act of pilgrimage had developed a sacred aura around Jerusalem, which gave it a unique place in the heart of Christians. The militarism of Western Europe meant that the lure of conflict and plunder would be welcome to the warlords of the region. And Islam was uniquely poorly placed to defend itself against any large invasion of its lands in the Levant. A plea for help had been made by the leader of the oldest empire in Christendom. All that was needed was a final call to arms. That call would not be long in coming.

CHAPTER 4

The Call to Arms

It is Tuesday 27 November 1095. Outside the east gate of the cathedral city of Clermont in France, a huge crowd has assembled. So vast is the congregation that it is too large to fit inside the cathedral, and is therefore forced to gather in a field. They are there because Pope Urban II has let it be known that he is to make a great proclamation of momentous significance. In his wildest dreams, Urban could not have imagined what effect his forthcoming statement would create, and how his words would unleash forces that were to instigate one of the greatest dramas in history.

When Alexius Comnenus, Emperor of Byzantium, had sent his letter pleading for help to the pontiff early in 1095, his envoys carried it to a meeting of the leading churchmen of the West at Piacenza, in Italy. The Pope had summoned a great council to the town, which was to discuss many of the major issues facing the Church. It was the first great convention that Urban had held, and he was determined to stamp his mark on his pontificate.

The envoys appear to have presented Alexius' case eloquently. Details of exactly what they said do not survive, but it is likely that they emphasised the fact that the Emperor had achieved much success in retrieving the lost lands of Christendom in Asia Minor, where the native Christian population had suffered greatly at the hands of the Turks. However, he did not have enough resources to single-handedly retrieve all of the territory held by the Infidel Turks. Help was needed from the West if a complete reconquest was to be successfully completed. Urban could exert great influence over Western Europe, and if he were to act as a focal point for recruiting aid from the warlords of the region then it was possible that a strong force could be despatched.

Urban listened intently to the request. It appears to have struck a chord deep within him. Although his motives for responding positively to Alexius' approaches must remain conjectural, several attractions to a pontiff are inherent in the scheme – particularly when it is remembered that Urban had only recently fought off the counter-claims of an Anti-Pope and needed to reinforce his authority at every opportunity. We need not doubt that, as leader of the Church in a deeply religious era, Urban genuinely believed in the spiritual efficacy of an expedition to defend Christendom, and to recover lost lands from the Infidel. There were also practical advantages. The Crusade was a way of directing the aggression of the Western warlords away from the lands of Western Europe, a region where their violence could do great damage to Christendom and seriously

Pope Urban II preaching the First Crusade at Clermont, 1095.

interfere with the well-being of the Church. If their warlike persuasions could be channelled towards the enemies of Christendom, then Western Europe might enjoy a period of relative peace and stability. If this were achieved, then all sections of Christian society – especially the Papacy – would benefit.

There was immense symbolism in the raising of armies at this period in history. Typically, it was the prerogative of kings and emperors to call their troops to arms. If Urban were to launch a Crusade, then he would be asserting his authority in a way that most of the leading men of Europe would understand clearly. It would be a tangible manifestation of the authority of the Papacy, of its determination to assert its right to pre-eminence in matters temporal as well as matters spiritual. The Investiture Conflict had by no means ended, and a public declaration by Urban that he intended to insist on prerogatives held in the past only by secular rulers was a clear statement of intent. If he could successfully direct the warlords towards objectives that he supported, then his authority would be greatly enhanced.

If Urban were to offer support, it would also be a useful step in the process of reconciliation between Eastern and Western Christendom. Although relationships between Rome and Constantinople had thawed in recent years, there still remained strong memories of the antipathy between the two in the immediate past. Many in the East were unsympathetic towards the Papal claim to supremacy in spiritual affairs, and there was a recent history of discord between East and West. In addition, doctrinal differences that might seem incredibly obscure to modern eyes, such as whether the bread used in the Eucharist should be unleavened or not, led to deeply felt theological division between East and West. If Urban could be seen

Christ leading the Crusaders. (Royal MS 19B XV, f. 37)

as the instigator of an expedition from the West to help Byzantium, then great progress towards reunification, or at least a deeper understanding between the differing elements of Christendom, might be achieved.

Accordingly, Urban embraced the scheme enthusiastically. Following the Council at Piacenza, Urban launched into a period of tremendous activity. He travelled extensively around Italy and France. At a time when kings, let alone pontiffs, were rarely seen by the masses, the effect was enormous. A new abbey was consecrated at Cluny, centre of the monastic movement in the West. As a symbol, it is difficult to think of anything that could be more significant. Urban's triumphal progress through France eventually led him to Clermont, where he publicly called the warriors of Western Europe to arms.

All this intense activity and preparation culminated at Clermont. Urban rose from his throne, on a platform facing the multitude, and began his speech. He told his audience that their brothers in Eastern Christendom had suffered greatly at the hands of a particularly virulent breed of Infidel. So great had been their tribulation that they had turned to the West for help. Even Jerusalem, the Holy of Holies, had been desecrated by the heathen. It was no longer safe for the followers of Christ to make their way to the place where He suffered and died for them. Could the Christian World stand by disinterestedly while pagan Turks mocked from behind the walls of Christendom's most sacred city? Could the true believer remain inactive while God wept for the fate of His city?

Urban proceeded to the crux of his message: it was the duty of the Christian to take up arms in the name of God, to indulge no longer in the wicked shedding of the blood of his brothers in Christ but to turn instead on the enemies of his faith. He must dedicate himself without reserve or equivocation towards the recovery of the Holy Land. Only then could God's Kingdom on Earth be restored.

As a speech, it is rich in rhetoric, strong with appeals to the emotion. Economical with the truth, it has all the makings of brilliant propaganda. The response to it was ecstatic. A huge cry ascended from the crowd, and triumphant proclamations of *Deus Le Volt* ('God wills it') resounded around the city walls. Waves of acclamation washed over Urban. Euphoria spread, and vast numbers of the crowd committed themselves to the enterprise.

It seems reasonable to assume that much private lobbying had taken place before these momentous events at Clermont. Judging by his actions shortly after the Pope's announcement at Clermont – at which he was not personally present – it appears that at least one important lord, Raymond, Count of Toulouse, was more fully appraised of Urban's intentions. It is also probable that many of the clerics who were close supporters of Urban would have known of his plans. Prominent among these men was Bishop Adhemar of Le Puy, who would assume a leading role in the days ahead and who was now the first to kneel at the feet of Urban. The Crusading movement had turned from speculative idea to positive action, and it had just found its first leader.

Several accounts of Urban's speech are extant, some of which at least appear to be from eyewitnesses. They are not entirely consistent, but the general tenor of Urban's proclamation would seem to be along the lines of the account given above. Certainly, several details appear to have held great significance. The Crusaders would go armed with the badge of the pilgrim, a tangible witness that this very military enterprise was to have deep spiritual motivation. This was to be a 'Holy War', a Christian *jihad*. Western society valued military prowess highly, and the development of this concept would help to legitimise it. It was a potent cocktail indeed.

To emphasise the spiritual nature of the mission, Urban both placed obligations on and offered benefits to participants. Those who took the Cross had to swear a solemn vow to set out subsequently on crusade; should they break it, then the full force of ecclesiastical censure would be unleashed, in extreme cases excommunication itself. However, the family and possessions of absentee Crusaders would be protected by the Church. While they were on Crusade, Crusaders would be subject to ecclesiastical rather than secular courts.

Vitally, those taking part would receive a Papal Indulgence in the form of remission of sins. Not only would participation in the Crusade be considered an act of penance, it would also help to earn forgiveness for the sins committed by the Crusaders in the past. To a society where punishment of sin in the afterlife was widely deemed to be an all too horrific reality, this was an enormous incentive. The very frailty of life meant that many were terrified of divine retribution in the hereafter. Urban's pronouncements in this respect were generous, stating that 'whoever goes to Jerusalem to liberate the Church of God may substitute the journey for all penance'. In the future, the concept of indulgence would develop to assume greater benefits but the rewards offered by Urban were, in the eyes of many, substantial.

The effects of Urban's speech at Clermont quickly radiated throughout much of France, and it soon became clear that the raw emotions unleashed by it would be very difficult to control. Urban would have expected that the response to his oratory would come in the main from militarily experienced men. Of course, there would also need to be a significant level of non-combatant support to these troops: blacksmiths would need to accompany the expedition; there would have to be a large number of drovers to tend to the beasts of burden; there would need to be priests with the army, and women to attend to the men's more worldly needs. In normal circumstances, these would be a necessary part of the force, but supplementary to the military men themselves. However, from the outset, the primary response to Urban's call was from 'ordinary' people. The great warlords were not, as a class, noticeably quick to respond. In fairness, it was impossible for them simply to abandon their interests in the West and throw themselves precipitately into the Crusading cause. It would take time to assemble their forces, and they would also need to make arrangements to ensure that their interests were protected while they were absent. All this militated against a quick response.

In contrast, many of the poorer sections of society were quickly gripped by the idea of the Crusade. Their zeal was fuelled particularly by itinerant preachers – a particularly influential force in society at this time – who took Urban's message to heart and built on it, engendering an outpouring of religious fervour in the process. The influence of Urban over these men was limited, and the response to the appeal at Clermont quickly became very difficult to control. Despite his enthusiasm, Urban had tried to limit participation in the Crusade, saying that none must go without the express approval of their spiritual advisor and even drawing up lists of those classes of people who should not set out on the expedition. However, it became increasingly difficult to enforce these restrictions.

The itinerant preachers were in a powerful position to influence the masses. For most of society, life was a long and painful struggle against poverty and hardship. Most of the people were poor, landless and exploited. Such men and women were the congregation of the itinerant preacher. The official Church was widely despised by the poor, its churchmen resented for the wealth that they controlled. Many of its bishops were rich and complacent, and appeared to pay little more than lip service to the principles that they espoused. Although the Reform Papacy made a determined effort to challenge these problems, it would be many years before significant inroads were made. The itinerant preachers were, in contrast, very poor, possessing little more than the clothes that they wore. As such, the poorer sections of society could easily identify with them.

The preachers foretold confidently that the New Jerusalem would appear on earth when the Old Jerusalem was restored to Christian ownership. They spoke of a golden land, a land of milk and honey, where the rewards to those who helped to regain the Holy City for Christ would be immense. So moving was their preaching that, to many, their descriptions appear to have assumed an almost

Peter the Hermit leading his army to Jerusalem. (Eg 1500 f. 45v Peter the Hermit, preacher for the First Crusades, 1095, early 14th century, Histoire Universelle *(c. 1286); British Library, London/Bridgeman Art Library, London/New York)*

literal significance. It often appeared that the distinction between the earthly and the heavenly Jerusalem had become distinctly blurred.

The most famous of these preachers was a man called Peter, who came to be known as 'The Hermit'. He was small of stature and swarthy in appearance. Dressed in the shabbiest of clothes and avoiding any meat in his diet, he approximates to the archetypal vision of John the Baptist. Despite being born to a knightly family, he insisted on travelling humbly on a mule. The crueller opponents of Peter would say that the animal bore an uncanny resemblance to its master. Despite – or perhaps because of – his unorthodox appearance, the response to the recruiting campaign that Peter launched after Urban's speech at Clermont was great. So charismatic did he appear to his followers that many of them sought to touch him, believing that, like Christ himself, mere contact with his cloak would miraculously cure the sick. Unfortunately, although these are excellent qualities for a prospective saint, future events would prove them to be poor indications of military prowess.

Peter may have been inspired by personal difficulties from his own experience. Some chroniclers aver that he had been turned back when he had previously tried to make the pilgrimage to Jerusalem. Whatever his motivation, his message fell on fertile ground. As he made his way through France and then into the Rhineland preaching the Crusade, thousands flocked to hear him, and they were greatly moved by his impassioned preaching. Urban's practical restrictions were soon being widely ignored, and a ramshackle army was formed as a result.

This so-called 'army' would be awash with old men, women and children. Even the men of fighting age were poorly armed, the cost of weapons being far beyond the means of most of the people. There were some low-ranking knights, but most of these troops, as well as being poorly armed, were poorly informed and blissfully unaware of the enormous challenge that lay before them. Further, without much semblance of discipline, this force would soon become uncontrollable.

The first expeditions, then, were formed largely of the peasantry of the West, although the 'Peasants' Crusade' talked of by historians of later times is a misnomer. In fact, several large, independent forces set out in the direction of the East, of which Peter's army was only one. The first to leave for the Holy Land was led by a man whose social standing is evidenced by his name. He was called Walter Sans-Avoir ('Walter the Penniless'). His expedition set out from the West just after Easter 1096, and made its way towards Hungary, arriving there on 8 May. The country was independent at that time, and its King, Coloman, was every bit a man of his era and could, if the occasion demanded, be ruthless in maintaining order. He granted permission for Walter to take his force across his country. The journey through Hungary passed without incident. By the end of the month they had arrived at Semlin, on the borders of the Byzantine Empire.

It was here that the discipline of the force, always likely to be extremely suspect, began to disintegrate. The Byzantine Empire was completely unprepared for its arrival. Aware of the amount of organisation needed for any major expedition, the Byzantines assumed that it would be many months before any help arrived from the West. Further, rather than a rabble of peasants, a well-armed force of mercenaries was anticipated. News of the arrival of this dubious-looking army was quickly forwarded to the nearest sizeable Byzantine garrison, which was in Belgrade. When the peasants began to reach Belgrade, the garrison's commander, Nicetas, had little idea of how to deal with this unexpected and alarming turn of events. He despatched a messenger post-haste to Constantinople, and awaited instructions from the Emperor.

The peasants quickly became frustrated. Armies of the time had little in the way of logistical support, and the lack of organisation within Walter's force made it particularly vulnerable. The only source of supplies for an army on campaign was the countryside through which it passed. Food would be bought if money was available but, if it was not, then provisions would be begged or stolen. Nicetas was unable to provide enough food to deal with the large number of peasants on his doorstep. As a result, they began to forage and pillage in the environs of the city.

Many of the stragglers among the peasant force were still making their way through Semlin, in Hungarian territory. It was here that the first flashpoint of the campaign occurred. Some of these peasants attempted to steal from the local market. The Hungarians were well prepared for such an event. The ringleaders were quickly rounded up, and disarmed. They were humiliated by having their armour draped mockingly over the city walls, and being sent on their way naked. It did not appear to be a major incident and there were no immediate reprisals – however, it would lead to unforeseen and unfortunate consequences in the not too distant future.

Semlin was a Hungarian town. Once across the Byzantine border, the force reassembled and continued on its way towards Constantinople. Alexius, successfully concealing his shock at the arrival of the peasants, told Nicetas to treat them well. He arranged for them to be escorted to Constantinople. Arriving there, they awaited the arrival of the larger force that was expected in their wake. Their behaviour, with the exception of the violence at Semlin and a few minor incidents, had been reasonable. In return, they had mostly been well treated. Sadly, this precedent would not be followed by subsequent expeditions.

Walter's force was primarily French. The next 'army' would be substantially German. The people of Germany had, in the first instance, greeted the preaching of Peter the Hermit with derision. However, his sincerity and oration had won them round. Large numbers joined his force, which would, it is estimated, eventually be twenty thousand strong. Peter led this group eastwards, mainly following Walter's route. Some lesser knights were in the force, and progress was good, averaging 25 miles per day. They reached Semlin on 20 June.

The local governor took fright at the huge size of this force. The atmosphere quickly became tense, particularly when the armour of the disarmed troublemakers in Walter's army was noticed, still draped over the walls. A minor argument broke out over, of all things, a pair of shoes. Given the already uncomfortable relationship between the new arrivals and the people of Semlin, from this small spark a major conflagration broke out. Full-scale rioting erupted, with the Westerners hammering at the gates of the citadel. In their frenzied blood-lust, innocent citizens were murdered. At the conclusion of this violent outburst, four thousand Hungarians lay dead.

Once their frenzy had subsided, the peasants were horrified by the potential consequences of their licence. Retribution would be swift and decisive. King Coloman would seek revenge first, and ask questions afterwards. The peasant force had to move on into Byzantine territory – quickly. On 26 June they hurried across the River Save and into the Byzantine Empire. Nicetas, aware of the threat of this force, sought to control their crossing. But the troops he sent to maintain order were seized and killed. Throwing off any pretence of self-discipline, the peasants then set fire to Belgrade. Nicetas appears to have been short of sufficient manpower to restrain them. The peasants then moved on to Nish, where Nicetas was able to take hostages to ensure the good behaviour of the Westerners.

For a time, it appeared that calm had been restored. Many of the local people were moved by the piety and faith evidenced by the army. Some even joined their ranks. It was a false dawn, however. In an act of gratuitous vandalism, the peasants burned down a mill. Presumably reinforced by now, Nicetas responded, in the first instance at least, in a measured fashion – he attacked the rear of the peasant force in an attempt to take more hostages. From this point on, events unfolded with a volition of their own. Rumours quickly swept through Peter's force that the Byzantines had launched an all-out attack. Numbers of them turned about to attack Nish. They were driven off but responded with a counter-attack.

It appears that the tolerance of Byzantium was exhausted by such indiscipline. The incident at Semlin, although it was a Hungarian town, was right on the border of Byzantine territory and trouble there could easily have spilled over the frontier. The riots in Belgrade had been a further extreme provocation. The trouble in Nish proved a step too far. Nicetas unleashed his troops on the peasants. The resultant battle, a conflict between well-armed Byzantine troops and the peasant force, was inevitably a one-sided affair. The limitations of Peter's army were cruelly exposed. Large numbers were slain, and many more taken captive. The latter were transported to dingy Byzantine prisons, destined to live out their days in damp and dreary incarceration many miles from home. Most of the inadequate monetary possessions of the force was also seized. Peter escaped with a tiny remnant of his force, five hundred strong – all that was left, so he believed, of his once mighty army.

The next day Peter's spirits were lifted when seven thousand survivors managed to rejoin him. As he continued his progress towards Constantinople, still more caught up with him. However, the true extent of the damage wrought by Nicetas and his men could not be disguised. Over a quarter of the force had gone, lost in an unnecessary fight of their own making, not against an Infidel foe but, rather, in conflict with troops of the Christian Emperor that they had come to help. As an omen for future co-operation between Byzantium and the West, it was a bleak portent. It also highlighted clearly the deficiencies of the peasants as a fighting force. Tragically, the obvious lessons concerning their limitations were not absorbed.

Thus it was a chastened force that approached Constantinople. Peter was very uncertain of his reception from Alexius – his force had, after all, behaved outrageously. Fortunately for them, the Emperor responded with magnanimity. So gracious was Alexius that Peter was moved to tears at his welcome; whether from relief or from gratitude is not clear. Small groups were allowed into Constantinople to view its wonders. Coming as many of them did from villages or small towns, the city must have made a huge impact on them. But the sightseeing could not last. The Emperor was in a quandary. If the force proceeded into Asia Minor, he must have been fairly certain that the Turks would annihilate it. On the other hand, if they stayed where they were, the Westerners might soon lose their discipline again, with unfortunate results for the city. Faced with such a choice, there was only one likely outcome. The force had to move on.

Alexius did what he could to help the peasants. Transport was provided to ship them across the Bosphorus. The Emperor advised that when they were across, they should wait for the other armies expected to follow behind them. It was a sensible suggestion, but the advice was ignored. In a desultory fashion, the army moved on to the abandoned town of Nicomedia. They plundered the countryside as they went, despite the fact that many of the local population were fellow Christians. Peter's force had joined with Walter's army at Constantinople, but there was a quarrel between the two contingents, and they split into separate groups once more. Broadly speaking, the French attached themselves to Peter while the Germans (who were also accompanied by a number of Italians) chose an Italian named Rainald as their leader. Nominally together, the two forces made their way to an old Byzantine military camp at Civetot.

The site had some positional advantages. It was surrounded by fertile countryside, and was close enough to the sea to be reprovisioned from Constantinople. However, the troops quickly became restive. The Germans and the French – who soon tired of Peter's leadership – began to raid the region around them. There was little co-ordinated opposition, which emboldened them further. They even dared to approach the largest Turkish city in the area, at

Nicaea. It was the capital of one of the leaders of the Turks in Asia Minor, Kilij Arslan. They did not ransack the city itself but they attacked the suburbs. Reports of atrocities followed, claiming that the Christians had roasted babies on spits. A force was sent to repel the Christians, but was beaten back.

Elated, the raiders returned to Civetot where they sold their booty to Greek traders. Tales of the success of this largely French expedition aroused the jealousy of the Germans, who determined to follow suit. A force of six thousand, led by Rainald, ventured forth on a foray of their own. They bypassed Nicaea and plundered the lands beyond. Eventually, they reached a castle at a place called Xerigordon. They succeeded in capturing it, and determined to make it a base for raiding the surrounding region. It was well provisioned and dominated the area from its lofty position on a high hilltop. Kilij Arslan was perturbed at their success and decided that they must be dislodged. His task would be made an easy one by the naïveté of the peasants.

The Turks approached Xerigordon on 29 September 1096. The Christians withdrew behind the large walls of the fortress. Unbeknown to them, however, a fundamental flaw in the design of the castle made it a potential death trap – the only water supply lay outside the walls. The besieged Christians had not compensated for this shortage of water and, unable to venture forth to restock their supplies, were soon tormented by thirst. As the raging sun beat down upon them and sapped their energy in this arid landscape, they soon turned to desperate measures. They drank their own urine and sucked moisture from the veins of their animals. This only delayed the inevitable, and the Christians were soon forced to seek terms. These were harsh in the extreme. The defenders were faced with a choice of conversion to Islam or death. To their credit, many chose the latter option. Despite their often-foolish actions, there is no reason to doubt the sincerity of their religious beliefs. Those that opted to convert were then taken away to a lifetime of captivity.

The army that had remained at Civetot knew nothing of this reverse. They were aware that the Germans had taken Xerigordon and had even heard – completely erroneously – that they had taken Nicaea. Turkish spies fed them the tale that the Germans had amassed immense booty in the process. Fuelled by stories of these successes, the army moved on from Civetot on 20 October, euphoric in anticipation of their undoubted triumph against the heathen Turk. It is reputed that over twenty thousand men were in this force, hungry to enrich themselves from a massive raid into Turkish territory. Only those who could not fight, the elderly, the infirm, the women and the children, were left in camp.

Barely 3 miles from Civetot, the road entered a wooded valley near the village of Dracon. Any commander who understood Turkish military tactics would have marked the spot as a prime site for an ambush. However, oblivious to such danger, the Christians blissfully continued their advance. Suddenly, the trees were alive with the war cries of the Turks. Within minutes, the Christians were surrounded by thousands of horsemen, whirling dervish-like around the fringes of the poorly prepared peasant army. They hacked and harried at the Christians, seeking for openings that appeared all too easily. Clouds of arrows enveloped the peasants, who were so great in number and so closely compacted that the Turkish horse-archers barely had to take aim. Resistance rapidly became sporadic, and then stopped altogether. The scene resembled an abattoir more than a battlefield. What remained of the Christian army broke and fled, rushing back towards the camp at Civetot.

The camp was just waking up. Suddenly, those that remained at Civetot were faced with a terrifying vision. Running frantically towards them was the residue of the huge force that had recently set out, running without discipline, without order, driven by stark terror. Close behind, in their wake, came the reason for their panic: a large Turkish force, descending nemesis-like on the camp. Within minutes, it was engulfed. Only the young and the beautiful, marketable commodities in the slave markets of the East, were spared. The rest joined the already large band of Christian martyrs.

A pitiful remnant managed to escape. With a courage born of desperation, they made their way to a nearby deserted castle. It was without gates, but the survivors hastily erected barricades. In a seemingly hopeless position, they resisted all the Turkish attempts to break in. One of their number had managed to escape the Turks and make his way back to Constantinople. Peter the Hermit, who had returned to the city shortly before the disaster at Civetot, and the Emperor Alexius were shocked at the terrible news. To his credit, Alexius reacted quickly and sent a force to relieve the Christians who were holed up in the castle.

They arrived not a moment too soon. The survivors within the castle walls had little in the way of food or water with them. However, as the Byzantines approached, the Turkish force evaporated into the surrounding hills. Starving and frightened, what remained of this brave but fated expedition was escorted back across the Bosphorus. Most of its leaders lay rotting on the bloodstained fields of Asia Minor, including Walter and Rainald. Of the knights that survived, nearly all were badly injured. It was a moving and pathetic end to their adventure. Their indiscipline and violence reflected the times in which they lived. Most had given up what little they had in a vain effort to reconquer Christian lands from the pagan enemy. They were convinced that God was on their side, and most had paid for their indiscretions with their lives.

Behind this first wave of peasant armies, a second followed, a far more sinister version of what had gone before. This latter group was led by men of dubious principle who matched military incompetence with lack of scruple. A disquieting side-effect of the Crusading movement was that it brought to the surface bigotry and fanaticism in Western Europe. It seems tragically inevitable that the Jewish communities of the West were the first to suffer from this. Their wealth was resented, despite the fact that they had been part of society in Western Europe for centuries. Christians were not allowed to charge interest on loans, but the Jewish community was exempted from this rule and many profited from this situation. A number of the Christian pilgrims to the East had to borrow heavily from the Jewish community for their journey. Antagonism would quickly degenerate into outright violence.

Ominous signs of what was in store became apparent early on. Peter the Hermit had approached the Jewish leaders in Rouen and suggested that their financial assistance would be an excellent goodwill gesture. Whether this amounted to low-key blackmail is not clear but others would soon be less subtle in their approaches.

Godfrey of Bouillon leading his men. (Fr 9084 f. 20v Knights on horseback, an illuminated page from the Crusades of Godefroy de Bouillon, Chronique de Guillaume de Tyr *(14th century); Bibliothèque Nationale, Paris/ Bridgeman Art Library, London/ New York)*

Ugly rumours began to circulate. Godfrey of Bouillon, one of the leaders of the 'official' Crusade that was being formed while the peasant armies were on their way, reputedly said that he would take his revenge on the killers of Christ before he reached the Holy Land. These stories led to a hasty response from some of the Jews, who hurriedly offered large sums of money to Godfrey as a placatory offering. He promptly accepted their offer, refuting all thoughts of ill will towards them. An important and dangerous precedent had been set.

For the Jews, sterner tests were to come. Several other Christian leaders emerged in Germany, among them two known as Volkmar and Gottschalk. A third, Count Emich of Leisingen, would commit terrible acts in the name of the Christian cause. Although the German Emperor Henry IV protected the Jewish communities in his lands, his protection was ignored by Emich. The Count and his followers attacked the Jewish community at Spier on 3 May 1096. The local bishop intervened and, although the outbreak of violence was contained, twelve Jews were killed. Some of the perpetrators of these crimes were caught and punished. However, worse was to follow at Worms. Rumours had spread that the Jews had killed a Christian in the town, and tension escalated quickly into open rioting. The army, assisted by the townsfolk, ransacked the Jewish quarter of the town. The bishop's palace, where many Jews sought refuge, proved inadequate protection. The doors were battered down and those seeking sanctuary were murdered.

Emich's force moved on to Mainz. The local archbishop, Rothard, locked the gates against it. However, the townspeople were sympathetic to Emich and the gates were reopened. The Jewish community once more sought shelter in the archbishop's palace but Rothard abandoned them to their fate. Given a choice of conversion or death, most opted to die. Some of those who converted subsequently recanted and they too paid the ultimate price. The chief rabbi in the town, a man named Kalonymos, escaped and asked for protection from Rothard, who was en route to his country villa. The archbishop tried to convert the rabbi. Enraged at his arrogance, Kalonymos attacked Rothard with a knife. His attack was unsuccessful, and he lost his life as a result of his actions.

Other terrifying but smaller-scale outbursts followed in Cologne, Trier, Metz and other towns, but the initial violence began to subside. Many of those in Emich's army, sated by their plunder, returned to their homes. Those who were left moved eastwards with him. They were preceded by two forces led by Volkmar and Gottschalk, who heard of Emich's actions and sought to emulate them. They had badly misjudged the situation. Volkmar's troops massacred the Jews in Prague and moved on into Hungary. King Coloman was by now well prepared for any problems. At the first sign of trouble, he turned on Volkmar's army. There was heavy loss of life. Similarly, there was another outbreak of violence when some of Gottschalk's men brutally killed a Hungarian boy. As a result, his men were disarmed. When further trouble followed, Coloman unleashed his soldiers on Gottschalk's army, slaying many of them in the process.

Emich's group was a more serious concern for Coloman. Even after many desertions in Germany, it was still larger than that of Volkmar or Gottschalk. Rather than attempt to control them within his borders, Coloman resolved to stop Emich entering the country altogether. A series of skirmishes, extending over a six-week period, ended when Emich managed to build a bridge over the river frontier into Hungary. The forces that crossed attacked a fortress at Weisselburg. They were much better equipped than the armies that had preceded them and their siege engines soon started to breach the walls. However, when it appeared that their efforts would be crowned with success, a sudden and unexplained panic broke out among them. Those inside the town were so inspired by this demonstration of irrational terror that they sallied forth and attacked the besiegers. Many of Emich's army fled. Most were killed, but with ironic injustice Emich himself escaped. He made his way back home with the remaining German knights, while the French knights in his army continued on to the East.

It had been a false and inglorious start. These armies, composed substantially of simple peasants, had started out with high expectations, convinced that their efforts had divine approbation. Their rotting corpses now lined the roads from Hungary to Asia Minor. If it were to succeed, the Crusading movement needed both military competence and good fortune. Neither quality was owned by these early expeditions. The strong emotions that they exhibited – bigotry, fanaticism and persecution – left a disturbing precedent for the future. The so-called Peasants' Crusade was little more than a sideshow to the Crusades proper. If for no other reason than the confusion it demonstrated in Christian theology, it was not an unimportant one.

CHAPTER 5

The Warlords Depart

Urban was a pragmatist. The Holy Land would not be recovered for Christendom merely by divine intervention. A strong and well-equipped military expedition was needed. In this respect, the peasants' expeditions had been unwelcome distractions. While they were taking place, in Western Europe much effort was expended in forming a powerful force to send to the East. This main Crusader army was due to leave in August 1096, once the harvest had been gathered in. Everyone going on the journey should take an oath before departure. The threat of excommunication hung over them should they abandon the journey before reaching Jerusalem. As a symbol of their divine mission, they were to wear a red cross sewn on to their surcoat.

Support from the warlords of the West was not unanimous or automatic. The Papacy was still a developing institution, and lines of communication were not good. Information did not move quickly or easily through the ecclesiastical hierarchy. Urban did his part by extensive lobbying in France, travelling widely in an attempt to heighten the profile of the Crusade. Some leading men were moved to support him. This was crucial. If a lord chose to support the cause, then his vassals would follow suit.

One of the first to commit himself was Raymond, Count of Toulouse. Approximately sixty years old, he had many connections with the royal family of Spain. He had participated in the wars in that country against the Moors. Despite his early promise of support, he appeared to be in no hurry to leave. He did not in fact depart until October 1096, when he set out accompanied by his wife and heir. He sold some of his lands to finance his journey. To set out on Crusade was an expensive enterprise, and many of the participants would have to sell assets before they could depart. Raymond's actions suggest that he hoped from very early on to be the secular leader of the Crusade, the counterpart to Bishop Adhemar, the undisputed spiritual leader of the expedition. Events would demonstrate, however, that Raymond lacked the charisma to command the Crusade; although he possessed courtesy and charm – attributes by no means common to his fellow Crusaders – his character was flawed by vanity, obstinacy and greed.

Raymond recruited an army primarily from his lands in the south of France, particularly from Provence. However, he was not the first to leave. Further north, another French lord, Hugh, the Count of Vermandois, had also raised a large number of men. Hugh was the younger son of King Henry I of France. He felt overshadowed by the more prominent members of his family. Like many other younger sons in this period in history, he possessed neither wealth nor any significant political position. He was extremely proud, and obsessively aware of his social status. Apparently a weak personality, he could be easily manipulated by others.

Adhering scrupulously to the timetable, Hugh left in August 1096. He sent messengers ahead of the expedition to announce his departure to the Emperor in Constantinople. He hoped that, by so doing, an appropriately regal reception would be arranged for him. He journeyed overland to the port of Bari in southern Italy. However, while making the short sea-crossing across the Adriatic, his ship fell victim to a sudden violent storm and was smashed to pieces on the shore. He arrived, a ragged and forlorn wreck, at the Byzantine port of Dyrrachium.

The governor of the city, John Comnenus, greeted him with cordiality but suspicion. Many within the empire were distrustful of the new arrivals. Mercenaries from the West had, in the past, hardly inspired confidence through their lack of loyalty. With perhaps understandable cynicism, a close watch was kept over Hugh. The Count apparently enjoyed the attention shown to him, but many of his entourage felt that he was being treated as a prisoner. In the meantime, Alexius despatched a high-ranking official, Manuel Butimites, an admiral of the Empire, to meet Hugh and escort him to Constantinople. Hugh was captivated when he arrived in the city by its many splendours, and by the lavish welcome afforded to him by Alexius.

However, behind the kindly greetings of the Emperor was a strong ulterior motive. As the first warlord from the West to arrive in Constantinople, Hugh might prove a useful ally. Alexius planned to gain influence over Hugh and, through him, hoped to assert similar authority over the Western leaders yet to

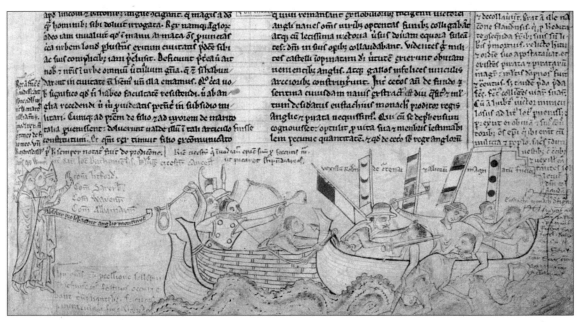

The perils of sea travel are vividly illustrated in this thirteenth-century chronicle. (MS 16, f. 42r)

arrive. Alexius knew of the importance of the oath of allegiance to Western society. In the feudal structures of Western Europe, each man had his lord, to whom he swore loyalty. Alexius wished to ensure that the Crusaders should use their arms to restore Byzantine lands to the empire, and not to build up dominions of their own. He hoped to ensure that they fell in with this plan by drawing from them an oath by which they would recognise *his* authority. Hugh was easily persuaded to comply, and also agreed to influence later arrivals to do likewise.

Unfortunately, if the Emperor thought that Hugh's ready acceptance would be typical of all the warlords of the West then he was sadly mistaken. The next army to set out for the East was led by a man of much stronger mettle, in the form of Godfrey of Bouillon, Duke of Lower Lorraine. His reasons for joining the Crusade were varied. Religious conviction certainly appears to have played a significant part in his decision, but so too did uncertainty over his future prospects in Western Europe. He came from an impressive pedigree. He was the second son of Count Eustace of Boulogne and Ida, a descendant of the great Charlemagne. Although he had been made heir to his mother's large estates, he had subsequently been deprived of them by the German Emperor Henry IV. Despite this, he remained a firm supporter of Henry and would eventually be given some of his lost lands back. He was appointed Governor of Lorraine, but appears to have performed poorly in this position. His administration was inefficient and generated much discontent. The Crusade therefore offered him a chance to recover some much-needed prestige.

Godfrey raised money for his journey by selling off his estates, and by pledging his castle to the Bishop of Liege. Along with the money that he obtained by subtle coercion from the Jewish community, this enabled him to raise a large and well-equipped army. With him were two of his brothers. Technically, his elder brother, Eustace III, the current Count of Boulogne, was more important than Godfrey but he appears to have had limited enthusiasm for the Crusade. He held large tracts of land in France, and his actions during the course of the First Crusade suggest that he longed to return home as quickly as possible. Godfrey accordingly took the prominent role in the leadership of this particular force.

Godfrey's younger brother, Baldwin, provided a total contrast. As the youngest of the three brothers, his prospects were distinctly limited. He had originally opted for a career in the Church, but the restrictive constraints of the cloisters proved completely unsuitable for him. He was driven by great ambition, as events in the future would show. He was the complete antithesis of Godfrey, in looks and in temperament. He was tall and dark, whereas Godfrey was fair and yellow-bearded. Baldwin enjoyed luxury whereas Godfrey preferred austerity. Godfrey had pleasant, winning ways while, in contrast, Baldwin appears to have been a man of cold and haughty disposition. His ambitions and his character were ill-suited to the role of a passive, younger brother. When he set out with Godfrey's army his wife and children travelled with him. He did not intend to return.

Godfrey led his force along the roads towards Hungary. When they reached its borders, he sought permission from King Coloman to cross the frontier. The King was understandably nervous about acceding to this request. His country had already suffered at the hands of a poorly equipped peasant army. A well-armed

A crusader army on the march. (From MS Hrabanus Maurus)

force could do much more damage. However, Godfrey met with Coloman and managed to allay his fears. The King agreed to let the Crusaders enter his country, but he insisted that Baldwin be handed over as a hostage against the force's good behaviour.

Baldwin was indignant but eventually agreed to this pre-condition. The army traversed Hungary quickly and without incident. Coloman complied with all the reasonable requests of Godfrey's army so that they would pass through his country as rapidly as possible. In return, the Westerners behaved themselves. As soon as they reached the River Save, the border with the Byzantine Empire, Baldwin was returned and the army of Godfrey went on its way. Despite the fact that it had taken place under a cloud of mistrust and suspicion, the exercise had been a successful one.

The advance into Byzantine territory was, in the first instance, equally uneventful. Belgrade was still deserted after its desecration by the peasant army. Nicetas sent out troops to escort Godfrey, and things at first went well. News of the friendly reception accorded to Hugh by Alexius Comnenus may have reached the Western army by this time. The leaders pushed on to Constantinople, hoping perhaps to profit from the Emperor's generosity. The bulk of the force remained behind at Selymbria, and without the restraining influence of their leaders their discipline started to deteriorate. Some began to riot but were restrained by ambassadors from Alexius. However, this was once again a precursor to more serious difficulties.

In Constantinople itself, Godfrey was disturbed by the attitude of Alexius. The Westerners did not understand the attitude of the Emperor, a misunderstanding that was reciprocated. Ahead of the Crusader armies lay much territory, currently in Turkish hands, that had once belonged to the Emperor. Should it be reconquered, Alexius (as the rightful owner of these lands in his opinion) wished the Crusaders to return them to his authority. In an attempt to convince Godfrey of the justice of his claims, Alexius sent Hugh of Vermandois to his camp to intercede on his behalf. Hugh tried to persuade Godfrey to take an oath of allegiance to the Emperor. Godfrey would have none of it. He regarded the German Emperor Henry as his liege lord, and he had already taken an oath of allegiance to him. His conscience would not allow him to accept meekly that he must recognise two masters. To give in to Hugh's exhortations would have been inconsistent with his character. It might also compromise his position with the leaders of the other Western forces that were yet to arrive in Constantinople, and it would therefore have been an unwise move politically.

Alexius was not the man to countenance such rejection. He understood the place of prominence that the oath of allegiance held in the social and political mores of the West, much more so than was the case in the Byzantine Empire. Persuading the Western leaders to take the oath was a key part of his strategy for ensuring that his interests were protected. If the Crusaders were to reconquer territory then Alexius might well have let them keep it, but only if they recognised him as their ultimate ruler. They could only be allowed to govern by his gift and on his behalf. In an attempt to force Godfrey to change his position, Alexius attacked him on his most vulnerable front – his food supplies.

A Medieval force carried little of its own food. It relied for sustenance almost exclusively on the country through which it passed. Consequently, when Alexius commenced a blockade against Godfrey's men, it was an extremely serious matter. The Emperor's anxiety increased as he received word that other Crusader armies were converging on his capital. Should they unite with Godfrey's army, their combined force could pose a significant threat. In an attempt to forestall their liaison, Alexius tightened the noose around Godfrey still further. Godfrey, however, was no mere puppet. Unable to accept further provocation, he attacked Constantinople.

Alexius was taken by surprise. Few in the city had expected the assault. In the event, the attack was beaten back with little difficulty. The fact that it had happened at all, however, sharpened the need to deal with Godfrey in the Emperor's mind. When ambassadors whom he sent to Godfrey's camp were ejected, Alexius resorted to force. Outnumbered by the seasoned Imperial force that Alexius despatched against him, Godfrey had to capitulate to the Emperor's demands. He took the oath of allegiance to Alexius and was rewarded with splendid gifts. Yet the episode underscored the deep misunderstandings between East and West. Alexius' desire to control the Crusaders is perfectly understandable from a Byzantine perspective, yet by the same token his attempts to manipulate Godfrey had made the Crusaders resentful and distrustful of the Greeks. Neither party was willing to accept the merits of the other's views, and in this atmosphere of conflict the seeds of future confusion and conflict were sown.

Once he had taken the oath, Godfrey and his men were quickly shipped across the Bosphorus. Other Western forces were soon at the gates of Constantinople. A large Norman force reached the city on 9 April 1097. At its head was Bohemond, the greatest adventurer of the day. Now forty years of age, he cut an impressive figure, a veteran warrior who was quick to exploit to his own personal advantage every opportunity that presented itself. He had been involved in many battles against the Byzantines during the Norman attempts to conquer parts of Alexius' territories, and had proved a troublesome and persistent adversary.

Most of Bohemond's lands were in the south of Italy, territory that had until very recently been part of the Byzantine Empire. His father was Robert Guiscard ('The Cunning'), who ranks among the foremost personalities of the Norman era. He had carved out a large territory for himself in Italy. Bohemond had inherited many of his gifts. Although he occasionally lapsed into over-confidence as a military leader, he was a skilled diplomat and, with his dashing clean-shaven appearance, someone who could charm other men into following him. In short, he was not the kind of man that Alexius could afford to trust.

The way in which Bohemond joined the Crusading movement exemplifies his personality. He was besieging the town of Amalfi in Italy; the peninsula was at that time riven with violent disputes. As soon as news of the Crusade reached him, he impulsively decided to abandon his assault on the town, and lead his army to the East. He assembled his force at Bari and left in October 1096. Included in this expedition were many Norman French, among whom was Bohemond's nephew, Tancred, who would play an important role in the future.

Bohemond sailed across the Adriatic and travelled thence by land to Constantinople. His political skill was evident from an early stage. He impressed on his troops the need to remain disciplined, in order to earn the goodwill of Alexius. Behind his actions appears to have been a desire from the outset to stake a claim as the overall secular leader of the Crusader armies – a course that was bound to lead him into outright conflict with the other prominent secular Crusaders, especially Raymond of Toulouse and Godfrey of Bouillon. He planned to ingratiate himself with Alexius with a view to gaining his support. By so doing, he hoped to advance his ambitions considerably.

Because of the order that he imposed on the army, Bohemond experienced little trouble from his troops on the way to Constantinople. Alexius responded by ensuring that the army was well provisioned and, apart from one minor skirmish when a few stragglers were harassed by Imperial troops, there were no difficult incidents as Bohemond and his men journeyed across the Empire. As he drew near Constantinople, Bohemond's behaviour continued to be exemplary. He sent envoys ahead of him to prepare for his imminent arrival. All the same, Alexius was extremely sceptical of his motives, and had every right to be. Indeed, Robert Guiscard had actually left Byzantium to Bohemond in his will, so firmly did he believe in the latter's claims to the Empire. Bohemond had fought long and hard in an attempt to enforce these claims in the past. Despite all this, he took the oath required of him without demur, and then entered into discussions with Godfrey and Baldwin, who crossed back over the Bosphorus for the purpose.

However, when Bohemond was alone with Alexius he spelt out the price of his support. Without embarrassment, he asked to be given command of the Imperial forces in Asia. Much as Bohemond's audacity might be admired, Alexius was far too wise to be bought so easily. Although he had no wish to antagonise Bohemond, he was also nervous of alienating the other leaders of the Crusade. He responded to Bohemond's approaches with a vague statement that he would certainly be strongly considered for the post when the time came to fill it. Bohemond realised that this was the best offer he was likely to get at this stage, and – contenting himself for the time being – he crossed the Bosphorus with his army on 26 April. His nephew, Tancred, however, had no intention of swearing allegiance to Alexius and slipped across at night to avoid the necessity of doing so.

Alexius' caution towards the Western armies was vindicated by the progress of the army of Raymond of Toulouse. His journey was a dreadful affair. Like the other armies, the land route to the East was chosen. But, although Raymond had had more time to prepare for the Crusade than the other leaders, the route he took suggests that he had not used that time wisely. The roads along which his army travelled were no more than tracks. Further, they passed through inhospitable terrain that was tailor-made for the ambushes of the aggressive Serb tribes who lived there. The journey was a nightmare experience, and attrition among the troops was high. Although there is no certain estimate of the numbers lost from Raymond's army during the early days of its progress, it would appear that the trials and tribulations experienced by the force had a dramatic psychological effect.

The army eventually arrived in Dyracchium where an escort was waiting to take them to Constantinople. There were several worrying incidents when the Imperial escort came to blows with the Crusader army. In one, the ecclesiastical leader of the Crusade, Bishop Adhemar of Le Puy, who was with Raymond's army, was wounded and captured. He was quickly released when his identity became known but the Crusaders were angry at the injury to the Pope's representative. The bishop was, in the interim, forced to stay behind in Thessalonica while he recuperated – his incapacity would have unfortunate repercussions in the near future.

Lacking Adhemar's restraining influence, discipline in the army rapidly declined. Several weeks earlier, Bohemond had passed through the town of Roussa, where he had legitimately purchased large stocks of provisions. Now, when Raymond's army looked to revictual in the town, there were simply no supplies left to buy. Infuriated by their inability to reprovision, Raymond's troops sacked the town. Alexius sent envoys to Raymond, telling him to hurry on to Constantinople. This, it transpired, only served to worsen the situation. Raymond pushed on to meet Alexius ahead of the main army, and without his presence order broke down completely. The troops left behind engaged in large-scale raids on the surrounding countryside. The Imperial troops escorting them fought back and, in the ensuing skirmish, bested the Crusaders, capturing their baggage in the process.

In Constantinople, Raymond was well received by Alexius, despite the problems that his army had caused. But once again, the oath of allegiance caused immense difficulty. Raymond saw himself as the secular leader of the expedition, a position that he believed was sanctioned by his perceived special relationship with Pope Urban II. He believed that he could not take the oath of allegiance without jeopardising the nature of that relationship. He was further concerned at the motives of Bohemond, and wanted to establish whether he and the Emperor had reached a mutual understanding about the future conduct of the Crusade.

In private, Alexius attempted to reassure him. It is probable that he tried to convince Raymond that he well understood the intrigues of Bohemond. It is after all extremely unlikely that the Emperor, who was a good reader of men, should not fully comprehend the nature of Bohemond's scheming, particularly given the open conflict between the two men in the past. Raymond responded by declaring that he had no difficulty in protecting the interests of the Emperor, but he merely wished to avoid serving under Bohemond. But this was not sufficient for Alexius – he could not let Raymond leave Constantinople without taking the oath. Raymond continued to resist, and an impasse was reached.

The situation was pregnant with threat. Bohemond, unnerved by the presence of Raymond, told Alexius that the Emperor could rely on his support should there be an open breach with the Count of Toulouse. Even Godfrey felt that

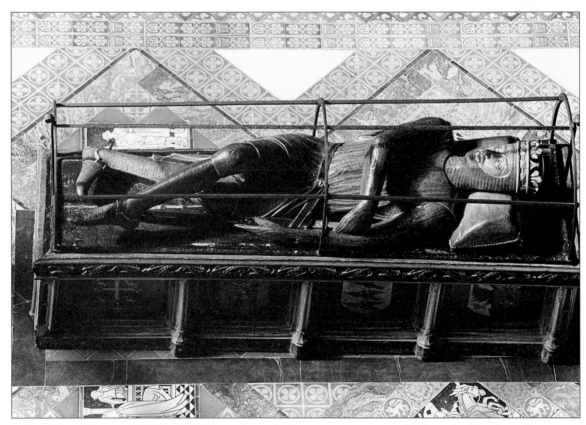

The tomb in Gloucester Cathedral of Robert of Normandy – a prominent crusader from the First Crusade.

Raymond was protesting too much. The veneer of Crusading unity, never much more than a superficial sham, was about to be exposed for the first time for the chimera that it was. Eventually, a compromise was reached. Raymond, particularly isolated in the absence of the still-recovering Adhemar, took a modified oath, whereby he agreed to respect the life and honour of the Emperor, and to do nothing that would jeopardise either. Adhemar further smoothed the choppy waters when he eventually caught up with Raymond at Constantinople. For the time being at least, a crisis had been averted.

One more force was yet to arrive before the armies collectively forming this First Crusade were complete. This was the most cosmopolitan group, in reality an amalgamation of smaller units combining to form a large but loosely-knit force. It was led by Robert of Normandy, the eldest son of William the Conqueror, along with Stephen of Blois and Robert of Flanders. Robert of Normandy was aged about forty, mild-mannered and ineffectual but not lacking in personal charm or courage. He had been at war for years with his brother William Rufus, the King of England. He funded his expedition by pledging the Duchy of Normandy to Rufus in return for ten thousand marks. The Church would not benefit particularly from this funding arrangement, as Rufus would finance it by the imposition of heavy taxes on its property in England. Robert was accompanied by many of the Norman nobility, as well as Bishop Odo of Bayeux. He also numbered knights from England, Scotland and Brittany in his army.

It seems that Stephen of Blois, unlike Robert of Normandy, had no great desire to accompany the Crusade. However, he was blessed of that occasional Medieval phenomenon, a strong and domineering wife in the form of Adela, daughter of William the Conqueror. If the chroniclers are to be believed, she had inherited much of her father's forceful temperament, and it was at her insistence that Stephen joined the Crusade. He was immensely wealthy and, for him at least, the costs of the expedition would not pose undue difficulty. He had with him many knights and Fulcher of Chartres, destined to be one of the great chroniclers of the First Crusade.

Robert of Flanders was the youngest of the co-leaders but possessed a striking personality. His father had been a strong supporter of Alexius, and had visited Jerusalem. Perhaps his father's journey was the motivation behind Robert of Flanders' decision to join the expedition. Throughout the Crusading period, the importance of family ties in electing to go on Crusade is a

Bishop Odo of Bayeux, seen here encouraging youths during the Battle of Hastings. Odo went on to accompany Robert of Normandy on the First Crusade. (The Bayeux Tapestry – 11th century. By special permission of the City of Bayeux)

recurrent theme. The First Crusade, for example, saw Bohemond and his nephew Tancred campaigning, along with the three brothers, Godfrey of Bouillon, Eustace of Boulogne and Baldwin. Family connection would continue to be important to the Crusading movement throughout its life.

Robert of Flanders provided the smallest of the three groups forming this force, but it made up in quality what it lacked in numbers. The army thus formed made its way to Italy, where Pope Urban gave it his personal blessing. In a desultory fashion, they then meandered to the Adriatic coast of Italy, where they waited for transportation. Robert of Flanders was seemingly impatient to move on, and made his way quickly to Constantinople, where he was received cordially by Alexius. Robert had no difficulties in taking the requisite oath of allegiance. Stephen of Blois and Robert of Normandy were much more lethargic. They suffered from their delay, as some of their troops lost patience and deserted. When they eventually crossed the Adriatic, a sudden squall capsized one of the ships causing much loss of life. The rest of the force subsequently made its way overland without incident to Constantinople, arriving in May 1097.

Here they were mesmerised by the opulence of the city. Alexius went overboard in his generosity to them, and both Stephen and Robert of Normandy took the oath willingly. As their army was the last to arrive, their force was allowed access to the city in small groups. The magnificence of Constantinople overwhelmed them. The West was characterised by squat and dark churches but, in contrast, the basilicas of Constantinople were vast and ornate. Everywhere explosions of light and colour burst forth from the city. Huge, airy palaces dedicated to the pursuit of pleasure provided another major difference in comparison to the gaunt, menacing castles of the West. The architecture of the city was an expression of wealth and sybaritic self-confidence as opposed to the military dominance that was characteristic of the West European landscape.

The sightseeing could not of course last indefinitely. When this last army finally crossed the Bosphorus, something like 5,000 mounted warriors and 30,000 foot soldiers and camp followers were gathered on its southern shores. The journey to this point was merely a preamble. The main event was about to begin. The army was about to embark on something of an adventure into the unknown and, whatever else one might think of the Crusaders, their actions represent a considerable step of faith. Although the region was not unknown to the West, the political uncertainties of Asia Minor meant that the map of the region had changed beyond recognition in the past thirty years. Much of the region was under Turkish control, and to add to their difficulties the Crusaders did not trust the guides provided to them by Alexius. If they were under any illusions about the difficulties ahead, these were soon dispelled by the bleached bones of the peasant army still strewn about the fields around Civetot, long since scorched dry by the blazing sun.

There were already serious questions to be asked of the Crusading movement. The whole concept of trust, for example, was a complex dilemma. A millennium later, it can be seen in the differing interpretations placed on events by the chroniclers of Byzantium and the West. Of course, the chroniclers of the day were not objective observers. They sought patronage from their chosen leader, and would therefore seek to represent him in the best possible light. Further, they often wrote their chronicles many years after the events they described had taken place. An excellent example of this is provided by Anna Comnena, whose work the *Alexiad* is our major Byzantine source. As the daughter of Alexius she was hardly likely to be objective, and her accuracy would surely not be helped by the fact that she wrote her narrative after a gap of thirty years.

For all this, there are certain recurrent themes that may be detected. The Byzantines criticised the Westerners for their poor behaviour, their barbarism and their duplicity. In return, the Western chroniclers distrusted the Byzantines and before long would be openly accusing them of treachery. If nothing else, the differences between the Eastern and Western chroniclers provide irrefutable evidence that the two halves of Christendom had completely failed to understand each other.

To those who cared to analyse the course of events so far, two problems would already be apparent. The first was that there was no unified command in the Crusader army. Each force had made its way to the East independently. At the first point of meaningful contact, when the leaders met in Constantinople, little time was lost before tensions became apparent. Raymond and Bohemond obviously saw each other as rivals, and the attitude of Godfrey towards either party was as yet unclear. Now they were in Asia Minor, the forces were still in reality individual armies. Events would show that Bishop Adhemar could exercise some sort of authority over the force, but it was never strong enough to keep the individual leaders completely under control. Each leader had his own motive, usually fuelled by selfish ambition. Before the Crusade was over, the evident lack of cohesion and common purpose would threaten the very survival of the expedition.

The second problem revolved around the misunderstandings between Byzantium and the West, which have already been mentioned. The oaths of allegiance that had been sworn to Alexius would become less effective as the miles increased between Byzantium and the Crusader army. In the minds of many of the Crusaders, suspicions were already firmly lodged, easily accessed in the event of future difficulties between the Empire and the Western army. The advancement of Byzantine interests counted for little with the Crusaders.

As stated above, the chroniclers of the day clearly noted these differing perspectives. Two brief extracts serve to illustrate the general outlook of each party. In the first, Anna Comnena outlines the Greeks' scepticism of Western motives:

[Alexius] feared their arrival since he knew their irresistible enthusiasm, their changing and inconsistent character and everything that is specific to the Celtic temperament with all its consequences. He knew . . . that they break their treaties without the slightest compunction . . .

In contrast, the Western chroniclers detected perfidy in the actions of Alexius. The anonymous author of the *Gesta Francorum* writes that:

The emperor, full of anxiety and boiling with anger, was thinking of how to capture these soldiers of Christ by cunning and fraud. But by divine grace, neither place nor time for mischief was found, either by the emperor or his men.

Despite these concerns, the Crusader army was positive and excited now that the real adventure was about to begin. They knew that sacrifice would be needed if Jerusalem were to be retaken for Christendom. Of the extent of the horrors ahead, though, few were fully aware. The Crusaders were about to embark on a journey during which they were to suffer incessant and ferocious attack from a fierce and determined Turkish enemy. Even worse, the vagaries of the Anatolian weather, from parched desert to snow-blocked mountain pass, lay ahead. And then there would be disease, the greatest enemy of all. Unimagined hardship stood before them. The army had little conception of the magnitude of the challenge ahead. It was just as well. If the Crusaders knew what lay between them and the recovery of the Holy City, it is likely that many of them would not even have started the journey.

CHAPTER 6

An Act of Faith

Above all else, the force assembled on the southern shores of the Bosphorus now faced a journey into uncertain territory. After the conquest of Asia Minor by the Turks the journey across the hinterland had become a perilous one. At one time the road system had been excellent and the country through which the troops were to pass would have provided an abundance of water and provisions. However, over twenty years had passed since the days of Byzantine rule and the order imposed by the empire on the region had long since evaporated. A number of petty kingdoms had developed in the wake of the catastrophe at Manzikert, and the infrastructure had disintegrated. These small kingdoms were constantly bickering among themselves. The fact that many of them came from Turkish tribes counted for little – if anything it enhanced the rivalry among them. Thus it was a disunited region through which the Crusaders were to pass, a territory that presented many dangers but, through the very disunity of the Turks, many opportunities as well.

The Christian army was in high spirits as plans were made. Such friction as there had been between Alexius and the Western leaders was, for the time being, not openly causing difficulties. And, as the undisputed spiritual head of the army, Adhemar provided a focus for the expedition. Even the military leaders, of whom there were so many, were at the moment working together, acting collectively in a council that had been set up to co-ordinate the army's moves.

The immediate priority was to decide on the route to the Holy Land. Maps that existed were often superfluous because of the ever-changing political situation in the region. However, there was no doubt about the first military target of the Crusade. The city of Nicaea stood beside the main road into the heart of Asia Minor. It was the capital of Kilij Arslan, one of the most important Turkish chieftains, and there was no way that it could be left intact, astride, as it was, the Crusaders' main line of communication. It therefore had to be captured.

The timing of the venture was fortuitous – a recurrent theme with the First Crusade. Kilij Arslan was absent, campaigning far to the east. He was involved in one of the interminable civil wars that characterised the Turkish tribes in the region. When he received news that the Crusaders were approaching his lands, he was not perturbed. After the debacle of the Peasants' Crusade, he had little respect for Western forces, and he had complete confidence that the men he had left behind to defend his territory would be perfectly capable of holding off the enemy. Ironically, the major contribution of the peasants' armies may have been that they provided a false yardstick against which other forces were measured, and which now lulled the Turks into a false sense of security. In addition, Kilij Arslan knew that Nicaea was surrounded with strong walls and any attempt to take it must of necessity be a long and painful process.

The Crusader army moved off at the end of April 1097 led by Godfrey of Bouillon in the absence of Bohemond (who was still in Constantinople), past the pitiful relics of the peasant forces rotting on the battlefield of Civetot. He showed commendable caution, widening roads and ensuring that an adequate number of scouts were always sent out in advance of the force. He even marked the way with white crosses to guide future expeditions. On 6 May the army arrived at Nicaea. The city walls, over 3 miles long and with two hundred and forty towers, had been built by the Byzantines. It would be difficult for the defenders to man such extended defences properly, but the Crusaders were nonetheless faced with a formidable challenge. To the west, the waters of the Ascanian Lake lapped against the foundations of the city walls. Godfrey encamped outside the north wall and Tancred, leading the Normans in Bohemond's absence, took up a position to the east of the city. The south was left for Raymond's army, which was still on its way.

Although inside the city in considerable numbers, the Turks were understandably apprehensive when they saw the size of the force arrayed against them. Messengers were despatched to seek assistance, but before any reinforcements could reach the city, Raymond arrived to complete the encirclement. Among the Crusaders, provisions were already in short supply – an ominous portent – but when Bohemond arrived from Constantinople he was accompanied by a generous amount of supplies from Alexius. The siege now began in earnest.

Turkish reinforcements arrived at the scene just after Raymond of Toulouse. They were quickly driven off. They withdrew to a safe distance, awaiting the arrival of a much larger force. Meanwhile, unbeknown to the Crusaders, Alexius apparently had an agenda of his own. He had no desire to inherit a ruin. Many of the inhabitants of the city had, less than a generation before, been part of the Byzantine Empire and the thought of a full-scale sack of the city must understandably have horrified him. His representative, Manuel Butimites, was authorised to negotiate secretly with the defenders.

These covert discussions were suddenly ended when news reached the Christian camp that Kilij Arslan was arriving with a large relieving force. It would appear that the full extent of the danger had shocked him from his complacency, particularly as his wife, children and much of his wealth were inside the city. He attacked immediately on his arrival on 21 May. The brunt of his assault was focused on the troops of Raymond, who, inspired by Adhemar, fought fiercely. Neither Bohemond nor Godfrey dared to send help as to do so would have invited an attack on their rear from the forces inside the city. However, Robert of Flanders did throw his troops into the battle, and swung the balance by so doing. Incessant Turkish attacks, and clouds of arrows from their swarms of archers, could not make a decisive impression on the Crusader battle lines. At the end of the day, the Turks withdrew, tired, demoralised and defeated, leaving Nicaea to its fate.

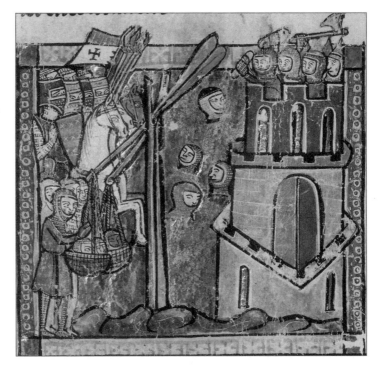

Bombarding Nicaea with the heads of captured Turks. (Fr 2630 f. 22v Crusaders bombard Nicaea with heads c. 1098, by William of Tyr (c. 1130–85), Estoire d'Outremer (12th century); Bibliothèque Nationale, Paris / Bridgeman Art Library, London / New York)

That fate was nowhere near as awful as it could have been. The Crusaders were understandably ecstatic at their success. True, the heads of the enemy corpses were cut off and catapulted over the city walls in a crude but terrifying example of Medieval psychological warfare. But attempts to breach the walls by mining were ineffective, and supplies still reached the city from across the lake. The Crusaders were therefore obligated to ask Alexius to provide a naval blockade, presumably much to his delight as it emphasised the army's reliance on him. On the arrival of this fleet, the garrison realised that there was no further hope of raising the siege. They therefore entered into further clandestine negotiations with Alexius, hoping to obtain good terms as a result.

Oblivious to these secret discussions, the Crusaders planned a final assault on the city for the morning of 19 June. One can imagine the feelings within the Christian camp on the eve of the attack; a mixture, no doubt, of excitement, fear, tension and anticipation. As the day of the assault dawned, however, these emotions were overwhelmed by others. As the Crusaders wiped the sleep from their eyes, they were greeted with the sight of the banners of Alexius fluttering proudly atop the city walls. A deal had been struck behind the Crusaders' backs.

There was inevitably ill feeling as a result. In practical terms, the Crusaders had been robbed of the material spoils of victory that the sack of the city would have given them, and for which they had already fought hard. Looked at from another perspective, it evidenced a lack of trust of the Crusaders that, however well justified, appeared to many of them to be manipulative and duplicitous on the part of the Emperor. For his part, Alexius tried to soothe their ruffled feelings. He gave large gifts to the Crusader leaders, and generous supplies of food were given to the rank-and-file. Yet even this had a price. Those lords who had not yet sworn an oath of allegiance were now required to do so. Prominent among these was Tancred, who initially continued to resist. Ongoing pressure forced him to concede and take the oath – subsequent events give the impression that he had little intention of keeping it.

However, despite some dissatisfaction among the Crusaders because of the actions of the Greeks, there was still considerable elation after the fall of the city. But while the alliance between Byzantium and Western Christendom did not suffer unduly, the relationship with Alexius undoubtedly became strained as a result of the way he had taken the city. It seems, too, that there was some degree of shock at the way in which Alexius treated the important Turkish captives taken in the city. Kilij Arslan's wife and children were taken to Constantinople where they were received with royal pomp; they were subsequently released and returned to Arslan without ransom. One of the chroniclers with the Crusade described the act:

> . . . the Emperor, who was a fool as well as a knave, told them to go away without fear; he had them brought to him at Constantinople under safe-conduct, and kept them carefully so that he could have them ready to injure the Franks and obstruct the Crusade.

Undoubtedly, Alexius' actions were wise in a political sense, but they were not understood by many of the Crusaders, who saw them as an attempt to harm their own interests.

Following the fall of Nicaea, the Crusaders were faced with difficult logistical decisions, particularly regarding the onward route that they should take. The problems of adequate provisioning were already significant and as more distance was put between them and Constantinople, these would inevitably increase. In order that the land through which they were to pass was not denuded of supplies, the army was split into two. This was logistically good sense, but militarily dangerous. The Crusaders were in a land they did not know well, characterised by rolling hills that provided wonderful opportunities for the Turks to employ their favourite tactic, that of the ambush. The situation called for caution, a virtue that the Crusader leaders did not possess in great measure.

The progress of the first army provided an object lesson in the need for discretion. This group was composed of the Norman troops of Bohemond, and the forces of Robert of Flanders and Stephen of Blois. It appears to have made little attempt to maintain communications with the second army. Their journey initially passed without incident. By 30 June, camp was set up deep inside Turkish territory at Dorylaeum. Early next morning, the break of day was heralded by the war cries of thousands of Turkish warriors circling the camp in the surrounding hills. There can have been little doubt of what this meant. Kilij Arslan had only been driven off at Nicaea, and he was far from a downtrodden enemy. Now he was attempting to obliterate the Crusader army.

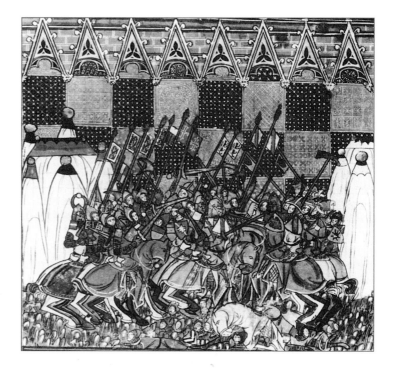

The Battle of Dorylaeum, 1 July 1097 – the first major battle of the Crusades. (MS Fr. 352, f. 49)

The enemy made a terrifying spectacle. The *Gesta Francorum*, which tells the story of the First Crusade, describes how 'the Turks made a fierce and sudden attack upon Bohemond and his comrades. These Turks began, all at once, to howl and gabble and shout, saying with loud voices in their own language some devilish word which I do not understand' (probably *Allah Akbar* – 'God is great').

However, Bohemond was an experienced warrior who had – to the good fortune of the Christian troops – lived through many a crisis before. The large numbers of non-combatants with his force were placed in the centre of the camp, which was well provided with water that they could help provide to the fighting men while the battle was raging. The tents of the camp were struck, and a messenger was despatched to find the second army, wherever it might be. He must have had an interesting journey.

Bohemond was in full control of the situation. His knights were ordered to dismount and instructed that, above all else, they must not break ranks. They were to fight where they stood. One small group disobeyed. Within moments they were in chaos, rushing back to the lines they had broken, severely cut up by the opportunistic Turkish forces. The lessons of Manzikert showed that disorganised forays against the Turks were bound to fail. Obviously the forty knights who disobeyed Bohemond had not properly studied these lessons and were quickly forced to return in undignified haste, badly bloodied by their disobedience and having made no impact on the Turkish forces whatsoever.

The advance of the day also saw the advance of Turkish fortunes. Arrows rained down on the mass of Crusader warriors. One wave of horsemen after another broke against the Christian battle line. The enemy force appeared to be attacking in enormous numbers and there was nowhere for the Crusaders to flee, surrounded as they were. They had to stand where they were, fight or die. Slowly but inexorably the defensive ring of steel contracted as it was driven further and further in on itself. The situation was now grim, and a martyr's death appeared to be the only available option. Whatever else modern interpreters may think of the Crusaders, they did not lack courage. They were not afraid to die.

At the point of deepest despair, salvation appeared. Around midday, small groups of warriors were sighted. They wore the badge of the Cross. Not a moment too soon, help had arrived. The effect on the Turks was significant, as it appears they were under the illusion that the army they had ensnared represented the whole of the Christian force. The arriving troops, the men of Godfrey, Hugh and Raymond, did not have time to form up in orderly fashion. As groups of men arrived they simply launched themselves pell-mell into the fray. Temporarily thrown off balance, Kilij Arslan could not prevent them from fighting their way through and joining forces with the other Christian warriors. The opportunity for counter-attack had now arrived. The Crusaders had withstood every assault that the Turks had hurled against them. Now it was time for the reckoning.

Buoyed up no doubt by the prospect of glory and wealth that victory offered, the Crusaders advanced on an extended front. The chroniclers of the day tell us continually that such an advance was an awesome sight, and one that struck terror into the enemy. Anxiety among the Turkish forces was transformed into blind panic when Bishop Adhemar arrived without warning with yet another force. He had carefully led this troop through the hills surrounding the camp and had somehow arrived unnoticed. In an action imbued with enormous symbolism, the warrior bishop was about to seal a great victory for the army of Christ. The Turks had no further stomach for battle, and broke. They fled so rapidly that they deserted their camp, leaving its treasures for the victorious Crusaders.

The battle at Dorylaeum was a tremendous victory, and one that greatly enhanced the prospects of the Crusaders. It opened up a route across Asia Minor, although the journey that was left would still extract a terrible price. The Christians had covered themselves with glory, but in the process had learnt something about their foe. He was not an enemy who would easily submit in the face of danger. He was disciplined, well armoured and determined, brave and ferocious in battle. Despite some earlier rumours to the contrary, he was indeed a worthy opponent. Some of the Christians recalled the legend that the Turks were descended from the Trojans, renowned as a great fighting race. This amounted to a psychological acknowledgement of their prowess as warriors.

Kilij Arslan continued his retreat methodically. In a classic demonstration of a scorched earth policy, water cisterns were systematically demolished and food taken or destroyed. The Crusaders, despite their victory and licking their wounds after the bloody cost of battle (among the dead was William, brother of Tancred), were yet to be faced with great deprivation. When they resumed their advance, they marched south to avoid a natural salt desert, little knowing that they were walking into a man-made one. In the six weeks following Dorylaeum, they came face to face for the first time with the physical torments that had thus far only

The Taurus mountains proved irresistible to Baldwin and Tancred.

threatened them. Short of food, water or any kind of physical comfort, the true nature of their challenge became apparent. It was comparatively easy to fight Turks. The militaristic society of the Franks, as the Crusaders were to be known to their enemies, understood warfare well. However, it was ill equipped to cope with the uncertainties of a country whose previous owners themselves were not fully aware of current realities.

Horses died by the score, unused to the extremes of temperature and emaciated by lack of food and water. Once proud knights were forced to march like common foot soldiers. On occasion, even dogs and sheep were used to haul the baggage. Fulcher of Chartres maintains that morale remained high and, if this is accurate, then the participants in this awful journey must have been inspired indeed. Whatever their true state of mind, it must have been an incredible relief when the town of Iconium was finally reached. The town was surrounded by orchards and well supplied by streams. It must have seemed an oasis. Even Raymond, who was ill and thought to be dying, made a remarkable recovery here.

The Crusaders recommenced their march through the hinterland, advancing deeper into countryside teeming with Turkish raiders. When they set out from Iconium, they soon had to beat off a Turkish attack. It was at this stage that real differences of opinion among the leadership started to arise concerning the best route to take. The bulk of the army moved north to Caesarea but two prominent men, Baldwin and Tancred, decided to cross the daunting Taurus Mountains to see what lay on the other side. For many, if not most, of the leaders, personal religious beliefs formed a strong motivation to their Crusading zeal. However, there were often other secondary but still important reasons that decided a man to take the Cross. And in the case of Baldwin and Tancred's decision now, those reasons were strong, personal and not necessarily religiously motivated.

For example, Tancred was inevitably overshadowed by his uncle Bohemond, successful, rich and powerful. Similarly, Baldwin stood in the shadows of Eustace and Godfrey. Both men were alive to the possibilities of aggrandisement opened up by the Crusade. Tancred was the first to leave for the mountains in September 1097, accompanied by a small force of 300 men. Baldwin closely followed with a much larger force of 2,500. Few non-combatants accompanied the armies, as this was primarily a raid in strength. Tancred, aided by the small numbers of men with him, took the quickest route and arrived before the city of Tarsus. Many of the population were Christians, and although the city was garrisoned by Turks, most of its inhabitants were sympathetic to the Crusaders. A sortie from the Turks was repelled but Tancred lacked the numbers to take the city by storm, and the fate of Tarsus was decided by the arrival of Baldwin's army.

Showing a quite understandable desire for self-preservation, the garrison abandoned the city. The populace opened the gates to the Crusaders eagerly, whereupon Tancred immediately entered and raised his standard on the city walls. However, Baldwin demanded that *he* be given ownership of Tarsus. Tancred was furious but, heavily outnumbered, was powerless to resist. It was a case of might equating to right. Angrily, Tancred acquiesced and left the city. The confrontation marked a major deterioration in the relationships of two of the foremost Crusaders.

The situation then became still worse. A party of latecomers arrived to join the now departed Tancred at Tarsus. They sought admission to the city, but Baldwin refused them. That night, while camped outside the walls, these stragglers were attacked and slaughtered to a man. Three hundred lives were lost through the thoughtlessness and myopia of Baldwin. The whole army was shocked by what had happened, and even Baldwin's closest supporters found it impossible to justify his actions. Only the arrival of a small fleet in the port, led by one of Baldwin's countrymen, Guynemer of Boulogne, deflected attention from him. Guynemer had shown the initiative to form a small fleet to help the Crusade. He was left to garrison Tarsus as Baldwin moved east. He stuck to the coast, a wise move as it meant that a supply chain of sorts could be maintained through the use of Guynemer's fleet. The importance of a maritime presence in the region throughout the Crusades should not be underestimated.

In the meantime, Tancred had moved on to the town of Mamistra. The Turkish garrison followed the example of that at Tarsus and deserted the town, which was taken without a fight. When Baldwin arrived at the town, Tancred was understandably suspicious of his motives. He consequently refused to admit Baldwin, but made sure that his army was provided with adequate provisions.

However, some of his men were not prepared to let the previous insult offered by Baldwin at Tarsus go unavenged and attacked his camp at night. They were outnumbered, and the assault was beaten back.

Both Tancred and Baldwin realised that great damage was being done by this petty infighting. The loss of life had been futile and destructive. They allowed themselves to be reconciled, although it would be reasonable to assume that beneath the surface resentment lingered on. The pressure was relieved somewhat when Baldwin was called back to the main army, responding to the grave news that his wife was dying and his children were seriously ill. Tancred also moved on, to the town of Alexandretta, which he took and garrisoned.

While this diversion was going on, further north the main army was about to meet a major challenge. After the heat of the desert hinterland, they were now faced with the difficult passage across the Anti-Taurus Mountains. Although challenged by the elements in the latter part of their journey, they were often hailed as liberators by the towns that fell into their hands. Turkish attacks were now driven back with relative ease.

On this stage of the journey, the Crusade benefited from passing through land held by the Armenians. The Armenians had in the past endured a difficult relationship with the Byzantines. For centuries they had enjoyed independent status, but the need to protect the crucial themes of Asia Minor had eventually led the Byzantines to annex the Armenian territories. The last states had been incorporated into the empire in 1064. The Armenians resented this, not unnaturally. They were also regarded as heretics by the Byzantines as they did not share the latter's Orthodox beliefs. Following Manzikert, when Asia Minor fell apart, Byzantine control of the Armenian territories was lost. The Armenians had suffered at the hands of the Turks, but despite their difficulties some small Armenian cities had managed to reassert a degree of independence in the vacuum left by the decline of the Byzantine Empire. They had sought help from the West in the recent past and, although they received little response, they were still well disposed towards the Crusaders. This considerably helped the expedition in its progress through the area.

However, if the Crusaders thought the worst was now over, the crossing of the mountains would sadly disabuse them. The journey revealed nature at its most brutal. Torrential rains washed away what little remained of the poorly maintained roads, already harmed by years of neglect. Horses, slithering in their frantic attempts to gain a foothold, fell to their deaths into sheer ravines, taking much of the baggage with them. Knights, once so proud of their magnificent armour, were now so weighed down by it that they tried to give it away to poor infantrymen. Thus it was a chastened and badly depleted army that finally descended into the valley at Marash. From here it progressed to the plains surrounding Antioch, one of the most ancient and holy cities of the Levant. It was here that the Crusaders faced their true test of fire.

CHAPTER 7

Weighed in the Balance

The great adventures of history are often characterised by a defining moment, a point at which the success, or indeed the survival, of the entire expedition seems to be in terrible doubt. At Antioch, the Crusading army teetered on the edge of a chasm into which it seemed it might fall, to certain destruction. Here it was weighed in a balance so finely poised that the smallest of adjustments would have tipped the scales irrevocably against it. Here untold horrors were to face them, horrors of war, of famine, of death. Here was Hell.

To understand fully what happened to the Crusade at this stage, the political state of the Levant must be considered. It would be the greatest of understatements to say that circumstances were confused. The Crusaders had already benefited from the chaos that existed during their journey thus far. The situation was at its most confused in the states to the east and the south of Asia Minor. A number of Arab chieftains had gained a degree of power in Iraq, causing great agitation there, so a co-ordinated response would not be forthcoming from that direction. And small Armenian city-states existed as far east as the Euphrates and even beyond, adding yet another dimension to the political turmoil in the region.

In the lands closest to Antioch, the prominent Muslim leaders were Ridwan of Aleppo and Duqaq of Damascus, who were rivals even though they were brothers. The death of Malik Shah had left a great vacuum in the area. Despite their kinship, Ridwan and Duqaq constantly conspired against each other in the violent civil wars following Malik Shah's demise. From Mosul, the Emir Kerbogha encroached on the territory of Ridwan, attempting to take advantage of the uncertainty caused by the conflicts in the region. Yaghi-Siyan, the ruler of Antioch, had recently fallen out with Ridwan, and this would affect the siege of the city.

Effectively, there was no cohesion within the Muslim states. Each city had its own ruler, who owned at best nominal allegiance to an overlord. In addition, the Turks in the region were involved in a long-running and bitter dispute with the Fatimids of Egypt. In the absence of a strong unifying leader, the Muslim Levant was completely divided. Ostensibly capable of resisting the advance of the Franks, the Muslims were too immersed in their internal disputes to respond to the danger that the Christian army posed.

The city of Antioch itself was steeped in Christian tradition. The word 'Christian' had first been used in this city. It was the seat of one of the most important patriarchs of the Orthodox Church. However, it is likely that such religious connotations were lost on the Crusaders when they saw the city for the first time. Surrounded by walls that snaked for miles around the perimeter, at places even climbing mountains, it represented a fearsome challenge. Although old, the walls had been kept in a good state of repair. They were high and regularly intersected by many towers, which provided the defenders with the opportunity to launch devastating crossfire against any attacking force. Further, the acreage enclosed within the city was huge, enabling it to be well provided with food from market gardens. There were ample supplies of water for the defenders, and the sheer length of the city walls made it impossible for the Crusaders to impose a tight siege.

The best opportunity for the Christian army would have been to attack immediately. At Antioch, as has been noted, Yaghi-Siyan was at odds with Ridwan and could not rely on his support. Therefore, a successful attack would be more likely if it could be mounted before he had time to find another ally. But only Raymond among the Crusader leaders advocated a quick assault. The troops were exhausted, and delay would enable fresher reinforcements to arrive.

There were also more selfish reasons for the hesitation. Further east, around Edessa, Baldwin was looking to carve out a principality of his own. Bohemond

Looking over the remains of the citadel of ancient Antioch.

wished to do likewise. However, to further this aim it was important that he was seen as the conqueror of Antioch. This would not be the case if Raymond's advice was followed and the city was to fall to an army under *his* command. Bohemond therefore counselled that the Crusaders should wait. Although obviously beneficial for Bohemond, for the Crusade as a whole the decision to delay was a grave error. For his part, Raymond well understood Bohemond's reasons for prevarication. Relations between the two were stretched to breaking point.

Meanwhile, Bohemond attempted to make contact with friendly inhabitants inside the city. There were large numbers of sympathetic Christians among the population (with the exception of the Syrian Christian element, who were opposed to the Orthodox emperors who had once, in generations past, been their rulers). A steady flow of information leaked out to the besieging army, providing the Crusaders with the hope that Antioch could be taken by treachery, the way that Yaghi-Siyan had himself taken it in 1085. Conversely, there were also spies in the Christian camp who told the defenders that the Franks were reluctant to attack. This emboldened the Muslims and they launched a series of disruptive sorties. They were further encouraged by news that a relief force was on its way from Damascus.

The siege of Antioch began on 21 October 1097. Initially, there were ample supplies for the Christian army, but this seemed only to breed complacency and the stores they accumulated to help them survive the winter would prove to be insufficient. Some minor successes further boosted confidence. The Turkish garrison at the nearby fortress of Harenc was lured out and massacred to a man. A Genoese fleet arriving at the nearby port of St Symeon brought reinforcements and supplies, although these were but token compensations when set against the supply shortage that was looming. As the besiegers became aware of their predicament, they were forced to search further and further afield for succour. Strong raiding parties were sent out from the city to attack while the Christian army was off guard; in response a large tower was built to help resist the Muslim attacks.

The first major crisis occurred when Bohemond set out on a raid at the head of 20,000 troops. Yaghi-Siyan knew of their departure, and of the consequent weakness of the forces left behind. Under cover of darkness, he launched a fierce attack on the Crusader camp on 29 December. The Crusaders were unprepared. For a while, the situation looked desperate. It was left to Raymond to save the day; showing skill and coolness, he reorganised his forces sufficiently to beat the attack back. The fleeing Turks were so hotly pursued by Raymond that the Christians gained a temporary foothold on a bridge into the city. But exhaustion eventually overcame them, and they were forced to withdraw.

Meanwhile, Bohemond met with mixed fortunes on his raid. Encamped at the city of Albara on 30 December, he was attacked at daybreak by the Turkish relieving force. The troops in the vanguard, led by Robert of Flanders, were surrounded. Defeat looked imminent, but at the crucial moment Bohemond unleashed his reserve and beat back the Turks. This provided a great fillip to those laying siege to Antioch as the relieving army was forced back from the city. Set against this, however, was the fact that the raid had found little in the way of provisions, the primary purpose of the foray, and the participants returned to the siege with hardly any tangible reward to show for their efforts.

The provisioning problems quickly became acute. Food became increasingly scarce, and large numbers of the Crusaders began to expire from malnutrition. Although the Crusaders held the nearby port of St Symeon and this enabled some supplies to be delivered from the exiled Patriarch of Jerusalem in Cyprus, it was not enough to make a significant difference. In desperation, Adhemar ordered a three-day fast to fortify the army spiritually. It made no real difference, as they had little to eat anyway. The defenders further taunted them by suspending the Patriarch of Antioch over the walls in a cage. Humiliated and hungry, the Crusaders probably did not imagine that things could get worse. They did. In February 1098 news reached them that a relieving force was approaching.

The situation presented opportunities for Bohemond. Taticius, the Imperial representative with the expedition, had abandoned the Christian army and was on his way back to Alexius. This had resulted in the prestige of the Emperor diminishing somewhat in the eyes of the Crusaders. Growing unrest was already spreading among the Franks concerning the role of Byzantium, and this cannot have been helped by Taticius' actions, which may well have been construed by some as a form of desertion. Bohemond – who was quick to employ his propagandists against Taticius – sought to avail himself of this turn of events. They significantly weakened the moral power of the oath that he had sworn to Alexius. He added to the strength of his position by insinuating that he was thinking of returning home, hoping to frighten the other Crusaders into a supportive position. His plans worked well and the task of fighting off the relieving force was allotted to his control.

On many occasions during the course of the Crusades, the Christian armies would be rash and ill disciplined. In this instance, however, the plan developed by Bohemond was masterful. By this time the relieving force was only 16 miles away from the city at Harenc. Halfway between this town and Antioch, the road narrows, bordered on one side by the River Orontes and on the other by a large lake. It was here that Bohemond chose to make his stand. The narrow front meant that the enemy, vastly superior as far as numbers were concerned, would be unable to exploit his advantage, while the hills marking the approach road would hide the Christian force until the last moment. Hopelessly outnumbered, Bohemond set about exploiting the only two tactical advantages left to him – surprise and nerve.

The plan worked magnificently. The Turks were completely taken by surprise. Before they could deploy their archers, the heavy cavalry of the Franks, with only 700 fit horses available, charged them. It did not break the Turkish line but it caused considerable confusion. This first assault, however, was merely a diversion. Its purpose was to lure the Turks to the place where the major part of the Christian army was positioned. The Turks, oblivious to this, tore after the tiny cavalry force. As they reached the point where the road narrows most, their large numbers inevitably constricted their movement. At this moment, the Crusaders charged again, but this was no feint. The crashing impact of this new charge created blind panic among the Turks, for whom the size of their force was now a positive disadvantage. In the ensuing rout, 2,000 Turks perished, drowned in the water in their haste to escape, or cut to pieces.

It was a spectacular triumph but one that relieved only the immediate crisis. A battle was won, but the prospects for victory in the war were still far from promising. Time had been gained, but the supply situation was worse than ever. The arrival of a fleet brought some relief, particularly much needed materials for siege engines, but as this was being escorted to the Christian camp by Bohemond and Raymond it was attacked by a large sortie from the city that, initially at least, succeeded in capturing the supplies. However, the counter-attack launched by the Franks drove the Turks into confusion. Many of the Muslims were trapped outside the city walls when the gates were shut, and it was rumoured that 1,500 died. The siege materials were also recaptured, which enabled it to be pressed more closely, and for the first time the defenders began to suffer real deprivation.

But now another danger loomed, the greatest yet. Kerbogha, Emir of Mosul, one of the most terrible of Turkish leaders, was on his way to raise the siege. Several powerful warlords from Persia and Iraq, as well as Duqaq, supported him. At the head of a substantial force, he presented the largest challenge of all to the Crusaders. Weakened by hunger, worn down by constant attrition against the Turks, there was a real possibility that they would not be able to resist another attack from the enemy. Help was to come from an unexpected source. The catalyst was Baldwin of Boulogne, presently 200 miles away in the city of Edessa.

Baldwin had not made for Antioch with the rest of the army. When he returned from his counter-productive disputes with Tancred, it was only to find his wife and children dying. On the march to Antioch following their demise he had protected the Crusaders' left flank. However, he was invited to help a local Armenian ruler, Thoros. The Armenians were a proud and independent people. They had a long and moving history, and following the defeat of Byzantium in the region had fought heroically to keep their traditions alive. Despite their Christian faith they felt little loyalty to the Emperor and they had long entertained hopes that their salvation might come from the West.

When Baldwin moved eastwards to help, he could at first argue that he had sound tactical motives for it, because it helped to shield the main force from counter-attack. Thoros was grateful for his presence and invited him to his capital, Edessa. Baldwin arrived there on 6 February 1098. Thoros, perhaps remembering that only twenty years before the Armenians had sent an impassioned plea to the Pope for help, needed the presence of Baldwin because he had been alerted that Edessa lay right in the path of Kerbogha's relieving force. He had every reason to be perturbed. He was not a popular ruler, and his attempts to foster ties with the Emperor had only served to further alienate his people. He believed that Baldwin could provide his regime with prestige and credibility. Baldwin's price was a high one. He would only support Thoros if he agreed to adopt him as his son and heir. Thoros agreed to this and in a strange ceremony during the course of which the two men rubbed bare chests, and Baldwin then repeated the gesture with the wife of Thoros, the adoption took place.

A further condition of Baldwin's support was that he be declared co-regent. Using his newly found power, Baldwin then launched a raid on the nearby town of Samosata; although not a complete success it at least severely limited the ability of the Turks to raid from the town. As the people of Edessa had been subject to frequent raids launched from here, it also helped to cement his popularity. Nothing breeds loyalty like success, perceived or real, and it was only a matter of time before plots were being devised with the intention of placing Baldwin in sole control of Edessa. Although we cannot prove his active involvement, it seems unlikely that Baldwin was unaware of the plans. Certainly, when a coup was launched on 7 March 1098, he accepted the position of sole ruler with alacrity. He advised Thoros to surrender without a struggle, merely guaranteeing his life. However, even this was forfeited when Thoros was captured trying to escape from the city and was torn to pieces by an angry mob.

Baldwin wasted no time in consolidating his position. His prospects were enhanced enormously when a large treasure trove was discovered in the citadel at Edessa. With this he effectively bought the city of Samosata. On his triumphal entry into that city, he found a large number of Edessan captives in situ and his subsequent release of them enhanced his reputation still further. He strengthened his standing even more by marrying a local princess, and maintained Armenians in positions of influence, hoping thereby to retain their loyalty.

Meanwhile, local Muslims were uneasy at the power Baldwin had accrued. Kerbogha himself was disquieted enough by Baldwin that he felt obliged to attempt to eliminate him on his way to Antioch. For three weeks his large army hammered at the walls of Edessa but, although Baldwin was too weak to oppose Kerbogha in open battle, equally he could not be dislodged from the city. Eventually, Kerbogha despondently raised the siege and resumed his progress towards Antioch. His delay would have dramatic repercussions.

The imminent approach of Kerbogha must have terrified the Crusaders at Antioch. Some openly showed their fear. Stephen of Blois, something of a reluctant Crusader, did not wait to face the enemy but fled back to tell Alexius that Kerbogha had destroyed the Crusader army – news that turned out to be premature and ultimately incorrect. In a dramatic turnabout in fortunes, by the time that Kerbogha reached Antioch the banners of the Christian army were flying proudly and defiantly atop the city walls. It had fallen into their hands through one of the most ancient and effective of all weapons – treachery.

Bohemond was behind the capture, and he would eventually be the major beneficiary of it. The guardian of one of the city's many towers was an Armenian named Firouz. Local gossip hinted that his wife had been consorting with a Turkish officer. When Firouz was also charged with illegally hoarding grain during the siege, he became embittered against his masters. Secretly, a message was smuggled to Bohemond, offering to deliver up the city into his hands. As an act of good faith, Firouz sent his own son as hostage to Bohemond. Like the master politician that he undoubtedly was, Bohemond kept this news from his fellow leaders until the last possible moment, never failing to emphasise how hopeless was their position. It was not until hours before the plan was to be put into effect that he took them into his confidence.

His plan was simplicity itself. The Crusader army would make its way east, towards Kerbogha. Under cover of darkness they would return, like the Greeks

The defeat of the Turks at Antioch. (MS Fr. 5594)

before Troy, to the perimeter of the unsuspecting city. They would then simply put ladders against the tower in which Firouz was situated, climb in and take the city.

Accordingly, early on a June morning in 1098, a herald made his way through the camp of the Franks. He told the army to prepare for a great raid to the east, which would commence that very evening. Large numbers of men armed themselves, and towards the end of the day a sizeable force decamped. Bodies of cavalry rode off down the road, followed by the foot soldiers climbing the hills. The defenders of the city noted their departure, and were pleased at the prospect of a trouble-free night.

However, any sense of relief felt by the Muslims inside Antioch was badly misplaced. When night had fallen, and the Franks were long gone from the sight of those in the city watch-towers, the departed Christian troops turned about. Shortly before dawn, they were once again outside the city. Quickly and quietly, ladders were placed against one of the towers. Groups of Franks swarmed up them, to be greeted by Firouz. For his part, he was concerned at their seeming lack of numbers, but he need not have worried. The Franks made their way unhindered to the city gates, which were swung open to admit the many troops who had assembled outside. Large numbers of men swarmed into the now defenceless town.

There was a tragic inevitability about the blood bath that followed. Mentally scarred by the months of frustration, sacrifice and suffering that they had endured, the Christians put to the sword every Turk they found, assisted, it should be added, by many of the inhabitants of the city. Houses were burnt to the ground, priceless treasures destroyed and thousands killed. Many innocent and friendly Christian inhabitants died in the confusion. It was a gruesome end to months of deprivation, but the prize was a great one.

At this point, however, whether or not the city would be held was quite uncertain. Although its former ruler Yaghi-Siyan had been killed while attempting to escape (his head was delivered to the Franks by the Armenians who killed him), many of the garrison had retired to the citadel that dominated the city. It was impossible for the Christians to take it, and equally impossible to stop the garrison communicating with Kerbogha. There were few supplies inside the city, and a long siege could not be countenanced. The only options were to fight off the relieving force or die. A rough wall was speedily erected to prevent the garrison in the citadel from attacking the city in a synchronised assault with Kerbogha and his army. When the latter arrived, the garrison did attack but was repelled. Kerbogha decided to starve the Franks out, and beat off a determined sortie from them.

The Crusaders waited for help from Alexius. He had in fact already started to move with a large army across Asia Minor. However, he stopped his advance when he was met by Stephen of Blois, who told him, erroneously, of the defeat of the Western forces. Understandably, Alexius would not lend his aid to a cause he believed lost and his first duty was to protect his Empire. Given the knowledge available to him, Alexius made completely the right decision, but when the Crusaders learnt of his actions they regarded them as an act of betrayal. His perceived desertion removed any lingering doubts about the validity of any oath of allegiance taken to him.

The Turks were by now launching violent assaults on Antioch, but help of sorts did arrive for the Christians, and from an unexpected source. Travelling with the army was a poor peasant, Peter Bartholomew. He claimed to have been visited by Christ himself, who told him that the lance that had pierced his side at the Crucifixion was buried beneath the cathedral floor in Antioch. Some were sceptical of the story, particularly Adhemar. Nevertheless, excavations of the cathedral took place and a small piece of metal was unearthed that was claimed to be part of the spear in question. Whether or not it was a hoax, its discovery lifted morale within the Christian camp enormously.

However, despite its psychological effects, Peter Bartholomew's contribution provided no practical improvements for the Crusaders. Matters reached such a pass that a delegation was sent from the city to discuss terms with Kerbogha. It was led by Peter the Hermit, in disgrace after trying to flee from the siege five months earlier. Whatever was offered by the Christian leaders was not acceptable to Kerbogha, and the siege was resumed. Short of supplies, the defenders of Antioch would starve if they stayed where they were. They were forced to seek battle.

On Monday 28 June the Crusader army marched out over the main bridge of the city. They were outnumbered, tired and hungry. Their foe had a reputation for ferocity in battle. The odds against them were hopeless. However, in six separate forces the Christians marched out, in what seemed a desperate and final act of defiance. They were led by Hugh of Vermandois, Robert of Flanders, Godfrey, Robert of Normandy, Adhemar and Bohemond with Tancred. Raymond, who was seriously ill, stayed inside the city to ensure that the garrison in the citadel was kept under control. Many of the knights walked, their stallions of war long since dead.

Weakened as they no doubt were, it appears that they still made an impressive sight. Kerbogha, when he saw the army, somewhat belatedly sought terms. His overtures were ignored. The battle began with the Turks adopting their favourite tactic, their horsemen retreating to lure the Franks out of position. As the Christians advanced, Muslim forces were sent to infiltrate behind them and attack them from the rear. However, Bohemond was in control of the situation and had left a sizeable reserve to cope with just such a move, which it did. Ignoring the Turkish arrow storm, the Franks pressed forward, urged on, some said, by the ghostly apparitions of knights on white horses with white banners positioned on a nearby hillside. The Turks fell back.

And it was now that the weakness of the Muslim Levant at this point in history was exposed. It was riven by petty internal rivalries; it lacked unity and cohesion. If divine inspiration was responsible for the Crusades, then it manifested itself most strongly in the timing of the First Crusade. Many of the Muslim leaders were inspired by self-aggrandisement rather than any sense of religious or political unity, and many of them still seriously underestimated the threat posed by the Crusade. In the heat of the battle at Antioch, the true extent of these internal divisions became apparent.

The Holy Lance outside Antioch. (Yates Thompson 12 f. 29 Battle scene outside Antioch, Bishop in mitre and mail probably Bishop Adhemer of Le Puy, by William of Tyre (c. 1130–85), Estoire d'Outremer (12th century); British Library, London/ Bridgeman Art Library, London/ New York)

A significant number of Kerbogha's Emirs feared him. Some believed that if he were to defeat the Crusade, his power would become absolute. Fearful of their own position, many decided to flee with their forces, leaving Kerbogha to his fate. In a somewhat desperate move, the suddenly exposed Emir set fire to the dry grass to prevent the Franks from advancing further. It was a futile gesture, and the last remaining Muslim leaders saw which way the tide was flowing and left the battlefield. Seeing the extent of his defeat, Kerbogha himself was faced with no option but to retreat also. The Crusaders pursued vigorously, killing large numbers of Turks in the chase. By the time that Kerbogha arrived back at Mosul, his army was a pathetic remnant of what it had been and his power was permanently broken. The garrison in the city, deprived of any further hope of relief, surrendered and was allowed to live.

Against all the odds, Antioch had been taken and held. Time after time, disaster seemed certain but the Crusade had grimly hung on. That it was a close-run race was not in doubt. Yet amidst the euphoria of victory, there were further worrying signals. The claim of Alexius to the loyalty of the army was now largely meaningless. The Emperor had, in the eyes of the Crusaders, deserted their cause. Most disturbingly of all, individual ambition, as demonstrated by Bohemond and Baldwin, now held sway over the strategic objectives of the expedition as a whole. The unity that was an integral part of the long-term survival of the Franks in the region was now clearly shown as the spectral illusion that it really was.

CHAPTER 8

Jerusalem the Golden

The capture of Antioch was a costly victory but it fired the Crusaders with renewed enthusiasm. The conquest of such a sacred place stirred the blood, and inspired many to push on to Jerusalem as soon as possible. However, not all of the army's leaders concurred with this view. Hugh of Vermandois had seen enough, and decided that the capture of Antioch was sufficient to fulfil his vows. Soon after the battle he began to retrace his steps through Asia Minor. Many of his troops lost their lives on the journey back; now more aware of the dangers posed by the Franks, the Turks were less prepared to leave them unharassed. After about three weeks journeying, Hugh reached Alexius at the end of July and passed on the news that Antioch was back in Christian hands. Alexius could do little to take immediate advantage of the situation. Between him and the Crusaders were hundreds of miles of hostile territory, as well as the huge natural barrier of the Anti-Taurus Mountains. It would take several months to prepare, and this was not a journey to make in winter; for the time being Alexius decided to stay put.

Bohemond was also not willing to push on to Jerusalem, as he had strong personal ambitions that would be best served by remaining at Antioch. He saw the city as the centre of an empire, with himself at its head. Many of the other leaders tacitly supported him in this aim, although some were reluctant to do so openly because of their promises of allegiance to Alexius. However, Bohemond's stance angered Raymond and the split between the two became more pronounced than ever. Ironically, Raymond – the man who above all others had resisted the oath to Alexius – now seemed to be the Emperor's greatest supporter. Bohemond controlled most of Antioch, but some important parts of it, especially the old palace of Yaghi-Siyan, were occupied by Raymond's troops.

Only one man appeared capable of controlling the potentially volatile situation – Bishop Adhemar. Tragically, immediately after the Franks had triumphed at Antioch, typhoid swept the city. Its foremost victim was Adhemar himself, who died on 1 August. This was a hammer-blow to the expedition. Throughout the journey, Adhemar had shown great skill in keeping the emotions of the Crusaders' leaders in check. Whatever disputes there may have been about who was the military leader of the expedition, there was no disputing that Adhemar had been its religious head. In addition, he had shown no little military prowess, and his decisive intervention at Dorylaeum had swung the battle irrevocably in the Christian army's favour. His loss was to have enormous repercussions.

The death of Bishop Adhemar on 1 August 1098. Adhemar had been a stabilising influence on the Crusaders, and his death came as a severe blow. (Yates Thompson 12 f. 34 Death of Bishop Adhemer of Le Puy with a group of figures, including a cross-bearer, an ecclesiastic and a man with a bucket and asperge, by William of Tyre (c. 1130–85), Estoire d'Outremer (12th century); British Library, London/ Bridgeman Art Library, London/New York)

In the aftermath of the epidemic, many of the leaders left the city. Bohemond went north to Cilicia, intending to conquer this region and add it to his sphere of influence. Godfrey was given the towns of Turbessel and Ravendel by his brother, Baldwin, while Robert of Flanders went to the port of Lattakieh to take possession of it. His rule, however, proved to be austere and unpopular and he was forced to leave the town, which was subsequently claimed for Alexius by one of his representatives. Food remained in short supply and several of the leaders, including Raymond, launched a major raid in an attempt to restock the army's provisions.

Meanwhile, a letter was drafted from the Crusaders to Pope Urban telling him of the death of Adhemar. In the absence of his restraining influence, there was a distinct change in the tenor of their representations, although their somewhat hostile comments may also have owed something to news of Alexius' alleged desertion having become known. Within the letter, the Orthodox Patriarch of the city, John the Oxite, was the subject of implicit criticism, and it was generally hinted that the Christians of the area were heretics. This was in stark contrast to the approach previously advocated by Adhemar. He had made it plain that he envisaged that the Roman Catholic Church would work alongside the native churches of the region, and had gone out of his way to be placatory towards local Christian communities. With his death, such moderate views became less acceptable, and some of the Crusaders insinuated that the Roman Church should replace the local churches rather than complement them. This did nothing to endear the Franks to the resident population.

Relations between Bohemond and Raymond continued to deteriorate. The troops began to grow frustrated by the seeming inertia of the leadership and threatened to take matters into their own hands. Raymond's troops intimated that they would resume the march on Jerusalem without him at their head if need be. The other leaders, fearful of the conflict between Raymond and Bohemond, instigated frank discussions between the two men. After a heated exchange of words, a compromise was agreed. Raymond would agree to abide by the Council's decision on the ultimate ownership of Antioch, provided that Bohemond would accompany him on the journey to Jerusalem. For his part, Bohemond would do nothing that would interfere with the prospects of the Crusade, even if by so doing his own personal ambitions were compromised. He was accordingly confirmed in possession of most of Antioch, with Raymond retaining the relatively small portion that he currently held.

It was vital that the inactive troops were given something positive to do quickly. As a result of the rather unseemly wrangling that had been going on, there was a grave danger that the momentum of the expedition would be lost before its ultimate goal was attained. It was therefore decided that the army should press on and attack the fortress town of Maarat an-Numan, which was a threat to the flank of the Crusader army. Two preliminary assaults were driven off with relative ease, and it became obvious that a full siege was necessary. Shortage of suitable materials with which to build the siege engines hampered the attack, and it was several weeks before a tower was erected that enabled the Crusaders to mine the wall and burst into the town.

Yet even now the rivalry between Raymond and Bohemond reared its ugly head again. Bohemond attempted to repeat his coup at Antioch by arranging that the populace of Maarat an-Numan should surrender to him in return for guarantees of their safety. In the event, this promise proved to be worthless, and most of the Muslims in the town were either massacred or enslaved. However, Bohemond refused to give the town to Raymond unless he would in return give up his claims to Antioch. By now, Raymond's men were completely disillusioned by this petty feuding and made it plain to Raymond that they should move on. For his part, he attempted to buy the support of the other leaders, with very little success. He seemed simply to lack the ability to inspire the confidence of other men.

The shortage of supplies now reached an unprecedented level. There were consistent, and possibly reliable, reports that the Crusaders were so short of nourishment that they resorted to cannibalism. Even their Turkish enemies were amazed at their resilience and fortitude, as the troops reached the limits of their endurance. In a gesture of contempt and defiance of their leaders, the troops demolished the walls of the town so that the army was left with little option but to push on. Even Raymond could not ignore so blatant a gesture. The time had arrived to complete the journey to Jerusalem. On 13 January 1099 Raymond led his troops away from the blazing town towards the Holy City, barefoot to emphasise his status as a pilgrim. Robert of Normandy and Tancred accompanied him. Robert of Flanders and Godfrey hesitated for a month but were forced by adverse opinion to follow in their footsteps.

Away to the north, Baldwin did not move. He for one would not hurry after the other leaders. He had experienced problems after his initially favourable reception at Edessa. New arrivals from the West, attracted to the city by tales of Baldwin's successes, could not understand his tolerance. They had little idea of local political realities and sought to impose their own values on Armenian society – a mistake tragically mirrored many times in the future. Baldwin's status started to decline when he introduced taxation at a level every bit as onerous as that previously imposed by Thoros. To add to this, over a period of time the Armenians had begun to lose influence, and it was not long before plots were being hatched with a view to the deposition of Baldwin.

Further south, the situation in the Holy Land had for a while been in a state of flux. The decline of the Turks in the area had created a vacuum that the ruler of Egypt, al-Afdil, was quick to exploit. When he heard of the defeat of Kerbogha, he invaded Palestine. The Egyptians had a mighty siege train with them and although Jerusalem, whose defences were immense, resisted for forty days there was an inevitability about the final fall of the city. The Turkish garrison was allowed to return to Damascus, and the Egyptians took possession. Once the Egyptians regained Palestine, they were not ill disposed towards the Crusaders and wished to reach an accommodation with them. In an attempt to fend off the Franks, they opened negotiations with them. The Franks had been advised earlier on by Alexius to reach an agreement with the Egyptians. Accordingly, some kind of understanding was secured. However, it meant little; the Franks would soon breach this accommodation by marching into Palestine.

Godfrey of Bouillon attacks Jerusalem in 1099.

Ironically, the next stage of the journey was for the Franks relatively uneventful. Their triumph at Antioch had secured their reputation and many of the leaders of the small semi-independent city-states that characterised the area were only too willing to provide cheap provisions if by so doing these ferocious Western warriors were encouraged to leave them in peace. The Crusaders decided to cut across country so that they could hug the coastal road, allowing their fleet to keep them supplied. The port of Tortosa was taken by trickery, a small force conquering the town by setting light to a large number of fires around the town at night to exaggerate the size of the army. The stratagem was so successful that when morning came the Crusaders were able to walk into an empty town, abandoned by a terrified garrison.

It was necessary for the Crusaders to obtain permission to pass through the land of the Emir of Tripoli. Ambassadors were invited into the town to discuss terms. While inside its walls, these envoys discovered that the city was extremely wealthy and appeared to be governed by a weak ruler. They believed that if he were threatened he would happily pay protection money to the Franks. Consequently, they attacked another of his towns, Arqa. It was a mistake. The town was stronger than anticipated, and the Crusader armies were not powerful enough to make a significant impression on its walls. There were in fact not enough troops to encircle it completely, although fortunately supplies were now adequate to ensure that the army did not have to endure great hardships. Up until this point, Raymond had been in the van of the expedition, but he was now caught up by Godfrey and Robert of Flanders at Arqa.

This turn of events was not totally welcomed by Raymond, as it meant that his overall authority over the army was no longer unchallenged. Another sinister development was the news that Alexius intended to travel to the Holy Land and had asked that the Crusaders wait for him. Raymond suggested that this request be complied with but he was out of step with the other leaders. They felt that Alexius had betrayed them and was merely hovering to pick clean the bones of the Muslim world when they had put in all the hard work. This perspective was not helped by the interception of a letter from Alexius to the Egyptians, which stated that he had not approved of the Crusade's invasion of Palestine. This seemed to provide decisive proof of his duplicity, and confirmed most of the leaders in their view that they were morally justified in rejecting the overall authority of Alexius.

While at Arqa, another important development occurred. For some time, the authenticity of Peter Bartholomew, the discoverer of the Holy Lance at Antioch, had been under challenge. (Indeed, these doubts had existed from the very beginning.) When Peter found the spear in the cathedral, Bishop Adhemar for one had been sceptical. After the death of the prelate, Peter claimed to have had a vision in which Adhemar had come to him and stated that he had spent a short time in hell because he had not believed the story. This antagonised many of the army, who revered Adhemar and were angered at this stain on his character. During the siege of Arqa, Peter announced that he had experienced another vision, in which he had been told that the army must attack Arqa immediately. Many of the Crusaders had by now had their fill of what they regarded as Peter's charlatanism. Peter was seen to be closely allied to Raymond, and his opponents saw this latest action merely as a cynical ploy to ensure that the city fell into Raymond's hands.

Many of the northern French now openly declared their disbelief of Peter's visions. Up until this point, many of the suspicions against Peter had been voiced surreptitiously; now they were declared openly. Several leading prelates came to Peter's defence. He himself genuinely believed in the divine origin of his visions. To prove his stories, he offered to undergo a trial by fire. Accordingly, on Good Friday he walked quickly through two piles of blazing logs. By the time that he had completed this terrible ordeal, he had been burned horrendously. He survived for eleven days in great agony, and then mercifully expired. The incident had a profound effect on the mood of the Crusade. Peter had been so closely connected with Raymond that the latter inevitably lost a good deal of credibility as a result of the situation.

The siege at Arqa carried on for another month. While they were there, the Franks were approached by envoys from the Egyptians. The Fatimid dynasty in Egypt was, as we have seen, implacably opposed to the Turks. Having recaptured the Holy Land, they wished to keep it as part of their empire. Accordingly, they renewed their overtures to the Franks, whereby they suggested that the Crusaders should retain the conquests they had made so far, while the Egyptians held on to Palestine. The Christians would be allowed free, uninterrupted passage to Jerusalem as pilgrims. Without serious consideration, this approach was rebuffed. But the Crusade would leave with Arqa untaken. The siege had taken a significant number of lives, and had been to all practical purposes a waste of time and resource. Raymond left Arqa in tears, his reputation badly damaged and his chances of being accepted as overall commander-in-chief all but gone. Fortunately, the Emir of Tripoli chose not to impede the Crusaders in their passage through his lands and they reached the border of Palestine on 19 May.

Palestine itself was not heavily garrisoned. It had not been in the hands of the Egyptians for long and only the major towns were defended by significant numbers of troops. The threat from the Egyptian navy though was very real and this posed great danger. The provision of supplies from the Christian fleet could be interfered with, and because of this it was imperative that the Crusade should move on to Jerusalem in all due haste. Many of the towns through which the Crusade advanced sought to avoid conflict by offering unhindered access and cheap supplies. Tyre, Sidon and Acre were all passed through with little incident, until the Crusaders finally arrived at the coastal town of Arsuf.

This was the point where they must turn inland, to take the last steps towards the city that had been the inspiration of their quest. The Franks would now be striking at the heart of the Holy Land, to the city that was for them the literal centre of the world. They stood on the verge of being the first Christian army in the city for half a millennium. They stopped at the town of Ramleh, a major Muslim town, unlike most of the towns in Palestine, which were either Christian or Jewish. The inhabitants of the place fled in abject terror, and amidst the subsequent celebrations the recently destroyed church was rebuilt. A new see was created with Robert of Rouen, a Latin priest, installed as its first bishop. This was a move of great symbolism. All of the bishoprics of the East were led by an

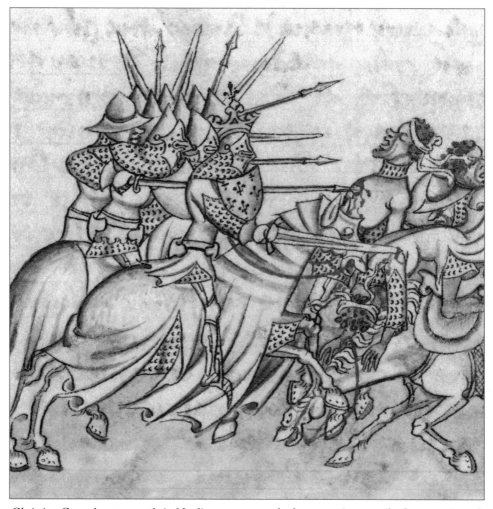

Christian Crusaders pursue their Muslim opponents – both on occasion mercilessly exterminated any whom they captured, in the name of religion. (MS Add. 21143, f. 90)

Orthodox bishop, and it had not been the initial intention of the Crusade that the Orthodox Church should be supplanted in the area. Now, for the second time on the Crusade (the first time was after the capture of Antioch) a Latin as opposed to an Orthodox bishop had been installed.

The Crusaders proceeded to the village of Emmaus, and while here they received a request for help from the people of Bethlehem. The population of this town was entirely Christian and they longed to be free of their Muslim overlords. When a force under Tancred arrived to grant their request, the entire population walked out in procession to greet them. To the Crusade, it was of course a wonderful moment; the birthplace of Christ was now restored to His people and only one greater prize remained.

On 7 June 1099 the Crusade reached the summit of the rolling hills surrounding the Holy City. From here, they looked down upon a sprawling metropolis, enclosed by imposing walls, with a skyline broken by the minarets of some of the most sacred places in Islam. They looked down in awe upon the place where Solomon had built his temple, upon the hill where Christ had died for the sins of the world, and down on the rock from whence Mohammed himself had ascended into heaven. It was without doubt the most important city in the world, awash with symbolism for three great religions. The sight must have been almost mystical to these men, who had walked through blazing sunshine and torrential rain, who had fought mighty battles against a seemingly innumerable foe, who had endured disease and famine on an apocalyptic scale. To many of them the very act of survival must have seemed miraculous when so many of their fellow pilgrims now lay in shallow graves along the road from Western Europe to Jerusalem. Surely they were indeed God's chosen people.

But much remained to be done if they were to take the city. The fortifications that protected it were immense, and its situation, surrounded on most sides by deep, impenetrable valleys, gave it an aura of invincibility. In ancient times, it had resisted the assaults of Rome itself for an inordinate length of time. Now, it contained a sizeable garrison of Egyptian and Sudanese troops. Further, its commander, Iftikhar, was an experienced general who had already taken a number of sensible precautions to protect the city.

Firstly, he had appreciated that the Crusaders, approaching in the height of summer and dressed in heavy armour, would be vulnerable if water supplies could be interrupted. He therefore had all the wells in the area poisoned. Consequently, the Crusaders had to draw water either from the nearby Pool of Siloam, dangerously exposed to fire from the defenders, or by travelling far afield, in which case they would be vulnerable to sorties from the city. Although there were no springs inside the city walls, there was plenty of water stored in cisterns, so the garrison would have few difficulties in this respect. Secondly, Iftikhar realised that the large Christian population of Jerusalem would be a liability during any siege. They were all evicted from the city, which not only removed the threat but also reduced pressure on food supplies and effectively protected those remaining from the danger of any shortages.

For various reasons, the Franks could not afford a long siege. They were short of provisions, and their numbers had been reduced drastically since they had left Constantinople. Many had died, and many others had deserted. Usually reliable sources state that the besieging force consisted of 1,200 knights and 12,000 foot soldiers. They were also aware of the danger of being trapped between the city and any relieving force. All this made it imperative that the city was taken as soon as possible. However, the lack of suitable building materials for siege engines caused great difficulties, while in contrast the garrison was well armed and used large bales of hay to limit the damage caused by the Christian artillery.

On 12 June an old hermit told the Franks that they must attack the next day but, although they followed his advice, their assault was beaten off. Failure was primarily due to the lack of siege engines, a situation relieved somewhat by the welcome arrival of a small fleet at Jaffa that brought crucial supplies of nails, ropes and other equipment to help in their construction. With the benefit of their local knowledge, friendly local Christians told the Franks that wood could be obtained from Samaria, and it was duly procured with the assistance of conscripted Muslim prisoners.

But despite this improvement in resources, the Crusaders continued to argue among themselves. Tancred claimed Bethlehem for himself, a move that created a genuine sense of shock among many. The Crusaders often felt that they were in a form of feudal relationship with God as their liege lord, and that any land taken in the Holy Land belonged only to Him. A final decision on human ownership of Bethlehem was deferred for the time being. However, this merely led to more serious arguments about who should rule in Jerusalem if it were captured. Even now men continued to desert, some bathing themselves in the Jordan to fulfil their quest before setting off for home.

Minds were distracted from this in-fighting by news that a large relieving force was on its way from Egypt. This prompted another vision, this time by a priest, Peter Desiderius. In his dream, he had spoken to Adhemar, who had castigated the Franks for their petty squabbles. He ordered that the army should fast, and then process around the city walls in penitence for their sins. The vision was

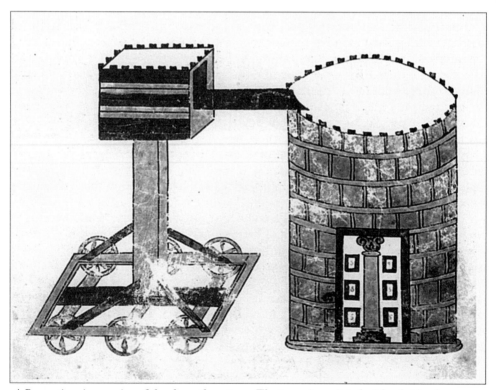

A Byzantine siege engine of the eleventh century. The tower is equipped with a bridge from which men could attack city walls. (MS Grec 2442, f. 97r)

widely believed, the fast duly kept, and the rituals culminated in a parade around the walls on 8 July 1099. This seemed to restore flagging spirits. Siege engines, constructed out of sight of the garrison, were now moved up, causing great alarm inside the city. It was decided that the assault would be launched in earnest on the night of 13 July. During the hours of darkness, the engines were brought ever closer to the walls. The following morning, fierce fighting broke out, the Crusaders suffering cruelly from the Greek fire of the defenders (a naphtha-based concoction that once lit was enormously difficult to put out), and responding with endless showers of missiles from their own artillery.

Raymond was the first to manoeuvre his tower close to the walls, but they were too heavily defended for any serious impact to be made. Godfrey reached the walls with his tower on 15 July, directing operations in person from the top storey. After some vicious fighting, two knights, Litold and Gilbert of Tournai, crossed the bridge from the tower to the battlements, and became the first to set foot on the city walls. A few men managed to join them. The number increased steadily from ones and twos to dozens. The city, although well defended, was simply too large for the defenders to be everywhere at once. As they were pushed back, more ladders were placed against the walls, and large numbers of Christians climbed up, now virtually unopposed.

Meanwhile, Godfrey sent men to open the gates, while Tancred worked his way to the heart of the city. He pillaged the Dome of the Rock, an act of sacrilegious significance to the Muslims. Large numbers of Muslims made their way to the al-Aqsa Mosque, which they hoped to defend. However, there was insufficient time to prepare its defences adequately before Tancred was upon them. They had no option but to surrender, promising to pay a heavy ransom in exchange for their lives. Elsewhere in the city, all sign of organised resistance rapidly abated, and vast hordes of the inhabitants rushed around in blind panic. Iftikhar retired with the small number of his men who remained alive to the Tower of David. He negotiated with Raymond that if they surrendered they would be allowed to leave the city in peace. Raymond honoured his promise, and they left unhindered.

They were the only ones. Three years of horror and deprivation were pent up in the souls of the Crusaders. What followed was a massacre on a virtually unprecedented scale. Everyone the Franks met in the city – man, woman, child – was put to the sword. The streets were awash with rivers of blood as the Christian army expiated its sins with the

An interior view of the Dome of the Rock.

lives of the Infidel. Thousands of apocalyptic warriors exploded into the Holy City in a horrific Bacchanalia of death and destruction. This was the ultimate logical conclusion of a spiritual policy that not only accepted war but also encouraged it as an act of penance, declaiming that the shedding of heathen blood was in itself a redemptive act. Fuelled by uncontrolled emotions, the massacre was of inhuman proportions. There was no room for Christ here. This was the God of the Old Testament, a cruel God without mercy.

The scene was horrific. The *Gesta Francorum* records that the leaders:

> commanded that all the Saracen corpses should be thrown outside of the city because of the fearful stench, for almost the whole city was full of dead bodies. So the surviving Saracens dragged the dead ones out in front of the gates, and piled them up in mounds as big as houses. No-one has ever seen or heard of such a slaughter of pagans, for they were burned on pyres like pyramids, and no-one save God alone knows how many there were.

And Fulcher of Chartres told how 'nearly ten thousand were beheaded in the Temple. If you had been there, your feet would have been stained to the ankles in the blood of the slain . . . neither women nor children were spared'.

Those Muslims who had relied on Tancred for protection were sadly disappointed. Christian knights broke into the al-Aqsa Mosque and killed those within to a man. Nor were the Jews excepted, and those that sought refuge in the synagogue were burned alive. To those not there, it seemed an act of shame; even other Christians were shocked by the ferocity.

In severely underestimating both the strength of the Crusader army and the fervour of its motivation, the Muslim world must hold some responsibility for the loss of the city. The Muslims were used to dealing with Greek Christians, who did not have the strength of purpose possessed by these barbaric yet resilient armies. They had insisted on continuing their trivial inter-state rivalries and their complacency towards the enemy had contributed to the sacrifice of Jerusalem. The terrible retribution visited on the city had been allowed to happen partly through their lack of a common purpose.

Meanwhile, on that first night in the captured city, the euphoria of the Crusaders, unencumbered by any feelings of guilt, must have assumed fantastic proportions. They had been outnumbered, short of supplies, seemingly unsupported by anyone in the area, even by the Christian Emperor who had asked for their help in the first place; the odds against them succeeding had been astronomical. To the world it must have seemed a miracle, attributable solely to the hand of God. Against all logic, a Christian bridgehead had been constructed at the very heart of the Muslim world. The major question now was how long it would stay there.

CHAPTER 9

The New Kingdom

During the course of the Crusade thus far, the priority had been survival. Long-term strategy inevitably suffered as a result. Ironically, the Crusaders had little idea about what they should do with their new kingdom now that they had taken Jerusalem. The most pressing problem was to appoint a ruler for the city. This was imperative for two reasons. Firstly, it was fully, and accurately, expected that the Egyptians would not meekly accept the status quo and would send an army to retake the city. The infant state would do well to survive its early days. The First Crusade did not end with the fall of Jerusalem, and there was much hard fighting to be done before its results could assume any vestige of finality. Secondly, it was equally as important that a leader be appointed to provide stability and guidance, so that a permanent infrastructure could be put in place.

Finding a suitable candidate proved difficult, and now the true extent of the loss of Bishop Adhemar became apparent. He would have had more chance of uniting the Crusaders than anyone else. A new legate, Daimbert, had been despatched by Urban to replace Adhemar. Daimbert was an unscrupulous, self-serving individual. He had not as yet arrived in the East. Those that knew him from his time in Spain, such as Raymond of Toulouse, regarded him as a man of great ambition not matched by talent. It was a poor appointment by Urban but he would not live to see the consequences of his mistake. Two weeks after the capture of Jerusalem, but before he knew of it, Urban died.

Perhaps the supreme irony of the First Crusade is that the two spiritual leaders who had made it possible did not live to see its final triumph. Urban was the man who had given the Crusade its initial impetus, and his ideas had been nurtured by Adhemar. Admittedly, they had not foreseen many of its repercussions, and in that sense their vision had been flawed. But Urban's oratorical skills, organisational abilities and energy had provided the drive that the concept of the Crusade had needed to evolve. Further, the collective discipline of the two men had helped to maintain a measure of control over the development of the idea. Without their hands at the helm, this potent combination of religious zeal and spiritually motivated warfare would become warped into bigotry and ignorance. Without a vision that sought to integrate rather than dominate the peoples of the conquered territory, the long-term prognosis for success was poor indeed.

The arguments concerning the rule of Jerusalem centred around whether such a uniquely sacred city should have a spiritual or a secular head. If Adhemar had lived, there can be little doubt that he would have been given the rule of the city.

But in his absence, no obvious ecclesiastical replacement was at hand. Therefore it was necessary to offer it to a secular leader. The first offer was made to Raymond by the Council. Raymond, however, did not accept. He argued that he would not be its king because it would be wrong for a mere mortal to assume such a pretentious title in God's own city. However, it has also been suggested that he believed that he did not have enough support among the broad spectrum of the Crusade's leadership to be sure of being an effective sovereign. His recent record, for example the debacle at Arqa, was not a good one.

Raymond seemed to believe that if he took this ostensibly moral stance, then all the other leaders would be obliged to follow suit. However, in this he had misread the situation. Of the other leading men, Bohemond was still in Antioch, while his nephew, Tancred, lacked the substance to be considered a potential ruler of such a hugely important city. Robert of Flanders had strength of character but was known to be keen to return home. Robert of Normandy also planned an early departure and was not a strong enough personality to be seriously considered. This left Godfrey of Bouillon. He was a devout man, famed for his piety and simplicity of living. He was generally a levelheaded individual and, although a compromise candidate, would be acceptable to most factions apart from the Provençal supporters of Raymond. After more deliberation, the kingdom was offered to him. Godfrey, showing commendable humility, refused to accept the title of king but it was suggested as a compromise that he be given the title of *Advocatus Sancti Sepulchri* – 'Defender of the Holy Sepulchre'. This amendment was agreed and Godfrey of Bouillon therefore became the first ruler of the newly formed Kingdom of Jerusalem.

Raymond was livid; he felt that he had been duped. He had been in occupation of the Tower of David in Jerusalem and now refused to surrender it to the new ruler. It was finally agreed that he would hand it over to the Bishop of Albara, who would hold it on trust until Raymond's grievances were properly examined. However, shortly after the Bishop of Albara gained possession of it, the tower was given over to Godfrey. This was the final straw for Raymond. His initial reaction was that he would return home immediately. He may well have meant it. The Crusade, which had promised so much for him personally, had brought only bitter disappointment. Raymond was not highly regarded by his fellow leaders, and he probably knew it. However, a more measured consideration of his actions suggested that he would be best served by keeping all options open. The success of both Bohemond and Baldwin in carving out a state for themselves gave him hope that he too could be successful in his aims. He withdrew to Jericho to await further developments.

It was fortunate indeed that Raymond did not rush away. The Egyptians had sent envoys to the Franks, berating them for their bad faith after the diplomatic contacts that had taken place between them. They left no doubts that they would attempt to expel the invaders by force. The new kingdom would need the help of every leader and every available man if this counter-attack were to be resisted. When news reached Godfrey that an Egyptian army was indeed on its way, he speedily assembled the other leaders. Eustace, his brother, and Tancred responded quickly, soon followed by Robert of Flanders. Robert of Normandy

1. A map of the world at the time of the Crusades, c. 1250, with Jerusalem at its centre. (MS Add. 28681, f. 9)

2. *Godfrey of Bouillon attacks Jerusalem in 1099, defended at this time by Fatimid Muslims.*

3. *An aerial view of David's Tower – the citadel at Jerusalem – where a small number of men survived Godfrey's attack.*

4. *The castle at Nimrod in the Holy Land. Built before the Crusaders conquered Outremer, the fortress was an important one on the road to Damascus through the Golan Heights.*

5. *Jerusalem; the Dome of the Rock and the city wall at dawn.*

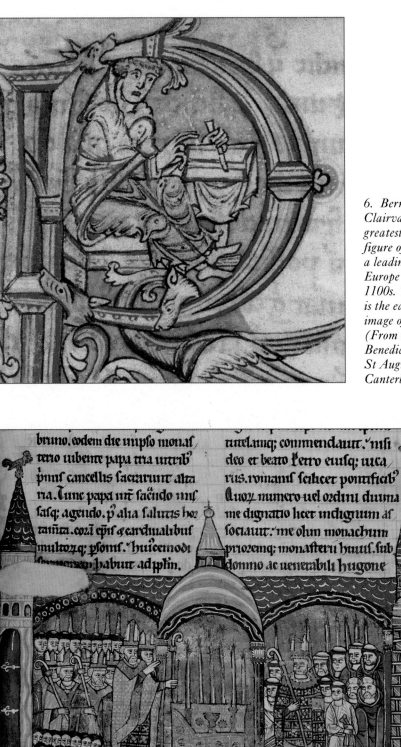

6. *Bernard of Clairvaux, the greatest clerical figure of his day, was a leading figure in Europe during the 1100s. This portrait is the earliest known image of St Bernard. (From the Benedictine abbey of St Augustine, Canterbury)*

7. *The consecration of the abbey at Cluny. This abbey was the centre of the monastic movement in the West, the revival of which led to many men taking the Cross. (Lat 17716, f. 91 The consecration of the Church at Cluny,* Chronicle of the Abbey of Cluny *(12th century); Bibliothèque Nationale, Paris/Bridgeman Art Library, London/New York)*

8. Alexius Comnenus, Emperor of Byzantium at the start of the Crusading movement. (From a mosaic in Hagia Sophia, Constantinople)

9. Baldwin II, King of the Franks, visits Manuel Comnenus, Emperor of Byzantium and grandson of Alexius. (Roy 15E I, f. 321v Baldwin II (d. 1131) visits Manuel Comnenus from a late 15th century French translation of the Latin History of the Crusades by William of Tyre (c. 1130–85), executed in France for Edward IV (1442–83), Estoire d'Outremer (12th century); British Library, London/ Bridgeman Art Library, London/New York)

10. *The Dome of the Rock, Jerusalem; built in the seventh century, the golden dome covers a rock revered by Christian and Muslim alike as the place where, respectively, Abraham prepared to sacrifice his son and Mohammed ascended into heaven.*

and Raymond prevaricated until they received confirmation of the threat from their own scouts. In fairness to them, when this was received they delayed no longer.

On their way to rendezvous with Godfrey, Eustace and Tancred obtained useful information. Some scouts had been captured from the Egyptian army, and they revealed that the Egyptians were now in Ascalon led by the Egyptian vizier al-Afdil in person. It would seem that they were overconfident, and their complacency exposed them to the risk of a surprise attack from the Crusaders. Even so, Godfrey was shocked at the size of the enemy force. He left Jerusalem on 9 August, but when he became aware of just how strong the Egyptians were, he instantly sent word to the city urging that every man who had not yet joined the army should do so immediately. The city was stripped bare of all available manpower, and only a skeleton garrison was left behind. There would be no second line of defence should the Christian army be defeated. An Egyptian triumph would mean inevitable destruction of the fledgling nation.

The army that the Crusaders were to face now was unlike any other yet seen. In contrast to Turkish forces, it was largely an infantry army and most of the horsemen with it were light cavalry armed with spears, rather than the horse-archers of the Turks. There may have been a few Turkish mercenaries in the force but there was little love lost between the Egyptians and their Sunni rivals. No formal support would therefore be forthcoming from the Turks, from whom, after all, the Egyptians had only recently recovered Jerusalem. In reality, the Crusaders possibly overestimated the threat from the Egyptians. So prompt were the Franks in raising troops that the numerical disparity that Godfrey had assumed was not, in fact, as great as anticipated. Further, the Franks had managed to build up their supply of horses, so many of which had been lost during the course of the Crusade, and they therefore presented a formidable mounted threat. On a one-to-one basis, an Egyptian infantryman would pose little threat to a Christian knight.

The Crusaders split themselves into nine groups and made their way apprehensively towards Ascalon. Fearing ambush, they themselves surprised the Egyptians, who had left their livestock largely unguarded, an error that the Franks were delighted to exploit. Only 300 men had been deployed to guard the herds and they were no match for the Crusader army, which probably numbered about 5,000 knights and 15,000 infantrymen. The guards were quickly driven away, and rushed to the camp of the Egyptian leader, al-Afdil, to warn of imminent attack.

The Egyptians gained little from the warning. As dawn broke on 12 August 1099, the Crusader army was in a state of readiness to advance on its enemy. Alarmed, Egyptian bowmen hastily despatched a flight of arrows at the massed wall of steel before them but before they could loose another the Christians advanced en masse. The disposition of the armies favoured the Franks. The sea protected their right wing, so that they could not be outflanked, negating the numerical superiority of the Egyptians. The Franks easily dismissed the enemy cavalry screen as they advanced down the beach. Soon after, they clashed with the infantry of the enemy, creating chaos among the Egyptian forces. Taken as a

The walls of Ascalon; the protruding columns were added by the Crusaders to strengthen the building.

whole, the Muslim army was outclassed and resistance quickly broke down. Not long after the start of the battle, their entire army was fleeing in disorder.

The lack of room to retreat told heavily against them, and many of the Egyptians died in the pursuit. Some sought to hide in a wood but perished when it was deliberately set alight. Others were crushed in the frantic rush to get inside the gates of Ascalon, and yet more drowned in the ocean. The Egyptian camp, outside the city walls, was ransacked, and a huge amount of booty taken. Defeat was total, apart from one thing. The city itself was still in Egyptian hands.

It was now, in this moment of victory, that Godfrey made an enormous error of judgement, which matches any other mistake of the First Crusade in terms of its shortsightedness and pettiness. The garrison in Ascalon was willing to surrender. It had been demoralised by the totality of the Egyptian defeat, and it retained little hope of successfully fighting off the Crusaders. And it remembered only too well the massacre at Jerusalem, where almost the entire garrison had been cruelly murdered. The one small group that had survived were the men of Iftikhar, who had surrendered to Raymond. Raymond had shown himself, in Muslim eyes, to be a man of honour and mercy. He was therefore the only man to whom they would offer their surrender.

A wise and magnanimous leader would have acceded to this request. Not only would it give the Christians the city – and with its position on the coast so close to

Egypt it was strategically very important – but it would also help to build bridges with Raymond, still a very influential leader. However, Godfrey would not acquiesce. He did not trust Raymond after the ill will between the two in Jerusalem, and refused absolutely to consider the proposed deal. Even Robert of Flanders and Robert of Normandy were stunned by his intransigence. Godfrey's support fell away and his army alone would be insufficient to take the city by force without the help of the other Crusader leaders. Negotiations fell through and the city remained in Muslim hands. It was to continue so for another half a century, a constant thorn in the flesh of the Christian state. It would only finally be captured after a great deal of Christian blood had been unnecessarily shed.

It was a black moment in the development of the Christian kingdom. Godfrey had shown a singular lack of vision in his actions, which sat uncomfortably against the image of humility that he had portrayed in the past. And matters did not improve when Daimbert eventually arrived. He had set out his stall clearly on his way from the West. En route to the Holy Land with a Pisan fleet, he had raided several islands owned by the Byzantine Empire. There would be little attempt at compromise between Orthodox and Roman strands of Christianity from this man. A fleet was sent by Alexius to chastise the prelate, but it failed to intercept him. An attempt by Daimbert to raid Cyprus was unsuccessful but he made his way to the coast of Syria. Here he arrived at the court of Bohemond. The Norman offered allegiance to him, doubtless recognising a kindred spirit when he saw one. An unholy alliance was formed, the first action of which was to persuade the Pisans to blockade the (Christian) city of Lattakieh.

This development, which did little to advance the cause of understanding and integration in the Middle East between the various forms of Christianity, coincided with the retreat northward of Raymond. He had cultivated close ties with Alexius following their earlier differences, and he was bitterly angry when he heard what Daimbert had done. Robert of Flanders and Robert of Normandy were equally disillusioned. They wished to return home, and to do so they would need the help of Alexius. The prospects of his assistance would not be helped by the actions of Daimbert. The leaders summoned the legate to their camp, where he was berated angrily. Bohemond was besieging Lattakieh from the land, and he hurriedly withdrew as a result of this opposition. Raymond entered the port and posted his banner next to that of Alexius, who regarded this as an acceptable compromise. Robert of Flanders and Robert of Normandy received offers of help from the Emperor as a result. The Governor of Cyprus provided a fleet, and the two leaders were feted when they stopped off at Constantinople. Both would be badly missed, particularly Robert of Flanders, although some of their men remained behind. Their return to the West would suggest that they had not travelled to the Holy Land for purely selfish motives. In addition, their flexibility in changing their support from Godfrey to Raymond after the action at Ascalon inferred that they had been objective in examining what was best for the Crusade at any particular moment. The kingdom could ill afford to lose men of this calibre.

Daimbert decided that his next step should be to travel on to Jerusalem. Bohemond decided to go with him, as he had not yet visited the city and it could be considered that he had not fulfilled his vows until he did so. Baldwin would also join them. Religious motives were not the only reason for this. Godfrey was not in a good state of health. For some time, the strains of leadership had been wearing him down. He was now very ill and it seemed probable that he would not live for long. Both men wished to register their claims for succeeding him should he die. Their journey was not an easy one. Raymond would not provide provisions for Bohemond's men although he did help Baldwin when he passed through Lattakieh. Many non-combatants accompanied Bohemond and Baldwin, and the Muslims who still remained in Palestine slaughtered large numbers of stragglers. The trip was made worse by unusually bad weather, but eventually, four days before Christmas, Jerusalem was reached.

The aftermath of the battle at Ascalon had seen an improvement in the kingdom's fortunes. Some of the ports on the coast remained in Muslim hands but the Franks now controlled much of the hinterland. Tancred had made significant conquests in Galilee. Godfrey decided to strengthen his position by offering allegiance to Daimbert, in return for which Daimbert confirmed him in his position of ruler of Jerusalem. Bohemond pledged his allegiance once more to the prelate, following which he was confirmed as Prince of Antioch. This was an astute move. By accepting his fief from Daimbert, Bohemond made himself a vassal of the Church and thereby under its protection. However, he knew that Daimbert would be too far away to exercise real control.

All of this added to Daimbert's prestige. He attempted to further his own personal standing by making himself Patriarch of Jerusalem. The post was already filled but such a minor obstacle did not concern him. It had recently fallen vacant when the Orthodox incumbent of the post had died in exile. A Latin, Arnulf, had been installed. He lacked any real authority, and now he was deposed on a technicality following claims that his election was not in accordance with ecclesiastical law. Daimbert's election as his successor was a mere formality. Baldwin, however, did not take an oath to him. Relations between the two appear to have been strained, and Baldwin made his way back to Edessa. We cannot be sure if Daimbert marked him down as a potential enemy. If he did not, he should have done.

A period of consolidation followed in the kingdom. Many of the cities that were still in Muslim hands bought protection from the Franks by the payment of tribute. Ascalon and Acre, for example, made such payments. Tancred was also successful in raiding and conquering yet more territory for the new nation. Ironically, just as Godfrey strengthened his position with regard to his Muslim neighbours, he was losing influence with the other Christian leaders. This followed blatant manipulation by Daimbert. He demanded that part of the port of Jaffa be given to the Church, and Godfrey meekly agreed. Next Daimbert demanded that he be given complete control of Jerusalem. At this, even Godfrey balked. A compromise was reached by which the situation would be reviewed if Godfrey should die.

The arrival in June 1100 of a Venetian fleet was welcome as it provided a potential counter-balance to the strong Egyptian navy. Godfrey hurried to the coast to meet it. On his arrival, he collapsed. Initially, he started to recover from this attack. He had planned to assault Haifa and the expedition for this was already assembled. Command was deputed to his cousin, Warner of Gray. Daimbert, who hoped to take over Jerusalem should Godfrey die, did not trust Warner and accompanied the expedition, believing that Godfrey was on the mend. It is unlikely that he would have left the city of Jerusalem if he thought that Godfrey was close to death.

With the benefit of hindsight this was a grave error of judgement. While on campaign, Warner himself fell ill. He was obviously incapable of taking any further part in the expedition and he was carried back to Jerusalem. His role here would subsequently prove vital to the course of events. When he arrived back in the city, a drama of epic proportions began to unfold. And Fate had decreed that Warner, in his last and greatest scene, would be the key player in it.

The performance began on 18 July with the death of Godfrey. He was a man who had many failings, evidenced by his arrogance after the battle at Ascalon. He had been weak and easily manipulated by Daimbert. Yet he also had a number of virtues, and his humility and simple living had won him many admirers. His death was greeted with genuine sadness. From hereon, events moved rapidly. Godfrey had confirmed in his will that the city should pass to Daimbert but few now had time for the strutting, egotistical prelate or his Norman friends. A plot had been hatched to overturn the wishes of Godfrey. Warner, himself terminally ill, occupied the Tower of David, the key point in the defences of Jerusalem. He then sent word to the chosen successor to Godfrey. The choice was obvious. One man had already carved out a province for himself further north. He had shown himself to be a formidable military leader, and he was related to Godfrey. That man was Baldwin, Count of Edessa.

Speed and secrecy were the ingredients essential to success. Messengers were hastily despatched north to inform Baldwin that Godfrey was dead, but news of his demise was kept from the campaigning army of the Franks. The expedition was eventually to hear of it from a passing Venetian fleet. Daimbert was shaken to the core by the tidings, and did not know what to do next. Eventually he did little, hoping that the legality of Godfrey's will would ensure that the city passed to him. He merely sent his envoy to Jerusalem, to claim the city formally for himself. But he had been outmanoeuvred, and his timing was hopelessly wrong. Faced with the intriguing wiles of Baldwin and his supporters, Daimbert was completely outclassed.

His miscalculations were compounded when he sent word to Bohemond at Antioch, offering him Palestine in return for his assistance. If this had been put into effect, most of the Christians in the country except for the Normans would have been outraged. Unfortunately for Daimbert, his messenger was detained by Raymond in Lattakieh. His papers were examined and the damaging missive was discovered. It could not have fallen into worse hands as far as the prelate was concerned. Unknown to him, however, further north a final, decisive blow was to be struck against his interests. In a typically rash venture, Bohemond had led a raid into Asia Minor to strengthen his position there. He had been offered a state in the country if he could drive the Turks out of Armenian lands. It was too tempting a prize for him to resist. But he had underestimated the size of the challenge, perhaps overconfident because of his successes on the Crusade so far.

Whatever the reason, Bohemond's resources were small and he led them right into a trap. They were cut to ribbons, and he himself captured. He was dragged off into imprisonment far to the north and too distant to be the subject of any rescue attempt. A messenger was sent quickly to Baldwin in Edessa, carrying the news that the Crusade's most formidable leader was a prisoner. This left Baldwin in a precarious position. The Turks would be buoyant at their success and he himself was greatly exposed on the northern frontier of the Christian territories. Baldwin knew what he needed to do. He did not wait to be attacked but he himself launched a raid into Turkish territory. Rescue of Bohemond was an impossibility but Baldwin's duty was to protect the Christian state. In the event, he called the bluff of the Turks. News of his advance preceded him and the Turks, content with what they had won, drew back. The immediate threat was removed.

When Baldwin had set out on this raid, he was unaware of events in Jerusalem. However, his accession was now virtually assured. Daimbert was widely discredited and when Baldwin approached Antioch on his subsequent journey to Jerusalem, the city opened its gates to him, greeting him as a hero. If the city of Bohemond himself recognised him as such, then it was inconceivable that all the other Christian cities would not follow suit.

One more significant event took place before Baldwin's arrival in Jerusalem, and this showed definitively that his star was firmly in the ascendancy. There is, near Beirut, a narrow pass between the mountains and the sea. Historically, it is famed for its strategic importance. Its situation made it difficult for an army to pass through if it were opposed, no matter how great its numerical superiority, and it had acquired the reputation of a Middle Eastern Thermopylae.

When he reached the pass, Baldwin's progress was impeded by a large Muslim force, supported by a fleet offshore. His attempts to force his way through were rebuffed and he was obliged to withdraw. During the night, he considered his options and devised a plan. He would use the weapons that, throughout history, have come to the aid of the underdog commander – the weapons of tactical ingenuity, surprise and daring. Baldwin was a man who would, in this instance, reap the maximum return from small resources. He resolved to play the Muslims at their own game, using tactics that had for centuries been the linchpin of Turkish strategy.

At the break of day, the Crusaders once more tried to press their way through the Muslim forces blocking their path. Unsurprisingly, they were driven back. They broke in panic, fleeing in terror before their enemy. For 5 miles, the rout continued, the Muslim forces exultant in their apparent victory, the Christian army in a state of pandemonium. Then, without warning, the Christian retreat stopped abruptly and their entire force was unleashed against the Muslims. The retreat had been a ruse, one of which the Turks would have been proud, and success was absolute. The Muslims were overwhelmed by the sudden turn of events, and faced about in confusion. There were so many of them that they could not deploy adequately in the press, and as the heat of battle intensified their situation was made worse by more of their forces joining in. Their position was hopeless and they fled in panic far into the mountains.

Baldwin continued this triumphal march to Jerusalem, his journey now resembling the progress of a hero. On his approach, the whole city streamed forth to meet him. A new legate, Maurice, who outranked Daimbert, had arrived in the East. He supported Baldwin. Opposition to such a display of popularity would be futile and Daimbert gave way to the inevitable, forced to accept that his dream of ruling Jerusalem would remain nothing but a reverie. He sought to ingratiate himself with Baldwin, who graciously accepted his spiritual suzerainty. It was the best that the prelate could hope for in the circumstances.

But there was only one real victor from these events, a man who had started life as a younger brother in the shadow of two older and more powerful siblings. It was an amazing turn of events for someone who had begun his career within the narrow confines of the Church. On Christmas Day 1100, eleven centuries after the birth of Christ, a new king was crowned in the Church of the Nativity at Bethlehem. The symbolism could not have been more apt. On the very spot that Christ was born, a new Christian era began, the start of a great Christian Empire on earth. And it would be led by Baldwin. For a man born with such humble prospects, he had risen to heights that his brothers could never hope to scale.

CHAPTER 10

Triumphs and Disasters

Like a newborn child, a new state is never more vulnerable than in its early days. Through a unique combination of circumstances, the Crusade had attained its ultimate goal but the Franks would have to work hard to protect their gains. They had launched their assault at a time when the Muslim Levant was more divided than ever before. If the Muslims should ever achieve any sort of unity, it would be desperately difficult for the Crusaders to fend off their counter-attack. Baldwin was no fool. Above all else he saw now that he must achieve two things: form a sound economic infrastructure to support the new kingdom, and consolidate the gains made to date. The former depended upon the latter, and this would not be possible without more men. Therefore, the paramount short-term aim was to encourage further expeditions to the East.

This need was exacerbated when, following the conquest of Jerusalem, several of the leaders, with many of their followers, returned home with their vows redeemed. To many, the restoration of the city to Christian hands was an end in itself. Some hoped to profit by conquering lands in the region, which they could then exploit, but many had no interest in this and large numbers made their way back to Western Europe. The Christian states were dangerously spread out, from Edessa to Antioch and from there down the Mediterranean coast. Situated threateningly along the border of this often-narrow strip of conquered territory were many small Muslim states. Other large and potentially hostile states, such as Aleppo, lay adjacent to the new kingdom. These were in a position to cut the arterial lines of the Frankish network of communications, a action that could quite possibly prove fatal. The independent Muslim states in the area would need to be destroyed or nullified, or there would be no peace for the new land that soon became known as Outremer – 'The Land Across the Sea'. Without peace the economy would not be built up, and the kingdom would not thrive.

Palestine had a particular problem compared to, for example, Antioch in that it was not well served with natural resources. Although it had some fertile places, often it was an arid country, in many areas poorly watered, and therefore it could not be self-sufficient. The recent upheavals in the region had also taken their toll on the environment. In contrast, the strategic position of Palestine was vitally important. It was located at a point where it could exert great influence over the trading routes between Central Asia and Egypt. Its situation on the rim of the Mediterranean also enabled it to play a prominent part in the import and export of goods between the Middle East and Western Europe. The trade routes of the

Mediterranean had been opened up by the development of the Italian city states, such as Venice, and Outremer's position as a possible link between the economies of the Orient and the West gave it great potential.

Many of those returning home to Western Europe took with them the message that more men were needed in the East. Importantly, although their memories of events were, in all probability, selective, their stories of the capture of Jerusalem touched a nerve in the Western psyche. There was genuine euphoria when news of it reached Europe. In the chronicles of all West European nations it is accorded a place of unique, almost mystical, honour, a supreme manifestation of God's power. There were many prepared to take up the challenge offered by its conquest.

The First Crusade was not one integrated movement (few Crusades were). As well as the Peasants' Crusade that preceded the main expedition, there was also a number of forces that followed on – another wave of manpower was indeed making its way eastwards. What was needed by the expedition were compact, well-equipped forces, capable of moving at speed. However, it was quickly apparent that the painful lessons that should have been learned from the bitter experiences of the past four years had not been assimilated; what evolved was frighteningly similar to what had gone before. There was no co-ordination of these forces, so the potential impact of a combined expedition was seriously reduced from the start. Their enemies could pick these armies off one at a time. Further, there were once again far too many non-combatants with them. The country through which they passed was incapable of feeding these slow-moving hordes. Perhaps this was a manifestation of victory disease; certainly the actions of this second wave are of an overconfident and arrogant nature.

The immediate response to the requests for men had come from three areas – Lombardy, France and Germany. The force from Lombardy was the first to set out. The Lombards had played a relatively inglorious part in the Crusades so far. Many had accompanied the Peasants' Crusade and had shared, for the most part, in the ignominious end of that misguided movement. Those who survived the trauma of its destruction had joined forces with Bohemond, who held a high place in their regard. However, the response to the appeal for reinforcements was not instantaneous. The vagaries of the winter weather militated against sea crossings in the tiny ocean-going vessels of the day, which were unsuited to anything but the most clement of conditions. Once the winter had ended, then there were crops to be grown and harvested, leaving only a small window of opportunity for the expedition to set out.

Consequently, it was not until the autumn of 1100, a year after the capture of Jerusalem, that the Lombards set off. They chose to follow in the footsteps of previous travellers and to make the short sea crossing of the Adriatic, followed by the overland journey to Constantinople. However, the expedition was not of a high quality. There were a few good fighting men in its ranks but also far too many vagabonds and opportunists. They proved impossible to discipline or control, helping themselves to whatever they needed without asking. Alexius must have been perturbed when he heard of the coming of this throwback to past expeditions. It was once again a quite different force than that which he really needed. Repeating the stance he had taken with previous groups of Crusaders, Alexius wished to move them across the Bosphorus as quickly as possible, but the Lombards were reluctant to comply as they knew that there were other forces following close behind with whom they wished to combine.

Alexius managed to develop good relationships with the force's leaders, the Archbishop of Milan and the Count of Biandrate, its spiritual and secular heads respectively. They were treated with all due respect and they appeared grateful for it. Not so their followers. Enraged by the shortage of supplies, they stormed over the walls of Constantinople and right up to the gates of the royal palace. Their leaders were horrified, and feared serious complications as a consequence of their violence. Fortunately, Raymond of Toulouse was back in Constantinople and on hand to mediate a solution. He was still on good terms with Alexius and used his good offices to defuse the situation, with the result that a potentially volatile confrontation was avoided. But once more the relationship between East and West had been strained. With the Crusading movement still in its formative stages, it did not augur well for the future.

The army made its way across to Asia Minor without further incident. Here they were soon joined by other forces, French and German Crusaders. Among the leaders of the French force was the disgraced Stephen of Blois, the reluctant Crusader and dominated husband. His wife, reputedly disgusted at his display of cowardice at Antioch, had never ceased to castigate him on his return home. To Stephen the easier option seemed to be to redeem his honour by returning east, rather than to be constantly upbraided for his behaviour by the redoubtable Adela. This combined force now started out on the journey across Asia Minor towards the Holy Land. Accompanying the expedition was a sizeable Byzantine element. To Alexius, however, Jerusalem was a distraction to the real objective, the recovery of Asia Minor. He wished to consolidate his hold on the area, to clear its roads of Turkish raiders and to make them safe to travel again. While this would, of course, help the Crusaders, who were still journeying to Outremer almost exclusively along the land routes, it was a mere by-product of Alexius' primary objective, that is, the consolidation of the Imperial infrastructure in the traditional heartlands of Anatolia.

In recognition of his experience and status, Raymond was elected leader of the army. This honour quickly proved to be a poisoned chalice. Before the army had travelled far, there were rumblings of discontent among the force. To many of the rank and file it was wrong for them to progress to Jerusalem while Bohemond remained in captivity. They argued vehemently that the army should alter course to mount a rescue attempt. They did so with what appears to be a complete ignorance of the geography of the country, the intensity of the climate and the fighting qualities of the Turks. To move north to attempt to release Bohemond would have been a distraction and a mistake. Yet once again the fallibility of Raymond as a leader was cruelly exposed. Seemingly powerless to resist their misguided demands, he meekly acquiesced. The army lurched to the north, heading in the vague direction of where they thought Bohemond might be.

The stupidity of the decision quickly manifested itself. The army was completely unprepared for the heat and aridity of the Anatolian plain. Wells were

Turks raiding in Asia Minor. (From Greek MS 135)

dry, food scarce and conditions as a whole unbearable. Men and women dropped in scores, carrion for the Turkish warriors waiting to seize stragglers. In contrast to the Franks, the Turks had learned their lessons well. Kilij Arslan may have underestimated the strength of the first armies; he would not repeat his folly. Cleverly, he withdrew his forces, luring the Crusaders further into unknown territory. He razed the countryside as he went, so that the Franks found nothing in the way of provisions. Other Turkish leaders, alive now to the dangers of the Crusading movement, sent their forces to help. The picture was a completely different one than that of a few years earlier. The Westerners, now acutely aware of the threat facing them, panicked and headed for the north coast of Asia Minor, hoping to make their way to one of the ports there in Byzantine hands. There was a great loss of face in this course of action but it was preferable to mass destruction.

Kilij Arslan had no intention of letting his prey slip away. His forces grasped every opportunity to take advantage of the demoralised Crusaders. On one such occasion, the Lombard knights fled in terror leaving vast numbers of infantry and non-combatants to be slaughtered. Raymond's prestige suffered as a result. Many of the army blamed him for their plight. Some felt that he had deliberately led them into an ambush, believing it be to part of some conspiracy hatched with Alexius, the known supporter of Raymond. The attacks of the Turks became ever more frequent. The army was forced to travel in a tight, compact mass, constantly prepared to resist enemy attacks. The nerves of the Christians were stretched to the limit as it became apparent that the increasingly aggressive Turkish attacks presaged a major battle.

It came at the small town of Mersivan, where the army arrived in August 1101, and began badly for the Christians when a band of Germans was destroyed in a

Turkish ambush. The Turks then employed their time-honoured tactics, sending swarms of horse-archers against the Crusaders, so that they, for their part, did not know where the next attack was coming from. Their nerve was not strong, and before long the cream of the Lombard cavalry was rushing headlong from the field. The majority that could not run were left to their terrible fate. Exposed hopelessly by the flight of the cavalry, those that remained were overwhelmed. Apart from those that would fetch a good price in the local slave markets, they were butchered.

The German and French contingents fought more resolutely but in a lost cause. Raymond himself was trapped on a hillside and resisted stoutly until knights led by Stephen of Blois and Stephen of Burgundy came to his aid. But his nerve was broken, and during the night he fled to the safety of the nearest Byzantine port and from there to Constantinople. On his arrival there, Alexius could barely contain his anger. The Crusaders had acted completely contrary to his advice, and the opportunities offered by the expedition had been thrown away. Thousands of lives were lost in a pointless exercise and the Turks had been given a significant lift to their morale as a result.

The next expedition to arrive was a small force led by the Count of Nevers. In contrast to previous armies, his was extremely well disciplined. During its march to Constantinople, there was never a hint of trouble. Alexius received them well, no doubt pleasantly surprised at their atypical good manners. The Count had hoped to meet up with his near-neighbour, Stephen of Burgundy, who at the time he arrived was a few hundred miles ahead of him with the Lombard army. The Count never managed to catch the first army, and he eventually stopped trying to do so, turning back to the road to the Holy Land, which he had wandered away from in his attempts to make contact. As he approached Heraclea, he was faced by a much larger Turkish force seeking battle. The French fought bravely but were overwhelmed. A few men broke out, eventually finding safety after a desperate journey. The others were killed or captured.

The last force to arrive in the area was led by William, Duke of Aquitaine, a sworn enemy of Raymond of Toulouse. It was a large force and included some prominent names such as Hugh of Vermandois, hoping to fully redeem his vows by reaching Jerusalem, and Duke Welf of Bavaria, at the head of a significant number of German troops. Their journey across Europe reverted to type and they proved difficult to control, but in spite of this they were still cordially welcomed by Alexius.

It would have been sensible for all these different expeditions to combine. However, the Crusades of 1101 are notable primarily for their complete lack of co-ordination. Never a strength of the Crusading movement, even by the standards of the day there was an appalling lack of communication between the Crusader leaders. Petty rivalry inhibited a united approach, and the momentum of the movement suffered as a result. This last force followed so closely in the footsteps of the Count of Nevers that the land had not had time to recover from his passage through the region, and there were consequently no supplies available. And inevitably, the sufferings of this force were made worse by incessant attacks from the ubiquitous Turkish horsemen.

Eventually it reached, and passed through, the town of Heraclea. On the other side of the town was a large river, which, when the men saw it, they rushed towards to quench their thirst. Unfortunately for them, this was exactly what the Turks had expected them to do. Large numbers of the enemy were secreted in the reeds surrounding the river. Unprepared and taken by surprise, the Franks' discipline quickly began to disintegrate. There was little chance to regroup. Huge numbers of dead once more littered the field of battle. Hugh of Vermandois, the veteran Crusader, was badly wounded but was carried away to safety. Sadly, he died when he reached the town of Tarsus, a proud man whose vow remained unfulfilled. Only a handful of men, including the Duke of Aquitaine, escaped.

The year 1101 was a black one for the Crusading movement. Materially, the effects were bad enough. The defeat of three armies represented a loss of manpower that the new states could ill afford. Shortage of men would be the curse of the Christian East, and such carelessness was inexcusable. But even this was secondary to the detrimental effect on morale. As success at Jerusalem was regarded as a sign of divine approval, so the losses in Asia Minor were regarded as the reverse. Such perceptions would quickly change the image of Crusaders from heroes into villains. This would have serious effects on the attempts to recruit more warriors in the West. For those that went on Crusade, the relationship between God and man was often regarded as a feudal one. Men offered their services to God and in return expected his protection. If He were not seen to honour the bargain, then they in turn would reconsider their obligations to make their pilgrimage to the East.

Fortunately for the Franks, the situation in Outremer itself, though volatile and potentially dangerous, did stabilise to an extent. The incarceration of Bohemond and the departure of Baldwin from Edessa to Jerusalem had left a vacuum that needed to be filled quickly. It was a heaven-sent opportunity for ambitious young men to exploit. One such man was Tancred. He had been expanding his conquests in Galilee, but Baldwin's presence in Jerusalem was close at hand in this area and Tancred knew that this would severely limit any opportunities he might have to manipulate events to his maximum personal advantage. But the enforced absence of Bohemond had left an opening in Antioch. Tancred was an experienced campaigner, despite his youth, and was closely related to Bohemond. He would therefore be an acceptable replacement in the eyes of the large and predominant Norman contingent in the city. This fitted well with Tancred's own desires; the city was, after Jerusalem, the most important in the region and it was far away from Baldwin. When the offer of Antioch was made to him, he accepted with alacrity. The only proviso he insisted upon was that if Bohemond were to be released in three years, Tancred reserved the right to take possession of his holdings in Galilee once more.

It soon became obvious that Tancred had many of Bohemond's characteristics. Negotiations to buy his own uncle's release were blocked by him. It appeared that he had been a superb pupil. It was also quickly apparent that he had inherited a distrust of Alexius. Open warfare broke out between the Normans and the Byzantines. Fortunately for Tancred, the disasters in Asia Minor proved to be a blessing in disguise. Following the catastrophic defeat of the new armies from the

West, the roads in the region were once again impassable so that Alexius could not bring his troops to Antioch to chastise Tancred. Tancred took further advantage by invading Cilicia and attacking Lattakieh, so long a coveted target of Bohemond.

Nothing, it seemed, would obstruct the progress of the ambitious young ruler. However, he finally overstepped the mark and, as a consequence, brought on himself the wrath of the Crusader leaders. Raymond of Toulouse had been anxious to try once more to establish a kingdom for himself. There was plenty of scope to carve out such a province from the vast expanses in Muslim hands. He readily obtained the leave of Alexius to chance his luck again. His ship put in to the port of Tarsus, which was held by Tancred. On his setting foot ashore, he was immediately arrested. He was forced to journey to Tancred, who berated him for his perceived desertion at Mersivan. This insult, coming from someone who may have been perceived as a young upstart, was too much for the other Crusader leaders to bear. Public opinion forced Tancred's hand, and Raymond was released, though not before Tancred had obtained his word that he would not interfere in northern Syria again.

If this seemed like the nadir of Raymond's career, its zenith would not be long in arriving. Another opportunity soon presented itself further south at Tripoli. The city formed a barrier between the county of Antioch in the north and the new state around Jerusalem in the south. It was presently ruled by a mild-mannered Muslim leader, Sheikh Fakhr al-Mulik. Despite his easy ways, his presence threatened communications between north and south and, worse still, if he were succeeded by a more militant ruler then the situation could quickly become extremely menacing. Accordingly, Raymond decided to attack the port. He was heavily outnumbered, accompanied as he was by only 300 knights. Duqaq of Damascus sent 2,000 men to help defend the city and the Crusader force was eventually at a numerical disadvantage of 20,000. Secure in the knowledge of certain victory, the Muslims nonchalantly commenced their attack. When they were resisted, they realised that victory might not be a formality. The steel wall facing them was more resilient than anticipated. Suddenly, inexplicably, they panicked. Their confidence high, the small Frankish force charged them, killing all in their path. Unbelievably, it soon became a rout in which thousands of Muslims died.

It was an incredible triumph, yet a force so small still could not contemplate storming the city. Raymond retired to consider his options. A subsequent assault aided by a Genoese fleet was unsuccessful. To provide him with a more permanent residence, Raymond constructed a mighty fortress, known as Mount Pilgrim. (Although Raymond, of course, would not be aware of the fact, it was to be the longest surviving Crusader castle in Outremer, not falling for 180 years.) The Emir of Tripoli could not leave it unmolested and, when it was finally completed in 1104, attacked it vigorously. The attack was beaten off but Raymond was badly burned in its defence. He never made a complete recovery, and died six months after the assault.

Of all the Crusaders, Raymond was perhaps the most unfortunate. His transparent vanity made it easy for people to dislike him, and he lacked the gift of winning their hearts. Yet for all his flaws, he had many qualities. He was an honourable man who, after his initial resistance, kept his oath to Alexius far better than any other Crusader leader. He could be merciful, as evidenced by his protection of the Muslims he captured at Jerusalem. Above all else, he was willing to sacrifice much to come to the East. He was successful in his own right in the West, but he never attempted to return there, and we may surmise from this that he was a man of principle. Despite his frequent quarrels with other men, his death was genuinely lamented. And it deserved to be, for he had more moral qualities than many of his contemporaries.

Further north, the situation was once more in a state of bewildering flux. Not for the first time, the catalyst of the upheavals that took place was Bohemond, although his part was an unwitting one on this occasion. Despite all the attempts of Tancred to interfere, a ransom for Bohemond was eventually agreed and paid. He returned to his principality at Antioch. Tancred had governed well in his absence, and had not tried to oust his uncle permanently. Nevertheless, Bohemond's return must have been a huge personal blow to him. While Tancred had ruled he had exercised ultimate power, an addictive drug for most men. Now, in an instant, the situation was transformed and Tancred was essentially back where he had started, as ruler of Galilee.

Meanwhile, Edessa was presently under the rule of Baldwin of le Bourg, cousin of King Baldwin. He was an intelligent man, and realised that he must win over his Armenian subjects, which he had attempted to do. Although on occasion his greed and avarice would alienate him from the people, at first he was not an unpopular ruler. He was also an opportunist. He managed to obtain money from his father-in-law, Gabriel of Melitene, by threatening to shave off his beard. Such a move would have been totally demeaning to Gabriel – the beard was a symbol of virility and power in these parts – and he was so horrified that he paid over the sum demanded to avoid disgrace.

The Franks were understandably anxious to protect their frontiers, and to expand more if possible. An initial step to this would be the taking of the town of Harran, placed alongside the main routes to the Euphrates and Asia Minor. A large force, headed by the rejuvenated Bohemond and Baldwin of le Bourg, set off to take the town. Tancred and Joscelin of Courtenay, a cousin of the Edessan Baldwin, were also with the force. The Muslims were seriously worried by these developments. The local Islamic leaders, once complacent, now felt the threat of the Crusaders only too acutely. A large army was gathered and hastily set off to meet the threat head on. The Crusaders were by now encamped outside Harran, reluctant to take the town by storm for fear that it be damaged too severely in the process. Even if a relieving force were sent to meet them, they were confident in their ability to fight it off.

When the Muslims appeared, the Franks quickly deployed for battle. The troops from Edessa launched the assault, and drove their opponents back. However, the enemy was merely feinting. In keeping with the Crusader approach to warfare, lessons painfully learnt had been forgotten. Confident of victory, the cavalry from Edessa rushed headlong across a river and straight into the trap set for them. There was no escape from the ambush waiting for them. Baldwin and Joscelin were captured, while Bohemond, seeing that the day was lost, decided that discretion was preferable to valour and rushed away from the scene. However harshly his actions may be criticised on moral grounds, it was the right course of action. To lose the entire army would turn disaster into irretrievable catastrophe. Bohemond and Tancred assumed rightly that the Muslims' next target would be Edessa.

However, the Muslims moved too slowly to take advantage of the Franks' disarray. Bohemond made his way to Antioch and Tancred took charge at Edessa. The Muslims were complacent, and were consequently unprepared when Tancred launched a night assault on their camp. Although born of desperation, the move was a stunning success and the camp was overrun. Edessa was saved and with it the northern Crusader territories. Following the withdrawal of the Muslims, the Franks were approached with a view to negotiating a ransom for Baldwin and Joscelin. Disgracefully, Bohemond and Tancred prevaricated. Their motives were transparently obvious, certainly to King Baldwin in Jerusalem, but their delaying tactics worked for the time being.

The set-back of Harran, coming so soon after the disastrous expeditions of 1101, had been a major blow. More men were urgently needed and Bohemond volunteered to go to Europe to raise them. Possibly he wanted to return home to ensure that matters there were being run properly on his behalf. Tancred, of course, was delighted as the reins of power reverted to him. Unknown to anyone, Bohemond would never set foot in Outremer again.

Ironically, however, Bohemond would still play a major part in the affairs of the region even when he was hundreds of miles away. On his return to Europe, he stirred up adverse feelings against Alexius. His Machiavellian dealings bore fruit. Bad reports about the Emperor had already reached the ears of the pontiff, Pope Paschal II. Already harbouring these negative thoughts, Paschal was easily persuaded to agree to a request that a Crusade be launched against Alexius. Within less than a decade, the ideals of the Crusading movement were already being prostituted, and the concept of the Crusade had taken its first step down a road that would lead to moral bankruptcy. It was a dangerous precedent to set.

Bohemond accordingly attacked the Byzantine Empire, assaulting first Dyracchium, on the eastern coast of the Adriatic. However, he had overestimated his prospects and was captured. He was taken before Alexius, who was correct but unsurprisingly cold towards him. Bohemond was forced to sign the Treaty of Devol, by which he was forced to hand over all his conquests to Alexius. Humbled, the proud Norman had no alternative but to agree, his prestige receiving in the process a mortal blow. He never went back to Antioch and died in the West in 1111. His ambition had been too great for his own good and, in an era of hypocrisy and double standards, he stood head and shoulders above most other men. He resembled another great but ultimately unsuccessful Crusader, Richard Coeur de Lion; for both, their diplomatic ineptitude negated so much of their military success. Yet Richard lacked the flair for subtle intrigue that characterised Bohemond; by the end, the latter had told so many half-truths and lies that he probably no longer knew himself exactly what to believe.

As was his wont, Tancred took full advantage of this latest diversion, and while Alexius was distracted, he consolidated his position. The Treaty of Devol, which applied to Bohemond's lands in Outremer as well as everywhere else, was haughtily ignored by him. He was no longer a great man's nephew. He was a great man in his own right.

This turbulent period of Crusader history was brought to an end by one final deeply symbolic act. The bastard son of Raymond of Toulouse, Bertrand, arrived to claim his inheritance in the East. Some of Raymond's lieutenants initially resisted his claims, but the support of King Baldwin won them over. Siege engines surrounded Tripoli once more and a naval blockade from Genoese and Provençal troops cut off the garrison. This time there was no escape. The city surrendered and on 12 July 1109 the banners of Toulouse at last fluttered in the breeze over Tripoli. It was the fulfilment of a dream, but Raymond of Toulouse, the man who owned the vision, was not there to see it.

CHAPTER 11

Consolidation

In addition to the turbulent events taking place at this time around Antioch, Edessa and the other northern Frankish territories, there was also much activity in Palestine itself. King Baldwin, whose prime need was for more troops, acutely felt the disappointments of the Crusades of 1101. Despite this, he did achieve much personal success, which added to his growing kudos. Rumours of a large caravan, laden with treasure, reached him and he resolved to attack it. The travellers in the caravan were taken completely by surprise and were killed or captured to a man. Soon after the prisoners were escorted away, a grieving Arab noble arrived at the spot where the caravan had been seized. His wife, heavily pregnant, had been with the caravan and he was certain that she had been lost. To his delight, he found her, accompanied by a maid, two camels, food and water – and a child. The Arab noble swore to repay the Christian king for his kindness. Baldwin would live to rejoice in the mercy that he had shown this woman.

Baldwin knew that to strengthen his kingdom he must capture the towns and cities that remained in Muslim hands, such as Acre, Tyre, Arsuf, Caesarea and Haifa. An opportunity arrived in April 1101. The arrival of a Genoese fleet offered him a potentially powerful ally. A deal was struck with the Genoese, by which they would retain a third of any booty taken if they helped him take Haifa. Just as importantly, they were also granted a street in the city in which they could trade. Resistance against this combined force was sporadic, half-hearted and brief. The inhabitants of Haifa sought terms, which were generous: those who wished to leave could, while the remainder stayed and became subjects of Baldwin. Baldwin felt inclined to be charitable because the city had surrendered after only a token resistance. The other side of the coin was witnessed when the town of Caesarea was targeted. It fell only after a hard fight. The sack that followed its capture was every bit as horrific, albeit on a smaller scale, as that of Jerusalem. Baldwin's approach was cold and calculated. His actions made clear that cities attacked by a Christian army were faced with a stark choice – peaceful surrender and mercy, or fierce battle followed by certain destruction.

Baldwin was soon troubled by the arrival of another Egyptian army. Ascalon, which would have been in Christian hands were it not for the stubbornness of Godfrey of Bouillon, provided the Egyptians with an excellent base. This new army was large, well disciplined and intent on a decisive confrontation. Baldwin was an astute king and statesman but was, it seems, sometimes an unreliable soldier. His tactical choices in the subsequent campaign were poor. There was an enormous

An Arab caravan on the way to Mecca. (Ar 5847 f. 94v Caravan going to Mecca from 'The Maqamat' ('The Meetings'), illustrated by Hariri, second quarter 13th century, Persian literary texts; Bibliothèque Nationale, Paris/Bridgeman Art Library, London/New York)

numerical disparity between the two armies: the Egyptians had 11,000 cavalry and 21,000 infantry against the Franks' force of 260 cavalry and 900 infantry. Yet despite the huge numerical advantage enjoyed by the Fatimids, Baldwin, whose first thought should have been to employ caution, rashly attacked on 17 May 1102.

He compounded his impetousness by allowing his horsemen to charge in five columns far in advance of the infantry, leaving the latter cruelly exposed to the Egyptian cavalry. Within moments of the collision between the Franks' cavalry and the human wall of the Egyptians, the former was swamped in the midst of a stabbing, heaving mass. The first two columns dissolved, decimated, their leaders dead with most of their men. The third column fought its way clear, and rushed back to Jaffa with the news that the King and his army were lost.

However, rumours of Baldwin's death were premature. Although he had not shown himself to be a master strategist in this campaign, Baldwin did not lack for courage. At the last crucial stage of the battle he called together his surviving men and knelt penitentially before the fragment of the True Cross that he had brought with him from Jerusalem to aid his cause. Then he turned his forces about, to face death or glory. Magnificently, they charged at the Egyptian host. Although heavily outnumbered, they were far better equipped than their foe. Gaps appeared among the Egyptians, which the Franks ruthlessly exploited, and before long the enemy were in full retreat. Against all odds, Baldwin had survived. The cost, however, had been heavy, with serious losses of cavalry, and major attrition within the ranks of the infantry, who had been cut up badly when left unprotected.

But Baldwin did not learn from the experience gained. The following year another Egyptian army attacked. The human resources at the disposal of the Fatimids were immense and they would not give up their lost territories without a fight. Several of the leaders who had survived the vicissitudes of the Crusades of 1101 had joined Baldwin in Palestine, among them Stephen of Blois and Stephen of Burgundy. Baldwin did not obtain proper scouting reports (an echo of Manzikert) and assumed that the army of which he had received reports was merely a reconnaissance force. He set out from Jerusalem with a corps of only 500 knights. As he rode into the plain around Ramleh, he was faced with a sudden shocking revelation. The force before him was no large raiding party. It was the full might of the Egyptian army. Even as this fact sunk home, his retreat was being cut off by groups of enemy cavalry.

The situation was grim. Baldwin was in no position to put up a fight. He was short of men, and his only hope was to find a defensible position close at hand, and trust that help would reach him. Nearby was a tower that Baldwin himself had erected and to this place he hurriedly retreated. He had no plan about how he could extricate himself from this precarious position. As he tried to think of a way of rescuing his army, his thoughts were interrupted. Surreptitiously, a lone Arab had made his way to the tower and he had an urgent message for Baldwin. He was a sheikh, and a year earlier Baldwin had spared the life of his pregnant wife when he had plundered a caravan in the desert. Now he was redeeming the debt he owed. Even as he spoke, the tower was being surrounded. There was no hope for the tiny army, but a lone rider might escape.

It may be surmised that Baldwin thought only briefly about the situation. He was brave but not foolish. Faced with reasonable odds, he might be prepared to stand and fight; but here there were no odds at all, only certainties. There was no chance of escape if Baldwin did not move immediately. He had to go now. He mounted his horse and made his way warily out into the night. A few Egyptians attempted to catch him but his magnificent charger was more than a match for them. One wonders if he gave any thought for those he left behind. When day broke, the hopelessness of their position was clear to those who remained. They fought bravely but against the inevitable. The end came when the Muslims set light to the tower. Among the dead was Stephen of Burgundy; with him died Stephen of Blois. The reluctant Crusader had died a martyr's death, the timorous acts of a weak life expunged in a final glorious moment.

The Egyptians were exultant. They made their way in a leisurely fashion to Jaffa. When they arrived there, they taunted the Christians inside the walls. Their triumph had been decisive and it appeared that the end of the short life of the kingdom had arrived. But even as they mocked, the despair of the Franks was translated to ecstasy. On the far horizon, a ship hove into view. As it got closer, it could be seen that it was flying the unmistakable personal banner of the king. He had made his way to Arsuf and commandeered a ship. Messengers had been sent post-haste to Jerusalem to reassure the Christians there.

This was truly an age of miracles. Only God could have rescued Baldwin. And just at that moment another miracle occurred. Without any forewarning, a large fleet came into view. It was an English fleet, carrying substantial numbers of English, French and German pilgrims. They were delighted to be faced with an instant opportunity to confront the Infidel. Bolstered by these new arrivals, Baldwin led his men out to fight the Egyptians on 28 May. The Muslim army was no match for this fresh force, and frantically retreated before it to Ascalon, leaving large amounts of booty to be taken in its wake.

Extraordinary as it was, this escape could not hide the fact that manpower shortages were still acute. The kingdom was forced to rely on short-term pilgrims from the West. Admittedly, there was still a considerable influx of these. It was still a major challenge to make the pilgrimage to the Holy Land, and its novelty remained fresh. This meant that large numbers of men would arrive at infrequent intervals. But they could not of course be relied upon. Only a few would stay and they did not therefore provide a permanent solution to the shortages.

The defeat of the Egyptian force allowed Baldwin time to consider the political situation inside his kingdom. Before he could build a stable nation, he must be ruler in his own house, and this meant being able to limit the influence of the Church in Outremer. This in its turn meant controlling, or at least influencing, the Patriarch of Jerusalem – not an easy feat with a man like Daimbert in the post. Accordingly, Baldwin attempted to remove him. However, the delegate that Pope Paschal sent to investigate the situation with Daimbert, Maurice, Bishop of Porto, was too weak, and would not take a decision. Aware of his vulnerability, Daimbert offered a gift to Baldwin. This was a message that the King understood. The two men were reconciled, and the papal legate returned to Rome, his adjudication ultimately not needed.

However, the reconciliation was short-lived. A year later, a gift was made to Daimbert, part of which should have gone to Baldwin but was not passed on. When the King discovered this abuse, he was only too ready to exploit Daimbert's greed. Here was a marvellous opportunity to get rid of the troublesome priest for good, and Baldwin was not the man to spurn such a chance. The misdemeanour was so blatant that Daimbert had little choice but to resign. He made his way to Tancred, hoping to use his previous contacts with Bohemond, Tancred's uncle, to good effect. But again his timing was awry. A new legate, Robert of Paris, had arrived to sort out the dispute. Baldwin prepared his attack. His weapons would be guile, his troops fellow leaders who detested Daimbert as much as he did. His one and only objective would be the complete and irrevocable subjugation of the Patriarch.

The evidence against Daimbert was too plain to be argued with. His removal from the post of Patriarch was confirmed and he retired in disgrace to Antioch.

From here he took ship to Rome, where he argued against the decision before Pope Paschal. Paschal, who was at that time under the influence of the persuasive tongue of Bohemond, gave way in the interests of a quiet life. Euphoric at this triumph and relishing his chance to gloat in Jerusalem, Daimbert was so overwrought that he fell ill and promptly died, his timing wrong until the bitter end. His demise was of inestimable assistance to Outremer. Unlike Daimbert, Baldwin realised that he must seek accommodation with the natives of Palestine and its immediate environs if the nation were to thrive. One of his first acts was to restore the rights of the local Christians that had been lost after the capture of the city, an act for which they were genuinely and openly grateful. Baldwin's vision of compromise was a vital ingredient in any recipe for success in the East.

Consolidation in Outremer continued with the capture of Acre in 1104. An attempt in the previous year had failed but Baldwin, again assisted by the Genoese, took it after strong initial resistance. The city capitulated on the offer of good terms. However, these were ignored by the Genoese, who brutally massacred many of the inhabitants after its capture. Baldwin was enraged by the presumption of the Genoese and almost retaliated against them, but desisted. Despite this sour taste after the fall of Acre, its capture was of huge significance. It was a deep-water port that was usable in all weathers, unlike most others in Outremer. It was to remain the gateway to the kingdom for most of Outremer's life.

Meanwhile, in the north trouble was brewing again. After the difficult times following the capture of Bohemond and Baldwin of le Bourg, the regions surrounding Edessa and Antioch had quietened down for a time. This was not because of any particular desire to live in peace and harmony but because the Turks were too busy plotting against each other to pay much attention to the Franks. A concerted effort by them must have critically stretched the Franks' resources but personal antipathies between the local Muslim rulers continued to outweigh wider strategic considerations once more. For the Muslims, a crisis point was reached in 1107 when the wily old campaigner Kilij Arslan fought one battle too many and was killed. It was a hammer blow for the Turks, whose immediate chances of unity died with him. However, for Tancred this was a major bonus. Alexius was seething at what he considered Tancred's duplicity. By rights, Antioch and the surrounding lands were his, but Tancred, with no sign of conscience, continued to disregard the oaths he had grudgingly made to the emperor. The death of Kilij Arslan made the routes across Asia Minor more dangerous than ever, and no Byzantine army would be able to approach Antioch for some time.

Joscelin of Courtenay and Baldwin of le Bourg still languished in a Turkish prison, but the time was ripe for their release. Their captors needed allies and money, and the two captives presented opportunities to acquire both. Joscelin was the first to gain his freedom after a large ransom was paid. To his great credit, he immediately threw himself into an energetic campaign to obtain a similar outcome for Baldwin. Initially, only a proportion of the requisite payment could be found. Joscelin offered himself as a hostage until the rest was found if Baldwin was released. His jailer, a man named Jawali, was so moved by the gesture that he

The ancient town of Antioch – modern-day Antakya in Turkey – seen from Citadel Hill.

agreed to comply with his suggestion. Joscelin was later released on condition that he settled the unpaid balance in the future which, being a man of honour, he subsequently did.

Sadly, Baldwin's troubles were not at an end. He wished to return to Edessa and take over as its ruler once more. However, the city was firmly in Tancred's sphere of influence and under the titular control of Richard of the Principate, a supporter of his. He was a cruel and unpopular ruler, but Tancred, Regent of Edessa in Baldwin's absence, acted true to form, and refused to return Edessa unless Baldwin swore allegiance to him. This Baldwin would not do, and he gathered together a force of Armenians to fight the issue out if necessary. Faced with this demonstration of strength, Tancred backed down.

The truce was brief. Baldwin allied himself with his ex-jailer, Jawali, in a war against Ridwan of Aleppo, who in turn asked Tancred for help. In October 1108 two Christian forces faced each other across a battlefield, each with Muslim allies at their side. It had taken a decade for the Franks to fall out with each other so completely that they were prepared to fight one another, seemingly oblivious to the fact that defeat of one faction must threaten the existence of the other. There were too few men for any troops to be lost with impunity. The battle was keenly fought but the tide eventually turned in favour of Ridwan and Tancred. Eventually Jawali's troops broke and fled, and with them went Baldwin and Joscelin. When Baldwin arrived back at Edessa, he suspected some of the Armenians of treason. In a vicious act that undid much of the good that he had done in better times, Baldwin rounded up and mutilated a number of them. Tancred did not attempt to take the city but great damage had nevertheless been done to the Christian cause.

When King Baldwin visited the siege of Tripoli in 1109, he took the time to arrange a reconciliation between Baldwin of le Bourg and Tancred, but the mere fact that he had to do so boded ill. The Christians needed cooperation and a shared vision. Nothing illustrates this better than events that took place in the following year. Baldwin of le Bourg now felt that only the major cities in his county could be defended and he decided to surrender the rural areas. Effectively, Baldwin was admitting that alone he could not hold the territory. During the evacuation of the countryside, large numbers of refugees were attacked and killed by the Turks, to the furious indignation of Baldwin. His heart ruled his head and his rash attempts to attack the Turks nearly ended in disaster.

Tancred continued to antagonise too many people. So incensed was Alexius at his on-going intransigence that he sought an alliance with the Caliph in Baghdad against Tancred. The approach was rebuffed, as it would have horrified devout Muslims as much as Christians, but the fact that Alexius would even contemplate such a move evidences the depth of the resentment that he felt. However, on 12 December 1112 the situation took a dramatic turn. Aged only thirty-six, Tancred died.

His life had been successful but inglorious. In an era of many selfish motives, Tancred was especially self-centred, and sought self-advancement at all costs. The Crusaders needed unity, as individually their paltry forces were inadequate against the vast resources of their potential enemies. Given this, Tancred's attitude to the redemption of both his own uncle, Bohemond, and Baldwin of le Bourg had been motivated purely by personal ideals, in stark contrast, for example, with the actions of Joscelin of Courtenay. Of course, other leaders had their faults, yet the death of Godfrey, of Raymond and of Bohemond all led to genuine mourning. Such a response was conspicuously absent when Tancred died, and in this silence lies his most fitting epitaph.

Tancred's successor in Antioch was named Roger, and to him would fall the crowning glory of the early life of the Crusader principality of Antioch. A great army of Muslims set out from the east intent on creating havoc. The Christians, comprising the forces of Roger of Antioch, Baldwin of Jerusalem and Pons, ruler of Tripoli, set out to confront it, significantly accompanied by a number of Muslim allies. The leader of the Muslim enemy retreated before this force, in a typical feint. Equally typically, the Franks failed to see through the ruse. Baldwin and Pons took their men homeward, confident that the threat had evaporated. They were wrong. As soon as they left the scene, the Muslim commander, Bursuq, turned around. Messengers were frantically despatched to urge the departed Christian forces to return. Time was of the essence for Roger, however, and he sent out scouts to monitor Bursuq's movements. They espied the enemy without being discovered themselves. Under cover of the hills, Roger crept towards Bursuq.

They reached a ridge bordering Bursuq's camp. The enemy was still completely unaware that the Franks were so close, and the camp was poorly guarded. Many Muslims were away foraging. Consequently, when the Franks launched their attack resistance was sporadic. The camp was overwhelmed and Bursuq was swiftly fighting for his life. He escaped with this but little else. His army was a broken force and he retreated eastward. Antioch was secure and would not be threatened again for some time. It was a significant moment indeed.

Around Jerusalem a semblance of stability prevailed. King Baldwin raided across the Jordan, and added to his kingdom an area that became known as Oultrejourdain. To protect this he built a number of castles, such as the great fortress of Montreal. His express purpose was to dominate the caravan routes that

The great fortress of Montreal.

criss-crossed the region. More forays strengthened his position still further, one of them reaching the Red Sea at Aqaba. The fortresses he built would be difficult to defend because of their geographical isolation, but at least served as an indication of the virility and confidence of the kingdom.

Domestically, King Baldwin's affairs were complicated. No issue had ensued from his Armenian marriage and, as the match had brought him little benefit, the king, not a man to be ruled by sentiment, considered whether another bride might bring him more advantages. A suitable partner would be Adelaide, a Princess of Sicily. She would bring important strategic benefits by her ties with the Normans of that island – a useful counterbalance against the Normans of Antioch. She was also extremely rich. When he considered all these assets, Baldwin instantly fell in love with her. A marriage was suggested and was agreed to by Adelaide; after all, few women are offered the chance to become a queen.

This of course left the minor obstacle of Baldwin's existing spouse, who was surreptitiously retired to a convent. She asked whether she could go to Constantinople instead, as her parents were currently living there. Baldwin agreed. On the arrival of Adelaide of Sicily in the Holy Land, Baldwin immediately deprived her of her treasure and used it to pay off his debts. It was an overt statement of the motivations behind his marriage plans. The wedding ceremony took place in the autumn of 1113. Given such an inauspicious start, it is no surprise that the marriage was not a happy one. Many people were deeply shocked by what appeared to be a bigamous liaison. The scandal became so great that it was suggested to Adelaide that she might like to return to Sicily. The barons of Outremer were unnerved by the terms of the marriage contract, which stated that Adelaide's son, Roger II of Sicily, would succeed to the throne. Unhappy though she must have been with the marriage, the summary method of Adelaide's dismissal in March 1117 bitterly hurt her pride and she left determined that Sicily would offer little support to Outremer in the future.

Despite these domestic problems, taken as a whole, after twenty years in Outremer the situation was not without promise for the Franks. Against many expectations, not only had the initial toehold in the region been held, it had been expanded. However, much depended on whether the state could survive the departure of a strong leader.

The year 1118 was one of obituaries. The first man to die was Pope Paschal. His primacy had not been good for the East. He little understood the region, and the attempts that he had made to enforce the submission of the Orthodox Church to Roman authority had been heavy-handed. Divisions between the West and Byzantium, fuelled by Bohemond's earlier influence with Paschal, had been exacerbated. In the same year, far to the east, another prominent leader, the Sultan Mohammed, ruler of the Islamic world, was summoned to Allah, an equally significant change to the political situation.

For his part, Baldwin was ambitious. He decided to strike at the heart of the Fatimid lands, into Egypt itself. He set out with a small force on an exploratory raid. While there, he was attacked by the deadliest of enemies. A tiny germ found its way into his system and the King found himself fighting a desperate battle for life. It was for him the final conflict. He struggled back to his kingdom but passed away on 2 April. The mourning was great and spontaneous. Even Muslims visiting the kingdom were moved. With the pomp appropriate to the status of a king, he was laid to rest in the greatest church of Christendom, the Church of the Holy Sepulchre. His loss was an immense blow. During his reign, all the ports north of Ascalon were captured for the kingdom. Not without blemish as a man, a soldier and a king, Baldwin had nevertheless led his realm through many crises and had managed to survive them, building a much stronger, more mature state than the one he had inherited. Ironically, Queen Adelaide was to die a fortnight later, exiled in Sicily.

But Baldwin's death was neither the last, nor the greatest, of that momentous year. On 15 August, Alexius, heir to the Roman Empire, a colossus of the world stage, died. His achievements were vast. He had inherited a once great but declining empire that had only decay and dismemberment to look forward to. By his qualities, as a warrior and as a statesman, he had breathed hope into the soul of a dying empire and had given it back its pride. It was in reality a futile revival, the hope of greatness that he brought was nothing more than an illusion. Yet he delayed the demise of his empire for three hundred years, and herein lies his greatest achievement.

It was in all ways the end of an era. The cast had been changed, and new players would join the drama. It was a time of change, of uncertainty, of self-doubt. It remained to be seen whether the plot would develop into a triumphant epic or into the darkest of Greek tragedies.

CHAPTER 12

Signs of Strain

It was very important that the gap left by the death of Baldwin should be filled quickly. The kingdom's predatory neighbours would interpret a long interregnum as a sign of weakness. There was no constitutional assertion that it was a hereditary fief, yet Western traditions encouraged many to regard it as one. Eustace of Boulogne was sent for but no sooner had the message been sent that many in Jerusalem began to have doubts. He was far away, and would not arrive for months, and he was known to be a reluctant Crusader.

The obvious candidate in his stead was Baldwin of le Bourg, a cousin of the late king and now an experienced ruler. He was an efficient if unlovable man, who enjoyed the support of many influential Franks, including crucially Joscelin of Courtenay. His arguments helped to persuade the Council to change its mind, and the invitation to Eustace was retracted. When he heard of their decision, Eustace graciously accepted it, no doubt with a hint of relief. Baldwin would be a strong ruler. He was full of energy, although he lacked the physical presence of his predecessor. However, he was a cold and calculating man, in short a ruler who would inspire fear, even respect but, with the exception of his wife, with whom he enjoyed a very close relationship, rarely love. He had strong mercenary interests and he would try to strengthen the local economy.

Meanwhile, Joscelin of Courtenay had a hidden agenda to fulfil. When Baldwin left Edessa to take up residence in Jerusalem, he appointed Joscelin as his successor. Although Baldwin's reign started positively, he was soon faced with a succession of problems that caused the kingdom to lurch from one crisis to another. The first of these was the formation of an alliance between Damascus and Egypt. The threat of this happening had always been the greatest fear of the Franks, and with good reason. It opened up the possibility of an attack from both sides of the kingdom that, if properly co-ordinated, would create immense difficulties. However, when Baldwin responded quickly and led an army to face the enemy, a stand-off was reached and much to the relief of everyone the expected assault did not materialise.

However, any hopes that Baldwin entertained of this being the end of his troubles were badly misplaced. A much greater challenge developed in the north when Ilghazi, a tough Muslim leader, invaded the county of Antioch. Alarmed, Roger of Antioch sent to Jerusalem for help. Baldwin's reply was swift, telling Roger that he must stay on the defensive until he arrived with help. It was sound advice but it was ignored. Roger glibly made a foray from the city, blithely assuming that he would be more than a match for his enemy.

It was a serious and, for Roger, a fatal mistake. He set up camp on the night of 27 June 1119. He was disquieted to receive reports that the enemy were very close at hand. Muslim spies within the Crusader camp reported to Ilghazi that the Franks were heavily outnumbered. Daybreak on 28 June found the Christian army completely surrounded. Roger's scouts confirmed that there was no escape; they would have to fight their way out.

The wall of steel encircling the Franks proved impenetrable. All the Franks could do was make a desperate attempt to push through the enemy lines; failure to do so meant certain destruction. The Frankish infantry were driven back, and became entangled with the cavalry. There was no way through for Roger or his army. Only a few isolated knights managed to hack their way out of the Muslim encirclement. Roger fought well but died in the battle. Those who were unfortunate enough to be captured were brutally tortured and then executed. Terrified at the prospect of an imminent attack from Ilghazi, Antioch regrouped under a new leader, Bernard the Patriarch. Fortunately, Ilghazi was slow to follow up on his victory and the city was for the time being safe. Baldwin assumed direct control of Antioch on his arrival there, but nothing could obscure the fact that a serious set-back had occurred. Roger could be replaced, but the destruction of so many men on what became known as 'The Field of Blood' would be a greater loss.

The Muslims failed to push home their advantage. A confrontation subsequently took place at the Battle of Hab, at which Baldwin was able to fight off the foe. But the need for a standing army was obvious. Since its birth, Outremer had relied on irregular influxes of men from the West to supplement its meagre resources. In 1118 several developments took place that would in the long-term provide a partial answer to the eternal problem. In that year, a new order was formed with the express aim of assisting pilgrims to the Holy Land. It was named the Order of the Knights Templar because its headquarters was situated at the al-Aqsa Mosque, on the site of King Solomon's Temple. They would be joined in their role eventually by the Knights Hospitaller, an order that had been based in Jerusalem for some time. The Hospitallers had originally been formed as a charitable, non-militaristic order with the aim of caring for pilgrims. Possibly following the Templars' example, they would, some years after the Templars were formed, develop a more aggressive stance, helping to alleviate some of the difficulties caused by the shortage of men, even though their change of attitude would not be unreservedly welcomed by the Pope.

It would of course be some time before the Orders would make a significant impact. Few records exist, from the early years of their existence, of how they developed. However, over the course of the twelfth century, they would assume a role of great importance. They based their code on the monastic rule instituted by St Benedict. They were required to pledge themselves to be obedient and chaste, and to reject material possessions. They would become a disciplined fighting force that would never retreat unless the odds against them were at least three to one, and they would fight to the death because if they were to be captured the Order would not ransom them. This would cost many of them their lives, as there was no point in keeping them alive if they were taken in battle.

The al-Aqsa Mosque, site of the headquarters of the Knights Templar.

Equally as important as the military effect of the Orders would be their contribution to the politics of Outremer. They would come to dictate policy in the Holy Land and to dominate weak rulers. Their position would be further strengthened because they would eventually owe earthly allegiance to none save the Pope himself, and were consequently often more powerful than the king. Grants of land would be given to them all over Europe, and they would become the richest organisations in Christendom. Their importance to the development of Outremer was immense. In Baldwin's time, though, these events were unforeseen.

The situation of the Franks in Outremer was not eased when they started to fight among themselves once more and Pons of Tripoli had to be forced to recognise the overall authority of the new king. Despite this, Outremer possessed one quality above all others – resilience. Throughout its life, it would stumble from one crisis to another. The vicissitudes of the kingdom would inevitably, over time, take their toll, and often seemed to form part of the inextricably linked chain of events that presaged the ultimate demise of Outremer. Within the space of twelve months, it would be faced with two of those events.

The first took place in 1122. Joscelin, who was popular with the people of Edessa, set out with a small army that came across a large Muslim force led by a man named Balak. Being heavily armed, and aware that his opponents were much more lightly protected, Balak immediately attacked. At this moment, a storm broke, making the ground a morass, impassable for the heavy chargers of the Franks. The more manoeuvrable Muslim force was able to pick off the immobilised knights, and Joscelin was dragged off into captivity.

This left Baldwin with the problem of finding a new ruler for the important city. Nominal control was given to Geoffrey the Monk. Baldwin stayed in the area to ensure stability but he was careless. He was preparing to go hunting when, on 18 April 1123, his poorly prepared troops were surprised and overwhelmed by a large Muslim force in the area. Baldwin was taken away to the castle of Kharpurt, a prisoner with Joscelin once more. But this set into train an extraordinary sequence of events. The people of Edessa were particularly fond of Joscelin and devised an escape plan. Dressed as local inhabitants with a grievance, they gained admittance to the interior of the castle. Once inside, they easily overwhelmed the garrison and freed the captives.

However, they were still far from safe. It was agreed that Baldwin would stay in the castle and defend it, while Joscelin would run for help. Joscelin made his way westward. Together with one companion he reached a swollen river. He could not swim across but he inflated two empty hog skins that he had with him and drifted over to the other side. He rushed to the nearest Christian town to enlist help, but he was too late. Balak had hastened to the castle as soon as he heard of its fall. Baldwin refused an offer of freedom if he surrendered, assuming – probably correctly – that this was a ruse. Balak therefore stormed the castle. Enraged with the audacity of the men who had taken his castle, within which his harem were resident, Balak hurled nearly all the captives to their deaths from the castle walls, including several members of his harem whom he suspected of sympathising with the Armenians who had taken the castle. Only Baldwin and two other important prisoners were allowed to live.

The capture of the King was a grievous blow but once again the survival instincts of Outremer revealed themselves. In Baldwin's absence, the Constable, Eustace Garnier, took charge. Not only did the nation survive, it continued to expand. Primarily responsible for this were the Venetians, who were now showing an interest in the area. They had been late to become involved in the region in contrast to the Pisans and, especially, the Genoese, who had to date shown some enthusiasm in Outremer. However, predictably, the Venetians quickly strove to make up for lost time. Asked to send help to the East, they responded with a large fleet, led by the Doge himself. They raided Byzantine vessels and towns freely en route but announced their arrival in Outremer by an overwhelming victory against an Egyptian fleet.

Once ashore, the Venetians evolved a scheme with the Franks to take the town of Tyre. Their price would be heavy: a street in every Christian town that they subsequently captured, with all that that meant in terms of trading opportunities; a third of Tyre itself; and exemption from customs duties. The prize on offer was so significant that the Franks accepted the bargain. The garrison resisted the assault but was soon starving. They negotiated good terms and agreed to surrender. Those who wished to leave were allowed to. The Franks were learning important lessons. There were too few Westerners to populate the country adequately, and they would need the help of the native inhabitants to maintain a viable economy. There was no question of the local population being accepted as equals, but the necessity of their contribution was tacitly being recognised.

King Baldwin was soon ransomed. It was an excellent sign that the kingdom had continued to thrive in his absence. For his part, on his return Baldwin undid little of what had been agreed in his absence. However, a new threat materialised in the form of il-Bursuqi, the Turkish governor of Mosul, who invaded Outremer in 1125. What followed in May, at the Battle of Azaz, was one of the most gruelling battles of Crusader history.

It is of great significance that Baldwin's small army of 2,000 infantry and 1,100 cavalry took the field with men from Edessa, Antioch, Tripoli and Jerusalem. Herein lay the secret of success in Outremer, the pooling of resources and a subordination of individual objectives to the greater aims of the state as a whole. This was the only possible basis for long-term survival. Baldwin was massively outnumbered but used his troops well. He stood firm against the powerful assaults of the enemy and, at the decisive moment, released his heavy cavalry in an overwhelming counter-assault. The shock was too great for the Muslims to resist, and in minutes they had disintegrated. Despite the ferocity of the initial Muslim attacks, the Franks' armour was impervious to them. The Islamic army became disheartened, and panic spread through their ranks like wildfire. Their defence collapsed. Two thousand Muslims were lost against twenty-four Franks. The booty captured was enormous and helped to pay off outstanding instalments on Baldwin's ransom. The hostages held as surety against this ransom – including Baldwin's daughter – were then released.

This was a tremendous boost to morale, to be followed soon after by news of the death of il-Bursuqi. He fell victim to a sinister group who had a penumbral influence on the life of Outremer on many occasions. They were Ismaili militants (the Ismailis were a branch of Islam connected to the Shiites and were, as such, traditional allies of the Fatimids). They were absolutely committed to their leader. Whatever was ordered of them, they obeyed without question. This often involved the murder of an enemy and, as there was usually little chance of escape, these acts were effectively what we would term suicide missions. In return for their obedience, they were taught that eternal life in paradise awaited them should they die a martyr's death, a land of indescribable sexual delights and everlasting contentment. Their alleged fondness for hashish gave them their name. The Anglicised version of this has become a well-known word in the English language; they were known as the Assassins.

The morale of Outremer was lifted by the arrival in October 1126 of a new warlord. He was Bohemond, son of the incomparable Norman warrior of the same name, who arrived to claim his inheritance. Only eighteen years of age, he had inherited many of his father's characteristics, striking good looks and great charm, as well as the more dubious attributes of rashness and ruthless, self-centred ambition. Time would show that he had not inherited one other great gift from his father – luck. But all this was in the future. The people were delighted to welcome him, especially Baldwin, who appreciated the need for new blood. It must have been a difficult task for Baldwin to rule in both Jerusalem and Antioch. He was punctilious in his treatment of Bohemond, giving him every due respect. He agreed that his own daughter, Alice, would marry Bohemond and the ceremony took place without delay, being celebrated with great pomp. It seemed a perfect match but it did not live up to its promise.

Baldwin also had to find a husband for his eldest daughter, Melisende. Her match would be especially important as, in the absence of a male heir, he was likely to become the next ruler of Outremer. No suitable candidate existed within the kingdom and so Baldwin sent to France to find one. It was suggested to him that Fulk, Count of Anjou, would be ideal. He was a widower and his younger son had just married Matilda, daughter of King Henry I of England. He was rich and powerful, and possessed a good military reputation. He was much older than his prospective bride but that was of little consequence. Fulk himself was delighted with the suggestion and the offer was also enthusiastically received in Outremer. Fulk was duly married to Melisende in May 1129.

By the time that he arrived, however, the region was once again in ferment. Toghtekin, ruler of Damascus, had died in 1128 and his death encouraged Baldwin to attempt to add Damascus to his domain. As he did not have the resources at hand to do this, he sent to Europe for help. His leading ambassador was Hugh of Payens, founder and Master of the Templars. On his arrival in France, Hugh spent much time with his cousin, Bernard of Clairvaux. Bernard was the greatest clerical figure of his day, even more influential than the Pope. He dominated the Papacy and was a leading figure in Europe for decades. He was a frail man physically, and a Crusade would have probably killed him. So he sought vicarious involvement, and engineered support for a large army to be sent to the East. But the expedition he helped to assemble was a major disappointment. Although it sailed to the East and reached a point only 10 miles from Damascus, it was not strong enough to attempt to take the city. However, this was secondary to the events that took place in Europe that had dramatic repercussions on the future history of Outremer. Bernard developed the image of the Templars as warrior monks. He gave them their own rule, and established their position in the ecclesiastical hierarchy. It was at his instigation that they would answer directly to the Pope. Effectively, this was the birth of the Order as a great power.

In Outremer, the arrival of Bohemond had proved to be a far from positive move. It was partly because of his self-centred actions that the expedition to Damascus failed; when it took place, he was too busy fighting Joscelin of Edessa to assist. After the expedition was abandoned, King Baldwin had journeyed north to castigate the two men, who were eventually reconciled. Nevertheless, the ambition of Bohemond was far from satiated. He knew that his father had for a time ruled part of Cilicia, and he attempted to recover the region for himself, as only a few towns remained of the original territories conquered. However, the force with which he set out to do this was small, and his scouting was desultory. He was taken completely by surprise when, in February 1130, a large Turkish force attacked him, and in the confusion of the mêlée he lost his life. By his death a great ransom was lost to the Turks, but even this did not dampen the enthusiasm with which the news was greeted by the Muslim world.

He left behind a two-year-old child, Constance, and an unprincipled wife. Alice, for her part, desired absolute power and did not appear to have many scruples about how she came by it. In the region now was a new Muslim power, a man named Zengi, whom the Crusaders would have good reason in the future to curse. Amazingly, Alice offered him homage if he would protect her. It was an incredible move, even though Alice's mother was an Armenian, not a Frank. However, she could not deliver on her promises. When she refused Baldwin admission on his arrival at Antioch, the elders of the city would not tolerate this open defiance and opened the gates to him themselves. Trembling in fear, the rebellious daughter was forced to kneel before her father, who promptly exiled her to Lattakieh.

However, Baldwin was worn out. He had lived an extraordinary life, first in Edessa and then in Jerusalem. He had spent two long periods in prison and had been tireless in his attempts to maintain the fabric of his kingdom. Now all this took its toll. He fell ill in 1131, and it quickly became clear that he was dying. Men may have doubted his nature but never his piety. His last act was to become a canon of the Holy Sepulchre, a move inspired in all probability by genuine religious feeling as much as by fear of the afterlife. It was his last action, and he died on 21 August 1131.

His old compatriot, Joscelin of Courtenay, soon followed him. While besieging a castle, he was hideously injured when a wall collapsed on him. There was no possibility of recovery. Joscelin lay dying when news reached him that a large Turkish army was threatening a nearby town. In a supreme act of courage, Joscelin resolved to die with style. He was carried on a litter at the head of the army that went to meet the Turks. Overwhelmed by the fortitude exhibited by this magnificent gesture, the Turks quickly departed. His job done, he expired by the wayside. The Crusaders may often have lacked scruple or judgement but none should doubt their bravery. If we believe that the Crusades have nothing to teach us, we should remember the heroic example of Joscelin of Courtenay.

These deaths left a large vacuum. Joscelin and Baldwin represented the last of the first generation of Outremer. There would be good leaders again in the future but all too often their reigns would be sandwiched between those of less effective men. The crowning of Fulk and Melisende in September 1131 could not disguise some uncomfortable realities. There was opposition to the new regime, centred on Alice. Antioch started to act in open defiance of Fulk's authority and the army that he sent to enforce it was refused passage by Pons of Tripoli. Nor did Fulk's domestic affairs help the situation. There were widespread rumours that Melisende was romantically connected with Hugh of le Puiset, a young nobleman. One of Hugh's stepsons, Walter Garnier, took such exception to the rumours that he challenged Hugh to a duel.

Hugh did not appear for this, and his non-appearance was read as an admission of guilt. However, news soon arrived that he had fled to Ascalon and had asked the Egyptians for help, but they deserted him. Hugh found himself alone and threw himself on the mercy of Fulk, who decided to forgive him. His sentence would merely be one of exile for a few years. However, Hugh would not escape so lightly. While playing dice in the port where he was waiting to board ship, he was involved in a fight and died shortly afterwards. Suspicion was cast on Fulk, a slur on his honour that he went out of his way to disprove. The unfortunate would-be assassin was sentenced to die a death that seems extraordinarily violent even for those harsh times. He was dragged into the market square and tied down. Then a leg was cut off. Boiling pitch was instantly poured over the gaping wound, causing more pain but prolonging life. When the assassin recovered from the shock, the other leg was cut off and the process with the pitch repeated. Finally, after both arms had been removed in the same manner, the limbless trunk was forced to confess its guilt and, mercifully, was decapitated.

Raids on Outremer became more intense. Antioch was attacked in 1133 and the attack was beaten off without great conviction. Two years later, Zengi captured a number of important border fortresses, threatening both Antioch and Tripoli. And Alice was still a difficult problem, offering her daughter Constance to the Emperor in Constantinople as a potential bride for his son Manuel. Finally, Fulk devised a plan to check her ambition. He sent in secret for Raymond of Poitiers, son of the Duke of Aquitaine, who was currently in England. Fulk planned to marry him to Constance, but secrecy was of the utmost importance. On his arrival, Fulk made out that Raymond was really interested in Alice. While Alice waited for him to come to pay suit, dressed in her most splendid finery, her daughter was forcibly married in the cathedral. Alice was powerless to change what had happened and she disappeared from the political scene from this point onwards.

Further raids took place in 1137. In the course of one of them, Pons of Tripoli was killed. In another Zengi captured Raymond of Tripoli. Fulk himself was holed up in the castle of Montferrand. He negotiated excellent surrender terms and withdrew with all his troops, merely abandoning the castle to his opponent. A relieving force was close at hand and Fulk may have regretted giving in so easily when he heard of its proximity. If so, he had little time to regret it. Stunning news had reached both the Franks and the Muslims from the north. The Empire was back.

When Alexius Comnenus died twenty years earlier, his son, John, succeeded him. His succession was opposed but John quickly established himself. It turned out that, although he lacked a prepossessing physique, he was a tough and determined character, a good soldier and an efficient administrator. Slowly, imperceptibly but inexorably, John started to recover land in Asia Minor. By 1137, his ambition had increased. He launched an assault on Cilicia. Then, without warning, he appeared before the walls of Antioch on 29 August.

To say that this came as a bolt from the blue is the greatest of understatements. For three decades, the rulers of Antioch had blithely assumed that the Emperor would never trouble them again. They had ignored without qualm the oaths of allegiance taken by the city's first rulers and confirmed by the Treaty of Devol. Now their bluff had been well and truly called. Raymond of Poitiers hurried back to the city, and frantically sought advice from Fulk. The King advised submission. The legal case was unequivocal and would brook no argument. The oaths had been taken in good faith, and must be honoured.

Faced with such counsel, Raymond had little alternative but to submit. John was magnanimous in accepting his submission. Raymond was offered a new territory, consisting of the towns of Aleppo, Shaizar, Hama and Homs. The only minor obstacle was that they were all currently in Muslim hands. That John intended to change this became apparent in 1138. Without warning, all Muslim traders in Antioch were arrested. Then an army of Imperial troops, supported by men from Antioch, Edessa and some Templars invaded Syria. However, the Franks were apathetic in their efforts as they felt that they were giving up a much greater prize in Antioch and, disgusted, John negotiated terms with Zengi. When the army returned to Antioch, riots broke out in which several Greeks died. John decided to leave for the time being. Superficially, he left his nominal vassals with a show of mutual respect. It was the shallowest of pretences. The two parties did not trust each other.

But the Byzantine withdrawal was not permanent. John returned in 1142, arriving suddenly at Turbessel. He then moved to Antioch, demanding that Raymond admit him. Raymond would not, so the Emperor took to subterfuge instead. He wrote to Fulk in Jerusalem, saying that he wished to visit the Holy City. This put Fulk in an embarrassing position as it could legally be construed that he was also John's vassal. He would therefore have to pay homage to the emperor. Fulk prevaricated, saying that his land was poor and could not support John's large retinue. He suggested that he journey to Jerusalem with a small group instead.

In the event, the visit did not take place. John was injured by a stray arrow in a hunting accident. The wound was minor but was not properly treated. It became infected and it soon became evident that the Emperor was dying of blood poisoning. He took steps to ensure that his youngest son, Manuel, should succeed him. There were elder sons but in John's view they were not as capable as Manuel. His assessment proved to be absolutely correct and Manuel became a good emperor. Having performed this last important task, John passed away on 8 April 1143.

This may have seemed like divine intervention to the Franks. The new Emperor would need to be near his capital to consolidate his position and Outremer would be left undisturbed for some time. Collectively, the rulers of the Frankish cities breathed a sigh of relief. Little did they know that they had exchanged one problem for another, and that the process of decline, which must lead inevitably to the demise of Outremer, had already begun.

CHAPTER 13

Counter-attack

So far, Outremer had weathered a number of tempestuous events, albeit with some difficulty. Through it all, the Crusaders had managed to remain on the offensive for some of the time. The Franks had lost no major cities as yet, but no new ones had been added to their dominions for a while, and there were many dangerous enemies scattered around their borders waiting for an opportunity to strike. But the greatest enemy of all was the enemy within – the Franks themselves.

The unity that the Franks so desperately needed was not encouraged by the fact that Fulk, although a committed leader, was not an inspiring one. There were notably more acts of defiance against the authority of what was a still young monarchy during his reign. And the situation did not improve. While out hunting on 7 November 1143, a rabbit broke cover in front of Fulk's horse, and he was thrown to the ground. As he hit terra firma, his saddle slipped and fell on his head. Fulk was badly injured, and died a few days later.

Now there were problems with the succession. Queen Melisende assumed command, acting theoretically as a co-leader alongside her son, another Baldwin. They were both crowned in the Church of the Holy Sepulchre on Christmas Day. The date was auspicious, full of symbolism and hope, but it would prove to be a misleading omen. Melisende constantly tried to dominate her son who, as he grew older, naturally rebelled against her authority (he was only thirteen when he was crowned). The result was that the declining respect for authority, already marked during Fulk's reign, accelerated.

On the borders of the Crusader states around Antioch and Edessa there were further signs of trouble. Raymond of Poitiers, Prince of Antioch, and Joscelin II of Courtenay, son of the great lord of the same name and current ruler of Edessa, were constantly at each other's throats. Both

The death of King Fulk. (MS Fr. 2628, f. 146v)

men inherited many of the vices, without many of the redeeming virtues, of the men who had previously ruled their respective cities. Raymond, who seemed to have an unfortunate habit of alienating men, invaded Cilicia, a move guaranteed to antagonise the Emperor in Constantinople. The disunity in the region was especially dangerous as Zengi was now increasing in power, and he would not hesitate to exploit any sign of weakness. The situation was pregnant with threat. Wise men would have heeded the warning signs and buried their differences, but such objectivity was in short supply. Personal ambition was the prime motivator of both Joscelin and Raymond. A disaster was waiting to happen. It would not be long in arriving.

The city of Edessa had always held a special place in the affections of the Crusaders. It had been their first major conquest away from Asia Minor. It had great religious significance because of its association with the Prophet Abraham. However, its position was – and always had been – precarious. The salient in which it was situated jutted uncomfortably into enemy territory and was susceptible to a pincer movement. Many of its people were Armenians, with the Franks markedly in the minority. Further, some of the other racial elements in the city, such as Syrians and Jews, were decidedly ambivalent about the Franks.

In 1144 news reached Edessa that Zengi had attacked one of Joscelin's vassals to the south of the city. It was a challenge that the Count of Edessa did not ignore, and he led out a relief force. However, Zengi had only meant to lure Joscelin out. While he was thus occupied, Zengi made for his real objective – Edessa itself. The sense of shock in the city must have been great. Although well fortified, there were insufficient men left in the city to man the walls adequately. The defence was in the hands of Archbishop Hugh, who had little military experience. The enemy was widely regarded as the pre-eminent Muslim leader of his day. Furthermore, he was a terrifying man. When he captured the city of Baalbek in 1139, he had massacred the garrison despite the promise of a safe conduct.

The defence was gallant but doomed from the start. The only hope was that a relieving force would arrive to drive the enemy away. Joscelin quickly decided that this was beyond the capabilities of his own small force and sent for help. However, his pleas to Melisende in Jerusalem were not answered quickly enough, and the army that she raised was too late in setting out. This left only Antioch as a viable source of aid. It is true that Raymond and Joscelin were mutual enemies. It is also true that over the years Joscelin had consistently tried to outwit Raymond. But the greatest truth of all is that the safety of Antioch was linked to the safety of Edessa. If Edessa were to fall, the risk to Antioch would be greatly increased. Aware of this, Joscelin therefore sent a request for help to Raymond.

Unbelievably, Raymond did not respond. It was myopia of the very worst kind. It signalled the death warrant of Edessa but also seriously compromised the security of Antioch. Unmolested, Zengi tightened the siege. He had miners with him, who dug away at the foundations of the city walls. After four weeks, on Christmas Eve, of all nights, part of the wall collapsed. Within minutes a stream of Muslims were rushing through the breach, lusting for blood. The people of Edessa fled to the old citadel, seeking safety. But its gates were locked and thousands were trapped between them and the mass of Muslims now in the city. Hundreds died where they stood before Zengi arrived to impose a form of order. The native Christians were taken to one side – they would be treated well. For the Franks, a quite different fate was in store. The women and children who would fetch a good price were sent to the slave markets. Everyone else was put to the sword. The massacres of Antioch and Jerusalem half a century before were amply revenged.

The loss of the city was a tremendous shock, and its effects were enormous. Strategically, of course, it was a bad reverse, but these considerations were secondary to the moral effects. For the Franks, it was the sharpest of blows to their self-confidence, while for the Muslims it was a wonderful boost and a reminder that the Franks were far from invincible. As a result of this disaster, Joscelin was consumed with hatred for Raymond. Outright antagonism replaced what had before been mere misplaced rivalry. Joscelin did not accept the situation but attempted to win Edessa back, actually breaking into the city at one stage. However, the citadel was too strong for him to take, and he was forced to retreat when he heard that another Muslim force was approaching, barely managing to escape after a sharp battle.

The architect of this Muslim revival did not live long to enjoy his triumph. Zengi was a mighty warrior but his cruelty made him many enemies. While besieging a small town, he severely rebuked one of the Frankish eunuchs in his army. The eunuch bitterly resented this and as Zengi slept, he stabbed him to death. Zengi's sons rushed back to his lands to safeguard their inheritance, while the corpse lay unburied. Their only interest in him was to rip from his finger the ring that symbolised power. His kingdom was then divided, Syria being taken by his son Nur-ed-Din. Zengi had been the first great Islamic protagonist in the struggle between Muslim and Frank. Nur-ed-Din would be the second.

The news of Edessa's fall was received with consternation in Jerusalem. It was the greatest set-back to Outremer so far, and it was important that steps were taken quickly to counter-act its adverse effects. Melisende sent her envoy, Bishop Hugh of Jabala, to the West to argue her case and to encourage the formation of another Crusade as quickly as possible. There were not enough men locally to initiate a fight-back and an influx of new blood was imperative. However, the portents for Hugh were not promising. The current Pope, Eugenius III, was in exile from Rome and had many problems of his own. Nevertheless, he welcomed the appeal for a new expedition warmly, as it would help to assert his authority. He would, however, need to choose his leaders wisely. The balance of power in Europe was sensitive in the extreme. Eugenius was constantly under threat from Roger II, the Norman lord of Sicily. The Pope's counterbalance against him was the German Emperor, Conrad of Hohenstaufen, who supported Eugenius and despised Roger. Therefore, the Pope was extremely keen that Conrad should stay in Europe to guarantee his safety.

The situation in France offered much more potential. King Louis VII would have made as good a monk as he did a monarch. He was almost obsessively pious, even by the standards of the day. Ironically, his wife, Eleanor of Aquitaine, was a hot-blooded woman who was reputed to have suspect morals. They made an ill-matched pair. Eugenius had a moral hold over Louis, who had recently burned down a church while on campaign, killing a large number of civilians seeking sanctuary inside. The atrocity, probably unintentional, had severely harmed Louis' reputation and he wished to redeem it. Any further persuasion needed would come from Bernard of Clairvaux, now at the height of his oratorical powers. The King was eager to go but many of his barons were less keen. The initial euphoria generated by the Crusading ideal was already starting to wear thin.

Organisationally, the Papacy had moved some way forward since the First Crusade. Eugenius now sold this new venture as a way for Christians to redeem their sins. The full range of dispensations was granted to those wishing to participate, and financial help was given in the form of interest-free loans. Bernard was the master schemer behind the enterprise. His links with the Middle East, for example through the Templars, stretched back several decades and he provided much of the impetus behind recruitment for the project.

Bernard cared not a jot whom he upset in the process of advancing the cause of the Crusade. An extreme ascetic, he berated the Church for its obsession with materialism. He wrote to Abbot Suger of St Denis in a blind rage, calling his new church of St Denis a 'vanity of vanities', demanding to know 'what is gold doing in this holy place?'. His attitude to the Christian's role in the Crusading movement was blunt and unambiguous. He summed up his ethos by stating that 'the Christian glories in the death of the Infidel because thereby Christ Himself is glorified'. He would obviously not accept rejection meekly.

All the leading men Bernard could reach were summoned to Vezelay where, along the lines of Urban's speech at Clermont, he would make an announcement that presaged the start of the Second Crusade. Thousands of red crosses were made available to stitch to the cloaks of those who agreed to go on Crusade. In the event, such a large crowd gathered that they could not all fit inside the cathedral and they were instead addressed in a field. Bernard's speech, although few details remain, must have been completely convincing. So many people came forward to offer themselves that Bernard had to rip apart his own cloak to make more crosses.

Eugenius' plan had so far worked splendidly. Louis was compliant and would undoubtedly protect the Pope's interests. However, at this stage things began to go wrong. A fanatic named Radulph starting persecuting Jews in the Rhineland, exploiting the anti-Semitic feelings that were never far below the surface. Bernard hurried to Germany to reproach the errant Radulph, who was a monk of his Cistercian order, and it would appear that the visit sowed an idea in his mind. He had been so successful recruiting in France, why not here in Germany? He must have been aware that Eugenius wished to keep Conrad in Europe, yet he chose to ignore the Pope's wishes. Convinced that he was communicating directly with the Almighty, he decided to obtain Conrad's commitment to the expedition.

The scene that followed is rich in drama. Conrad was one of the strongest men in Europe, yet Bernard berated him like a teacher chastising a pupil. Bernard started mildly enough, attempting to persuade Conrad by subtle arguments. Conrad proved impervious to this approach. When this failed, Bernard resorted to intimidation. He exploded in an incredible tirade, reminding Conrad that he only owned what he had because it had been given to him by Providence, and in return the Emperor was obligated to protect the cause of Christ. It was an amazing outburst. Only a man of truly epic stature would have dared to deliver such a diatribe. His arguments proved so strong and his presence so dominant that Conrad capitulated, probably terrified that if he did not do so he would be struck down by a thunderbolt from heaven.

When news of this reached Eugenius, he was furious. The departure of Conrad would leave Italy an open door to Roger of Sicily. Eugenius did not speak to Conrad for a long time after. We do not know what his comments to Bernard were, but we may perhaps assume that even the Pope dared not rebuff him. In consequence of these events, two armies set out for Outremer. Both were large forces. Conrad took 20,000 men, while Louis led 15,000. True to form, they did not heed the lessons of earlier campaigns. Their ranks were swollen by many non-combatants who seriously depleted food supplies without offering much benefit in return. They also decided to use the land route to the East rather than the sea route, which would have been much safer. If they had done so, a great deal of trouble would have been avoided.

Emperor Manuel learned of the new Crusade with concern. The track record of previous expeditions was, of course, not good, marked with blatant disregard of the rights of Byzantium's citizens. Further, Manuel had been involved in several wars against the Turks that he now had to abandon as he was forced to return to Constantinople to monitor the progress and behaviour of the new Crusade. Truces were arranged with the Turks, and Manuel hurried back to his capital to prepare for the arrival of the expedition.

The Germans were the first to arrive, having set out in May 1147. They passed through Hungary without incident but once in the Emperor's territory they began to misbehave. Men took what they wanted without paying, and whole villages packed up their possessions and moved out of their way rather than risk losing everything. Matters became more serious when a German noble who had fallen was left to recuperate. As soon as he was unprotected, he was robbed and killed by local brigands. Frederick of Swabia, nephew and heir of Conrad, was incensed (he would become better known as the Emperor Frederick Barbarossa.) In a disgraceful and sacrilegious fit of pique, he burnt a Greek monastery to the ground, killing the monks whom he found there. In revenge, local inhabitants started to kill any stragglers they came across.

Manuel was understandably perturbed by the advance of this large army, apparently – even by Conrad's admission – out of control. The Emperor had no wish to see them in Constantinople. He therefore suggested that Conrad should take the direct route to Asia Minor. Conrad would not be told what to do, and continued his advance towards the city. When he arrived, he was billeted in a royal palace. He made such a mess of it that within a week he had to move.

The French army was ambling along behind at a leisurely pace, which is unsurprising as in its ranks were some of the leading ladies of the royal court. On the whole, they behaved better than the Germans. Among their number was one Everard of Barres, Master of the Templars; the Order's discipline would impress greatly during the forthcoming campaign. The local economy was already under great strain, as the Germans had denuded the region of provisions. Further, the local inhabitants did not welcome the French. The fact that they were a Christian army on Crusade was irrelevant – the people of the country saw no greater virtue in having their possessions stolen by Christians than by Muslims.

Manuel's attempts to encourage the French to go straight to Asia Minor were again unsuccessful. Fortunately, by the time the French arrived most of the Germans were already across the Bosphorus. A further matter of concern for the expedition was that, on the few occasions that French and German leaders had met to date, there had been great enmity between them.

While Louis was in Constantinople, Manuel tried to bring him under his control. Conrad had already taken an oath similar to the one taken by Raymond of Toulouse, but Louis would not agree to do the same. He felt it was demeaning to his regal status. However, an opportunity presented itself to Manuel when a Flemish member of Louis' force caused a riot. Louis was shocked and hanged the culprit. However, Manuel would not be appeased and deprived the French force of rations. Faced with starvation, Louis was impelled to give way to the Emperor's demands.

The Crusade leaders now had to decide what route to take. The Germans were in the van, and therefore were the first to choose. The French could learn from

The entry of Louis VII into Constantinople. (Fr 6465 f. 22 Entry of Louis VII into Constantinople with Emperor Conrad III during the Crusades, 1147–9, Chronicle of France or of St Denis *(14th century); Bibliothèque Nationale, Paris/Bridgeman Art Library, London/New York)*

their experience. Manuel's advice – and it was good – was that the armies should stay near the coast. The advantages of this were two-fold. Firstly, the coastal regions were largely in the hands of Byzantium, and secondly the Byzantine fleet could provide a supply line whatever the state of the land through which the forces passed. But his advice was not taken. Apart from a group of non-combatants, who heeded the suggestion, the German army decided to take the direct route through the heart of Asia Minor. It was a catastrophic decision.

It was not long before the horror of passing thorough hostile territory manifested itself. Constantly harassed by Turks, thirsty, hungry and tired, the troops soon had cause to curse Conrad. They eventually reached a point near to the field of Dorylaeum on 25 October 1147. Here they found a small stream, in normal circumstances not worthy of note but on this occasion appearing to be an oasis. Without discipline, the army broke ranks and rushed towards it. However, a large Turkish force was watching them. Seeing the way that the Germans were disintegrating, they realised that Allah had given them a great opportunity. This they did not allow to pass by. Within minutes, clouds of arrows were falling into the tangled mass of the German army. Behind the horse-archers, swarms of horsemen rushed in with their swords, slicing heads from shoulders and limbs from torsos. It became a rout of gargantuan proportion. Conrad's bodyguard fought its way out to safety and Frederick of Swabia escaped. But the losses were of truly immense proportions, nine out of ten men being lost.

Louis was quick to learn the lessons of this appalling disaster. He adhered to the coastal route along with the pathetic remnant of the German force, who joined him. Humbled, relations between the two armies temporarily improved. However, the exertions of the campaign and the depression of defeat were taking their toll on Conrad. He fell ill and was shipped back to Ephesus. It was to prove a turning point for him. The Emperor Manuel was there and was interested in medicine. He took an active part in the care of Conrad, who recovered. As a result, the two men became good friends. Meanwhile, Louis continued on his way. The Crusade was unhappy that prices seemed to rocket in the towns as they passed through, but this was nothing more than the economics of price inflation, for which Manuel could not be blamed.

The Crusaders had more reason to question the commitment of Manuel to their cause when they reached the city of Antioch-in-Pisidia, part of the Imperial territories in Asia Minor. A Turkish army was encountered outside its walls. When the Turks got the worst of the fight, they retreated for safety among the Greeks inside, an act of perfidy by the Byzantines in the eyes of the Crusaders. This accusation is difficult to refute. True, Manuel had not asked for the Crusaders to come but he had been fighting the Turks before they arrived. He would not hesitate to obtain any benefit he could from the Crusade, yet he seemed prepared to do little to help it. To the Crusaders, he appeared to be trying to be all things to all men, and they did not like or understand it.

From this point on, progress was increasingly tough. There was mountainous terrain to cross. Further, there was a major scare when the force was split into two by the indiscipline of the vanguard. A sharp fight ensued, from which the French only escaped with some difficulty. When they reached Attilia, Louis decided that he could no longer travel by land, and boarded ship to continue the journey to Outremer. Unfortunately, there were not enough ships at hand for the bulk of the army to follow suit. Other noblemen copied their king's example as soon as they could, but most of the foot soldiers were left to continue the arduous journey across country. They suffered considerable loss before half of them arrived at Antioch.

Here Louis rejoined them. The wealthy entourage that travelled with him found Antioch a delight, a rich city inhabited by rich people and as such a refreshing contrast to what they had seen in Asia Minor. The army could not decide what to do next. The locals offered conflicting advice. The inhabitants of the city wished them to attack the Muslim stronghold of Aleppo, while Joscelin, the Count of Edessa, wished them to retake his city. As the recruiting drive for the Crusade had drawn heavily on the need to retake Edessa in its propaganda, Joscelin's view was not unreasonable. The city had long been a Christian possession and if it were retaken a huge boost to Christian morale would ensue. On the other hand, the capture of Aleppo had been an objective for many years, and if it were to fall then there would be a strong buffer zone around Antioch. Both objectives had merit. Amazingly, neither of them was chosen.

It was a fact of life that the Franks in Outremer needed to win the support of some of the local Muslim population to survive, and on occasion formal alliances were formed. Recently, the Franks had entered just such an agreement with Unur, Emir of Damascus. Unur was alarmed at the growing power of Nur-ed-Din. As such, he was a man whose friendship the Franks should have cultivated, but such strategic subtleties were lost on the Franks in Jerusalem, who merely coveted the wealth of Damascus. It was true that if Damascus were held by a hostile leader, it would be a worthy target. By capturing it, a wedge would be driven between Egypt and Syria, and an alliance between the Muslim forces of those two regions had always been the greatest strategic nightmare of the Franks.

Louis was, indeed, cajoled by those in Jerusalem to attack Damascus. When he arrived in the Holy City, he rejoined Conrad, who had completed his journey by sea. After much discussion, Damascus was agreed as the primary objective. However, because of the current political situation, now was not the time to attack this city. But newcomers from the West were not fully aware of the political situation, and cannot be blamed for being misled by men, in this case the local leaders, who we must hold responsible for the decision, and who ought to have known better.

The greatest Frankish army yet seen in the area set out for Damascus in July 1148. Unur at first refused to believe that his city was their target. All too soon, however, the veracity of the rumours that he had heard was evidenced. The Franks, arriving on 24 July 1148, installed themselves in the lush orchards around the city. These were filled by guerrilla warriors, who harassed the Christian army unmercifully. Within the city, the Damascenes were in a state of panic. The force facing them appeared to be very strong. Unur was left with no option but to ask Nur-ed-Din for help. He was being driven into the arms of his greatest enemy.

Before long, the fall of the city, once seemingly certain, became less imminent as reinforcements poured in. Morale inside the city shot up as a result. This was further improved by the strategic naïveté of their assailants. The Franks, discomfited by the incessant attacks from the guerrillas, decided to move out of the orchards. The site of the new camp was appallingly chosen. They moved to an area with no vegetation; unfortunately, they failed to make the mental connection between lack of vegetation and lack of water. There was none for miles. And to make matters far worse, the leaders of the Crusade were bickering among themselves. The city was not yet theirs, but they were already arguing over who should rule it.

The reality of their now precarious situation began to dawn on the local Franks, including King Baldwin. It was probable that any Christian ruler in Damascus would be an appointee of Louis, most likely Thierry of Flanders. The barons of Outremer therefore would not significantly benefit from the city's fall. Further, the potential damage to their relationships with local Muslims may have occurred to them, albeit far too late. Whatever the real reason, they became slack in their prosecution of the siege and argued for a return to Jerusalem.

Louis was stunned. The finer points of their arguments were lost on him, but deprived of local support he had to raise the siege. Bitter, and convinced that the local leaders had been bought off by Unur, on 28 July he set out on the return to Jerusalem, angry, frustrated and disillusioned. The retreat was punctuated with constant assaults from the cock-a-hoop Muslims and many good lives were lost. The siege had lasted for four days and had achieved nothing but great damage to relationships between all the major parties. It was only good fortune that the debacle had lasted for so short a time that Nur-ed-Din himself was not in Damascus. Worst of all, however, was the obvious truth that the Franks in Jerusalem and the Christian leaders of Western Europe were now decisively out of step with each other.

Conrad soon returned to the West, entering an alliance with Manuel against Roger of Sicily. Louis stayed awhile, unwilling to go back to France with so little return for so much effort. It was also likely that he would be involved in complex and embarrassing divorce discussions when he went home. Rumours abounded about the sexual liaisons of Eleanor while she had been in Antioch. Little could he know that the role of his wife in the Crusading movement was far from over. When Louis did eventually go back, he was filled with a burning desire to avenge himself on the man he held responsible for the failure of the expedition – the Emperor Manuel. His ambition would not be fulfilled but it was nevertheless another nail in the coffin of relationships between Eastern and Western Christendom.

What became known as the Second Crusade had been a disaster. The resources put into it were huge. In contrast to the men who led the First Crusade, mostly middle-ranking members of the nobility, the leaders of the Second were at that time the two greatest kings in Western Europe. Thirty-five thousand men had set out, and only a fraction returned. The disaster had been caused not by a lack of commitment but because of the non-existence of a coherent strategy. In this, the First Crusade had been fortunate – for many, there had never been any doubt that Jerusalem was the ultimate goal. But once that goal had been achieved, a new objective was needed. Such focus did not exist and for that reason, above all others, the Second Crusade had failed. That a clear objective did not register among the men who came from the West was perhaps understandable, but that it was not present in Outremer itself was a source of great concern for the long-term viability of the Crusader territories.

Herein was the lasting legacy of this abortive adventure. Christendom was not yet in disarray but was descending towards it. Many from the West regarded the real enemy as being in Constantinople, not Damascus, Cairo or Aleppo. This misguided view would reap a bitter harvest. In contrast, there were strong unifying factors among the Muslims. The Crusaders had been living on borrowed time, relying on the disorganisation of the Muslim world for their existence. From this point on, the very survival of Outremer would be under threat. Time was running out.

CHAPTER 14

An Ill Wind

The knights of Outremer desperately needed a period of peace and stability in order to regroup. They did not get it. The kingdom was about to be hit with a series of body blows that would threaten its very survival. Within a few years of the totally unsatisfactory end of the Second Crusade, three Crusader states were to be deprived of their leaders, all of them dying violent deaths or being tortured, mutilated and incarcerated in dank, dreary Muslim prisons.

There appeared to be only one focus for all Nur-ed-Din's actions over this time; the removal of as many troublesome Franks as possible. Previous Muslim leaders had generally shown a desire to profit from the ransoms they demanded for their important captives, but the son of Zengi seemed intent on nothing save elimination. The first to suffer was Raymond of Poitiers, Prince of Antioch, as glamorous a noble as there was in the Frankish East at that time. In 1149 he received news that Nur-ed-Din was besieging one of his fortresses. He set off with a force to relieve it.

When the Muslim ruler saw the relief force arriving, he initially misjudged its size and began to withdraw. However, a more measured assessment showed that he enjoyed a significant numerical superiority. He then sought to obtain the maximum tactical advantage. The Crusaders spent the night of 28 June encamped at a desert oasis known as the Fountains of Murad. Despite its idyllic appearance, it was to become a death trap. During the night, the camp was surrounded. The Crusaders awoke to find that there was no way through the Muslim lines. Raymond's scouts had obviously not been deployed well, if indeed they had been deployed at all. There was no option other than to fight their way out.

Unfortunately for the Franks, they had to charge uphill with sand blowing in their faces, their heavier armour becoming more of a hindrance than a benefit. What followed was a massacre. Several principal men, including the leader of the Assassins, who was assisting Raymond, perished in the slaughter. So too did Raymond himself, struck down by a great warrior named Shirkuh. In an act of supreme humiliation, his corpse was decapitated, and his skull boiled dry and sent in a silver case to the Caliph in Baghdad. When he received news of the catastrophe, Baldwin, only nineteen, hurried to Antioch to provide stability. He urged that Raymond's widow, Constance, should marry again as quickly as possible.

Further disasters followed. Joscelin of Edessa was now a leader without a capital, and a count only in name. He held the town of Turbessel still but only with a tenuous grip. Now all his possessions would be lost to him. He had entered into a truce a few years previously with Nur-ed-Din but it had only been accepted because it suited the Muslim leader's plans at that time. A succession of raids had disturbed Joscelin and he decided to travel to Antioch to enlist help. While en route in April 1150 he was briefly parted from his escort (to respond to a call of nature, according to one chronicler). It was a fatal move. Following close behind the party were a band of brigands waiting for an opportunity to strike. That opportunity had arrived.

The bandits overpowered the isolated leader and dragged him away. They wished to receive a handsome ransom in return for his release. But when Nur-ed-Din was made aware of what had happened, he sent out riders to find the brigands and to buy Joscelin off them. They were successful in their mission and Joscelin was taken back to Aleppo. He was led out in front of a hostile crowd and publicly blinded. He would never taste freedom again, and spent the last nine years of his life in a miserable Muslim prison.

This was the ideal time for Nur-ed-Din to reconquer all the lands held by Joscelin. Joscelin's wife, the Countess Beatrice in Turbessel, gallantly fought off the subsequent Muslim assault. However, it was now clear to all but the greatest optimists that the Franks could no longer adequately defend their isolated possessions in this region. The defence of what was left of the salient would only divert resources from other more important areas. At this moment, the Emperor Manuel entered the scene. He offered to buy what was left of Joscelin's dominions from Beatrice. The countess referred this offer on to Baldwin in Jerusalem. The Council could see that there was no future in retaining the dismembered territories. They had no love for Manuel, but accepting the offer was seen to be marginally the lesser of two evils. The deal was struck, and the Franks withdrew from the territories.

The psychological effect must have been enormous. Edessa had been regarded as one of the greatest prizes of the First Crusade and the kingdom's first two monarchs were both counts of the city. The Second Crusade, which had been started primarily because of the reaction to its loss, did not even attempt its recapture. Now not only was the city lost forever, but so were the surrounding fortress towns. The Franks departed with nothing more than a whimper. It was a huge humiliation and should have been a salutary lesson to the Franks not to underestimate the power of a reunited Muslim world. But it was a lesson that would not be learned. Even Manuel could not hold on to the towns that he had purchased and within a year they were all lost. Nur-ed-Din's career seemed at its pinnacle, but it would yet rise further.

King Baldwin must have been a deeply worried man. Now his family was to add to his problems. There seems to have been something about the women who lived in Outremer that made them renounce the life of hearth and home, where they would meekly take their place in the background. The kingdom had more than its share of ambitious and ruthless women. Princess Constance of Antioch was one example of this phenomenon. Baldwin offered three suitable suitors for her hand to choose from. She rejected them all.

Constance had in mind something quite different for her future. The rulers of Antioch had to date done all they could to distance themselves from the Emperor in Constantinople. They felt that only by doing this could they retain their independence. Constance, therefore, must have created a good deal of consternation when she asked the Emperor Manuel to provide a suitable partner. Manuel was delighted to do so, but misjudged Constance badly. He nominated a man called John Roger, who was totally obedient to his wishes. He was of Norman extraction, and would therefore be acceptable to the people of Antioch, in Manuel's view. However, he was approaching the wrong side of middle age. For a young princess who had been married to a dazzling man like Raymond, this proposal was completely unacceptable and was, once more, rejected.

Another family crisis then distracted attention. Baldwin's aunt, Hodierna, was the wife of Prince Raymond of Tripoli. She became the target of persistent rumours concerning her morals. Her husband became jealous as a result and tried to make her change her active social lifestyle for a quieter, almost conventual, one. However, there was little chance of Hodierna acceding to this request. The marital disharmony grew and rumours about it spread to Jerusalem. Baldwin set out to Tripoli in an attempt to patch up the marriage, and Raymond and Hodierna were persuaded to try and restore their relationship. It was deemed a good idea that Hodierna should take a holiday in Jerusalem. She accordingly set out with the queen from Tripoli. Her dutiful husband accompanied her on the first mile of the trip.

As he returned through the city gates, he may have noticed a small group milling around. The men, pretending to be disinterested bystanders, were in fact Assassins. Suddenly, they threw aside their disguise and overwhelmed Raymond and his escort. Baldwin was still in the city, and became aware of the commotion in the streets. He rushed out to be told that Raymond was dead. In blind fury, the Franks slaughtered every Muslim they found but the real murderers escaped. Baldwin assumed control of the city for the time being.

Baldwin was being severely stretched in both a personal and a military sense. As well as Jerusalem, he effectively ruled in troubled Antioch and now Tripoli. Fortunately for him, although Nur-ed-Din tried to take advantage of the situation he was not able to do so. Baldwin also experienced a further complication in that he was still only joint-ruler with Melisende. For her part, she had no intention of giving up her status. She was helped by the unclear constitution of the kingdom. However, Baldwin would not tolerate sharing power with his mother for much longer, and his frustration soon became apparent.

Melisende suggested that she and Baldwin should both be re-crowned on Easter Day 1152, to confirm their standing. Superficially, Baldwin agreed to the plan but, at the last moment, he withdrew from the ceremony and two days later attempted a dramatic coup. He kidnapped the Patriarch of Jerusalem, who was virtually forced to crown him sole ruler in the Church of the Holy Sepulchre. However, as the ruse lacked dignity and subtlety, it initially failed to cement Baldwin's position as sole ruler.

Baldwin therefore resorted to persuasion. He used the argument that the power of Nur-ed-Din meant that the kingdom needed a sole leader. In fairness, this was a valid point. However, Baldwin did not have absolute power, being merely an elected king and therefore simply the kingdom's foremost baron. He consequently had to rely heavily on his Council, which consisted of the leading nobles in the land. Many of these men tended to pursue their own personal objectives and this led to a disunited front. As the Franks still formed a small presence in the kingdom, the pooling of resources was vital but unfortunately rarely practised.

Baldwin's claims did not meet with universal approval and an unsatisfactory compromise was reached whereby he would have Galilee and the north of the kingdom while his mother retained Jerusalem. Belatedly, though, some of the nobility came to see the logic of Baldwin's claim that having a sole ruler would make the state stronger. The turning point came when Melisende's leading supporter, the Constable Manasses, was captured by some of Baldwin's troops and forced to return to the West in exchange for his life. Her support crumbled away and she was forced to concede defeat. No further action was taken against Melisende but her influence was effectively ended.

The Crusader territories in Outremer in the mid-twelfth century.

Baldwin sought to build quickly on his triumph. For some time, Egypt had been disintegrating internally. The Franks had long harboured ambitions in that direction. In itself, there was nothing wrong with this. Egypt was indeed weak, and it was also rich. However, the objective started to become an obsessive one. The Franks were so dominated by thoughts of Egypt's capture that they virtually ignored the huge menace developing at their backs in Syria. There was insufficient resource in Outremer for both capturing Egypt and fighting off the resurgent Muslim threat from further east.

There remained one port in Palestine itself still in the hands of the Egyptians – Ascalon. Of course, at one point Ascalon had been as good as offered on a plate to the Franks, without bloodshed, and since the time that Godfrey of Bouillon had spurned that opportunity the port had continued to pose a consistent threat to Outremer. Its coastal position meant that the Egyptian fleet could keep it provisioned even when the land routes to it were closed. Its capture would therefore represent a considerable coup.

Baldwin decided that Ascalon must be taken. He received the support of his Council in this aim, and most importantly also of the Hospitallers and the Templars. The Military Orders were becoming increasingly influential. The chance to fight for Christendom struck a chord with a society where both religious and militaristic values were highly prized virtues. For many men, fighting for God presented a much more attractive proposition than spending one's life in a cloister. The Crusading concept had legitimised religious violence, and the Military Orders had developed the notion of divinely inspired warfare still further. They would soon own many of the castles in Outremer, and they were also becoming very rich, across Europe and not just in the Levant. It was the supreme irony that while individual knights were expected to renounce material possessions, the Orders to which they belonged became ever more wealthy. Their wealth, along with their direct answerability to the Pope, gave them immense power. They did not serve the King of Outremer and could not be ordered by him to act in any particular way.

Fortunately for Baldwin, the Orders were keen to see Ascalon fall. Consequently, the whole army of Outremer appeared before the walls of the city on 25 January 1153. However, the fortifications were in an excellent state of repair. The Egyptians were well aware of the strategic importance of the port, and would defend it strongly. The Crusaders for their part were equipped with siege engines that, in theory, could be pushed up against the walls and then used as a platform from which their infantry could pour into the city. In practice, they would have to cross ditches and moats while the defenders bombarded them with Greek fire. The siege went on for months, and

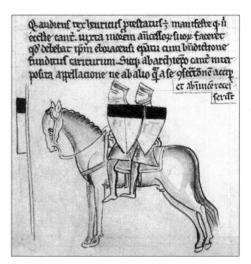

Templars sharing a horse (MS 26, f. 110v)

there was no sign of any weakening in the walls despite the constant battering of the Crusader artillery.

The Egyptians could not reinforce the city by land but their fleet was still strong. The Franks were boosted when an influx of pilgrims arrived at Easter eager to help. However, when a larger Fatimid fleet hove into view, the Christian ships meekly dispersed. Apparently, chivalry was not so appealing when the odds were heavily stacked in favour of the enemy. As it turned out, the Fatimid fleet brought only food, and no extra men arrived to help the defence.

A breakthrough came in an unexpected way. In July a siege engine was moved uncomfortably close to the walls. The garrison was very disturbed at the danger it represented and during the night crept out of the city with a view to destroying it. They managed to set the siege engine alight, and before long it was blazing fiercely. But what elation the Muslims felt was soon transformed to despair when the strong wind fanned the inferno against the city walls. The intense heat started to crack the stones, and by morning a considerable breach was opened, with a host of expectant Franks waiting to pour through it.

And then occurred one of the most incredible acts of folly of Crusading history. The Templars would, over time, develop a reputation for excessive pride and if their actions at Ascalon were anything to go by it was quite merited. Although the Templars were widely feared, even among the Muslims who had developed a strong disliking of the bearded warriors (most Western warriors were clean-shaven at this stage), it would appear that they had started to believe their own publicity. The Templars positioned by the breach apparently decided that all they need do was walk in and take possession of the city. Forty of their number entered the city, while other Templars prevented any other troops from joining them. The defenders were panic-stricken until they saw that the Templars were alone. They turned around, and swamped the arrogant knights, who were overwhelmed in minutes. The breach in the wall was repaired and the corpses of the dead Templars were hung over the walls to mock the assailants.

It was a terrible blow to Templar pride and almost as big a shock for the rest of the army. Baldwin wavered and considered abandoning the siege, although he was talked out of this. In truth, the garrison was tired and had little hope of relief. The success over the Templars had given them a welcome boost, but it had not materially improved their position. A particularly fierce artillery bombardment in August decided the issue. The garrison realised the hopelessness of its position and sought terms. For his part, Baldwin was not unrealistic. His main objective was the city itself and a massacre of the garrison was not important to him. He offered good terms, and he would abide by them. His conditions were accepted on 19 August; as a lengthy trail of refugees made its way unmolested towards comparative safety, the Christians walked in to take possession.

It was a worthy triumph, but one that the Franks did not have long to savour. Nur-ed-Din had been asked to help in the defence of Ascalon but assistance from him had not materialised. The reason for his inaction suddenly became obvious. His eyes were elsewhere and, while the Franks were distracted by Ascalon, Nur-ed-Din would make a move for the city he really coveted. For some while, he had wanted Damascus for himself. Unur was now dead and his successor was weak.

Nur-ed-Din sent his envoy to Damascus demanding entry, an order that was predictably refused. Following this rejection, Nur-ed-Din responded with calculated fury. The city held out against the large army he sent to besiege it, but without real conviction. One night, while the city slept, a Jewish woman opened the gates to admit Nur-ed-Din's troops, who soon quashed all resistance.

It was a tremendous victory for Nur-ed-Din, far outweighing the capture of Ascalon. The fall of Damascus was a portent of the greatest possible danger to Outremer. The Franks now held just a thin coastal ribbon, and hard up against it was a Muslim kingdom that was powerful, aggressive and, most dangerous of all, united. The Franks had lived in comparative safety while their Muslim neighbours had existed in a number of small, disunited states, but once that disunity was overcome the resources available to the Muslims far exceeded those of the Franks. If they wished to survive, the Crusaders needed to be especially on their guard now.

In the meantime, Constance of Antioch had found a husband, a somewhat surprising choice given the range of candidates available to her. He was a minor nobleman who had come east with the Second Crusade. He had no real prospects at home in France so he had decided to seek his fortune in Outremer. He was nominally a subject of Baldwin and had shown himself to have some courage in battle. His name was Reynald of Chatillon and if Baldwin had possessed the slightest inkling of the part that he would play in the future of Outremer he would have sent him packing in the first galley back to Marseilles. However, he did not suspect the true nature of Reynald and accordingly gave his approval to the match.

The newly-weds' first task was to face the wrath of Manuel. Constance ought to have consulted with the Emperor before appointing a co-ruler in a city that was nominally his. Manuel feigned anger in a successful attempt to encourage Reynald to help him in an expedition against the Armenians. Reynald grew tired of the fighting quickly and performed a sudden volte-face, throwing his lot in with the Armenians. They had spotted easy pickings elsewhere, and the fact that their target formed part of the Byzantine Empire would not unduly bother them.

The island of Cyprus had, to date, been little disturbed by the Crusades, despite its close proximity to the shores of Syria. The Imperial fleet had effectively deterred would-be invaders. In contrast to the mainland, it was a haven of relative tranquillity. It was rich, the pace of life was slow and the local leaders were complacent. Their complacency was cruelly exposed when, without warning, Reynald landed on the island with an army. The news should not have been a complete surprise. King Baldwin knew of Reynald's plans and sent warning of it to Antioch but his messengers were too late to intervene. Reynald's attempts to finance the expedition were hardly subtle, even by Crusader standards. He sought money from Aimery, the Patriarch of Antioch, and when it was refused he had beaten the prelate violently. His head wounds were then liberally laced with honey and the Patriarch was left tied up outside in the Levantine sun, a magnet for the many insects in the area. A day of this helped loosen the purse strings of Aimery, who subsequently fled to Jerusalem at the earliest opportunity.

The local Cypriot militia initially won a small victory against the invaders but the ultimate result was a foregone conclusion. The militiamen were eventually defeated heavily and the island devastated. Monasteries were destroyed, monks slaughtered, nuns raped. Vast amounts of booty were taken. The wealthy prisoners were taken to the mainland by the Franks; the rest – the old, the young, the poor – had their throats cut. It was a disgraceful atrocity, perpetuated against a peace-loving Christian people who, incidentally, were subjects of the Emperor just as Reynald was supposed to be. Reynald does not appear to have thought through the repercussions of his actions. Perhaps he thought that Baldwin would tolerate his indiscretions and that Manuel was too far away to punish him. If indeed he believed this, he was a poor judge of character.

Baldwin for one was outraged. Public opinion in Outremer was incensed at the way that Aimery had been treated. The King may also have feared the reactions of Manuel. Indeed, this may have been one of his reasons for sending to Constantinople to ask for a bride, as he was as yet unmarried. The Emperor responded by offering his niece, Theodora, a girl of thirteen with a maturity beyond her years and a classical figure to boot. Baldwin was entranced by her and, apparently genuinely smitten, accepted. Before he met her, he had a reputation for promiscuity but he was to become a devoted husband.

Reynald, meanwhile, lived off his ill-gotten gains. The situation in Outremer had become relatively tranquil. Baldwin had recently defeated Nur-ed-Din in battle and, anyway, the Muslim leader was ageing and noticeably slowing down. Further north, Reynald's partner in crime, Thoros of the Armenians, was equally content, confident that he had escaped retribution. Two years had passed since the decimation of Cyprus and nothing had happened in response. One fateful day in October 1158, Thoros was resting in his palace, having returned to Armenia. His relaxation was disturbed by a frantic messenger, with terrifying news. He had just passed a group of horsemen less than a day's ride away. Among them was the Emperor of Byzantium. Behind them was an army of massive proportions. It was unlikely that they were there on a hunting expedition. And if they were, their prey was probably human.

Thoros was terror-stricken, and rightly so. A dreadful retribution was imminent. In an instant, his wealth and power became secondary considerations to life itself. He fled to the mountains, leaving virtually everything behind. News of the Emperor's proximity then reached Reynald, now back in Antioch. He searched frantically for an escape route, but few options were available to him. He had already made a host of enemies in his short time in the region. Only one choice was open to him, and this, in an unusual display of sagacity, he adopted. He had to throw himself on the Emperor's mercy. He sent messengers to Manuel, offering to deliver the citadel of Antioch over to Imperial troops. But this would not be enough for Manuel, for whom nothing short of total humiliation would suffice.

Reynald acted the required role perfectly. Inspired by the adrenaline produced by the prospect of imminent death, Reynald played the part of his life. He entered the camp of Manuel, dressed as a penitent, bareheaded and barefoot. He threw himself at the feet of the Emperor, who made him lie there for five minutes –

a period that, to Reynald, must have seemed like as many hours. Then, after some of the sweetest moments of his life, Manuel acknowledged the presence of this repentant sinner. He would allow him to live, and he might even allow him to retain his presence in Antioch, but there would be conditions and they would not be negotiable.

A few days later, King Baldwin arrived. We can only surmise whether he would rather have seen Reynald executed, but anyway it was too late to influence that particular decision. Whatever his views, he presented himself to Manuel. The meeting between the two was an enormous success, both of them enjoying the other's company. At least one positive outcome had accrued from the mayhem.

Manuel wished to carry out one more act of great symbolism. He wanted to enter Antioch in such a way that no one could doubt his pre-eminent authority over the city. Reynald's henchmen tried to avoid this further humiliation but the Emperor had none of it. On Easter Sunday 1159 Manuel entered the city dressed in Imperial splendour, arrayed in his finest garments, lavishly covered in precious jewels and preceded by his Varangian Guard. He towered over the crowd on his charger, which Reynald, on foot, led by the bridle. Other Frankish lords walked beside him, including Baldwin, minus his royal diadem.

It was a great triumph for Manuel but he missed his moment. The Franks now expected him to unleash his forces against Nur-ed-Din and would gladly have joined him. This could have increased his prestige as the secular head of Eastern Christendom. However, Manuel had other less ambitious considerations. He merely wanted to protect Anatolia from further incursions, and was therefore happy to accept a truce with the Muslims after an initial show of force. The Franks watched this scenario unfold with a sense of betrayal. They had misread the Emperor's intentions for sure, but to them it was another sign of Imperial weakness. Another grievance was stored up for future reference.

Manuel then returned home. Reynald reverted to type swiftly, with dramatic personal consequences. In November 1160 he was made aware that there was a large party of Syrian herdsmen nearby with substantial unprotected flocks. This was too tempting a target to resist, and he set out quickly to intercept them. The herdsmen were completely incapable of defending their flocks and substantial booty was indeed captured. Reynald meandered lethargically back towards Antioch, unaware that some of the herdsmen had summoned help from Aleppo. He was totally off guard when this force caught up with him, and he was overpowered and unceremoniously dragged off to Aleppo. He would not be free again for sixteen years.

Antioch was thrown into a state of constitutional uncertainty. On the advice of Baldwin, Constance eventually offered the city to her son from her first marriage, who became Bohemond III. Manuel was not happy when he heard of this as, by rights, this decision rested with him. However, he distracted himself by looking for another wife to replace the one that he had lost not long before. He courted Melisende of Tripoli. The city was ruled by her brother, Raymond, who appeared to be delighted at the prospect of becoming the Emperor's brother-in-law. Large sums of money were spent to provide her with suitable finery to impress the Emperor. But the joy turned to anger when Manuel changed his mind and opted instead to marry Maria, daughter of Constance of Antioch. It seems that Melisende could not cope with the shock; she became ill and died shortly after.

She would soon be joined by King Baldwin III himself. Early in 1162 he was passing through Tripoli when he fell ill. He moved on to Beirut, where he died on 10 February. As he was a strong man, rumours that he was poisoned by his Muslim enemies were rife but were never proved. It was a blow to the kingdom, deprived of a young king (he was only in his thirties) in the prime of his life. Many of his acts had been wise beyond his experience and he had the potential to become a great ruler. Now the Franks would have to try to find an adequate replacement. On the whole they had been lucky with their kings so far. The question now was how long could that good fortune – or was it divine approbation – last?

CHAPTER 15

The Crescent Ascendant

The obvious candidate to take Baldwin's place was his brother, Amalric, Count of Jaffa. However, in an electoral monarchy such as that in Outremer it was by no means certain that he would be chosen. As it happened, the peers of the realm did demur. Their reluctance to accept Amalric as the new king revolved around his marriage to the Lady Agnes, to whom he was closely related. There had been controversy over the match at the time of their wedding, and the barons of Outremer now resurrected it. The upshot of their concerns was that they would not accept Amalric as their ruler unless he divorced Agnes. This proved to present few difficulties to him, provided that the rights of his children by the marriage were recognised. Once these problems were resolved, he was duly proclaimed king.

Amalric lacked some of the sparkle of his late brother. Although he had a good legalistic mind and was physically attractive, he did not possess the charm of Baldwin. All in all, he would find it hard to court popularity. However, he did have some strategic insight. He developed the policies of the kingdom towards both Byzantium and Egypt. With regard to the former, he realised that Outremer needed the help of the Emperor to protect it, and thus on his part, Amalric offered unstinting support to the Emperor, and over time would provide much assistance to him.

The linchpin of Amalric's strategy though was Egypt. It provided an important counterbalance to the might of Nur-ed-Din, and it was imperative that he be prevented from taking rule there. Were he to do so, the Kingdom of Jerusalem would be surrounded, exposed to a lethal pincer movement whereby its puny resources would be overwhelmed by the strength of the enlarged Damascene empire. But unfortunately the Fatimids were no longer in control of their internal affairs, and within Egypt, chaos reigned. When Ascalon fell, there was much pressure on the vizier of the country, Abbas. He was soon embroiled in a plot involving his son, Nasr, and the Caliph, al-Zafir. The Caliph and Nasr were involved in a homosexual relationship and the Caliph suggested to Nasr that he should murder his father. When Abbas got wind of the scheme, he reversed the roles and instead arranged for Nasr to assassinate the Caliph. This Nasr did by stabbing him to death when he was off his guard. In the recriminations, the Caliph's own brothers were accused of the murder and executed.

However, many in Cairo saw through this ruse, and the governor of upper Egypt marched on the city. Support for Abbas and his son melted like snow on a spring day. Faced with staying in Cairo to meet certain death or fleeing, father and son chose the latter. They escaped Egypt successfully but when they emerged from the Sinai desert they were attacked by Franks from the castle of Montreal. Abbas was killed in the fight that ensued, but Nasr survived and was taken by his Templar captors to their fortress. While he was there, he was educated as a Christian and he subsequently converted. However, news of his capture reached Egypt and the authorities there offered a large sum to the Templars if they would return him. Forced to choose between their Christian duty and monetary gain the Templars had few qualms in opting for the latter. Nasr was sent back to Egypt where he was tortured and mutilated by the family of al-Zafir and then hanged.

This was not the end of the chaos in Egypt, merely an aperitif. Several viziers came and went in a short period of time, until a man named Shawar took the post in 1162. Just a year later he was replaced by another vizier, Dhirgam. Surprisingly he did not eliminate Shawar. He lived to regret his leniency.

In that same year, Amalric thought that his time had come to exploit the weakness of Egypt. He used as his excuse the fact that Egypt had agreed to pay tribute to the late King Baldwin, but had never fulfilled its commitments in this respect. Leading a large army, Amalric reached Pelusium but unfortunately he had mistimed his expedition. The Nile was in flood and by opening their dikes the Egyptians could immerse the land. Powerless against the forces of nature the Franks were forced to withdraw. At least they returned to good news for a change. Nur-ed-Din had used Amalric's absence to attack the strong castle at Krak. Unusually, the Franks' response had been swift and united. An army composed of forces from Antioch, Tripoli and Byzantium had marched to the rescue and chased Nur-ed-Din off with a badly bloodied nose.

In Egypt, Shawar intrigued to regain his lost power. Nur-ed-Din was the obvious person to turn to for help. However, an approach to him would involve a major gamble. Once involved in Egyptian politics, Nur-ed-Din was unlikely to retire meekly again. After any coup he would want to retain his influence within Egypt and maybe even to rule it. However, Shawar did not, or perhaps could not afford to, concern himself on that score. Once he had recovered his position, he would worry about getting rid of Nur-ed-Din. In 1164 a deal was struck. Nur-ed-Din sent a large army led by his greatest warrior, Shirkuh, and his young nephew, Saleh ed-Din Yusuf. As Saladin, the nephew would become the most famous of Crusader adversaries.

Nur-ed-Din attacked the fortress of Banyas to distract the Franks. While they were concentrating on repelling that assault, Shirkuh led a large army across the arid Sinai desert. The plan was excellent, both in theory and practice. They slipped past the Franks unnoticed and overwhelmed the unsuspecting forces of Dhirgam at Pelusium. Dhirgam attempted to flee from Cairo but it was too late. He was caught by the fickle population before he could make good his escape. His head was struck off and his decapitated trunk was left to rot in the streets.

Once Shawar was installed as vizier again, he attempted to get rid of Shirkuh as quickly as possible. He stated quite blatantly that the service of his army was no longer required, but Shirkuh did not meekly acquiesce to this dismissal. He moved his army to the town of Bilbeis, just 40 miles from Cairo and in a position of menace. Shawar was not disconcerted however. He merely examined his options as to whom he could manipulate next. He decided to seek the help of Amalric and offered a large sum of money to the King if he would help. This was a great attraction to the Franks, who would not only enrich themselves by the agreement but who also had no wish to see Nur-ed-Din in charge of Egypt. It made strategic as well as economic sense to support Shawar.

Amalric duly sent an army that besieged Shirkuh in a desultory fashion for three months. Eventually, with the garrison hungry and the Franks tired, a truce was agreed. It suited the purposes of both the Franks and Shirkuh. The Franks had only undertaken to evict Shirkuh from Egypt and they had therefore kept their side of the bargain, while Shirkuh left with his army intact. There were good reasons for the Franks to hurry home anyway. Disaster had struck in their absence.

Nur-ed-Din had invaded their territory and laid siege to the castle of Harenc. An army led by Bohemond III of Antioch, Raymond of Tripoli, Thoros of Armenia and Constantine Coloman, a Byzantine commander, had marched out to meet the threat. When Nur-ed-Din knew that this large force was nearby, he raised the siege.

The Christian army set off in hot pursuit. On 10 August 1164 they closed on Nur-ed-Din at Artah. With a small force of 600 horsemen, Bohemond drew close to the Muslims. More experienced voices warned him to beware of

A fifteenth-century portrait of Saladin – already by this time a figure of romance. (Add. 30359 f. 86 Saladin (1138–93), Sultan of Egypt and Syria from the 'Six Ages of the World' represented by historical personalities from Adam and Pope Boniface VIII, Italian, 15th century; British Library, London/Bridgeman Art Library, London/New York)

trickery but, with the confidence of youth, he ignored their advice. He charged headlong at the enemy. The other Christian leaders followed him, not wishing to be thought cowards. Nur-ed-Din's forces broke in panic and were pursued into a valley by the Christian cavalry, oblivious to the dangers inherent in the situation. Without warning, the retreating Muslims stopped and turned about. Behind the Franks, previously quiet hills and scrub were filled with a multitude of war cries. The Franks were trapped in between two forces, hopelessly outnumbered and outmanoeuvred. It was not a battle, it was butchery. There was no escape for the Franks, who were struck down in their hundreds. Wounded men were despatched on the spot. Only the rich were allowed to live, to be exchanged for ransom. Bohemond, Raymond and Constantine were all taken to Aleppo as prisoners.

Antioch was open to the Muslims. It would be saved by the invisible hand of the Emperor. Nur-ed-Din had no wish to antagonise Manuel, who was titular owner of the city, and he even released Constantine for a small ransom. Conversely, Bohemond would only be released after a very large sum was paid and Raymond would not be set free for any price at this precise moment. So perturbed was Baldwin by the reverse that he did the only sensible thing he could and sought to strengthen ties with Manuel. He sent to Constantinople asking for a bride. His divorce was proving to be a cloud with a political silver lining. However, Manuel was in no hurry to respond and, for the time being, Baldwin was left kicking his heels.

In Egypt, Shawar's position was soon under threat again. Shirkuh did not miss the opportunity to plead with Nur-ed-Din to be allowed to return to the country. Eventually, at the beginning of 1167, another expedition was sanctioned on religious grounds, the Caliph in Baghdad declaring a holy war by the Sunni Muslims against the heretic Shiites in Egypt. Shawar received word of the threat and appealed to Amalric for help. Once again, the Franks could see the strategic desirability of this, but they dallied too long and Shirkuh managed to slip pass them through the Sinai desert once more. The greatest threat to his army came from the elements and his force was nearly lost in a sandstorm. However, they managed to weather the storm, and descended upon Egypt like a host of avenging demons.

Meanwhile, Amalric had shown considerable speed in sending an army after them. As soon as the Frankish forces were close to Cairo, Shawar sent delegates out to meet them and escort their representatives into the city. For their part, they were totally overwhelmed by the city, by the soaring splendour and sumptuousness of its palaces and by the magnificence of its mosques. They were only too glad to cement an alliance with the Egyptians. It was agreed that a large force should cross the Nile to confront Shirkuh, who was sheltering in the shadow of the Pyramids. The force sent outnumbered the Sunni army but was composed mainly of lightly armed Egyptian infantry. Shirkuh retreated south at first, eventually setting up camp in the ancient ruins of Hermopolis. Here, in the decaying splendour of a long-gone Egyptian civilisation, he decided on his plans. His tactics would be simple and entirely predictable to any student of Turkish warfare, but unfortunately the Franks and their Egyptian allies obviously were not pupils of this particular science. The Frankish-Egyptian army seemed to think that their numerical superiority would strike terror into the heart of Shirkuh and that his troops would rush in panic into the desert, never to be seen again.

On 18 March 1167 the allied army launched a ferocious attack on the Sunni force, and Shirkuh's army appeared to give way. However, a watchful observer would have noted that only the centre gave ground while the flanks stood firm. The allies were being sucked into an ever-larger indent in the Sunni lines. Suddenly, as they had done a thousand times before and would do a thousand times again, the centre stopped retreating while the flanks enveloped the rear of the allied force. The leaders were accompanied by a strong bodyguard and fought their way out, including Amalric who had been told to fight that day by a vision the night before from St Bernard. Hundreds of others were not so fortunate and were scythed down.

THE CRESCENT ASCENDANT 143

The defeat, although heavy, was not decisive. Cairo was still protected by a large garrison and was in no danger. Shirkuh himself realised this, and started to raid the western bank of the Nile, eventually arriving at Alexandria. The citizens had no love for Shawar and let Shirkuh in, welcoming the Sunnis as liberators. However, Shirkuh soon found himself trapped by a much larger force. He broke out, leaving a garrison under Saladin, hoping to entice the besiegers away by resuming his raiding. But Shawar knew full well how important Alexandria was and would not move. Finally, Saladin sent a messenger to Shirkuh telling him to return. Another truce was agreed in August 1167. During the discussions leading up to this, Saladin made a particularly favourable impression on the Franks with his courtesy and manners. The terms were not harsh, and both sides departed with honour substantially intact. It was probable that no one was deluded by this charade. A battle had ended but the war was far from over.

On his return to Jerusalem, Amalric considered the best way forward. He developed two main strands to his strategy. The first was to give more power to the Military Orders. Manpower was in short supply and there were further worrying signs that the Crusading concept was losing its appeal in the West. Shorn of the influxes of men that expeditions from Western Europe provided, albeit erratically, alternatives were needed. By this time, there were a large number of castles in Outremer. Many were already manned by the Military Orders. Amalric continued, and built on, this approach. By so doing he hoped to take maximum advantage of what was in effect the kingdom's standing army. There were of course drawbacks in this approach. The Orders were already powerful – they would soon become arrogant. With their master, the Pope, thousands of miles away, they had great local autonomy, which they would not always use wisely.

The second strand of Amalric's policy was to continue the process of improving relations with Constantinople. Manuel had at last found a bride for Amalric, Maria Comnena, grandniece of the Emperor. She was a charming creature, whom Amalric was pleased with. However, not long after their marriage relations were threatened by the arrival in Outremer of Manuel's cousin, Andronicus Comnenus. He had already been in Antioch, and had created a furore there by seducing Philippa, the sister of Bohemond. At the time, Bohemond had complained furiously to Manuel, who was equally angry and summoned Andronicus back to him to explain himself.

Andronicus ignored the summons and continued on to Outremer. Here he met another cousin, Theodora, widow of Baldwin III. They were too closely related to be involved romantically, but chose to disregard this social convention. They were apparently instantly attracted and were soon openly living together. Manuel got wind of this, and was incensed. He sent a cursory message to Amalric that Andronicus must be returned to Constantinople. Given the close ties between Emperor and King, Amalric almost certainly would have complied if he could, but he was not able to. The two lovers had fled the city to Damascus, where they had been well received.

The weaknesses of Egypt were now blindingly obvious to all. Within Outremer, many voices were demanding that the leaders of the kingdom mount an expedition to take the country for themselves. Amalric could see that this scheme had more chance of success if supported by the empire, and accordingly he commenced negotiations with Manuel. However, the discussions were protracted, and many of the barons in Outremer lost patience. The arrival of a sizeable new force under the Count of Nevers gave renewed impetus to the plans to attack Egypt, and large sections of the community demanded that the invasion was delayed no longer. Most of the nobles were behind these calls, as well as the Hospitallers. Faced by such powerful advocates, Amalric capitulated and the expedition set off without the forces of Manuel.

There was one notable group of absentees. The Templars argued that Amalric had made an agreement not to be aggressive towards Shawar, an agreement that should be honoured. In reality, their moral difficulties were probably secondary to the economic drawbacks of the scheme as far as they were concerned. The Templars had important trading links with Egypt, which would be lost if the invasion took place. Amalric therefore set out without them. The Count of Nevers died before the army left, but his men still enthusiastically supported the plans. Shawar was incredulous when he heard that the invasion was on its way. To him, the Franks appeared duplicitous, though given his own far from honourable manoeuvrings in the past he should not have been surprised. He was threatened from all sides, as his son had already been involved in clandestine discussions with Nur-ed-Din. Nevertheless, he resolved to fight against the threat posed by the Franks.

The first major town in the path of the Franks was Bilbeis, which was reached on 30 October 1168. This held out more strongly than anticipated but fell after three days. There was a sizeable Coptic Christian element in the town who were not naturally antagonistic towards the Franks and who did not like Shawar. Cultivated wisely, their support could help in the conquest of Egypt. However, such strategic considerations did not figure uppermost in the psyche of the force; in a frenzy of destruction large numbers of the inhabitants were killed, and the Franks thereby failed to grasp the opportunity to be treated as liberators. The story was similar when the town of Tanis fell.

In Cairo, Shawar was terrified. The Crusader army advanced to its suburbs and, rather than let these areas fall into Crusader hands, Shawar set fire to some of them, threatening to do the same with the rest of the city. Amalric let it be known that he would leave if the price was right, and negotiations to discuss what this price might be were started. Before these were far advanced, stunning news arrived from the north. A huge army led by Shirkuh was on its way to drive the Franks out. Shawar had swallowed his pride, and asked for their help. It was a bitter pill for the Franks. The army could not stay where it was, and hurried back to Outremer to defend the kingdom. Recrimination was rife among the leaders, some of whom felt that Amalric should have been more interested in finishing off the Egyptians than seeking to obtain financial benefit. However, there was one far greater disadvantage that would accrue to Outremer as a result of the failed mission. Shirkuh and his forces had no intention of leaving Egypt this time. Within weeks, Shawar had been killed by Saladin. Egypt was now in effect a puppet state, ruled from Damascus.

In Constantinople, Manuel was stirred from his apathy, realising that the balance of power in the region had now shifted disproportionately. He sent a large fleet to Cyprus and from there to Outremer to help the Franks to drive Shirkuh out. But the Franks were downcast by their retreat from Egypt, and months were wasted while they put their house in order. The Greek fleet only carried provisions for three months and these were already running out before the Franks had started on their way back to Egypt. Further dissension occurred between the Byzantines, who wished to complete the journey by sea, and the Franks, who wished to take the land route. It was nine months after leaving Egypt in his hasty retreat before Amalric set out again in October 1169. At least three months had been wasted in the complacent organisation of the project.

Nevertheless, there were still good hopes of success. Shirkuh had died on 23 March 1169, and Saladin was now ruling Egypt, but he was as yet untried and inexperienced. Furthermore, the Turkish and Kurdish supporters of Saladin were hated by the native Egyptians, and a revolt led by Nubians had only recently been ruthlessly suppressed. The Franks started well, completely deceiving Saladin, who had expected them to make for Bilbeis again. They attacked Damietta instead, a large and strategically vital port at the mouth of the Nile. However, it was strongly defended. A large chain was strung across the river preventing the Greek fleet from sailing upstream. The Greeks urged all-out assault but Amalric hesitated, awed by the defences. Reinforcements were poured in by the Muslims to strengthen the city, and the Christian army began to run short of provisions. The Franks and the Greeks blamed each other for their problems.

The final blow to this unenthusiastic enterprise came when fire ships were launched towards the Greek fleet, causing considerable damage. Soon after, a deluge drenched the camp, which became a quagmire. Cold, hungry, wet and disillusioned, it was now plain to the Christians that they had failed. A glorious opportunity had been thrown away, partly because of the total inability of Greek and Frank to co-operate. Only two results emerged from the debacle, neither positive. Firstly, another chapter was added to the growing litany of mistrust between the Eastern and Western Christian factions. This would soon reap a bitter harvest. Secondly, the position of Saladin was now undisputed. Rather than weakening his grip on power, the expedition had strengthened it. The payback from this would be even more bitter and even more immediate.

Both Manuel and Amalric were wise enough to see that they must try to avoid mutual recrimination. Common interest dictated that the alliance between them must continue. Amalric visited Constantinople, where he was received with sincere warmth. There was a lull in the pressure on Outremer when an earthquake rocked the region on 29 June 1170, and the local Muslim leaders were more occupied in rebuilding their shattered fortifications than attacking the kingdom.

Even more promisingly for the Franks, relations between Nur-ed-Din and Saladin were strained. Nur-ed-Din was alarmed at the growing power of Saladin, which he suspected, with good reason, would encourage him to challenge his supremacy. Matters reached a head in 1171 when Saladin set out to attack the Crusader stronghold of Montreal. By doing this without asking for Nur-ed-Din's approval he was far exceeding his authority. The siege was prosecuted fiercely and the fall of the castle appeared imminent, but a most unexpected benefactor would save Montreal. Saladin was disturbed by news of shocking significance; Nur-ed-Din was nearby and he was coming to see why Saladin was ignoring his authority. Urgently, Saladin sought council. His younger followers argued that now was the time to throw off his allegiance to Nur-ed-Din but older men urged caution. The final word went to Saladin's father. He would not betray his trust and neither should his son. Chastened, or perhaps realising that he was not yet powerful enough for a confrontation, Saladin made placatory overtures to Nur-ed-Din. The latter accepted the approaches, though we may be sure that the experienced campaigner would not be fooled by the gesture. In any event, for the time being, the defenders of Montreal were left in peace.

The following year, Raymond of Tripoli was released. This helped the King, as it meant that he had one less city to rule personally. However, he needed new friends. The new political realities of the region were evidenced by discussions that went on between Amalric and a group of potential allies at this time. The Assassins had approached Outremer for help. They hated Sunni Muslims far more than they hated Christians and the loss of Egypt was a terrible disgrace. They even offered to convert to Christianity as a sign of good faith, asking in return that they be relieved of the requirement to pay tribute to the Franks.

Amalric realised that the price was worth paying, but the Templars did not share his views. Consequently, a local Templar, Walter of Mesnil, ambushed the Assassin delegation, murdering them in cold blood. The Templars would suffer if the deal went ahead, as they were the ones currently receiving tribute, and this may well have been a critical factor in their actions.

Amalric was enraged. He demanded that the Grand Master, Odo of Saint-Amand, hand over Walter for punishment. Haughtily the demand was refused, Odo arguing that he alone would judge a Templar. Showing a disregard for constitutional issues that would have served other kings of Jerusalem well, Amalric seized Walter anyway and threw him in jail. The Assassins accepted this as a sign of good faith from the King, but the sordid affair evidenced deep problems within the structure of Outremer. The Templars had acted as if they were above the law – which indeed they were legally – and had put self-interest before the greater good of the state. It was another instance of the declining moral validity of Crusader ideals. Before long, far worse examples would follow.

Despite these difficulties, the start of 1174 showed the kingdom in relatively good shape. But the year was not to end that way. The first blow to the Franks, though they would not have seen it as such, came with the death of Nur-ed-Din on 15 May. He was en route to Egypt where he had planned to attempt the subjugation of Saladin. He may well have succeeded, as many leading Egyptians disliked Saladin. Indeed, Saladin had already considered fleeing to Ethiopia or Arabia. Before long, Saladin, now with a free hand, would assume control of the entire Muslim crescent around Palestine, a situation alive with threat for the Franks.

Amalric attempted to exploit the chaos that followed Nur-ed-Din's death. He entered into an agreement with al-Muqaddam, the immediate successor to the late Muslim leader in Damascus. As a result of this, all Frankish prisoners in Damascus were to be freed. Well pleased, Amalric started back to Jerusalem but fell ill on the way. It became obvious that he had dysentery and, although he made a brief recovery after being bled by a doctor, he soon suffered a relapse and died on 11 July 1174.

Amalric had been a worthy king, who in time could have aspired to greatness. His vision exceeded that of many other rulers of the kingdom. His contribution to Outremer should not be underestimated. In one thing only had he failed, and that was no fault of his. A few years earlier his son and heir, Baldwin, had been playing a children's game, watched by the historian William of Tyre. The children were seeing how hard they could pinch each other without registering pain. Without fail, Baldwin won. To his horror, the reason why dawned on the historian. Baldwin was winning not because of fortitude but because he had fallen prey to that most awful of maladies, leprosy.

Now this thirteen-year-old leper was to be king. His ravaged body was all that stood between Outremer and the ascendant star of Saladin. It would take the combined efforts of everyone to guide Outremer through the period of turbulence that lay ahead. Bravery, machismo and resilience were abundant in the kingdom, yet the man who looked for unity of vision and purpose, the qualities that were really required, would have sought in vain. And unless some of these qualities were found quickly, it did not take a prophet to foresee that a terrible day of reckoning was at hand.

William of Tyre at work, from the twelfth-century Estoire d'Outremer. *(Possible self-portrait of William of Tyre (c. 1130–85), writing at his desk,* Estoire d'Outremer *(12th century); Bibliothèque Nationale, Paris/Bridgeman Art Library, London/New York)*

CHAPTER 16

Towards Disaster

Saladin could not believe his luck. A tenacious opponent had died and had been replaced by a disease-ravaged juvenile. Coming so soon after the demise of Nur-ed-Din, it must indeed have seemed that Allah was smiling on him. Amalric's death gave Saladin confidence, and he resolved to march on Damascus, which he took easily. Further north, other cities such as Aleppo did not accept his suzerainty, but the state of the Muslim world around the eastern Mediterranean contrasted starkly with the disunited lands of Outremer. The reign of King Baldwin IV would be epitomised by petty infighting, leading the realm down a long and slippery path that would take it to the brink of oblivion. In fairness to Baldwin, he stoutly fought to overcome his disabilities, showing great courage and fortitude. Ultimately, his efforts would be in vain, undone by his own bodily weakness and the spiteful vindictiveness of his nobility.

Baldwin invited his mother, Agnes, back to court. As a minor he still needed maternal support. It would transpire, however, that if Baldwin were cursed with serious physical challenges then his problems were doubled by his mother. She was a haughty woman, who interfered with the affairs of state and sought to advance the interests of her favourites. There were many of these, and the court was soon rife with rumours of her promiscuity.

Agnes came back to court two years into Baldwin's reign. Even by this time, it was already riven with different factions. Problems were apparent as soon as Baldwin inherited the kingdom. Given the King's age, a regent was needed and one of Amalric's leading supporters, Miles de Plancy, coveted the position. But de Plancy died in a mysterious assault while he was in Acre. The obvious candidate to be regent in any case was Raymond of Tripoli. He was related to the royal bloodline and he was an experienced ruler in his own city. However, although he had a number of supporters, many others were bitterly opposed to him. For Raymond was a man who sought accommodation with the Muslims, and his vision was not shared by all. The attitudes of some significant sections of the community in Outremer were fundamentalist in nature, and notable among such hard-line attitudes was the stance of the Templars.

Around Aleppo, events were taking place that would result in an unexpected twist of fate for the kingdom. Saladin had been vainly trying to take the city, and its ruler at this time, a Turk named Gumeshtekin, asked for the help of Raymond and the Assassins. Raymond was delighted to assist and he distracted Saladin by attacking the town of Homs on 1 February 1175. So grateful was Gumeshtekin that he offered two important prisoners as a token of gratitude. The release of one, Joscelin III of Courtenay, was potentially embarrassing as he was a lord without a province. He was the son of the ill-fated Joscelin II of Courtenay. He still bore the title of Count of Edessa, although the lands around the city had long been lost to Christendom. He had been captured some years previously in a Muslim raid. The other, Reynald of Chatillon, had been a conceited and egotistical schemer when he was captured. Events were to prove that prison life had done nothing to change him.

Reynald was quickly intriguing again. He allied himself with the hawks within the kingdom, especially the Templars. Opposition to Raymond's regency became more open and more consistent. His cause was not helped by an incident involving an ambitious young man, Gerard of Ridfort. Raymond promised Gerard that he would give him the hand of the next available heiress in marriage. Unfortunately, when such an heiress became available, another suitor approached Raymond and offered him the weight of the lady in gold if he would give him her hand. As the lady in question tended towards the plump, this was a very attractive offer that the Regent did not spurn. Gerard was incensed with this rebuff and made a mental note of it, hoping to obtain retribution in the future. He joined the Templars and devoted his energies to rising through their ranks. He became a prominent member of the organisation, on the verge of great power within its hierarchy. Sadly for Outremer, his energy was not matched with wisdom and his influential position meant that he could cause immense damage to the kingdom.

Saladin was distracted from the affairs of Outremer for a while whilst he sought to consolidate his position in Syria. One group in particular attracted his attention. The Assassins despised him as the despoiler of Shiite Egypt and continually created problems for him. Saladin finally ran out of patience and laid siege to their headquarters, an impenetrable looking castle at Masyaf. The siege was suddenly raised for no apparent reason, but rumours abounded. The leader of the sect, a man named Sinan, who was better known as 'The Old Man of the Mountains', was attributed with powers that were almost supernatural. Even today, Ismaili Muslims speak of him with awe. The legend grew that one morning Saladin awoke to find a poisoned cake next to him of a type only baked by the Assassins. Saladin's tent was closely guarded; it was as if a phantom had ghosted past the sentries. The message of the cake was crystal clear. Even in his own tent Saladin was not safe; if the siege were not raised, then Saladin and his family could expect to be assassinated. Whatever the truth was, Saladin never troubled the Assassins again.

The distraction was welcome to the Franks. Baldwin needed to find an heir, as he himself would never sire one. Currently, his sister Sibylla was next in line to the throne but according to the conventions of the country she could not rule alone. A suitable husband was found for her, one William Longsword, who was related to both King Louis of France and the German Emperor, Frederick Barbarossa. Although he was older than his bride, he still cut a glamorous figure. The marriage was happy enough but short-lived as William died a year after they were married from a disease contracted in Outremer.

Masyaf castle, headquarters of the Assassins.

A depiction of Louis IX at Acre, receiving embassy from the Old Man of the Mountains, leader of the Assassins.

Baldwin was now of age and ruling in his own right. He quickly needed to find another husband for Sibylla, for the balance of power had shifted against the Franks. In the previous year, Byzantium had suffered a defeat every bit as decisive as that of Manzikert. With Nur-ed-Din dead, the Turks in Asia Minor had again asserted their independence. Law and order in the region disintegrated once more. The major troublemaker was another Turk named Kilij Arslan, whom Manuel decided must be brought to order. He announced his intentions by writing to the Pope, encouraging the formation of another Crusade, and then marched with a large army into the heartland of Asia Minor.

Kilij Arslan was alarmed when he heard of Manuel's actions and sought peace but the Emperor would have none of it. However, a salutary lesson was taught him when the vanguard of his army was badly cut up by the troops of Kilij Arslan. Manuel's cousin, Theodore Vatatses, was killed and his head paraded in triumph around the Turkish camp. Manuel pressed on regardless, eventually entering a narrow valley at Myriocephalum on 17 September 1176. Manuel's wiser advisers urged caution. The terrain was ideal for an ambush and the Byzantine force was ironically almost too well equipped, as the large number of siege engines with them hampered movement.

But others, more rash, urged Manuel to scorn this advice. Manuel, not a great warrior, allowed himself to be persuaded. There was an old fort at the far end of the valley, in front of which some of the Turks were carelessly parading. The vanguard of the Imperial army entered the valley, pushing on confidently down the narrow road. The Turks retreated and the Greeks hurried after them. They were being led into a trap, which was sprung suddenly and without warning. Hordes of Turks materialised as if from thin air and descended on the Greeks. For their part, the Byzantines could not reposition themselves quickly enough to repulse the attack. Cohesion quickly broke down, and Manuel's resolve failed him. Seized by panic, he fled from the valley with his bodyguard, leaving his men behind to die. The defeat was absolute. Although Manuel survived, his army was destroyed.

At sundown the Sultan halted the carnage. Surprisingly generous terms were offered. Manuel could return to Constantinople together with the remnant of his army. The only condition was that he must destroy two fortresses he had recently built in the area. Manuel was in no position to argue. Many of the Sultan's men were amazed at the generosity of the terms. Perhaps Kilij Arslan himself could not come to terms with the scale of victory. Certainly, his real interests lay further east. However, Manuel appears to have been a broken man. Never again would an emperor intervene directly in the affairs of Syria. The bastardisation of the Imperial army, evidenced by the increasing use of mercenaries by the Greeks, and the disintegration of the theme system, had now led to a decline in military power that was irreversible. This became apparent even to the Franks, who realised that in future they must fend for themselves.

Manuel tried to restore his tarnished image by encouraging the Franks to send another army into Egypt. The timing seemed right for this as a large force had arrived from the West led by Count Philip of Flanders, son of an old Crusader, Thierry of Flanders. A large fleet was sent by the Emperor to help but the project quickly became a fiasco. Baldwin was not healthy enough to lead the army and so a replacement had to be found. When Philip was offered the position of commander he prevaricated. After he had offered a number of excuses for not leading the army, he eventually admitted that he had only come out to Outremer to find suitable brides for members of his family. The Greeks sailed off in disgust, weary of the Franks' indecision. Against this backdrop, the plan to invade Egypt was stillborn. Philip left Jerusalem and wandered around the counties of Tripoli and Antioch where he was involved in a few minor forays before making his way homeward.

Emboldened by this display of confusion, Saladin decided that it was high time to attack Outremer. He set out at the head of a large force on 18 November 1177. The Templars tried to block him at Gaza but he merely bypassed them and pushed on toward Ascalon. The situation was a serious one. Baldwin had just risen from his sick bed but although he was frail of body, he had a great spirit. He gathered together all the men he could find, just 500 knights. Encouraged by a portion of the True Cross that they carried with them, they rushed to Ascalon and entered it before the Muslim host had arrived.

Saladin decided that he would leave Baldwin holed up in Ascalon and pushed on to Jerusalem. Although the latter city was well fortified there seemed to be insufficient manpower to resist an assault. The prospect of achieving everlasting honour and glory by taking the Holy City seems to have blinded Saladin and made him complacent. He paid little attention to the tiny army of Baldwin or the Templar forces at his rear. Unknown to him, Baldwin had requested the Templars to join him. They responded quickly and Baldwin led the small force rapidly towards his capital. The Muslims had relaxed their discipline, and were unprepared when, on 25 November, the Christian force approached. Saladin's army was crossing a ravine, near the castle of Montgisard, and he had apparently deployed an inadequate screen of scouts. Consequently, Saladin was completely off-guard when, from nowhere, the Franks came charging into the rear of his forces.

There was no line of battle formed within the Muslim force. Some of them ran away even before the first shock of the Franks' cavalry charge hit home. Those who stood firm were quickly fighting for their lives in a disorganised mêlée. They were soon overwhelmed. Saladin himself only escaped through the exertions of his bodyguard. So complete was the surprise that the issue was not in doubt. Those who survived fled the battlefield back to Egypt. Many of them threw their weapons aside in order to move more quickly. Even in the Sinai desert their troubles were not ended. Nomadic Bedouins picked off the stragglers by the score. Without doubt, this was the low point of Saladin's career to date. His reputation was in tatters, and he had been taught an extremely painful lesson. The Franks, though, were elated; the apparent ease and completeness of victory seemed to have been divinely inspired.

Saladin needed to spend time in Egypt to restore his credibility. However, there was no doubt that he would be back and that he would be a tougher opponent because of his defeat. The Muslims had been overwhelmed because Saladin was overconfident and he resolved not to act in this way again. In 1179 he raided Outremer once more. In the initial clashes, Baldwin narrowly escaped capture only because some of his nobles sacrificed their lives for him. Despite this, when Baldwin received word that a booty-laden Muslim force was due to pass near to him, he determined to intercept it. Saladin, however, was made aware of his plans and resolved to confront the Franks in battle.

The Franks espied the Muslim army at the head of a valley near to the River Jordan on 10 June, 1179. Although experience suggested caution, there was one group who would not contemplate a careful approach. The pride and vanity of the Templars would again lead to defeat. The Grand Master, Odo, would not countenance talk of careful tactics, which spoke to him of cowardice. With God at their head, the Christians would be invincible. Proudly, the Templars began a headlong charge at the Muslims. Within minutes, those who survived were streaming back. If the enemy managed to survive the initial shock of the cavalry charge, then the Crusader offensives quickly fell apart as the horsemen lost their co-ordination.

Baldwin's other troops, most of whom had stayed put when the Templars embarked on their suicide mission, were confused by the Templars rushing back towards them. The Muslims were close behind, and the Crusader line quickly started to disintegrate. Baldwin, along with Raymond of Tripoli, escaped to the safety of the castle at Beaufort but many others perished in the chaotic aftermath of the battle. Odo was captured, but in line with Templar philosophy he refused to allow any discussions for his ransom to take place. It was for him a fatal decision. He was thrown into a dismal prison where he expired within the year. Thus the leader of one of Christendom's greatest Military Orders died, his body weak through malnutrition, disease and perhaps pique, a demise attributable in no small part to the exaggerated view he held of his own power.

In an attempt to secure the succession, further discussions concerning Sibylla took place. The most likely candidate for a husband appeared to be Count Baldwin of Ibelin. He was well known and respected in Outremer, and Sibylla appeared to be genuinely in love with him. But then the Count was captured by Saladin. Baldwin could not raise his ransom but thought that if he were allowed to travel to Constantinople to speak to Manuel he could obtain the necessary funds. Manuel, a man who enjoyed grand gestures, was moved by his tale and gave him the money. Baldwin happily returned to Sibylla to claim his prize.

Unfortunately, this fairy-tale romance did not have a happy ending. Sibylla was cold towards the Count when he returned. She argued that she could not, as a lady of honour, marry a man who was so heavily in debt to the Emperor. However, this disguised the real truth. Some years previously, a noble named Aimery of Lusignan had arrived from the West determined to make a career for himself in Outremer. He was, it was rumoured, involved romantically with Agnes, the former wife of the late King Amalric. He mentioned to her that he had a younger brother, Guy. Agnes was so enamoured by the picture that he painted of this paragon of virtue that she decided he would make the perfect match for Sibylla.

So persuasive was Agnes in her discussions with Sibylla that her daughter fell in with the scheme. The deal was agreed and Guy, who was still in France, set sail for the East. He was indeed a handsome man and Sibylla resolved that she would have no husband but him. Politically, however, this was very difficult. Guy of

Lusignan was a man who as yet had insufficient standing to rule Outremer, but if Sibylla's young son were to die he would be next in line to inherit the kingdom. The romance of the situation did nothing to persuade the Council, who were singularly unimpressed by the prospect of being ruled by an individual who was little more than a youth. But the casting vote lay with King Baldwin who, although equally unconvinced, lacked the strength of character to resist Sibylla's appeals and consented to the match.

Even now the drama was not yet over. Rumours swept the court that Guy was occupying Sibylla's bedchamber on a regular basis, and as the couple were not yet married, King Baldwin was incensed at the slur on his family honour. However, the interests of the Lady Agnes, the Templars and Guy were now hopelessly enmeshed and the Templars would not allow Guy to be punished. Baldwin allowed himself to be placated by their submissions to him and the matter was dropped. The marriage was celebrated at Easter 1180.

Lady Agnes and the hawks around her were now in the ascendancy, a situation particularly evidenced by an unsavoury wrangle in 1180 over who should become the new Patriarch in Jerusalem. The hard-liners in the kingdom wanted a man called Heraclius to take the post. Although he was a supporter of Agnes, he was reputed to have very loose morals. In the ballot for the post, Heraclius only came second. The King promptly ignored this result and installed him anyway. The problems of having a weak king, in the shadow of his mother, were becoming apparent. Agnes mercilessly persecuted her enemies. One of them, William of Tyre, the chronicler of the Crusades, was forced into exile. He died in Rome, some said the victim of poison.

Sadly, such vicious accusations were all too believable. The barons were becoming a law unto themselves, particularly Reynald of Chatillon. He had married Stephanie, a rich widow who held Oultrejourdain. He consolidated his position here for a time, keeping an unusually low profile. The major fortress of the region was at Kerak. It stood on a large hill, dominating the road from Damascus to Egypt. Some castles of the Frankish East, because of their fine masonry and craftsmanship, are objects of beauty. Kerak was not one of them. It spoke only of strength and menace, a great glowering monster of a castle overshadowing the travellers who were forced to travel on the road beneath its walls.

In this evil place, Reynald bided his time. Baldwin and Saladin had signed a truce in 1180, as both parties needed time to refresh themselves. The truce encouraged goods to flow along the caravan routes that bypassed the castle at Kerak. Other caravans travelled from Damascus along the pilgrim routes to Arabia. The concept of pilgrimage, or *hajj*, was even more deeply engrained in the Muslim psyche than it was in the Christian one. Hosts of pilgrims made the pilgrimage to Mecca regularly. In 1181 a particularly large caravan was travelling to Mecca when Reynald suddenly fell upon it. The pilgrims were virtually defenceless and were easily overwhelmed. Reynald plundered the caravan, and even considered pushing on to attack Medina but thought better of it.

Saladin was indignant, and demanded compensation from Baldwin. The King himself was far from pleased and demanded restitution from Reynald. But when

The castle and town of Kerak, with the road to Egypt visible below.

Reynald refused, Baldwin meekly backed down. Even when Saladin took hostage a large party of Christians, who had unwittingly put into Damietta, Reynald would not budge. His intransigence resulted in a war that the tired land could ill afford. In the conflict that followed there were several bruising encounters but neither side gained a clear advantage. However, the unavoidable fact was that in any prolonged war of attrition the Franks, for whom manpower was always a desperate problem, must come off second best.

Fortunately for Outremer, Saladin was preoccupied elsewhere and it was at about this time that he finally took Aleppo on 18 June 1183. He even besieged the great city of Mosul, though without success. However, he did add Edessa to his territories. He was, naturally enough, a great threat to many other Muslims and some sought an alliance with the Franks against him. Common interest dictated the Franks should react favourably to these approaches and several raids were launched, one reaching Damascus itself. But, these actions were insignificant compared to the ongoing process of conquest in which Saladin was involved.

Given the trouble he had caused in 1181, one would have thought that Reynald would become more circumspect but not a bit of it. He now embarked on several schemes that were even more ambitious than those in which he had previously been involved. He built a small fleet of galleys and manned them with some of his own men and some local pirates. He then besieged the port of Aqaba and attacked any ship that he came across. Two acts caused particular outrage. He attacked and sank a ship of unarmed Muslim pilgrims, and then assaulted Mecca itself.

It must be conceded that Reynald cannot be accused of hypocrisy. The Crusading concept revolved around disdain for the Muslim religion, and many Christians would not consider the breaking of an oath made to a Muslim as a breach of trust. However, the moral justification is irrelevant when weighed against the potential harm that could be done by these acts. Reynald's methods inflamed and united the Muslim world. The states that surrounded Outremer, all Muslim, bitterly resented what he had done. The immediate response from Saladin was to send out a fleet to intercept any Christian ships that they could find. Large numbers of prisoners were taken, and then sent to Mecca to be publicly beheaded at the height of the celebrations surrounding the Muslim pilgrimage. Reynald himself escaped but he was making himself immensely unpopular.

He returned to a kingdom in crisis. The King was so ill that he could not move. He was unable to help when Saladin launched another invasion in 1183. Guy of Lusignan was given command of the army, a daunting challenge for a man so inexperienced. Saladin had left Cairo some time before and had made his way to Damascus. Unknown to him, he would never see Egypt again. Guy raised as large a force as he could with the local barons and the Military Orders both providing troops. The two armies came face to face in Galilee.

For some time they stared at each other, neither side wanting to make the first move. Many of the hawks in the Christian army urged an all-out attack but other more cautious voices, notably that of Raymond of Tripoli, advised against this and their approach was eventually adopted. Guy's cautious tactics were deplored by the hawks, a fact that would have serious consequences a few years hence. When he saw that the Franks would not fight, Saladin moved back to Syria. However, the Franks did not take advantage of the breathing space. While he had been seriously ill, Baldwin had handed Jerusalem over to Guy and had gone to live in the coastal town of Tyre, which had been held by Guy. Now that the King felt slightly healthier, he asked for Jerusalem back. Guy haughtily refused. Ill or not, Baldwin would not countenance this sort of opposition. Angrily he summoned the Council and demanded that Guy be deposed. Baldwin named as his successor in Jerusalem another Baldwin, the son of Sibylla by her first marriage. For the time being, he resolved to fight against his illness and resume government himself.

Guy took himself off in a huff to Ascalon, and threw off all pretence of allegiance to the King. He had powerful allies; both the Templars and the Hospitallers appealed to the King to reinstate Guy, but he would not consider it. The squabbling did little to help the kingdom as a delegation led by Heraclius was waiting to go to the West to try and whip up enthusiasm for another Crusade.

However, there was a prestigious social event imminent that might help to restore the morale of Outremer. Reynald's stepson, Humphrey of Toron, and

The castle of Kerak and the desert beyond.

Isabella, sister of King Baldwin, were to be wed and a great feast had been arranged at Kerak. Many important guests made their way to the edge of the wilderness and the gaunt fortress. The King was not among them, which would prove to be very fortunate. The marriage was duly celebrated and sumptuous banquets were enjoyed by the guests. Reynald took a brief tour around the local environs outside the castle to see that nothing untoward was going on, when he was suddenly almost engulfed by hundreds of villagers driving their livestock towards the castle. It quickly became apparent that matters were badly awry. The news broke that Saladin was even now within striking distance of the fortress with a large army at his back. Reynald was shocked, as he had received no warning. He only just managed to return to the castle before the Saracens were in view. The castle was only saved by the brave self-sacrifice of a warrior who stood guard over a bridge until it could be demolished behind him.

A messenger was despatched in haste to Baldwin in Jerusalem. Meanwhile, the wedding feast continued, with some of the food being sent out to Saladin. In a courteous response, he asked to know in which tower the newlyweds were sleeping so that his artillery would not attack it. Fortunately for the Franks, the castle was immensely strong. It was cut off from the town it dominated by a dry moat some 90 feet deep. A steep glacis protected the foot of the walls, which were squared off with strong rectangular towers. Adequately provisioned, the castle could hold out for years.

Reynald was fortunate. When Saladin heard that a relief force was headed for the castle, he called off the siege. The duplicitous Franks had escaped punishment again but Saladin had a long memory and Reynald was firmly ensconced in it. Sadly, after this traumatic start, the marriage itself was not happy and Isabella suffered cruelly at the hands of a domineering mother-in-law. She may have found some consolation in the fact that she was reasonably well looked after by her mild-mannered husband.

Early in 1185 it became obvious that Baldwin's uphill struggle against his terrible malady was nearing its close. His will was announced to the court. On no account was Guy to be Regent; that honour should go to Raymond of Tripoli. His nephew, Baldwin, was to become King when he was old enough. His guardianship was offered to Raymond but he refused it; should the boy die – and he was not strong – then suspicion would almost certainly be directed at his guardian, and Raymond was not ignorant of this fact. Joscelin of Courtenay was given the honour instead. The very public will was timely, for a few weeks later this brave King was called to rest at last.

Baldwin's reign had been a disaster for Outremer, although this was not due to his personal efforts. He gave all that he had in the cause of his kingdom, but his physical shortcomings meant that this was not enough. Baldwin did not have the strength to combat the powerful personalities within his kingdom who sought to advance their own interests. Never had the country been more disunited. Outremer had always had a strong ruler to keep its competing factions under some kind of control, but now that control had gone. Against this, the Sunni Muslims were on the whole united behind one man, a man with vision, persistence, intelligence and, most of all, resources. Never had the kingdom's enemies been so strong. In reality, barring a miracle, Outremer was doomed to die.

CHAPTER 17

Death and Resurrection

Baldwin's will was accepted and Baldwin V was crowned with all the dignity that could be mustered for a young child. Raymond took over as Regent with surprisingly little initial opposition. Besides the threat from Saladin, a drought had hit the country and crop yields were low. Most people accepted that a truce was needed. Fortunately, Saladin was equally keen on the idea as he was experiencing difficulties from various rebel tendencies within his ever-growing dominions.

The real danger to the Franks came from the continuing decline of Byzantium. Manuel died on 24 September 1180, to be succeeded by an eleven-year-old boy, Alexius. His mother became Regent but she alienated the people, and the old adventurer Andronicus Comnenus was invited to depose her. This he did. However, he proved to be ruthless and cruel. Ordinary people and the nobility alike were subjected to persecution. Fear stalked the land, and Andronicus inspired a level of detestation rarely witnessed before in the history of the Empire. His hold on power became tenuous in the extreme.

The end came for Andronicus when a Sicilian army invaded the Empire. Andronicus lost his grip on power and a mob seized him, paraded him through the city on a camel, tortured him and finally killed him. His cousin, Isaac Angelus, was declared his successor. He would prove to be ineffectual and irrelevant, a pale shadow of the emperors of old. This declining Empire, living on the memories of past glories, would no longer be able to intervene effectively in the affairs of Outremer, and the Franks would suffer for it.

For the moment, the Franks were oblivious to the effects that these events would have on their future. Baldwin V had always been sickly and it was no surprise when he died at Acre in August 1186. The terms of the previous king's will were unambiguous. If the young king were to die, it was stated that Raymond should act as Regent until such a time that the four leading men of the West – the Kings of England and France, the German Emperor and the Pope – could arbitrate on whom should be the successor, the candidates for that post being the Princess Sibylla and the Princess Isabella.

Raymond was with Baldwin when he died, accompanied by Joscelin of Courtenay. Joscelin suggested that Raymond should return to his base at Tiberias and summon the barons of the kingdom to review the situation. The idea seemed a sound one to Raymond, and he fell in with the plan. But when he had gone, Joscelin sprang into action. He accompanied the child king's body to Jerusalem where it was quickly interred. Then he occupied Tyre and Beirut and declared Sibylla queen.

Raymond was furious, and decided that he would still summon the barons to Tiberias. While those who had responded were there, they received an invitation from Sibylla to her coronation. She had won powerful allies. Reynald, quick to scent profit, was for her, as was Heraclius. The Templars also offered their support. They were now led by the same Gerard of Ridfort whom Raymond had insulted a few years earlier, and Raymond well knew that he could expect little help from this quarter. The Grand Master of the Hospital, however, would not declare for the queen and reminded the others that they had taken oaths to support Raymond. Such scruples did not concern them and preparations for the coronation went ahead.

The insignia of the monarch was stored in a locked chest; one key was held by the Patriarch and the other two by the Masters of the Military Orders. In disgust, the Grand Master of the Hospital threw his out of the window. It was retrieved and the chest unlocked. Sibylla's husband, Guy of Lusignan, was so unpopular that in the resultant coronation Heraclius would not crown him, and Sibylla had to perform the act personally. As they left the Church of the Holy Sepulchre, Gerard of Ridfort could contain himself no longer. Aloud, he declaimed so that all within earshot could hear that his insult had been avenged. His words were the clearest statement yet that petty personal ambition was still the dominant motivating factor in the kingdom.

The barons who had opposed the coronation now had to decide on their next move. They concluded that they would put Humphrey of Toron forward as the ruler of Outremer, as he was the husband of Princess Isabella. Unfortunately for their schemes, Humphrey was a weak man who wished for an easy life. He slipped away from their camp to that of Sibylla and Guy, where he paid homage to the newly crowned couple. This removed any leverage that Raymond may have had. Even his strongest supporters saw that the choice was now between a grudging acceptance of the status quo and civil war. The barons therefore journeyed to Jerusalem where they too paid homage, although one of the leading nobles, Balian of Ibelin, was perfunctory in this respect to say the least, and Raymond could not bring himself to do this at all.

A great deal of ill feeling had been generated by this unsavoury affair. Raymond had been seriously alienated by what had happened. What the kingdom most needed at this stage was a time of reflection and peace so that angry emotions could subside. It was crucial that the time bought by the truce that was in place with Saladin was used to consolidate. Only a fool would jeopardise this opportunity. Reynald of Chatillon was just such a man.

Reynald's downfall would be the temptation offered by the rich caravans that regularly passed close to his lands, and which had already proved too strong on previous occasions. A particularly lucrative opportunity presented itself when a caravan on its way to Cairo came within reach of him. Once again, he could not resist the bait and his men seized it. It was the richest prize yet won by Reynald, and not one that he would be prepared simply to hand back. Despite the fury that he must have felt, Saladin responded in a measured and placatory fashion, merely asking that Reynald return what he had taken. Reynald's reply was predictably negative. Saladin therefore put his complaint before King Guy, who agreed that he had been wronged and asked Reynald to comply with Saladin's reasonable requests for restitution. However, Guy was in the debt of his errant baron and, when Reynald refused, the King had little choice but to support him.

Other Frankish leaders quickly attempted to distance themselves from Reynald. In Antioch, Bohemond III renewed his truce with Saladin, and Raymond of Tripoli sought to reach an accommodation with him. The hawks in Jerusalem were incensed at what they regarded as the treasonable approaches of Raymond, who had sought to have his wife's lands in Galilee exempted from any punitive action taken by Saladin. They assembled an army to bring the Count of Tripoli forcibly back into line. Before they could leave their camp, however, Balian of Ibelin rode in. Angrily, he asked the King what he thought he was doing. After forcefully expressing his views, he managed to gain Guy's permission to attempt to effect a reconciliation. Balian led the group that set out with this purpose, which also included the Masters of the Hospital and the Temple. It was particularly important that Raymond and Gerard of Ridfort could resolve their differences.

Not long after the party had left, Raymond received a delegation from a force of Muslims who sought permission to cross his lands. This put Raymond in a quandary. He did not wish to jeopardise his truce, but he saw that the force was well armed and might well engage in conflict. If this happened, then Raymond would be berated by many of the Franks as a traitor. He compromised; the Muslims could cross his territory but they must do so in daylight, and they must return on the same day that they came. These terms were accepted. Raymond sought to exonerate himself from any claims of treachery by sending out messengers to warn any whom they might meet that the force was in the area.

Unknown to either party, these Muslims were on a collision course with the Templars who had accompanied Balian. They had become separated from Balian, who had had to break off to conduct some business transactions. He set out to rejoin them on the morning of 1 May 1187. However, when he reached the castle of le Feve, where he had expected to find his men, he came across only two sick knights. Balian's concern grew as the day advanced. Searching for the knights, he was on the road to Nazareth when he spotted a solitary figure in the distance. As the figure drew nearer, Balian felt sick of heart. It was a Templar knight, alone and, judging by his appearance, he had been in a fight. The absence of any companion by his side suggested that the outcome had not been favourable.

The story that the knight related was a chastening tale of pride and stupidity. When the knights had reached Nazareth, they had met one of Raymond's messengers. News of the Muslim force in the area fired the imagination of the Grand Master, Gerard of Ridfort, who determined to strike a blow for Christendom. He summoned all the Templar knights he could find in the immediate vicinity. His appeal was responded to by the local Marshal, James de Mailly. Confidently, the small force thus assembled left Nazareth, telling the local inhabitants to follow them and help themselves to booty from the corpses of the Muslims they had killed.

They came across the Muslims watering in a valley near Nazareth, at a stream known as the Springs of Cresson. There was an enormous numerical imbalance between the forces. The Muslims had 7,000 men, the Christians 140 knights and 300 infantry. This disparity merely served to inspire Gerard with prospects of a miraculous victory. Others demurred, but Gerard accused them of cowardice. James de Mailly haughtily replied that he was no coward but, before the day was out, Gerard would show himself to be one – a claim that would prove to be all too true. Gerard's jibes succeeded in cajoling the others to follow him.

So keen was the Templar Grand Master to reach the enemy that he compounded his folly by letting the cavalry charge far ahead of the infantry. The Muslims were initially surprised but easily regrouped. Their huge numbers were decisive and the small Christian force was overwhelmed. Three knights escaped, the rest were killed or captured. As James de Mailly had predicted, Gerard fled the scene when he saw what the outcome was likely to be. Perhaps this was the greatest tragedy of all. This vain and arrogant man was free, able to exercise his faulty judgement again should the opportunity arise. The next time he offered foolish council, the effect would be deadly.

Although not final, the results of this latest episode were extremely serious. The knights lost could not be replaced, and the Franks had been given an object lesson in humility. Perhaps there was just one positive consequence for them. When the Muslim force retreated past Raymond's castle on their way back, they carried the heads of Templars on their spears. Understandably, the sight shocked Raymond. He realised that he could no longer sit on the fence, and came down firmly on the side of the Franks. Guy had the good sense to receive him warmly. The reconciliation had not come a moment too soon. Saladin had assembled a huge force, the largest he had ever commanded. An outpouring of anger, directed especially towards Reynald of Chatillon, had caused a tidal wave to sweep the Muslim world; this one man's greed, his arrogance and his contempt for Islam had achieved, for a short interlude, the unification of Outremer's enemies. The whole expedition took on the appearance of a *jihad*. It was essential that the Crusaders face such a great threat with a united front.

Saladin crossed the Jordan and attacked Tiberias. The town fell easily but the castle, defended by Raymond's wife, Eschiva, stood firm. Saladin settled down for a siege. There were several responses available for the Franks. The most obvious was to rush to Tiberias to raise the siege, but according to some of the chroniclers several important men, including Raymond, counselled against this. The leaders in Acre met to consider what to do. Guy summoned all the magnates of his realm to him. The Orders, smarting after the humiliation at Cresson, were especially keen to comply. The net result was that Guy assembled the largest force ever gathered by a king of Outremer.

The story of what follows is as confused as any in the annals of Outremer. The lack of objective analysis already noted among the chroniclers is acute. The account given here is a view based on the narrative of Ernoul. He was associated with Balian of Ibelin and as such was not ill disposed towards Raymond of Tripoli; any account of his is therefore not necessarily an objective one. Further, it is believed that his version of events was subsequently added to. But Ernoul was probably present at the battle and consequently has the virtue of being an eyewitness. His account forms a coherent view of what might have happened, although many of the important details are contradicted in other sources.

The arguments of Raymond, and several others, made good sense. If the Franks stayed on the defensive then Saladin would be forced to advance across dry country during the hottest period of the year, or withdraw. Either way, the realm would be protected. Saladin's army was mostly made up of men who would want to return home after a short campaign. If Saladin's assaults were driven off, then the Franks could use their large army to pursue him. However, there were strong objections raised against this cautious form of action. Predictably, the loudest voices were those of Gerard of Ridfort and Reynald of Chatillon.

The hawks won the argument. The army moved up-country as far as Sephoria, where it was still well situated. There were plentiful supplies of water here, and the Franks were close enough to the Muslims to create anxiety. While the force was camped at Sephoria, a messenger arrived from Tiberias. The Countess begged the King to send help. Her sons, at Raymond's side, understandably were convinced that the army should go to their mother's aid. However, Raymond still argued against any further advance, and in a far stronger way than he had done before. The countryside between Sephoria and Tiberias was parched at this time of year. Water supplies were inadequate for a force this size and the army would be dangerously exposed to attacks from the Muslims. He, of all people, had a personal involvement in the situation but that made his arguments all the more convincing. Guy was persuaded by him and resolved to stay put.

This was not the end of the drama. When all the other leading men had left, Gerard of Ridfort sought an audience alone with Guy. His purpose was to change the King's mind. Guy had been severely criticised for his failure to attack Saladin during the campaign of 1183. It may be that he felt he had to prove his credentials as a king by going on to the offensive. Further, he was never very good at resisting strong personalities. Accordingly, Guy acquiesced. The army would march on to Tiberias. When Raymond heard the news he must have been horrified but to his credit he stayed with the army and joined it in its advance.

The troops had not travelled far when the Muslim attacks began. Men were picked off as they straggled, and hordes of horsemen constantly wheeled in and out of the Franks' lines, causing considerable damage. These assaults were nothing, though, compared to those of a far stronger enemy – the hostile and omnipotent Palestinian sun. There was no shade from it, and no water to quench the thirst that it induced. Men started to fall by the wayside, easy prey for the Muslim cavalry.

After many miles of this hell, the Franks trudged wearily up a road that led to two peaks known as the Horns of Hattin. These stood guard over the town of Tiberias, which was visible below. Tantalisingly, next to the town shimmered the waters of the Sea of Galilee. Between the water and the Franks stood the huge Muslim host, barring their way through to the life-giving liquid. Their only chance was to push on immediately. Exposed to a long night without water, the energy and the confidence of the Christians would be completely sapped before battle was joined. Gerard de Ridfort informed Guy that his men would go no further. They had been badly shaken by the persistent assaults of the Muslims throughout the day and were too tired to press on. Raymond, for one, did not doubt the import of this decision. He cried aloud to Guy: 'The war is over; we are all dead men, the Kingdom is finished'.

Throughout the night the Franks were taunted by the Muslim forces that now encircled them. To compound their misery, the Muslims set fire to the scrub surrounding the camp of the Franks, sending smoke and flames through the terrified ranks of the soldiery. The thoughts of the Franks can only be surmised, and it must have been a terrible night.

As the sun rose over the Sea of Galilee on 4 July 1187, it presaged the birth of a new order in Outremer. The Franks, surrounded as they were, had no option but to fight. The Muslims launched fierce attacks against them, forcing home their assault with vigour and energy, the vitality of their offensives fuelled by the certainty of victory. It was all too much for the Christian infantry, many of whom were now crazed with thirst and attempted to fight their way through to the lake. They were engulfed by the Muslim host. Hundreds were slain and the rest captured. Those taken prisoner lay lethargically in the sun, their thirst still unquenched.

King Guy demanded that Raymond lead a cavalry charge to break out and escape. This was successful, although later Muslim chroniclers, perhaps with the benefit of hindsight, insisted that they were allowed to escape. At least there would be some men left to continue the battle for Outremer. They made their way to Tyre, to await further instructions. Raymond was accused by some of cowardice for deserting the army and leaving it to its fate. Certainly his knights showed little desire to return to the fight once they broke out; they must have

King Guy of Jerusalem fails in his attempt to defeat Saladin. (MS 26, f. 140r)

been completely demoralised by this stage. It is true also that Raymond had little reason to love King Guy or his supporters. When weighed up, the evidence suggests that he showed timidity, although his actions stop short of the outright betrayal of which he stands accused by some of his most bitter enemies.

On the field of battle, the Christian infantrymen were soon either captured or dead, and the light horsemen were also disposed of. Only a small band of knights fought on around the royal standard. They were forced halfway up the hill, their horses dead or dropping with exhaustion. They slowly retreated to its summit, where they defiantly erected the royal tent. They fought magnificently. Several times it was thought that they had been overrun but they retaliated in a desperate defence, without hope or prospect of escape.

Suddenly, above the ebb and flow of battle, a cry went up. The royal standard had fallen and with it fell Outremer. The Christian knights collapsed where they were, beaten by exhaustion and fatigue. To the amazement of their captors, many of them were not wounded, their armour impervious to the blows of the enemy. But the time for fighting was over. Now it was time for retribution.

The leading Christians who had been captured were taken to Saladin's tent. Among them were King Guy, Reynald of Chatillon, Gerard of Ridfort and Humphrey of Toron. Saladin offered a goblet of water to the tired and shattered King. This was an act of enormous significance; Saladin was treating Guy as a guest and he could therefore expect to live. Guy in turn passed the goblet to Reynald. Ominously, Saladin pointed out that this act was performed by the King and not by Saladin – Reynald was therefore a marked man.

Saladin berated Reynald for his perfidy. He was particularly outraged by his attacks on pilgrim caravans. On one occasion Saladin's sister had been captured. Gossip suggested that Reynald had ravaged her. Reynald was an arrogant man and did not know when to keep quiet. Haughtily, he refused to show any sign of repentance for his actions. Incensed, Saladin left the tent. According to some chroniclers, he returned soon after, reached for a sword and removed Reynald's head from its shoulders. Whether Saladin actually killed him personally we cannot be sure, but whoever was responsible, Reynald was dead.

The other leaders were led away to captivity. The ordinary soldiers were taken to the slave markets of Damascus; there were so many of them that they were virtually worthless. Saladin on the whole acted mercifully, but there was one exception. All Templar and Hospitaller knights bar one were massacred. The honour of carrying out the slaughter was given to a party of Muslim Sufis, apprenticed youths who aspired to become holy warriors. Saladin, in a letter that he wrote soon after the battle, summed it up well when he said that 'the wolf and the vulture kept company, while death and captivity followed in turns'.

Other Christian chroniclers give a very different view of Hattin and the events leading up to it. According to them, Raymond deliberately led the Franks into a trap. Ambroise, the writer of a contemporary account, accuses Raymond of enticing the Franks into an ambush by prior agreement with Saladin. The Genoese made the same charge to the Pope. However, many chroniclers agree that Raymond originally argued against the Franks setting out. This course of action was the one best designed to protect the Christian army and, if true, provides strong circumstantial evidence that Raymond was not guilty of treason. The evidence, though, is not overwhelmingly convincing or clear. Bitter recrimination followed in the wake of the disaster.

The one Templar to survive the battle, and Saladin's brutality, was the one who perhaps most deserved to die – Gerard of Ridfort. Saladin had further use for him. He was now intent on the annihilation of Outremer. As his army advanced into the kingdom, it squeezed the lifeblood from it. The simple truth was that the Franks had gambled everything at Hattin, and they had lost. Every available man had been called up, denuding the castles and towns of the garrisons that would be needed if the Muslims invaded, which they now did. Outremer was under sentence of death.

Tiberias was the first to fall, its gallant Countess well treated by the chivalrous Saladin. Acre was surrendered shamefully, with only the merest hint of resistance, by Joscelin of Courtenay, a pale imitation of his braver and more illustrious predecessor. Jaffa fell to an army from Egypt after a fierce fight. Next to fall was Ascalon. King Guy was paraded in front of the city and told to order the garrison to surrender. They derided him, and refused. However, when the defenders saw that no help was likely to come they too surrendered on good terms. The saddest loss of all was Gaza, the garrison of which was led by a Templar knight. Gerard of Ridfort was told by his captors to tell the city to give in. In an appalling abuse of his position, and completely contrary to the Templar code of honour, he complied. The Templar defenders had little choice but to obey the commands of their Master, which they had sworn to do when they were made members of the Order. It was no wonder that the kingdom was in such a parlous state when it was run by men like this.

The greatest prize of all was, of course, Jerusalem. Balian of Ibelin was inside the city. He was only there because he had been given a safe conduct by the Muslims. The citizens begged him to lead the defence. Balian would be breaking the terms of the safe conduct if he did so but eventually gave in to their entreaties. So embarrassed was he by his breach of faith that he wrote to Saladin, explaining his actions. Saladin recognised him as a man of honour and did not bear a grudge against him for his actions. The resistance anyway was doomed to fail. Initial attacks were repulsed but miners created a breach in the walls. The fall of the city was inevitable and the Patriarch Heraclius advised Balian to seek terms.

Balian concurred and negotiations began. Saladin again was merciful and offered freedom to the citizens of Jerusalem if they would pay a fine of 100,000 dinars. This amount was far beyond the resources of the city and a compromise was reached whereby for 30,000 dinars, 7,000 citizens would be set free. Saladin entered the city on Friday 2 October 1187, the anniversary of the day in the Muslim calendar when Mohammed had been transported to heaven from Jerusalem. Many of the inhabitants, especially the Orthodox Christian community, saw the Muslims as liberators.

The city struggled to raise the requisite ransom. The Treasury was emptied to help but the Hospitallers and the Templars were grudging in their aid. Worst of all was the action of the Church. The Patriarch gave none of the Church's wealth as part of the settlement, save to buy his own freedom. He paid the 10 dinars for his own release and then, laden with gold, passed a stream of weeping and terrified Christians being taken into captivity because they could not buy their release. The sight of the pathetic captives moved even the Muslims. Al-Adil, Saladin's brother, asked for the gift of 1,000 prisoners. As soon as they were given to him, he released them. Saladin also gave gifts of a similar nature to Heraclius and to Balian. Even the widows and orphans of the city were given money to help to support them. It was an object lesson in Christian kindness from a Muslim leader.

Some of the Muslims were so incensed when they saw the vast amount of wealth that some of the richer members of the clergy were taking with them that they wished to seize most of it for themselves. However, Saladin would not hear of it, saying, 'We must apply the letter of the accords we have signed so that no one will be able to accuse the believers of having violated their treaties', an ironic comment, perhaps, on the actions of men such as Reynald of Chatillon.

Most of the kingdom then fell to Saladin. Castle after castle was lost and before long Antioch and Tripoli were the only cities of any substance that remained in Christian hands, and they were far to the north. But also there was the city of Tyre, up to this point a smaller city that offered no threat. Saladin's failure to conquer Tyre would be the biggest political and military mistake of his career. Most of the leading barons who had survived Hattin now made their way there, despite the fact that negotiations for its surrender were well advanced. It was at this point that a ship came in carrying a newcomer, Conrad of Montferrat, brother-in-law of Queen Sibylla. He was fleeing from Constantinople, where he had been implicated in a murder. The timing of his arrival was opportune. He had a good reputation, and was brave though ruthless. He provided a focal point around which the Christians could rally. The surrender negotiations came to an abrupt end, and Conrad took over the defence of the city.

So staunch was his resolve that when his father, who had been captured at Hattin, was brought before the walls and told to instruct Conrad that he must surrender or he would be executed, Conrad still refused to give in. Moved by this defiance, Saladin did not carry out his threat. He instead moved on to take Ascalon. When he returned, his army was tired and wished to go home. Saladin was confident that Tyre provided no threat, and could be taken at any time. He also did not believe that any expedition from the West would be sent to rescue the tiny rump of the Kingdom of Jerusalem that remained.

This was a huge miscalculation and indicated that Saladin had not yet fully understood the tenacity of the Franks and the place that the Holy Land held in the consciousness of the West. To say that all was well with Outremer would, of course, be a complete distortion of the truth. Yet its death, once certain, had been delayed. He did not know it but, because of his lack of what might be termed a killer instinct, Saladin had just lengthened the life expectancy of the kingdom by another century.

CHAPTER 18

Playing for Time

The beleaguered Franks of Outremer now needed one commodity above all others, and that was time. Time to regroup, and time for help to arrive from the West. And help would come. Saladin had misread the psychology of the Occidental world. The Holy Land held for many in the West a mystical status.

When news of the fall of Jerusalem reached the West, it was reacted to with unprecedented grief and shock. A wave of emotion washed across Western Europe generating an impulse for another Crusade to recover the city that was virtually unstoppable. One of the first to hear the dreadful tidings was Pope Urban III. He was unwell and, according to some chroniclers of the day, the shock killed him. Pope Gregory VIII, destined to have a short but eventful primacy, succeeded him. In a frenzy of activity, he inundated the rulers of the West with pleas for help. He reminded them that the fall of Edessa forty years previously had been a warning that they had chosen to ignore, and by implication they were therefore partly accountable for the fall of the Holy City. He stated that 'We ought not to believe, however, that these things have happened through the injustice of a violent judge, but rather through the iniquity of a delinquent people.' Redemption could only be achieved by recovering Jerusalem for Christendom. A complete range of papal rewards would be made available to all those making the journey.

Gregory resolved that the clergy should set the example. Strict fasting was introduced as an act of penance. He decreed that the rulers of the West should restrain from fighting each other for seven years. This was no mere gesture. The King of England, Henry II, and his French counterpart, Philip Augustus, hated each other with an absolute and sincere passion. The two had been engaged in an undeclared war for a considerable length of time, the conflict made more heated by the frequent treachery of Henry's sons, particularly Richard, the second eldest.

Because of this conflict, when the Patriarch Heraclius had come to the West several years previously no substantial practical help had been offered to Outremer. But the visit had had some small effect. Henry had been sufficiently moved by Heraclius' oratory to offer significant sums of money to help the Franks in the East. A large payment had in fact reached Jerusalem before it fell, and this had helped to purchase the release of many of those captured. In military terms, however, little immediate help could be expected from a king who was old by the standards of the time, whose family was rent by internal division and who detested the King of France, who would almost certainly be the co-leader of any Crusade.

The dramatic aftermath to Hattin transformed the situation. The threat of disaster, which the West European states had complacently ignored in the past, had become an awful reality. Although Gregory died after just two busy months as Pope, his successor, Clement III, shared his determination. He lobbied for the support of the German Emperor, Frederick Barbarossa. This in itself illustrated the seriousness of the situation, as the Papacy and the Holy Roman Empire had traditionally been bitter rivals. Such rivalries now had to be forgotten, as the requirements of the situation dictated that the vast resources of the Empire could not be ignored.

In January 1188 Joscius, the Archbishop of Tyre, arrived in France. By this time, Henry II's son, Prince Richard, had already taken the Cross. Such an action was totally in keeping with the character of this man of large gestures. Delighting in war as an art form, and very sympathetic to the Templars, Richard was obsessively devoted to matters military. The chance of building his reputation by recovering the Holy Places of Christendom was a bait that he found irresistible. However, both King Henry and King Philip were slow to follow his example.

The arrival of the Archbishop was decisive. Moved by his impassioned pleas, the monarchs resolved to put aside their differences and to raise armies to fight for the Holy Sepulchre. There would be three: an English army identified by white crosses on their surcoats; a French force with red crosses; and a Flemish contingent with green crosses. Henry also levied a tax, known as the Saladin tithe, on his subjects. This would be charged at a rate of 10 per cent of all revenues. But money, although useful, was not the primary consideration. Men were the urgent need, and some other forces were already on their way to help the gallant defenders of Tyre. Notable among them was a fleet sent by King William II of Sicily. The arrival of these reinforcements was enough for Saladin to call off his siege of the mighty Hospitaller fortress at Krak des Chevaliers.

Saladin still held King Guy captive but released him in July 1188. It is unlikely that this was just a chivalrous gesture by the Muslim ruler. By releasing the King, he made him a factor in the politics of the region once again, and thus increased the likelihood of the Franks continuing to argue among themselves. If this were Saladin's wish, it would be amply fulfilled.

Guy made his way to Tyre, demanding to be recognised as king. Conrad would have none of it; Guy had lost the kingdom through his incompetence and had only been elected ruler in the first place by ignoring the very specific terms of Baldwin IV's will. Anyway, Conrad was enjoying the power that his defence of Tyre had won, and had no intention of meekly stepping aside now that Guy had returned. In frustration, Guy erected his camp right outside the walls of Tyre. Fortune smiled on him. A fleet from Pisa arrived at this moment and was rudely received by Conrad. In contrast, Guy greeted them with all the charm he could muster. The Pisans were so impressed that they offered their support to Guy, and were soon joined by the fleet from Sicily.

It was at this juncture that Guy, that weak and easily manipulated king, decided to embark on one of the bravest and most unlikely ventures of all Crusading history. The supporters of Conrad watched incredulously as Guy's small army broke camp and made its way south. Offshore, the ships from Pisa and Sicily

Krak des Chevaliers, from the south-west.

guarded its flank. The road that the army followed led, as the defenders of Tyre well knew, to Acre, which was now defended by a garrison much larger than Guy's force. It was strongly fortified and surrounded on two sides by water. The other two sides sheltered behind huge, impenetrable walls. No one knew why Guy was heading this way, but they were all sure that it was not to attack Acre for to do so would be tantamount to suicide.

Saladin was engaged further north, attacking the castle of Beaufort. Its owner, Reynald of Sidon, was a fascinating character. When he knew that his castle was to be attacked he made his way to Saladin. He was a charming individual, who spoke fluent Arabic. He explained to Saladin that he secretly favoured his cause and, in fact, he was even planning on converting to Islam. He would happily surrender his castle to Saladin but his family was not with him and they would be persecuted if he meekly handed over the fortress. All he needed was time.

And so time passed, until Saladin felt that he must force the issue. Reynald, who was in Saladin's custody, was taken to the castle and told to order the garrison to surrender. In Arabic, he did so. Just in case they did not understand, he repeated the message in fluent French. The garrison refused to surrender. Saladin was no fool, and quickly worked out why. When Reynald had shouted his instructions in French, he had ordered the garrison to resist. While he had been negotiating with Saladin, the garrison had been strengthening the defences of Beaufort. All Saladin could do now was blockade it. Reynald was taken to Damascus but even here managed to charm Saladin, who did not punish him too severely for his subterfuge.

It was at Beaufort that Saladin first heard of Guy's escapade. Although he wished to crush the threat immediately, his advisors talked him out of it. They argued that Guy, if he were foolish enough to head for Acre, could easily be trapped between the garrison and Saladin's army at a later stage. Saladin, who was unwell, agreed. This would prove to be another error on his part, and it would help the Frankish fight-back to begin.

The garrison of Acre must have been stupefied when on 28 August they saw Guy erect his tents a mile away from the city. They thought it was a ruse but were disabused of this idea when three days later the Franks attacked the city. There was no serious possibility that the assault would succeed, but the offensive actions of Guy encouraged newcomers to the East to unite with him. Within a few weeks, small groups of Danish, Frisian, Flemish, French and German troops had joined him. These were not official armies but were led by zealous individuals and, collectively, they began to pose a greater threat than had originally been perceived.

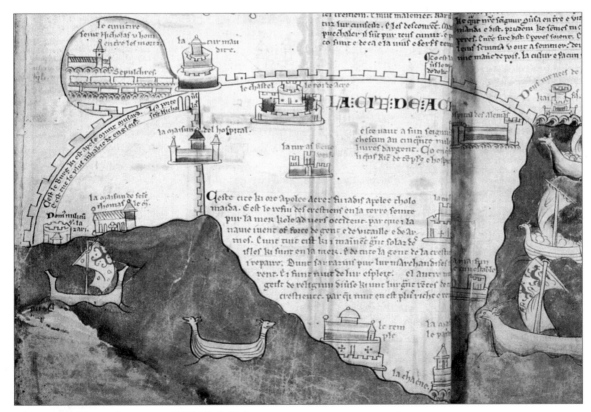

Acre in the thirteenth century. (MS 26, f. iiiv)

Saladin was concerned enough to send an army to Acre. Although he made contact with the defenders, his attacks on the Franks were repulsed. In Tyre, Conrad was also alarmed. Guy had seized the initiative from him by his aggressive stance and supporters were flocking to his cause as a result. Conrad was forced to concede that, to save face, he must join the Franks at Acre, although he quickly qualified this by stating that this did not mean that he accepted Guy as king.

On 4 October the Christians at Acre launched a fierce assault on the Saracens. It was a vicious, hard-fought slogging match, with the Franks initially successful. Saladin's right wing feinted in an attempt to lure the Christians out of position. It was so well executed that Saladin himself was fooled. Believing that his army was breaking, he denuded his forces in the centre to reinforce the right, a move that created chaos. The Franks attempted to press home their advantage and at one point almost took Saladin's tent. However, the Muslim left held firm and pushed the enemy back. In the ensuing confusion, the Franks were forced to retreat.

There was one exception to this. Gerard of Ridfort, who had been released by Saladin, seemed to be of the opinion that he could defeat the Muslims single-handed. He stood alone in front of the retreating Franks, daring the Saracens to come at him. For a moment, the enemy stood transfixed, bemused by the foolhardiness of the Templar. Then in a huge unstoppable torrent they rolled over him. Easily captured, he was taken to Saladin who decided that it would be better for everyone if the world was rid of this arrogant man. Gerard was duly executed, an act which was probably of much more help to the Franks than it was to the Saracens.

Saladin was the victor of this battle but not decisively. The Franks remained strongly entrenched, and their confidence must have been improved by their performance. Saladin's forces, not strong enough to remove them, surrounded their camp. The besiegers became the besieged, attacked by some of the strongest weapons available; hunger, disease and adverse weather. They also lost command of the sea, preventing any re-provisioning from this direction.

Fortunately for the Christians, more substantial help was on its way. Frederick Barbarossa had been the first to set out from the West in May 1189 with a massive army. He was an old man but still an imposing figure. Tough, ruthless, stubborn and autocratic, he was the epitome of a Medieval king. His men revered him, as much through fear as affection. He threw himself body and soul into the raising of support around Europe for the Crusade. He then sent three important letters. The first was to the Emperor in Constantinople asking for supplies. The second was to Kilij Arslan, leader of the Turks in Asia Minor, telling him not to prevent the Germans from crossing his land. This was received in an amiable way, though it was highly doubtful that the Turks would avoid trouble if they could profit from it. The third letter was to Saladin, demanding the return of all the lost territories of Outremer. Saladin was disarming in his reply but obviously did not agree to such a request.

The Germans passed through Hungary with little incident. However, following the pattern of previous expeditions, once inside Byzantine territory trouble loomed. The Emperor at that time was Isaac Angelus, a man of cunning but little tact. He was insecure and very conscious of his weaknesses, which were many. One of his first acts as emperor had been to obtain an alliance with Saladin. He had even sent a message of congratulation to him when he captured Jerusalem. This was not by any means an act of perfidy, as the Orthodox Church in the city had been poorly treated by the Latins and would be better off under Saladin's enlightened regime. However, it would hardly endear the Emperor to the Germans.

The situation was not improved by the fact that Frederick had been present during the catastrophic Second Crusade. Many of the survivors of the disastrous journey across Asia Minor unfairly blamed the Byzantines for the choice of route. Further misunderstandings arose when the German army was attacked by Slavs in the Balkan regions through which it now passed. Although the Slavs were unruly tribesmen at the best of times, Frederick still blamed the Byzantines for this. When he subsequently negotiated a safe passage for his army with the Slavs, Isaac, for his part, considered him to be fraternising with rebels.

Frederick Barbarossa.

The crisis point came when Frederick reached the town of Phillipopolis. From here, he sent two ambassadors ahead to Constantinople to ensure that everything his army needed was ready. Isaac foolishly imprisoned the two men as hostages. It was an enormous mistake. Frederick was no weak Hugh of Vermandois, or outnumbered Godfrey of Bouillon. He was the greatest monarch in Western Europe, with a huge army at his back. His response was swift and decisive. His son, Frederick of Swabia, seized the town of Didymotichum and messengers were sent back to Germany to raise a fleet to sail to the Eastern Mediterranean with the intention of teaching the Greeks a lesson.

Now terrified, Isaac meekly capitulated. He was forced to hand over hostages of his own. There was no doubt about who would be the senior partner in this particular relationship. The only concession that Frederick would make was agreeing to cross over to Asia Minor at a point further away from Constantinople than the Bosphorus. He would not hurry, however. Winter was fast approaching and he did not want to spend it dangerously exposed to bands of hostile Turks on the far shore. Instead, he chose to see the year out in relative comfort, ensuring that Isaac spent an uncomfortable few months looking over his shoulder.

When the army eventually shipped over to Asia Minor, Frederick maintained iron discipline over it. The terrain was as inhospitable as ever and provisions hard to find but, generally, excessive deprivation was avoided. Predictably enough, Kilij Arslan did not desist from creating difficulties for the Germans. However, the size of the German army forced him to employ marauding tactics, picking off isolated stragglers. There was a sharp battle at Konya but the Germans drove the Turks off. Here, they refreshed themselves in the fertile gardens that surrounded the town.

From there, the army advanced towards Seleucia. On 10 June 1190 Frederick moved ahead with his bodyguard to the plains that surround the city, making for the River Calycadnus. Shortly after, disturbing rumours began to reach the troops at the rear of his army – something had happened to their Emperor. Gradually, the fog of uncertainty lifted to reveal an appalling tragedy. Frederick Barbarossa had been found lying on the bed of the river, weighed down by his armour. It was unclear what had happened. Possibly his horse had shied for some reason and thrown him into the water, or maybe the shock of immersing himself in the cold flow had been too much for an elderly frame. Whatever the reason, when Frederick's body was recovered, no breath of life remained in it.

The army was shattered, deprived of its figurehead. The Emperor was the fulcrum of their hopes, and there was nobody on hand to fill the massive void that his death had created. Frederick of Swabia lacked the strength of personality to restore the sense of impetus to the force. In addition, many of the German leaders wished to return to their homeland. A new reign could mean a time of instability there, and many decided that it was inopportune to be absent. Large numbers of

The River Calycadnus, where Barbarossa drowned.

the troops made their way home, the will and commitment squeezed out of them by this massive blow. Those who remained escorted the body on its way to Antioch. Frederick's corpse was pickled in vinegar so that it could be buried in Jerusalem when the city was recovered.

What remained of the army was given a hospitable reception in Antioch. Ironically, this proved to be the final straw. Dazzled by the opulence of the city and bewitched by its wealth and good living, the Germans would go no further. Bohemond was delighted to integrate any who wished to stay in his army. Saladin was equally pleased. In his view, Allah was intervening again. The final humiliation for the Germans occurred when the late Emperor's corpse began to disintegrate, as the improvised embalming fluid proved ineffective. The remains were hurriedly deposited in the vaults of the cathedral at Antioch, with the exception of a few bones that, it was hoped, would one day repose in Jerusalem. Frederick of Swabia resolved to complete the journey to Palestine but it was a pitiful remnant of a once mighty army that accompanied him. He eventually arrived at Acre in October 1190.

However, there was by now another substantial force on its way. The catalyst for its creation was the death of Henry II, who died, romantic chroniclers asserted, of a broken heart after his favourite son, John, turned against him. Henry had been too old and too calculating to join the Crusade and this precluded King Philip of France from going either. His death removed this obstacle. Henry's son, Richard, who succeeded to the throne as his elder brother was now dead, was a completely different proposition. He was determined to earn power and glory by reconquering Outremer.

Richard was crowned King on 3 September 1189. His coronation was marred by a riot, and was followed with the now traditional persecution of the Jewish community in England as part of the hysteria released by the preparations for the Crusade. Richard took full advantage of the opportunities offered, charging the Jews protection money for looking after them while at the same time fining those who persecuted them. Richard is an intriguing character who has caused much debate among historians. He was a product of Henry's II's marriage to Eleanor of Aquitaine, that same lady who had once been married to Louis of France and who had accompanied the Second Crusade. What is certain is that his main interest in England was for its usefulness as a source of income. He never spoke a word of English, being born in, and by nature attached to, France. Yet this has not prevented him from being seen as one of England's greatest heroic figures.

With Richard now committed, Philip was forced to follow suit. He would lose face with his subjects if he did not respond to Richard's gesture. The combined forces of the two men would provide a formidable army but it would be an uncomfortable alliance. To say the least, both men had been inconsistent in their attitudes to each other over the years, at one point being extremely close friends and at another ruthlessly plotting each other's downfall. It also seemed that Richard, with his pretensions of grandeur, was a far more enthusiastic Crusader than Philip, who appeared to be at best a perfunctory pilgrim.

The two men met at Vezelay on 4 July 1190 to discuss plans for the journey. It was agreed that they would travel by sea, this now proving by far the safer option.

The size of the combined forces meant that they could not travel together, and as it transpired, Philip would arrive in the East before Richard, who would have an eventful journey. From the beginning, some of the Franks in Outremer were unnerved by the imminent arrival of Richard. Conrad cannot have failed to notice that the Lusignans were vassals of the English king, and that as a result Richard was unlikely to be an impartial mediator in the dispute between him and Guy.

Conrad therefore needed to strengthen his hand. He was given the chance to do this when Sibylla and her children by Guy died of disease. Constitutionally, it could be argued that Guy was only king because of his relationship to Sibylla, and therefore the throne was definitely no longer his. Conrad sought to improve his chances further by marrying the late Queen's younger sister, Isabella. Only two problems prevented this. The first was that Isabella was already married; the second difficulty was that so was Conrad. Such minor obstacles were unlikely to inhibit a man such as him.

He approached the first difficulty by pushing for an annulment of Isabella's marriage to Humphrey of Toron. Many of the barons despised Humphrey for his weakness, and because he was, on occasion, effeminate. He lacked the backbone to resist Conrad's scheming. On the other hand, Isabella proved more truculent. For all his frailty, Humphrey was a kind and considerate husband, and his generosity of

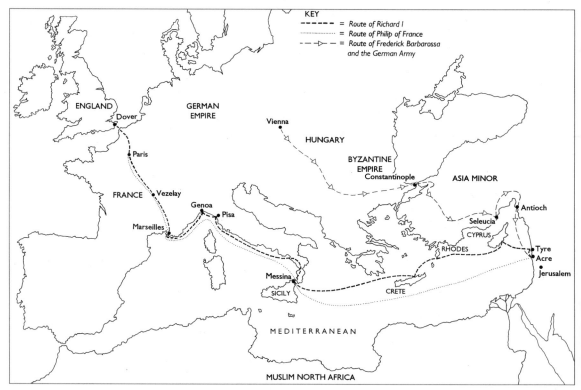

Major expeditions of the Third Crusade.

spirit was no mean virtue in the age in which he lived. He was also of a similar age to Isabella, whereas Conrad was much older. The proposition did not attract Isabella.

But the first part of the plan was finally accomplished, not without the help of Isabella's mother, who pressurised her daughter to agree to the annulment. As far as his own marriage was concerned, Conrad had an even more straightforward solution. He chose to ignore the marriage as if it had never happened. In this, however, he had reckoned without the intervention of one man – Baldwin, the current Archbishop of Canterbury, who had hurried to Outremer in advance of Richard. The Patriarch Heraclius was ill and asked Baldwin to arbitrate on the matter for him. Knowing well that Richard supported the Lusignans, Baldwin refused to recognise the annulment of Isabella's marriage. He then told Conrad bluntly that any formal liaison with her would be bigamous. He would therefore have nothing to do with the scheme.

Conrad therefore turned to the Papal Legate, the Archbishop of Pisa; by offering trade concessions to the Pisans he hoped, in return, to receive the Archbishop's support. The Archbishop weighed up his obligations to his city against those of his conscience, but this was no real contest. He ensured that the appropriate annulments were granted so that the match could go ahead. Baldwin was livid, and hurled excommunication against anyone who had opposed him. However, suddenly and conveniently, he died, leaving the field clear for Conrad to progress his plans.

Guy did all in his power to reverse the decline in his fortunes, even challenging Conrad to a duel. Conrad refused. The disputes did nothing to help the recovery of Outremer. Another winter arrived, accompanied by famine. Sickness ravaged the Crusader camp, claiming as one of its victims Frederick of Swabia. A recently arrived Austrian noble, Leopold, attempted to take over as leader of the Germans. In contrast to the sufferings of the Crusaders, the garrison was as strong as ever. Saladin still watched the camp like a hawk, looking for the merest chink in its defences to exploit. It seemed that all he had to do to win was simply to stay where he was. Plague and pestilence were doing the work of thousands of Muslim warriors.

It appeared that the fight-back had fizzled out, a gallant venture that had lost its momentum. Unless there was a dramatic and quick reversal in fortunes, the kingdom would finally slip over the abyss into complete oblivion. What was needed was another hero to inspire the troops to renewed efforts. Conrad and Guy both had successful moments, but they were fleeting and generally out of character. The reputation of King Richard was as yet unestablished, and hopes had been dashed before. The history of the Crusades was littered with tales of failed expectation, of men like King Louis of France and Frederick Barbarossa who had promised much but ultimately failed to deliver.

The little that men did know of Richard was nevertheless encouraging. He was committed and brave, well versed in the arts of war and accompanied by a strong army. Combined with Philip's force perhaps a miracle would happen and Saladin would be ejected. Demoralised, debilitated and disillusioned, the weary troops around Acre prayed for Richard's coming. His arrival could not happen a moment too soon.

CHAPTER 19

A Ray of Hope

The voyage of King Richard to Outremer could hardly be described as uneventful. At times it appeared that the warrior-king was going out of his way to ensure that his troops were not rusty when they finally arrived in the East. His journey began quietly enough. Richard and Philip's armies made their way to Lyons, and then the French and English troops went their separate ways as planned. They were to reunite in Sicily. The English were to take ship at Marseilles and cross the Mediterranean but Richard would not stay with them. He was a notoriously bad sailor, and he opted to hug the coast of Italy before landing in the south of the country and crossing the straits of Messina.

Richard was not a man who was liberal with his affections, as is evidenced by his treatment of his father. However, he was very close to his mother and also to

Richard the Lionheart embarks on the Third Crusade.

11. *Trumpeters lead a Muslim celebration, possibly with the Sultans' Guard. (Ar 5847, f. 19 Celebration of the end of Ramadan, from 'The Maqamat' ('The Meetings'), illustrated by Hariri, second quarter 13th century, Persian literary texts; Bibliothèque Nationale, Paris/ Bridgeman Art Library, London/New York)*

12. *Frederick Barbarossa,
King of Germany (1152–90)
and Holy Roman Emperor
(1155–90), and his sons.
(Ms D 11 Barbarossa and his
sons, German,* Weingarten
Chronicles *(1179–91, Landes
Bibliothek, Fulda / Bridgeman
Art Library, London / New
York)*

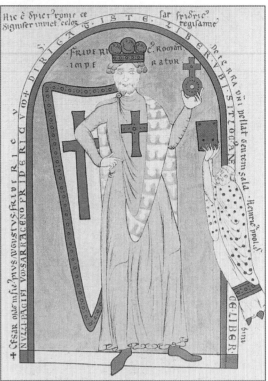

13. *Barbarossa played a key role in the
Crusades, encouraging the rulers of
Europe to give their support. (MS Vat
Lat 2001, f. 1r)*

14. *The Damascus Gate at Jerusalem, one of the ancient gateways to the city. (From a print by David Roberts, dated 14 April 1839)*

15. *The facade of the eighth-century al-Aqsa Mosque, Jerusalem, one of the many buildings within the city that witnessed bloodshed and slaughter during the Crusades.*

16. *Jerusalem: the south-east corner of the city wall, and the al–Aqsa Mosque.*

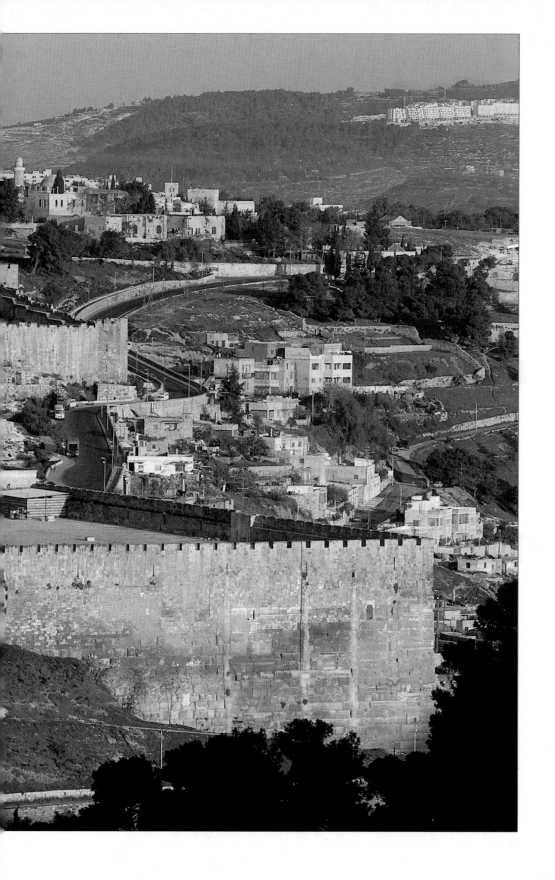

17. A German manuscript showing, in the centre, Frederick Barbarossa with his sons Heinrich and Philipp, and, below, Frederick en route for the Holy Land, c. 1189. (Codex 120 II, f. 143r)

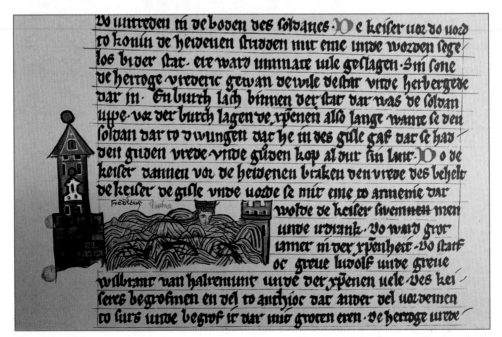

18. This manuscript illustration depicts the tragic death of Frederick Barbarossa. Little more than a year after his departure, he drowned in the River Calycadnus on his way to Seleucia.

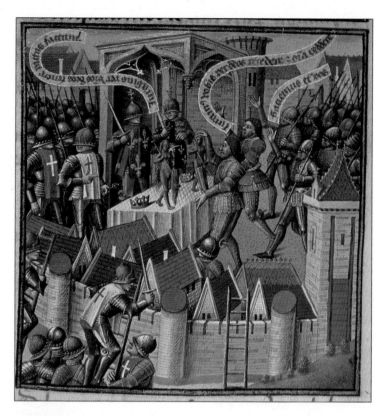

19. The capture of Acre, 1191, when Richard I triumphed over Saladin. (The capture of Acre, the crusades, 1191, by Vincent de Beauvais; Bibliothèque de Chantilly, France/Bridgeman Art Library, London/New York)

20. Richard of England is captured on the way home from the Crusades – an ignoble end to his Crusading dream. (Codex 120 II, f. 129r)

21. The Church of the Holy Sepulchre, Jerusalem.

his sister, Joanna. She had been married to the same King William II of Sicily who had already sent a fleet out to help the Franks of Outremer. When William died, the current incumbent of the throne of Sicily, Tancred of Lecce, did not deal with his widow especially well. We do not know exactly how Tancred reacted when he heard that the violent elder brother of the shabbily treated Joanna was en route to his island, but it may be safely assumed that it was not the most cheering news he had ever received.

Tancred of Lecce had not been meant to take the throne of Sicily. The legitimate successor was Constance, daughter-in-law of Frederick Barbarossa. However, many Sicilians did not take kindly to the thought of being governed by a German. This concern was shared by the Papacy, who would have to contend with a very powerful German Empire surrounding its lands if the move went ahead, and the Pope himself was implicated in his rise to power. Through the machinations of these interest groups, the crown was offered to Tancred. But Tancred had not ruled well or sensibly. He kept Joanna in confinement and deprived her of most of her wealth. He also deprived Richard of the legacy that the late King had bequeathed to the Angevin dynasty in England. Richard loved wealth, and he doted on his sister, so his feelings toward Tancred are not difficult to gauge. As he travelled through Italy, and as more details of Tancred's actions came to his attention, his fiery temperament was increasingly aroused by the wrongs done to him and his family.

As he approached the last leg of his journey, nearing the point where he would have to make the short sea crossing from the mainland to Sicily, Richard spotted a magnificent bird of prey outside a peasant's house. The King enjoyed hawking and immediately helped himself to the bird, as he would have done in his own kingdom. Unfortunately, the local villagers, not being his subjects, did not know him and beat him senseless. Richard would have been extremely angry by the time that he reached Sicily.

Tancred was rightly concerned. Richard had sent word ahead, demanding that Joanna's wealth be returned. He arrived at the town of Messina and was announced by a blaze of colour and the blare of trumpets, in contrast to the austere King Philip, who had arrived shortly before, virtually unnoticed. Richard was installed outside of the town and Joanna was released and sent to Richard. If this was supposed to improve relations, it failed dismally. Tancred's hand of friendship was met with an iron glove. Richard seized a town on the coast opposite Sicily and housed Joanna there and then raided a Greek monastery nearby. A tempest was brewing that threatened to overwhelm the shaky regime of Tancred.

On 3 October 1190 riots broke out involving some of the English army. Representatives were sent by Tancred to defuse the situation but just as it seemed that some kind of mutual understanding was being reached, Richard was infuriated by the taunts of a number of the local citizens. Richard appears to have been capable of two forms of anger, the one violent and impulsive, the other pre-meditated and calculated; on this occasion, it seems to have been of the latter variety.

For some reason, the gates of Messina had been left ajar. In a movement that was so quickly executed that it can hardly have been unplanned, the English troops poured through. Before any effective resistance could be organised, the city was overrun. Richard was now effectively the ruler of Messina, and to ensure that there were no doubts on this score he erected a huge tower, provocatively called *Mategrifon*, 'the curb on the Greeks'.

Philip was as alarmed as Tancred was by these developments, and sent him offers of help should he need it. However, Tancred was cunning. He knew that the French King was a friend of the Hohenstaufen dynasty in Germany and could manipulate the situation to his advantage. In contrast, Richard had no such loyalties and if Tancred could rebuild his relationship with the English monarch, he could be a useful ally. He negotiated using an approach that was most likely to impress Richard – he offered him financial inducements. Richard met his approaches favourably, his enraged principles placated by the promise of profit. A treaty was duly agreed between the two men.

This was a bitter blow to Philip, but it was nothing compared to subsequent developments. Despite persistent rumours of homosexual liaisons that involved, among other people, King Philip, Richard was expected to marry. For some years, he had been betrothed to Alice, sister of Philip but the marriage had not taken place. Moreover, the gossipmongers of the day insisted that Richard's father, King Henry, had taken more than a platonic interest in the lady. Now, Philip felt that it was high time that the marriage was celebrated. Richard refused, citing the promiscuity of Alice as the cause of his reluctance. However, his stance was disingenuous. Queen Eleanor, Richard's mother, had secretly been looking for an alternative bride and she had found one, Berengaria, a princess of Navarre. Although she held no physical attraction for Richard, he could appreciate the strategic benefits that the match would bring and consequently gave his approval.

When Philip became aware of these dealings, he was understandably enraged. He sailed out of Messina as soon as he could, only to be driven back to port by adverse weather conditions. Reluctantly, Philip decided that living in close proximity to Richard for a few months was preferable to taking his chances with the fickle winter weather of the Mediterranean. He said nothing more but brooded inwardly on the insult that had been offered to his family.

At the end of March 1191, Philip set sail again. The day after he left Messina, a ship arrived carrying the lovely, bemused and ultimately unhappy Berengaria. Shortly after this, Richard decided that he too should leave for Outremer. As he sailed eastwards, the weather worsened and the fleet was scattered. Richard eventually landed on the coast of Rhodes, undoubtedly in a black humour after a severe bout of seasickness. But the ship carrying his bride and his sister Joanna was nowhere to be seen.

In fact, the ship carrying the two women had been driven towards the coast of Cyprus. Berengaria's ship managed to anchor offshore, unlike the two accompanying vessels, which were wrecked. They sent ashore to ask for supplies and received back the polite request that they should land so that they could be better protected. Joanna refused, taught from her bitter experience with Tancred not to trust anyone. She judged the ruler of Cyprus perfectly. He was a usurper named Isaac Comnenus. As soon as his suggestions were rebuffed, he dropped his pretence and cut off all supplies to the ship as well as erecting fortifications opposite it.

A few days later, Richard's fleet appeared off the coast of Cyprus. The weather continued to be unfavourable and Richard suffered from yet more seasickness. When he heard how his sister and bride had been received, he flew into a rage, this time of the impulsive kind. He landed his men near the port of Limassol. Isaac was not popular; he had taxed his people exorbitantly and had given them no reason to love him. His day of reckoning had arrived as the population greeted Richard as a liberator.

Thrown off balance by these developments, Isaac Comnenus sued for peace. Negotiations went well and agreement was reached, but when Isaac saw how few men Richard had with him he broke off the discussions. Sadly for him, his timing could not have been more disastrous. Shortly after his decision, a fleet appeared off the island. It was led by King Guy. Philip had already arrived in Outremer, and was reacquainting himself with his old friend Conrad of Montferrat. Guy wished to ingratiate himself with Richard and was delighted to offer his men to him. For his part, Richard saw that a great opportunity had presented itself. Without these troops, he was confident that he could teach Isaac a lesson; with them, he believed that he could conquer the island.

Richard and Guy set about their task with alacrity. Castle after castle fell to them, and Isaac soon sought terms. His only condition was that he should not be put in iron chains, the standard fate for prisoners at that time. Richard happily agreed. Isaac's shock when he surrendered can only be imagined – Richard kept his part of the bargain by providing silver chains for his captive. The conquest was a huge strategic success. Cyprus was located directly opposite the coast of Outremer. It was fertile and crops grew in abundance. It was destined to play a great part in the history of the Christian East for centuries to come.

Richard made the most of his new kingdom. His new subjects were taxed more than they had ever been. He also helped himself to the huge treasury that Isaac had built up over the years. In fact, he was so enamoured of the island that he decided to marry there. However, these events were mere distractions from the main reason for his presence in the region and eventually he set sail for Tyre. Ominously, when he arrived the garrison would not admit him. They were under the influence of Conrad, and Richard was obviously supportive of Guy. Swallowing his pride, the King of England therefore sailed south to Acre, arriving in May 1191. His arrival there was an enormous boost for the Crusaders. There had been sharp exchanges aplenty since the siege began, but neither side had threatened a decisive breakthrough. Philip had, on his arrival, tightened the stranglehold on the city, but more was needed if the city were to fall.

Saladin was still camped a few miles away. If the Franks threatened a breach of the walls, the defenders simply signalled him to send more troops to their aid. The diversion they created would draw the Franks away, leading to stalemate. Richard's arrival tipped the scales. His ships strengthened the blockade of the port, a strategy that would deprive the garrison of revictualling opportunities and thus help substantially in the bid to force it to its knees.

Richard brought zeal and energy to the siege. It was needed to encourage the Crusaders to make one last push. The assault had run out of momentum and, methodical as he was, Philip was not the man to restore it. However, at his best

Richard was a great motivator of men, particularly in a military environment. The besiegers were aware of this, and his arrival was greeted with the lighting of huge bonfires in spontaneous celebration. He immediately set to his task with a will, inspiring the men to ever-greater efforts. Even when struck down by disease, he directed operations from his sickbed.

Despite their outward hostility towards each other, Richard was keen to understand Saladin better. He suggested that the two men meet. Saladin refused but sent his brother, al-Adil, in his stead. For three days the fighting stopped as the two men talked. However, no real progress was made and it was important to bring matters swiftly to a head. The Christian leaders were already falling out with each other, arguing, among other things, about whether Cyprus should be divided between Philip and Richard (it had been agreed at the start of the Crusade that all conquests would be split). While all this counter-productive bickering was going on, Saladin had received reinforcements. The Crusaders needed a breakthrough soon.

However, the fortitude of the defenders was weakening. An attempt by Muslim forces to break through the Franks' lines and relieve the city failed. Soon after on 3 July 1191, the French made a breach but could not follow it up. A few days later, the English attempted to take the city while the French were dining. The garrison could take no more and determined to surrender on the best terms possible. While their envoys contacted the Crusader leaders to begin negotiations, a swimmer surreptitiously made his way to Saladin to tell him what was happening.

Saladin was alarmed at this news. He told the swimmer to return with instructions that the garrison must fight on until help could break through. But the defenders had lost all hope and decided that they must give in. The terms offered were hard. The defenders of Acre could keep their lives and their freedom only if Saladin could provide a huge ransom and release a large number of Frankish prisoners, among whom were some particularly important individuals.

Another messenger was despatched to Saladin telling him of the garrison's decision. He was horrified when he heard of it, and sent the courier back with an instruction that the city must not capitulate. He was too late. Even as he gave the order, Saladin saw the banners of the Christian kings flying atop the city walls. Saladin accepted the decision graciously. He was a man of honour and now that the deal had been struck he would attempt to adhere to it.

The timescale set by the Franks was extremely challenging. Raising so much money in a short period of time would be difficult. Assembling the Frankish prisoners quickly would be even more so. Saladin did all that he could to comply but, although a large sum of money was raised and many prisoners were brought together, it proved logistically impossible to assemble all those prisoners who had been named. Richard's envoys noted the absentees and asked Saladin where they were.

In reply, Saladin stated that they would soon be assembled and that, in the meantime, he would release all the prisoners who had been gathered and would offer hostages to guarantee the return of the remainder. Richard's representatives were not empowered to agree to these changes to the conditions and undertook to discuss the matter with their king. On receiving their report, Richard found

Acre submits to Philip and Richard I.

himself in a quandary. He wished to push on and maintain the impetus that the capture of Acre had given to the Crusade, but he could not do so if he were encumbered with the thousands of Muslim prisoners then in his possession. To compromise would be alien to his character. If nothing else, Richard was a man who considered most issues as black or white. He decided to order the unthinkable. He would murder every prisoner that he had, including the women and children.

In later times, Sir Winston Churchill would describe Richard as: 'in politics, a child. The advantages gained for him by military genius were flung away through diplomatic ineptitude.' Sadly, he was right. The subsequent slaughter took days to complete. It should be noted that all the Christians asked to participate did so with enthusiasm. Once again, the new arrivals from the West had little appreciation of what was politically necessary in Outremer. Fed by the Church on a staple diet of which one ingredient was that all Muslims were inherently evil, these sinful penitents attempted to redeem themselves by the shedding of innocent blood. There was nothing contradictory in their attitude. Although the Christianity of Medieval man was a deeply personal affair, it was increasingly shaped by the teachings of the Church, particularly now that the Papacy was becoming more organised in its attempts to provide the lead on spiritual matters.

There was absolutely no contradiction or hypocrisy in the way that the Christians acted; given the dogma that lay at the core of the Crusading ethos it was an inevitable consequence. Of course, those Muslims who witnessed the scene did not share this view and attempted to intervene. However, they were driven back and forced to watch helplessly as the slaughter continued.

It is dangerous to take a moral view on the massacre. Such barbarity was not restricted to the Franks; after all, the Muslims had slaughtered the Templars after their victory at Hattin. And it was a logical extension of the glorification of violence in Christ's name that was integral to the development of the Crusading movement. But even ignoring the moral implications, the diplomatic effects of this act were immediate and transparently obvious. By his actions at Acre, Richard condemned many Christians to death. Many commentators, Christian as well as Muslim, agree that Saladin was a chivalrous man but he was understandably enraged by this atrocity. For a while, every Christian captive, male or female, could expect nothing save death, often prefaced by an awful ordeal by torture.

The massacre of the Muslim prisoners, coming as it did as part of a pattern of Christian intolerance, ensured that the war in Outremer would be one fought to the death. It was disunity that had allowed the Franks to capture Outremer in the first place but the Franks, by a series of tactless acts, were forging unbreakable bonds of hatred, among the native Christians of the 'wrong' persuasion and the Muslims alike. Their actions would weld their enemies into a coherent whole that would eventually overwhelm the tiny Occidental ruling caste. When retribution finally arrived, it would be terrible and without pity.

Whatever doubts exist about his judgement, Richard now became the driving force behind the campaign. Philip considered that by taking Acre he had redeemed his Crusader vows and was now eager to return home to France. Among other things, he had unfinished business to attend to there regarding territorial disputes with Richard. The latter had also alienated the leader of the Germans, Count Leopold of Austria. After Acre has fallen, Leopold had raised his standard alongside those of Richard and Philip as a means of symbolising the involvement of the depleted German forces in the capture of the city. Angrily, Richard denounced his presumption and threw the banner into the ditch surrounding the city. Leopold furiously prepared to return to his homelands, swearing vengeance. His chance for revenge came more quickly and directly than he can have expected.

To an extent, Richard's attitude here is explainable. Leopold and the Germans had played a minor role in the fall of Acre. Leopold himself had arrived late, and inherited only the insignificant rump of the vast German force that had set out. The raising of his standard was more than a mark of prestige. By this act, a man symbolically staked his claim for a share in the riches of a captured city. Richard prized wealth highly, and his ire would have been aroused by Leopold's arrogance. Nevertheless, his instinctive reaction typifies his faults. By refusing to deal tactfully with the situation, Richard made a lasting enemy of Leopold and lost the support of his troops, however few, for the rest of the Crusade.

Philip and Leopold accordingly made preparations to leave. Philip sailed homeward for France on 3 August 1191. A significant proportion of the French army stayed, under the command of the Duke of Burgundy. However, Philip's departure emphasised a lack of commitment on his part to the Crusading movement. He had satisfied public opinion by embarking on this Third Crusade in the first place. Now he had fulfilled what was expected of him. He had also been unwell for some time and the conditions in Outremer had aggravated his health problems. His departure was a great opportunity for Richard at a personal level. Although the French would retain nominal independence, there was no doubt that Richard was now the effective military leader in Outremer. The forces of the kingdom would look to him for their example and their inspiration, a chance that Richard meant to exploit to the full. Here was a chance to achieve his deepest ambitions of power and glory, to attain fulfilment of his greatest desires.

In his next move, Richard indeed showed the true genius of a master military strategist. He could, it is true, be a fool. It was, for example, no accident that he lost his life besieging a minor castle in France without his armour on, an occasion when he simply underestimated what he considered to be second-rate opposition. But here and now, when he was faced by a true challenge, the real man emerged. At such times he became the complete military professional.

Given the euphoria following the capture of Acre, there must have been great pressure to march immediately on Jerusalem. But Richard well understand that, if he captured Jerusalem, he would also have to retain it. To do that, there needed to be a solid line of communication from the city to the tiny coastal enclave that presently represented the extent of the Kingdom of Jerusalem. A base nearer the Holy City was therefore required and, accordingly, Richard decided that he must next march on Jaffa. Nothing was left to chance. Whenever possible, the supply train of the army would march next to the sea so that the heavy cavalry could protect them from attack on the landward side while the navy performed a similar function from the other flank. All unnecessary non–combatants had to stay behind. This caused great consternation, particularly the removal of the women. Many of the men grumbled, the French were decidedly lukewarm about the adventure and Conrad of Montferrat refused point blank to go.

Despite their apathy, the persona of Richard was sufficient to drive the initiative forward. On 22 August Richard rode out at the head of the army on its way south. The conduct of its progress was meticulous. It travelled slowly to ensure that the fleet kept up. There were regular stops so that the troops could stay fresh. However, despite the well–laid plans, as the march progressed the armies were subject to ever-more regular and aggressive Muslim attacks. Stragglers were seized, tortured for information and then brutally disposed of in revenge for Acre. On one occasion, the French force was nearly overwhelmed when it fell behind the main army.

But these raids did not seriously impede the Franks, and Saladin was aware that a pitched battle would need to be fought if he were to prevent them from reaching Jaffa. He searched now for a site to favour his forces and found what he was looking for just north of the town of Arsuf, where there was a plain over which his cavalry could be deployed. On its edge was a forest, which would cover his force. It was here that Saladin resolved to stand and fight. Richard knew that a major confrontation was imminent and sought a truce. However, the two sides had very different objectives and the subsequent discussions that took place with al-Adil did not bear fruit. Richard wanted nothing less than the complete restitution of all the lost lands of Outremer, a price that Saladin would not pay. Battle was unavoidable.

The rigid discipline that Richard had imposed had protected the Franks thus far. The incessant Muslim attacks had encouraged many of the Christian army to retaliate. The Muslims wished this to happen, so that they could exploit the gaps created in the Christian ranks as a result. It was an old tactic, used many times previously, but this time Richard was too canny to be duped by it. He insisted that the Franks did not break their line until he gave the order to do so.

As day broke on 7 September, orders were given to the Christians to break camp and march the 6 miles that remained to Arsuf. The army was protected on its landward side by a screen of infantry, particularly crossbowmen. Inside them rode the cavalry, the Templars in the vanguard, followed by Angevins, Poitevins and English troops. Then came the Flemish and French troops and, at the rear, the Hospitallers. Next to the sea were the baggage train and yet more infantry, protected as ever by the fleet offshore. As the day progressed, the Muslim attacks became more intense. It became apparent that this was no mere skirmish. The plain was alive with an enveloping swarm of enemy cavalry, who concentrated their attacks on the rear, hoping to separate the Hospitallers from the rest of the army.

The Crusader line held its order, although the pressure was intense. Many horses fell under the Muslims' arrows but their riders walked onwards, their armour making them impervious. The crossbowmen returned the attacks with interest, the power of their bolts far exceeding that of the Muslim missiles. The infantry kept together and no gaps appeared. But the pressure of battle inevitably started to tell. The Hospitallers begged to be allowed to fight back, but Richard told them to wait. He had no intention of wasting his force by indulging in piecemeal attacks. When the moment came to strike, it would be co-ordinated and overwhelming.

Eventually, the waiting became too much for two Hospitaller knights. They dug their spurs into their steeds and charged at the enemy. It was a catalyst for the rest of the Hospitallers to follow suit. Fortunately for them, Richard was just about to give the order for the charge. He quickly took control of the situation. Some of the cavalry became temporarily entangled with the infantry but Richard managed to extricate them. Along the entire Christian line, a great ripple effect was observed as horseman after horseman set his sights on the Muslims. This was no disorganised rabble, spending its energies foolishly by fighting as small groups; this was a mighty wave of steel that would overwhelm anything in its path. The Muslims knew that to stay where they were meant death, and this particular Muslim army was not prepared to court martyrdom.

Even the Muslim chroniclers admit that what followed was a rout. Faced by this horrifying sight, the Muslim forces evaporated. Thousands fled headlong from the battlefield. Because of their greater mobility, many escaped and casualties were not disastrous. Militarily, the army lived to fight another day. The importance of the victory was its effect on morale. Saladin had been defeated in open battle, showing that the victor of Hattin was far from invincible.

Conversely, Richard's stock was enormously high. It seemed that at last there was a Christian leader who could give the military impetus needed to recover the kingdom. The performance of the troops had been magnificent and showed what the Franks could achieve if their efforts were co-ordinated and controlled. There was at last optimism in the land, a rare commodity in recent years. Three years previously, only one town south of Tripoli and a handful of castles were left to the Franks. Now Acre was recaptured, and Saladin had been defeated. There was still much to do before Outremer was viable again, but there was at least a solid foundation on which the decimated kingdom could attempt to rebuild. Through the darkness a glimmer of light had shone, a ray of hope to the battered Frankish nation.

CHAPTER 20

Breathing Space

In the immediate aftermath of the battle at Arsuf, the road to Jerusalem seemed to be open. Despite this, Richard showed uncharacteristic caution. Saladin's army was still largely intact, and rather than press on Richard chose to consolidate. It is difficult to assess whether he was right to do so. This was a great opportunity to retake Jerusalem, as the morale of the Muslims had been badly dented. On the other hand, Richard may by now have been aware of the intrinsic weaknesses of Outremer. There needed to be a permanent solution to the nation's difficulties, otherwise the moment that Richard and his troops departed, all the gains made by his efforts would be lost.

While he pondered over his options, the army moved on to Jaffa. It was in a paradisian setting, surrounded by lush orchards with abundant provisions. The army became indolent, and began to lose its self-control. Harlots from Acre moved down the coast to join the men. Desertion became a problem, and significant numbers of men returned to Acre. King Guy was sent to persuade them to return but typically failed to move them. Eventually, Richard went to Acre himself and berated them. Only then was there a significant response to the appeals to return.

Richard, too, had other distractions. The people of Cyprus, who had seen him as a liberator, had long been disabused of their misconception. Richard's governor on the island had died, and there were now rebellious undercurrents among the people. Cyprus needed strong government and eventually Richard sold it to the Templars, with whom he had always been in sympathy. He was also concerned at the level of support for Conrad of Montferrat, a man much feared by the Muslims. And he must have known that his ambitious younger brother, John, would be likely to attempt to take advantage of his extended absence from his kingdom, probably with the support of King Philip of France. He decided therefore to seek a diplomatic solution.

Thus Richard made overtures to Saladin, initially of a typically extreme nature. Saladin was to return all his conquests. It was especially important that he restore to the Franks the fragment of the True Cross taken at Hattin. He had threatened to bury this under the doorway of a mosque in Damascus so Muslims could trample on this emblem of the unbelievers. Of course, Saladin would not contemplate agreement to such unrealistic demands. However, Richard did not give up and sent back his ambassadors with a quite bizarre proposition. Under the terms of Richard's proposals, Joanna of Sicily was to marry al-Adil, Saladin's brother. As a wedding gift, she should be given all the coastal cities now ruled by Richard. By this unlikely alliance, the nation would be united and peace restored.

It was an incredible offer, which would be anathema to Christian and Muslim alike. Saladin himself accepted immediately, believing that it was nothing more than a humorous prank. But Richard appeared to be in earnest. When she heard of the scheme, Joanna – who had not been involved in the discussions thus far – was incensed and would have nothing to do with it. Richard suggested that al-Adil should convert to Christianity but the Muslim prince scoffed at such an idea. The enterprise was stillborn, as it was doomed to be all along.

Meanwhile, other negotiations had been taking place. Conrad had made his own approaches to Saladin through the medium of Reynald of Sidon. Saladin sought advice of his council, wanting to know whether he should side with Conrad or Richard. They argued that he should support Richard, as he was unlikely to be in Outremer for too long. Saladin's double-dealings soon became public knowledge. Richard's representative, Humphrey of Toron, saw al-Adil out hunting with Reynald and realised that other discussions were taking place.

By now, the time for talking had passed anyway. Winter was approaching and Richard needed to restore the esprit of his army. He decided to march on Jerusalem. Saladin had disbanded half of his men, many of whom were keen to return home, but he had summoned fresh troops from Egypt in their stead. As Richard began his march, the weather turned. Violent squalls made the countryside a quagmire. Many of the stores were destroyed. Troops were exposed to driving rain and bitter cold, with little shelter. Despite these trials, every mile they moved nearer to Jerusalem so their spirits rose. Hopes and expectations soared.

But Richard already knew that he could not hope to hold Jerusalem even if he took it. Saladin had large numbers of men in the field, many of whom were still fresh. Richard could end up caught between the garrison of Jerusalem and Saladin's army. And if the city fell, he would be trapped inside with little hope of additional supplies reaching him. So he called off his advance and returned

A tilting competition between Saladin and Richard. (Add. 42130 f. 82 King Richard I of England tilting at Saladin, begun prior to 1340 for Sir Geoffrey Luttrell (1276–1345), Latin, Luttrell Psalter *(14th century); British Library, London/Bridgeman Art Library, London/New York)*

towards the coast in January 1192. Richard took this decision at Beit-Nuba, just 12 miles from the Holy City.

The retreat was a bitter blow to his men. They were convinced that the city could be taken and did not understand the strategic merits of Richard's decision. The French were especially disillusioned. They had received no pay from Philip for months, and Richard had been forced to meet their wages instead. Now even the king's coffers were running short and he could afford to pay them no longer. For many of the French, this was the final straw and they began to desert in droves. A large number went to Acre, intending to board the first ship back to France.

Richard was aware of the despondency of his force, and appreciated that some offensive action would help restore momentum and focus. Therefore, he decided to march to Ascalon, which had been abandoned by Saladin. Given its strategic position, it would be a valuable addition to the small territory now held by the Franks. Accordingly, Richard marched south and took residence in the city, unopposed. It was not an ideal location. The city's harbour was not good, and the supplies that were brought by sea could only be landed irregularly. Nevertheless, it was a distraction and at least gave his men some positive task to perform.

By this time, the need for an accommodation with Saladin had become acute. Richard had received definite news that his brother, John, was causing many problems in his absence. In addition, the Crusaders in Outremer were as disunited as ever and Richard's envoys were dismayed to discover that Conrad was still talking to Saladin. In particular, the presence of Balian of Ibelin among Conrad's entourage gave cause for concern. If such a prominent man, and one much respected by the Franks, was openly supporting the recalcitrant Conrad, it suggested real problems ahead.

It was now imperative that the issue of the succession was finally faced. Richard called all his nobles together and asked whether they wished Conrad or Guy to be their king. To his shock, they opted unanimously for Conrad. Acquiescing to the decisiveness of their views, Richard agreed to offer the crown to Conrad and in recompense sold Cyprus to Guy. The Templars who owned it had proved completely incapable of effective government and were happy to fall in with this scheme. Messengers were rushed off to tell Conrad of his good fortune, and a coronation was arranged in Acre. Conrad was a serious man, and prayed fervently that if he were not capable of ruling the country, the crown would be taken away from him.

He prayed too earnestly. In the town of Tyre where Conrad resided were two new converts to Christianity. As Conrad was out walking to meet his friend the Bishop of Beauvais, the two men approached him, ostensibly to hand him a letter. As Conrad took it from one of them, the other took a knife from his robe and thrust it deep into Conrad's body. Help rushed to his aid, but it was hopeless. One of the assassins was killed on the spot, the other was tortured before being executed. They were servants of Sinan, the Old Man of the Mountains, who had sent them to dispose of Conrad. Some of the Franks thought that Saladin had encouraged the assassins, but others felt that Richard had been the instigator of the heinous act. However, this seems improbable. Richard's character demanded strong, transparent action and such intrigues were not his normal way of conducting his affairs. Nevertheless, some made the accusation with conviction and the allegations would cause much harm to Richard at a later stage.

The truth is probably more prosaic. Some months previously, Conrad had captured a Muslim ship carrying pilgrims. He had ransacked the cargo and thrown the pilgrims over the side to drown. The pilgrims were Assassins, and his murder was probably in revenge for this act. Whoever was responsible for the killing, it created a constitutional crisis. Conrad's widow, Isabella, had just lost her second husband and she was not yet in her mid-twenties. It seemed to many that another husband was desperately needed. Richard sent his young nephew, Henry of Champagne, to assess the situation. Being young and an eligible bachelor, the people saw him as an ideal husband for Isabella. He demurred, unsure of Richard's response and afraid of upsetting social convention which decreed that widows should not remarry for at least a year.

Richard, however, was delighted when he heard of the proposal and gave his wholehearted approval. The harsh realities of the situation dictated that any social convention should be ignored in these exceptional circumstances. The two were accordingly married. It was a good match. Isabella quickly warmed to her attractive husband and for his part he treated her with kindness. It was for the time being a satisfying end to a sad tale.

Within the Muslim world at this time dissentient elements were once again at work. While Saladin's attentions were distracted elsewhere dealing with these troublesome factions, Richard made a lightning raid on the fortress of Daron, some miles south of Ascalon. The fighting that ensued was bitter but ended in triumph for Richard. After the capture of the fortress, many of the defenders were thrown over its walls to their deaths and the rest were dragged off into captivity. The success was a major boost to the Franks. As was so often the case, its significance on moral grounds far exceeded its practical effects. The Franks once again pressed Richard to march on Jerusalem. And now, the King agreed to their requests. However, his enthusiasm for the cause was limited by practicalities and, believing that Egypt was the Achilles' heel of the Islamic world, he may well have preferred a campaign there.

When the army had once again reached Beit-Nuba in June 1192 Richard vacillated, unsure of his chances of success. Despite hesitation over his main objective, though, he did surprise a large Muslim supply caravan in the area. So vast was the store of food taken, as well as the horses and camels, that Saladin seriously considered abandoning Jerusalem. He did not doubt that Richard would attack and, as the Turkish and Kurdish elements in his army were at each other's throats, he was not sure of his own men. However, after some consultation, the Muslim leader decided that he would stand firm. All the wells in the area were poisoned to ensure that the Franks were without water, even if they had food.

Meanwhile, doubts still weighed heavily on Richard. The Masters of the Temple and the Hospital both reminded Richard that the city would soon revert to Muslim control when he left. There was continuing news of unrest in England. There were altogether too many reasons militating against an attack on the city. Richard climbed a hilltop and, from its summit, caught an unexpected glimpse of Jerusalem from a distance. He instantly shielded his eyes, unable to bear even a distant view of the city that had meant so much to the Crusading movement but would never, he knew, be his.

A few days later, the attack was abandoned. After a month at Beit-Nuba Richard decided to return to the coast to arrange a truce before he left for home. There were jeers from the French troops who remained as they mocked his timidity. Demoralised and angry, not to mention confused, the Christian army trudged wearily away from Jerusalem. Once back on the coast, Richard recommenced talks with al-Adil. There would be no bluster this time. Richard merely wanted to keep the towns that had been reconquered. The stumbling block, though, was Ascalon. It was far too important to be left in the hands of the Franks. But Richard would not agree to forego his claim to it.

The King was now weary and began to lose interest in the desultory negotiations. Saladin read this as an opportunity, and made a sudden march on Jaffa while Richard was moping in Acre. The garrison was heavily outnumbered. After three days, a breach in the wall was made and the garrison agreed to surrender. However, Saladin's troops quickly got out of control and began to pillage the town. Saladin advised the garrison to lock itself in the citadel for their own safety.

Unknown to the Saracens, the defenders had sent a messenger to Richard, telling him to come quickly. Stimulated by the scent of battle, Richard's fatigue was forgotten and he sprang into action. He gathered together every warrior he could at such short notice and requisitioned every ship then in Acre. When he arrived off Jaffa, he could not see if the garrison had capitulated or not. A brave monk swam out to his ship to tell him that the Franks were still in possession of the citadel.

This was all the encouragement that Richard needed. He stormed ashore at the head of a motley force of 2,000 Italian marines, 80 knights and 400 archers. His main army was still miles away. He was not even properly armoured and his entire force had only three horses. The Franks' greatest weapon, the cavalry charge, would not be available in this fight. Despite these problems, Richard threw himself into battle. The garrison attacked from the rear of the Muslims and, trapped between these two forces, the enemy broke. Unaware of all this, Saladin was in his tent talking to representatives of the garrison, arranging terms for their capitulation. Suddenly, a servant burst in to tell him what had happened. Saladin tried to hide the situation from the Franks in his tent but the pandemonium outside told its own story.

Saladin withdrew, but when he considered his numerical superiority he decided to attack the next day. As the sun came up on 5 August 1192, an alert sentry in the hastily erected camp of the Franks caught it glinting off the points of thousands of Muslim spears. He sounded the alarm and the camp frantically prepared to receive the enemy. Richard ordered that sharpened tent pegs be driven into the ground to inhibit the Muslim cavalry. The attacks when they came were ferocious but this was Richard's finest hour. He was everywhere, directing the defences, leading counter-attacks, inspiring his men. When his horse was killed under him, his sheer courage so overwhelmed Saladin that he sent a replacement to him. If a man could inspire the admiration of his enemies like this, then how much more should he do so among his allies? Yet herein lies Richard's contradiction. So magnificent in action, decisive and irresistible in battle, he could not transfer his prowess to politics. The victor of so many battles, he never once learned the secret of conquering men's hearts.

But on this day, Richard was unbeatable. All day long the waves of Saracen horsemen were repulsed. Then, when Richard thought the enemy was tiring, he had his archers loose a sharp volley at them. Following this, he led his heavily outnumbered force in a ferocious charge. The sight of this colossus racing towards them was more than the enemy could bear. Saladin withdrew his troops and returned to Jerusalem.

It was an astounding victory, probably Richard's greatest. It was won by sound tactics and coolness under fire but, above all else, raw courage. But it is significant that it had been won in a defensive battle. For all the promise of the Third Crusade, all that was left to the Franks was a rump of the state that they had once held, a pale reflection of what was expected when the Crusade was launched. Deserted by Philip and the Germans, despised by many of the French who were left, betrayed by his brother in England, it was Richard's last throw of the dice, magnificent, chivalric but irrelevant. His health rapidly went into decline. His return to England could be delayed no longer.

A truce was finally agreed with Saladin, who would not budge on the question of Ascalon. Ultimately, Richard was forced to demolish the walls of the city. Those of his army who wished to visit Jerusalem were given free access to do so by Saladin. Richard did not join them. In his heart, he knew that he had failed. He took ship for the West on 9 October, 1192, sailing from the chronicles of Crusader history and into the pages of legend, to spend years incarcerated in the castles of the enemy he made on Crusade, Count Leopold of Austria.

His departure left the small Crusader kingdom seriously exposed. However, help was at hand and from an unexpected source. It was only since the days of Nur-ed-Din that Syria and Egypt had been under the control of one Muslim leader. The sheer force of Saladin's personality had kept the two territories combined, but he was noticeably slowing down. His health had deteriorated and the pressure of ruling this large and divided empire was taking its toll. He returned from his campaigning to attempt to catch up with the vast amount of routine administrative tasks that were now outstanding. His health worsened, and he began to complain that he felt tired. In 1193, soon after Richard's departure from Outremer, Saladin left Damascus to meet the pilgrim caravan returning from Mecca. On his return, he fell seriously ill. It soon became clear that he was dying.

Even before he expired, his sons (there were seventeen in total) were disputing their inheritance. It was an unsavoury and unfitting end to a marvellous life. Although he could be ruthless, Saladin stood out above all men of the Crusades as a man of his word. His gentility, mercy and generosity often infuriated his own people. He deserved a better end than this. A man of simple tastes, and devout beliefs, he slipped peacefully away on 3 March, fully reconciled to the faith that he had fought so hard to protect, and for which he had been such a powerful, yet often gentle, ambassador. There are many stories extant that tell of Saladin's courtesy and chivalry. His personal secretary, Baha al-Din, tells of a woman whose child had been stolen away from the Frankish camp, who came to see Saladin. She related her story to him:

Saladin; regarded by Muslim and Christian alike as a man of his word.

Yesterday some Muslim thieves entered my tent and stole my little girl. I cried all night, and our commanders told me: 'the King of the Muslims is merciful, and you can ask for your daughter back.' Thus have I come and I place all my hopes in you.

Saladin's eyes filled with tears and he sent men out to recover the child, who was restored to her grateful mother later that day. The story may be apocryphal. It is, however, consistent with other tales of Saladin that are told both by Muslim and Christian chroniclers, such as the story of Saladin sending his doctor to Richard when the King was ill, or his treatment of the widows and orphans of Jerusalem after its capture. He was a man possessed of a degree of humanity seemingly far above that demonstrated by most other men of his time, be they Muslim or Frank.

On Saladin's death, his empire quickly began to disintegrate. Overall control of it had been given to his eldest son, al-Afdal. He was arrogant and overbearing, and quickly alienated his brothers by his condescension. His patronising and suspicious attitude led to many of his brothers declaring independence from him. One brother took Egypt, another Aleppo. The power broker in these events was al-Adil, who came through these unsatisfactory events unscathed. The arguments among the brothers gave the Christian enclave in Outremer a period of relative tranquillity.

Meanwhile, Henry of Champagne, though not born with the mark of greatness, was none the less performing well in his new role as ruler. He negotiated successfully with the Muslims, and with his own people he became genuinely popular. However, he could not totally avoid internal unrest. He fell out with many leading clerics in 1194 when he insisted that his appointee should be the new Patriarch of Jerusalem. Possibly because of this he was never officially crowned king, although most men did accept him as their leader. Henry also had difficulty with Guy of Lusignan. There was a plot against him in 1193, behind which was Guy's brother, Amalric. Amalric was thrown into prison for his pains, a brave step by Henry as his opponent was a powerful man.

The problem conveniently solved itself when Guy died in May 1194. Cyprus was bequeathed to his brother Geoffrey, but he had returned to France. In his absence, the people of the island pushed for Amalric as their leader. Reluctant to comply at first, Henry eventually agreed. Amalric wisely saw that he should forget his past disagreements with Henry and generally cooperated with him. However, he had no intention of declaring himself a vassal and decided that he needed another sponsor to support him. The choice was not easy. It would be impossible to approach the Emperor in Constantinople in this respect, as he regarded the island as his. After considering all the alternatives, Amalric decided to approach the German Emperor, offering to become his vassal in exchange for his support.

It was an astute move. German involvement in the Crusades so far had been unimpressive and this suggestion offered them the chance of making amends. The Emperor, Henry VI, was delighted to agree to Amalric's approach, sending his own Chancellor, Conrad of Hildesheim, to crown him personally. He even sent a sceptre with Conrad to add an air of regality to the coronation ceremony.

On the mainland, Henry of Champagne was also looking for allies. He received interest from a most unlikely quarter. The Assassins had recently lost Sinan, their leader. They invited Henry to their headquarters to discuss an alliance. Here, in the giant fortress of al-Kahf, high up in the craggy Nosairi Mountains, a bizarre scene was played out. To prove the loyalty of his men, the new Assassin leader ordered one of them to throw himself to his death from the castle walls. Without hesitation he obeyed. The scene was then repeated several times with other men. Eventually, Henry begged the Assassins to stop. The point had already been made with graphic clarity.

From here, Henry went to Antioch and then to Armenia. Although on the periphery of the main events in Outremer, the region was in ferment. Bohemond of Antioch, who had made his own truce with Saladin, had fallen out with the Armenians over a fortress that had once belonged to the Templars at Baghras. The Lord of Armenia, Leo, had claimed it for himself after it had been captured by the Muslims and then deserted, but Bohemond fought against his claim. Leo invited Bohemond to his capital to discuss the issue further. When he arrived, Leo promptly threw him in his dungeons.

For his part, Henry attempted to negotiate Bohemond's release. It was agreed that Bohemond would be set free without ransom but Leo would retain Baghras. To cement the relationship, Bohemond's heir would marry Leo's niece, Alice. Leo, in the meantime, was also scheming elsewhere. He followed the example of Amalric and asked the Germans for support. Although initially the Emperor was unsure whether he would provide it, further negotiations involving the Pope, whereby the Armenian leader agreed to adopt the practices of the Latin Church in his country, convinced him to change his mind.

Their increasing involvement encouraged the Germans to launch another expedition to Outremer. When the Chancellor Conrad set out to crown Amalric in Cyprus, he had with him a large force. The rank and file mostly went straight to Acre while the leaders stayed in Cyprus for the coronation. They eventually arrived in 1197. Henry of Champagne was not pleased to see them. He had done nothing to encourage the Germans to show an interest in the area and feared they would be a destabilising influence. He had been carefully nurturing more friendly links with the neighbouring Muslims and he was concerned that these newcomers from the West would once again jeopardise the peace of his small country.

His suspicions were well founded. Hardly had the Germans arrived than they raided Galilee, searching for a Muslim enemy, any Muslim enemy, to fight. Their intrusion aroused the local Muslims and caused them to unite – they had been arguing among themselves for a time. As the Germans infiltrated the country further they became acutely aware that the hills ahead of them were covered with a mass of Muslim warriors, intent on defending their land. There was not even a fight. The mere appearance of the enemy sent the German cavalry charging back to Acre in panic, leaving the infantry to their own devices. Henry of Champagne personally had to lead a force out to recover them.

However, al-Adil, who was at the head of the Muslim forces, determined that he would not disperse the large force at his disposal without a fight. He declined to confront Henry of Champagne directly but swung his force south towards Jaffa. The town was weakly defended and Henry rushed to help it. Sadly for Outremer, tragedy struck. Henry had assembled his army and, on 10 September 1197, he was waiting in an upper room to lead them to battle. He was distracted when a delegation from Pisa entered the room to see him and he stepped back through an open window. His dwarf, Scarlet, rushed to pull him back but could not. Both men fell to their deaths in the courtyard far below.

The kingdom learned of Henry's death with sadness. Isabella was completely devastated. However, the council would not let her personal feelings detract from matters of state. They determined to find yet another husband, her fourth, as quickly as possible. The Germans felt that they had the ideal candidate. Aimery had recently lost his wife and was therefore available. They suggested that he take the hand of Isabella. He had vast experience of the politics of Outremer. And, most importantly for the Germans, he was a vassal of their Emperor.

Initial opposition came from an unexpected source – Amalric himself. He eventually agreed with one condition; Isabella's existing daughter would not inherit Cyprus if he died. The terms were accepted and the marriage went ahead. Amalric had ensured that the rule of Cyprus and the rule of the Kingdom of Jerusalem would remain completely different things.

Amalric ruled from 1198 to 1205 and his reign, more accurately described as a regency, was one of consolidation. The peace with al-Adil was maintained and two towns, Beirut and Sidon, were even recovered for Outremer. However, as Jaffa had been lost soon after the death of Henry, this was only partial compensation. For their part, the German troops soon lost interest and returned home. Before they left, Conrad of Hildesheim set up a new order. As the Teutonic Knights, they would play a great part in the future, although their sphere of influence would be on the German frontiers rather than in the East. Apart from this event, the German expedition had been a failure. Their military performance was derisory, and the fiasco did nothing to restore German prestige.

Further north, Antioch was in turmoil again. Bohemond's heir, Raymond, died and this meant that his young grandson from Raymond's marriage with the Princess of Armenia was next in line to rule should Bohemond die. The latter was already old, and the people of the city did not look forward to the events likely to happen after his death. There would probably have to be a regency, and it would be dominated by Armenians, and the many Germans now in the city, influenced by their friendly contacts with Leo of Armenia, would not allow this process to be interfered with.

The castle at Sidon.

However, Bohemond had another son, also named Bohemond. He was ruler of Tripoli and had inherited a flair for intrigue from his illustrious ancestors. He schemed with the Templars, who wanted the castle of Baghras back. He also bribed the Hospitallers and granted generous trading concessions to both the Pisans and the Genoese. However, he could not buy over the Papacy. Pope Innocent, whose spiritual leadership the Armenians had only recently recognised, had no wish to antagonise them. Despite the protestations of the Templars, the Pope's support lay with the Armenians. However, when Leo proved to be extremely inflexible in subsequent negotiations, even Innocent changed his view. Accordingly, when Bohemond III died in 1201, he was replaced by his son who became Bohemond IV. Fortunately for him and his supporters, at this crucial moment Leo of Armenia was distracted by a large Seldjuk raid into his territory and could not intervene.

On the whole, Amalric's reign passed without incident. A man with a sound legal mind, he helped to tidy up the messy constitution of Outremer. He avoided military bravado, which suited the now pre-eminent al-Adil, who was attempting to became sole ruler of the Muslims. He could see that the small Frankish state was exhausted and offered little real threat; on the contrary, it offered excellent trading opportunities. And most of the Franks now knew that another major

Crusade was unlikely. Occasionally, a small group of zealots would arrive from the West, cause a lot of local difficulty by their machismo, and then return dejected to Europe after the inevitable military defeat that followed.

However, there were rumours of a new expedition on its way, although it was taking some time to organise. This Crusade would not arrive in Outremer though. The army that was sent was about to strike a blow at the heart of Christendom. Its actions would expose large parts of Eastern and Central Europe to Muslim rule. A new god had appeared, the god of money. The Crusading ethic, an ideal of dubious moral validity, was about to be prostituted completely.

CHAPTER 21

The Death of Idealism

The story of the Crusades is as much a chronicle of the mistrust and misunderstanding between Western and Eastern Christendom as it is about the battle for the Holy Land. From the moment that the two first came into contact, it was apparent that a massive chasm had sprung up between the different cultures. Despite their Christian roots, the two shared virtually nothing in common, in philosophy, in politics, in their attitudes to the world and their respective places in it.

It is important to emphasise that the Crusades were just one of the symptoms of the problem, and not its sole cause. The real doctrinal differences that existed between East and West could not fail, in this deeply spiritual age, to cause difficulties. These problems were exacerbated by tensions in political and economic spheres. For centuries there had been disputes between the two halves of Christendom, of which the wars between Byzantium and the expansionist Normans were just one example. As late as 1154, the Byzantines unsuccessfully invaded Italy. And in 1185 the Greek city of Thessalonica was burned by the Normans. The economic expansionism of the West in the Mediterranean inevitably brought the two cultures into conflict. Significantly, relationships between Byzantium and Venice, which had been good at times in the past, deteriorated alarmingly towards the end of the twelfth century. In the midst of these problems, the Crusades only served to fuel the tensions that already existed.

The influence of the maritime states of Italy, especially Venice, began to be particularly resented in Byzantium. The Venetians had built a prominent position in the world of trade by being the commercial conduit between the hungry markets of the West and the sought-after goods of the East. They exploited this position to the full, along with other Italian states such as Genoa, Pisa and Amalfi. Their influence created resentment in Constantinople.

The first meetings between the Eastern Empire and the Crusaders were fraught with difficulty, with the two parties not having a shared vision from the outset. Godfrey of Bouillon had tried to attack Constantinople, and Raymond of Toulouse had refused to pledge himself to the Emperor. Bohemond I had superficially sided with Alexius but had thrown off his allegiance quickly. Antioch would be a constant thorn in the side of the Byzantine Empire.

The situation deteriorated still further during the twelfth century. Manuel Comnenus was never forgiven for refusing to lead the combined Christian forces against the Muslims when he had the opportunity, and the Germans blamed the

Byzantines for the choice of route that led to the disasters of the Second Crusade. Similarly, there was a perception that the Byzantines had been obstructive when the Germans were marching to the East on the Third Crusade. There was also the recollection that the Emperor had congratulated Saladin when Jerusalem was retaken. These were just some of the misunderstandings that abounded. Many of the popular myths held were at best half-truths, misleading but widely believed. It is obvious from the chronicles of the time that in many quarters there were deep-rooted suspicions of Byzantium.

Philosophically, the differences were immense. Generalisations are dangerous but on the whole Western Europe was a realm of black and white, with little scope for the politics of compromise. In the view of many, there was right and there was wrong – there was no middle way. This was diametrically opposed to the world view of the Byzantines, which held that it was necessary to cohabit with all manner of strange bedfellows (and, interestingly, the Franks in Outremer had quickly learnt to enter into alliances with such unlikely partners as the Assassins). In their global vision, the art of diplomacy and subtle negotiation was as valid a weapon as the sword or the spear – and often more effective. In this philosophy they were masters, and because of it the Eastern Empire had outlived its Roman counterpart by seven hundred years.

Centuries of religious disagreements had exacerbated the situation. Western Europe often regarded the Byzantine Church as bordering on the heretical, its morals loose and corrupt (although immorality was hardly a stranger to the Latin Church), and its vision at odds with that of the Papacy. The wealth of the Eastern Empire was also envied, and it appeared that the West, with its less developed civilisation, suffered from an inferiority complex when it came into contact with cities such as Constantinople or Cairo for the first time.

But the dislike that the Westerns felt for the Byzantines was reciprocated. The Western armies who had descended upon Byzantium since the days of the First Crusade had regularly helped themselves to whatever they wanted. In fairness, all this happened just a century after Viking marauders – many of whose none-too-distant relatives went on Crusade – had been destroying the abbeys and towns of France and England, slaughtering monks, nuns, bishops and even kings without compunction. It would be naïve to think that attitudes would change quickly in such a short space of time.

The people of Byzantium particularly resented the fact that many of their Emperors had adopted Western customs and attempted to obtain Western brides to further their strategic alliances, inevitably disadvantaging many of the leading families of Byzantium. Constantinople was a city rent by internal intrigue and once it had lost the all-powerful ruling family of Comnenus, it was governed by an Angelus dynasty that had used the forces of xenophobia to remove its predecessors.

Given this groundswell of mutual antipathy, of which the Crusades is just one illustration, it was unavoidable that there would one day be a major confrontation between Byzantium and Western Europe, particularly as the former was in a state of noticeable decline and therefore less well placed to defend itself. For since the disaster of Myriocephalum in 1176, Byzantium had deteriorated alarmingly.

A succession of second-rate Emperors had assumed control, under whose disordered leadership the infrastructure of the once mighty Empire crumbled. Byzantium was wide open to a major attack. In the vacuum left by the decline of Imperial power, Western Europe perhaps recognised the opportunity for easy profits. Given the aggressive culture of the West in recent centuries, it was not at all unlikely that Byzantium itself would be attacked.

Despite the disappointed expectations of the Third Crusade, there still remained some interest in the West in launching another expedition to Outremer. However, the motivation was becoming more a chivalric than a spiritual one. The dominant character of the Third Crusade was Richard of England, a man who had, by the standard of the time, a slightly unusual approach to religion; he had, after all, suggested that his sister should marry a Muslim. Although capable of unorthodox piety, Richard was driven more by concepts of fortune and glory than other factors. Others desired to mirror or outshine his exploits and, set against this, it is perhaps no coincidence that the next serious Crusading initiative came about, according to some accounts, as the result of a tournament.

This tournament took place in November 1199, and was hosted by Count Tibald of Champagne at his castle on the Aisne. Following the jousts, the conversation turned to the need for a new Crusade. Family loyalties were often an important factor in deciding who went on Crusade, and the Count was brother to the late Henry of Champagne, erstwhile ruler of Outremer. He also had connections to both King Richard of England and King Philip of France. In the area at this time was a travelling priest, Fulk of Neuilly, a man of fiery oratory. He was invited to address those present and did so in rousing fashion. He reminded them that it was an outrage that Jerusalem remained in Muslim hands, speaking so persuasively that by the time he ended, his audience was determined to launch an expedition.

There was by now a new incumbent of the Papal throne, Innocent III, a pragmatic, business-like man. In common with Urban II, he saw that a Crusade held potential for expanding the power of the Papacy, and was therefore keen to encourage any such ideas, provided that the Church retained influence over its actions. To ensure that this was so, it was important that the secular leadership were prepared to recognise his ultimate authority. Innocent did not discourage the monarchs of the West from joining the Crusade but there was little enthusiasm from them. A man of some standing was still required to give the venture the requisite credibility. Count Tibald would be the ideal candidate. He had enough prestige to gain support from other men of influence but at the same time would not feel powerful enough to challenge Innocent's authority.

To encourage men to join the expedition, Innocent granted a very comprehensive and generous indulgence. While man could seek penance for his sins in a variety of ways, ordinarily there was no guarantee that God would be merciful. An indulgence gave a much stronger commitment that mercy would be granted. Urban II had been generous in the spiritual benefits offered at the start of the First Crusade, but Innocent's rewards exceeded them. There were, however, conditions. The Crusader must confess all previous sins and be absolved

Pope Innocent III; a fresco in the lower church of Sacro Speco, Subiaco.

from them. He or she then had to abstain from all serious sin in the future. If they were to commit further sins after their pilgrimage was completed, then penance had to be sought once again.

The precise conditions surrounding an indulgence were often unclear. Theologians argued on occasion over whether the indulgence was effective from the time that the vow to go on Crusade was taken, or from when the vow was redeemed – for example, when the Crusader visited the Holy Sepulchre. Regardless of the conditions attached, the indulgence was undoubtedly a major factor in the taking of the Cross. Innocent's terms acted as a significant attraction for many who joined this latest Crusade.

Fulk of Neuilly traversed France to encourage others to join the Crusade. Although he was successful in this aim, he encountered little of the spontaneous abandon that had characterised the First Crusade. This was altogether a more organised response – but none the less welcome for that. After the experiences of earlier expeditions, it was made clear that there was no place for non–combatants who used up valuable resources, offering little in return. If success was to crown the venture, this must be a professional military undertaking, organised methodically.

There was little significant input to the force from Germany, apart from the Rhineland. The hub of the force came from France and the Low Countries, both traditional recruiting grounds. Apart from Tibald, Baldwin of Flanders was prominent among its leadership – he would play an important role in later events. Louis, Count of Blois, and Simon de Montfort were also involved, the latter a man who was to be involved in one of the darkest travesties of the Crusading ideal. There were also several leading bishops but no kings. Richard of England was dead and his successor, John, was locked in combat with Philip of France. This meant that neither monarch would provide other than token support to the Crusade.

However, assembling the force was only part of the problem. It was essential to provide transport, and this would cost a great deal of money. The disintegration of Byzantium meant that the land route across Asia Minor was impracticable. Even if this were not so, one of the lessons of the Third Crusade was that journeying by sea would be far preferable to travelling overland, being quicker as well as safer. It also meant that the troops should arrive in a much fresher condition. The Count of Flanders had his own fleet but the others would need to find transport of their own. This would be an expensive option. It was eventually agreed that the Venetians would provide transport for the not inconsiderable sum of 85,000 marks. They would also provide provisions for a fixed period of time. Fifty galleys would be provided to add firepower to the force, for the far from token payment of half the conquests made.

At this time, the most likely destination for the Crusade appeared to be Egypt. Richard of England had argued that it was the weak point of the Muslim dominions. He may well have been right; it was easily accessible by sea, and it provided the Muslim world with much of its wealth and agricultural produce. And it had only recently been integrated into the Syrian super-state that Saladin had created and its Shiite Muslims were historically at odds with the Sunni strand of Islam. Internal dissent could therefore theoretically be exploited to the advantage of the West.

However, there now was set in motion a sequence of events that was to have dramatic repercussions to the Crusade and its final destination. The first was the inconvenient death of Count Tibald. This meant that a new leader had to be found. The man chosen to replace him was Boniface of Montferrat, brother of Conrad. He had many connections with the Holy Land and was an obvious

The castle at Sahyoun, Syria, captured from the Franks by Saladin in 1188.

candidate. But he was an independent and powerful man, closely allied to the current ruler of the Germans, Philip of Swabia. The Germans had been involved in power struggles with the Papacy for centuries, and as such Boniface would be no mere puppet. The Crusade, which Innocent had helped to instigate, had, by the unfortunate mischance of divine intervention, moved out of the Pope's orbit of control.

In common with many of his countrymen, Philip of Swabia was no lover of Byzantium. He was married to the daughter of a deposed Emperor of Byzantium, Isaac Angelus, and as such had more reason than most to be opposed to the current regime in the city. His father-in-law had lost his throne in 1195. He was not a good ruler and his subjects, inflamed by his extortionate taxes, engineered a rising that ended with Isaac thrown into jail after losing his eyes.

Isaac's son, named Alexius, was more fortunate. He was kept under house arrest but otherwise was not significantly deprived of his liberties. During the winter of 1201, he had escaped from his relaxed imprisonment in Constantinople and made his way across Europe to the court of his brother-in-law, Philip. Alexius was by most accounts a feckless youth, undeserving of much sympathy. Nevertheless, Philip offered him hospitality. Present at this family reunion was Boniface of Montferrat, the leader of the Crusade – a fact that was to have sinister connotations at a later stage.

The Venetians were an important factor in this expedition. They had little affection for the Byzantines. They were an immensely powerful and wealthy player on the European stage. The current Doge was a man named Dandolo, who was virtually blind. Venice was providing the transport for the campaign, and had committed itself to enormous expenditure as a result. Many new ships were built specifically for this venture. The complex economics of the situation meant that each Crusader was to pay an individual sum towards the overall cost. However, the calculations relied on a certain number of Crusaders assembling in Venice if the Venetians were to be paid off in full. When the force gathered in June 1202 there was a huge shortfall against the numbers anticipated. According to the chronicler Villehardouin, many Crusaders had made their own way to other ports. Those that did meet in Venice found that they were expected to increase their contributions towards the costs.

Despite strenuous efforts to raise the required amount, a significant deficit remained. But the Venetians came up with a compromise. They had recently lost the port of Zara in Dalmatia to the Hungarians. If the Crusaders would help them to retake it, then Dandolo would provide the transport if the Western leaders agreed to pay off the outstanding amounts from the proceeds of the Crusade's future conquests.

This proposal proved acceptable and the fleet accordingly made the short crossing across the Adriatic, laying siege to Zara. Innocent was beside himself and sent an urgent message to the Crusaders, forbidding them from attacking the city. This was ignored. The city resisted but for only a few days. When it fell, on 15 November 1202, it was subjected to the full horrors of a sack. When he heard of this, Innocent fell into a blind rage. It was a direct rejection of Papal authority and he would not let it go unpunished. He used the most powerful weapon available to him. A Bill of Excommunication was hurled at the Crusaders – not just the leaders, but the entire expedition. Later, he withdrew this from all but the Venetians, whom he held responsible for the diversion.

And it was here, at Zara, that there was one final and fatal twist of fate. The army wintered in the city. On 25 April 1203 Alexius, son of the deposed Byzantine Emperor, turned up at the city. He entered into discussions with the leaders of the expedition. When the rumours of these discussions entered the public domain, the reason for his presence became clear. In return for the promise of large rewards, the Crusade was to divert to Constantinople and restore the city to Alexius. By no means all the Crusaders agreed with this choice, and indeed there was dissent against the plan for some time. However, it was finally resolved that the army, or those members of it who wished to go, would fall in with the scheme.

In Constantinople, the Emperor in power, Alexius III, was amazed when the Western fleet arrived before his city on 24 June. There was only so much that he could do to interfere with the Crusaders. The native troops who had been the backbone of the Byzantine army were no longer available, and it had declined greatly in recent years. The mercenaries who had replaced them (many of whom were Franks) were not of the same calibre and were unreliable. The Emperor therefore did nothing, hoping that the problem would disappear of its own volition.

The Franks attacked some towns on the Asian shore and then turned their attention to the city itself. The Crusaders believed that the Emperor was so unpopular that his people would capitulate meekly, but they were mistaken. The people of Constantinople mockingly asked who Alexius was, making their views of the pretender's claims all too clear. The blood-ties of the inhabitants to Byzantium and their lasting enmity against the West led them to resist Alexius. Conflict was now inevitable.

According to Robert of Clari, who wrote an account of the Crusade, it was Doge Dandolo who led the call to arms. The Venetians led the subsequent assault, their archers clearing the shores of the Greeks who attempted to prevent the Western army from landing. Once ashore, the Franks attacked the Galata Tower, from which a huge chain was suspended across the harbour entrance, preventing the fleet from making further progress. The tower was taken, and the chain was broken. It was then agreed that the Venetians would pursue the attack by sea, and the rest of the army would attack from the land. Attempts by the Greeks to prevent the siege from being tightened failed. On the night of 16 July, terrified, the incumbent Emperor Alexius gathered together as much wealth as he could and fled.

The authorities in the city reacted quickly. They proposed to release the blinded Isaac from prison and restore him to the throne. They would make his son Alexius co-ruler, and by so doing they hoped to deprive the Franks of an excuse to sack the city. It was a clever ploy, reprieving the city for the time being. The deal was struck but it was not long before the young Alexius showed himself unworthy of his exalted position. He tried to bribe the Franks with lavish presents but quickly started to denude his treasury. At the same time, his attempts to force

The interior of the church of Santa Sophia, facing east.

the Byzantine clergy to conform to Latin rites created a groundswell of resentment in the city.

For their part, the inhabitants hated the Westerners. The arrogance of the latter and their attempts to force Western customs on the Greeks were bitterly deprecated. The Franks frequently roamed the city wildly, and on one occasion a French knight burnt down a mosque because it offended his religious sensibilities. The fire burned out of control and destroyed other buildings. Alexius quickly stopped trying to take control of events and his blinded father was incapable of doing so. The city drifted like a rudderless ship, without control or direction.

It would now take the merest spark to light a huge conflagration. It came in February 1204. Alexius had not fulfilled his promises to the Crusade leaders and a delegation went to him to demand that he do so. The population was incensed at their presence and manhandled them. The mob, always a powerful element in Byzantine politics, then rushed to the holy church of Constantinople, St Sophia, and formally declared that Alexius was no longer their Emperor. Authority was given over to a man named Alexius Murzuphlus. For some time, this individual had been courting the favour of the now powerless Alexius. Now he turned on him, breaking into his palace and throwing him into prison, where he was soon executed. Isaac's fate is uncertain. He may have died shortly before these events: he was certainly dead soon after.

The Crusaders were not slow to pick up the gauntlet thrown down to them by the city. They attacked on 6 April 1204, but were beaten back. So elated were the Byzantines at the failure of the attack that they presented their bare buttocks to the Crusaders as a sign of derision. On the morning of 12 April 1204, the Western army reassembled for its final assault. Flying bridges were suspended from high up in the Venetian ships, from which soldiers could pour onto the city walls. The ships advanced towards the ancient walls of Constantinople, and a fierce artillery assault was launched. Attempts to set fire to the defences with Greek fire failed. In reply, Greek catapults hurled rocks at the Venetian ships, which were well constructed enough to avoid serious damage.

The fight was fierce but eventually one of the Venetian ships succeeded in placing itself next to the walls. From it, a knight managed to cross over onto the wall itself. He was soon joined by others, until a foothold was gained. Other areas of the wall fell to the Crusaders, and the outer defences of the wall were breached. This still left the inner line of defences, which was formidable. It appeared to be holding when consternation broke out inside the city itself. Flames were seen that quickly spread out of control. In the panic that ensued, all pretence at defence soon evaporated and the Westerners poured into the city. The short-lived Emperor Murzuphlus escaped as quickly as he could, and the leaders of the Crusade made their way to the royal palace.

There was little organised resistance left to overcome and all appeared calm. The next morning, the Crusade leaders met. They now commanded the richest city in Christendom with a large army expecting some form of payment. That payment would be simple and shocking. For three days the city would be delivered up to their men, to do with as they wished.

Thus began one of the most horrific and disgraceful scenes in Crusader history. An orgy of obscenity was unleashed. Blind-drunk soldiers staggered round the streets, terrorising the citizens. They helped themselves to whatever they desired, drink, treasure, women. Young nuns were raped in their convents, women struck down with their children. The material destruction was horrendous and often sacrilegious. The body of the Emperor Justinian was stripped of its funeral jewellery. Churches were ransacked and despoiled of their treasures. The final indignity for the city occurred when the doors of St Sophia itself were hacked off and stripped of the gold and silver that gilded them. Some more fortunate examples of the rich heritage of Constantinople were pilfered by the appreciative Venetians, but the heritage of millennia was otherwise destroyed by the uneducated and uncaring Franks. A chronicler who was present, Villehardouin, stated that such booty 'had never been obtained in any city since the world began'. It was an awful act, without provocation, without purpose, without pity. One of Christendom's greatest and most noble cities was raped by a Christian army. It was an abhorrent disfiguration of everything that the Crusades were supposed to stand for.

After three days, order was restored. The Crusading ethic had taken a sinister lurch. Innocent himself was profoundly shocked when he heard the details of what had happened. In bemused tones, he asked 'how is the Greek Church, so afflicted and persecuted, to return to ecclesiastical union . . . when she sees in the

Latins only an example of perdition and the works of darkness?'. However, he would in time come to appreciate the potential for power that was offered him. Within a decade, he would use this change in direction to obtain his own unscrupulous ends. It was Innocent who launched the Crusade against the Albigensians, an event that helped to legitimise the killing of other Christians.

The Franks proceeded to carve up the Byzantine Empire. They appointed as their leader Baldwin of Flanders. But they could not hold onto their gains for long. They were heavily defeated by the Bulgarians, and Baldwin was captured and died in captivity. The deposed Byzantines set up a rival empire, based around Nicaea. The dynasty would eventually retake Constantinople in sixty years' time. The only long-term gains for the Franks were a duchy in Athens and a principality in the Morea. The share of the spoils even then caused controversy, the rich apparently making themselves much richer and not letting the poorer Franks share proportionately in the spoils. Robert of Clari stated that 'the very men who should have guarded the treasures seized the golden jewels, and anything they wished for . . . there was nothing for the poor knights, nor for the soldiers who helped to win it'.

There were inevitably winners and losers from the capture of the city. Venice greatly strengthened its position, taking several important Aegean ports and the island of Crete. The Muslims were also helped by the squalid infighting and would take advantage of it. On the other hand, it was obviously a hammer blow for the Byzantines. Resilient to the end, they would claw their way back from the brink but would exert themselves so much in doing so that they would die of exhaustion. The greatest losers of all, though, were the peoples of Eastern and Central Europe. Without Byzantium as a buffer they would be defenceless when the Ottoman Turks finally took the city three hundred years later, going on to reach the heart of Europe. To blame this on the Franks would be a gross exaggeration but their attitude towards Byzantium did nothing to protect Christendom.

Nor did the Crusade's actions bring anything but harm to the Franks in Outremer. They were initially delighted to hear that the city had fallen, believing that the news would terrify the Muslims. However, their belief that the vast resources of the empire would be diverted to help them was naïve and wrong-headed. In reality, the resources of the Empire had been overutilised in keeping Byzantium alive. An unforeseen consequence of the capture of the city was that many Franks took land in Greece, diverting many who might otherwise have journeyed to Outremer. Allied to other factors, this meant that the shortage of manpower in Outremer now reached crisis proportions.

Throughout Western Europe, the news was mostly greeted with rejoicing. Even Innocent III was initially congratulatory. It was not until full details of the pillaging of the city reached him he was moved to great anger. He sent a ferocious letter to the Franks in Constantinople, itemising the crimes that had been relayed to him and castigating their perpetrators. He heard how a prostitute had sat on the throne of the Patriarch and sang bawdy songs. He learned with horror that his own legate had absolved the Crusaders from their vows to travel to the Holy Land. He appeared to be deeply shocked by the full enormity of what the Crusaders had done.

Yet Innocent was an expedient man. He had been troubled by a sect of heretics in southern France known as the Cathars. Among other heresies, they proclaimed the Pope Anti-Christ. Such open defiance of Papal authority would not be tolerated and the Pope had a readily available solution. He would summon a Crusade, not against Muslims but against heretic Christians. Every Crusader would receive the full range of spiritual benefits available to those journeying to Outremer. Why should a man make the dangerous trip across the Mediterranean when he could achieve as much in Provence? Many Christians were delighted to support Innocent in his Crusade against people whom they too regarded as heretics.

When this Crusade set out in 1209, it was led by a Cistercian monk, Arnald-Amalric. Its first port of call was the city of Beziers. The citizens would not open the gates. Anxiously, the soldiers given the task of storming the city asked how they would recognise those who were heretics and those who were not. Even now, centuries later, the answer that this man of God gave has not lost its capacity to shock and is among the most chilling in history: 'kill them all, God will recognise his own'. And when the city fell, they did, including the huge congregation of women and children attending mass in the Roman Catholic church. Others took up the mantle of Arnald-Amalric in the Crusade that followed, especially Simon de Montfort who persecuted the Cathars mercilessly. To such depths had the Crusading ethic sunk.

The 'facts' behind the taking of Constantinople are among the most hotly debated in Medieval history, even today. Schools of thought have tended to divide

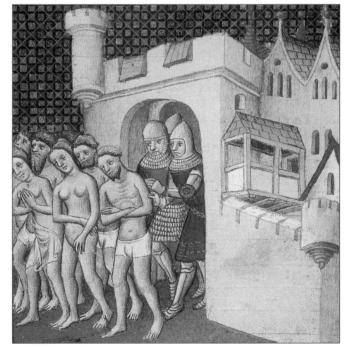

Expelling Cathar heretics from Carcasonne. (Cott Nero E II pt2 f. 20v The expulsion of the Albigensians from Carcasonne: Catharist heretics of the 12th and 13th centuries, from 'The Chronicles of France, from Priam King of Troy until the crowning of Charles VI', by the Boucicaut Master and Workshop, Chronicles of France, 1388; British Library, London/Bridgeman Art Library, London/New York)

into two camps; those who believe that the taking of Constantinople was a cleverly conceived conspiracy and those who argue that it happened as the result of a series of accidents. The debates behind the motivations of each party involved, particularly the Venetians, the Germans and the body of the Crusade, have raged literally for centuries.

But one fact is indisputable. The idealism of the Crusades was always suspect and, from the very earliest days of the movement, there are many examples of how it became a demonic and warped distortion of the Christianity from which it claimed to stem. But this distortion found its most blatant and hideous expression when Constantinople, a Christian city with a magnificent heritage, was plundered of its treasures and its heart. At times like this, Christ Himself must have watched in sorrowful bewilderment at the acts that were committed in His name.

CHAPTER 22

Debacle on the Nile

Outremer did not benefit from the Fourth Crusade at all. It remained a pale shadow of what it had once been. However, in this lay its salvation. The emaciated kingdom posed so little threat to the Muslims that they left it in peace. If they were to attack, they chanced creating the impetus for another Crusade. On the other hand, the small enclave presented good economic opportunities, which al-Adil was happy to exploit.

When Amalric died, his heir, Maria, was too young to rule. When she became Queen in her own right in 1208, after a short regency, it was important that a husband was found for her. A delegation was sent to Europe to find an appropriate spouse. However, the proposition was no longer attractive to many of the eligible men of the West and it took two years to find a suitable match. Even then, he appeared a poor catch. He was John of Brienne, a penniless knight recently embroiled in scandal, and sixty years of age. Nevertheless, he was considered an intelligent statesman, and a brave man. To make him appear more acceptable, both King Philip of France and Pope Innocent made generous gifts to him. The barons accepted him and he arrived in Acre on 13 September 1210, to be married the next day to the young Queen Maria.

John guided the realm along the road to relative recovery. He worked well with the Military Orders, who came to respect his wisdom and skill. He continued the policy of appeasement towards al-Adil, and a truce with the Muslims was confirmed. However, this was merely a front, for he had sent letters to Innocent asking that another expedition could be readied to arrive in Outremer when the truce expired. In 1212 Maria died after giving birth to a daughter, Yolande. This was disconcerting for John, who only ruled because of his marriage. Maria's death considerably weakened his position.

John's appeals for aid from the West did not go unheeded but the

John of Brienne arriving in Acre. (MS espagnol 30, f. 4–5)

first group to respond was unlikely to help reconquer any lost territories. It was composed of children and its story, though irrelevant to the struggle in the East, provides one of the most tragic tales of the Crusading movement, as well as giving an insight into the gullibility and literal beliefs of the Medieval mind.

In fact, several groups of children were involved. The first was from France, and had been motivated by a shepherd-boy named Stephen. He appeared at the court of King Philip and began to preach a Crusade. Philip, unsurprisingly, was not convinced at the efficacy of his preaching and bade the boy, who is thought to have been about twelve years of age, return to his flocks. However, Stephen would not be so easily dissuaded. He was an extremely persuasive orator, without any inhibitions. He continued his efforts outside the gates of St Denis, France's holiest church. He cajoled his listeners to follow him to the East. If his listeners truly had faith, he said, they need not worry about transport because the very seas would dry up in their path. Many were impressed and he attracted a large following, particularly among people of his own age. He led his entourage to the port of Marseilles, to the edge of the sea, where he waited for the waves to retreat meekly before him.

Of course, no such thing happened and his dream was shown to be but a mirage. Many of his followers gave up and turned back – they were surely the lucky ones. Those who remained persuaded the captains of various ships in the harbour to give them transport. Some of the vessels were subsequently wrecked, and most on board were lost. The rest dropped anchor when they were surrounded by Muslim privateers. The generous sea captains had, it transpired, been in league with the Muslims. The pathetic remnant of the misguided expedition was shipped across to the slave markets of Algeria, their fate a mystery until twenty years later when a survivor, who had somehow ended up in Egypt, returned to the West.

Despite this tragic outcome, Stephen's example was emulated. In Germany, a juvenile named Nicholas appeared at the Cathedral of Cologne, and began to preach. However, his approach was markedly different. While the French army planned to conquer the heathen, Nicholas proposed to convert them. A huge host joined him and set off towards Italy. Two contingents were formed. One, under Nicholas, crossed the Alps, undergoing a truly horrendous ordeal. An enormous number died before they reached Genoa. Here, after some initial scepticism, the Genoese felt pity for the children, inviting them to stay. Similar attempts to force the sea to retreat were made by this group, also with predictable failure, after which many of the children decided to stay in Genoa. A small group continued to Pisa. Nicholas himself travelled to Rome, to meet Innocent. The Pope was nothing if not a pragmatist and much as he admired Nicholas' courage he knew no good could come of it. He told him to go home.

The second party was no more successful. It travelled across Switzerland and down the eastern coast of Italy to Brindisi. Some of its number may even have obtained passage from here to Palestine but many, by now disillusioned, set off towards home. Most of them never saw their parents again. They in turn blamed Nicholas' father for giving him grandiose ideas and strung him up in revenge.

It was not through misguided ventures like this that help could come. Innocent ordered his legate, Robert of Courcon, to travel through France, breathing life into the campaign for recruitment. Unfortunately, he attracted a motley assortment of thieves, lepers, prostitutes and old men and women. Letters of complaint were sent to Innocent by the French authorities, and he was forced to restrain Robert.

Innocent sensed that an injection of energy was needed to give the Crusade impetus. He summoned a council, at which he urged many of the leading men in Western Europe to commit themselves to the project. He was a convincing speaker, and succeeded in rekindling enthusiasm. Indulgences were confirmed for all those who took part and financial assistance was organised. A methodical man and a thorough organiser, Innocent ensured that the enterprise would not rely on faith alone. Preachers were despatched throughout Western Europe to generate support. Transcripts of Papal proclamations were posted in the cathedrals and churches of France, Italy, England and any other country owing nominal spiritual allegiance to the Papacy.

Innocent was also a realist. There would be no attempt to mount a joint expedition between the Germans and the French. The national rivalries dividing these countries were too great for such a coalition to be workable. However, he felt confident enough to write to al-Adil, telling him that a great army was on its way and suggesting that it might be better if the Sultan were to surrender gracefully the Christian lands he held.

However, there were powers that even Pope Innocent could not resist. At Perugia, in May 1216, he was taken ill. The intercessions of his priests on his behalf were to no avail, and he died on 16 July. He had been every bit a man of his time, ruthless, resourceful, energetic, persistent. He had undoubtedly been the driving force behind the Crusade. It would be difficult to find an equally charismatic leader to fill the void that his passing had created.

Now an old cardinal, Savelli, was elected Pope and took the name of Honorius III. Preparations for the Crusade continued but with disappointing results. A pitiful contribution came from Scandinavia and a small party from Ireland made its way directly to Palestine. John of Brienne must have been distinctly uncomfortable, knowing that Innocent's strident rhetoric to al-Adil was not being backed up with material resources. The most significant response came from King Andrew of Hungary, an obsessive collector of religious miscellanea and relics. Although it appears incongruous that he should be helping this Crusade when one of his cities, Zara, had been sacked by the Fourth Crusade, he had an ulterior motive. His queen was related to the Latin ruler of Constantinople, who was childless, and he wished to stake a claim to the inheritance.

There were also forces led by Duke Leopold of Austria and King Hugh of Cyprus, individually not large but enough to make a useful contribution if they worked together. Al-Adil sent men to monitor these troops when they arrived in the East but these forces withdrew quickly when they saw that the Christians outnumbered them. However, the Christian armies were beset by age-old problems. Each individual contingent would only obey the orders of its own commander and only a few minor towns were taken. King Andrew added a few relics of doubtful pedigree to his collection before returning home, the Cypriots left when their King died and that was that. The enterprise petered out.

However, this was a mere precursor to the main expedition, which would indeed target Egypt. A large Frisian fleet arrived in Outremer in April 1218 with the comforting news that a sizeable French force was waiting to sail from Italy. John of Brienne fell in with the plan to invade Egypt, the fall of which, it was widely believed, would be the prelude to the recapture of Palestine. Al-Adil was slow to recognise the threat, possibly complacent after the long period of tranquillity that the region had enjoyed. Perhaps he was lethargic because the expedition of Andrew of Hungary had achieved so little. His response to rumours of the army that was supposedly on its way was at best insipid.

The Franks in Outremer left Acre on 24 May 1218, on board the Frisian ships. They put in at Athlit to stock up with provisions. Here they found the most magnificent example of military architecture ever erected by the Franks. The castle of Athlit was a masterpiece. Built on a promontory jutting into the sea, it was separated from the mainland by a ditch that could, if required, be flooded. The vast area enclosed within its walls meant that ample supplies could be stored, and plenty of fresh water was available. The outer wall was 20 feet thick and 50 feet high, nearly twice as high as its more famous contemporary at Krak des Chevaliers. When it was under siege two years later 4,000 people would find shelter within its walls. At the present time, it may have seemed apposite that the fleet anchored in the shadow of what could be construed as a symbol of the virility of Outremer's revival. However, this is incongruous. The castle did have offensive aspects but Athlit had the appearance of a place of last resort, a citadel within which a defiant last stand could be made. Its very existence was in stark contrast to the offensive, expansionist attitudes that had once driven the kingdom.

Nevertheless, Egypt was completely off guard when a small number of Christian ships arrived off the port of Damietta. After waiting in vain for the rest of the force to arrive, the men on board decided to put ashore. They landed on the west bank of the Nile, and quickly sighted a fleet on the horizon, carrying King John of Outremer, Duke Leopold of Austria and the Masters of all the Military Orders, who had arrived from Athlit.

The town of Damietta was some 2 miles upstream. As was the case in 1169, when the Crusaders had previously attacked it, a co-ordinated land and naval attack was vital if the town were to fall. The river approaches to the town were protected by a large chain, stretched across from the east bank to a tower close to the west bank. This tower would be the target of the first assault. It did not fall when the attack was launched, and it became apparent that a degree of initiative would be necessary to take it. The Crusaders came up with an engineering solution, a siege tower that floated, supported by two ships. From this, the attackers could launch a sweeping enfilade from the top storey down onto the defenders, and troops could cross from the tower to the battlements across planks carried for the purpose.

The idea seemed sound, and the tower was built. It was covered with leather to improve its defences. Scaling ladders were attached, and it was launched into action on 24 August 1218. The fight was fierce, with the defenders battling desperately. After twenty-four hours their efforts slackened, and it became clear

The castle at Athlit (above), and the western walls of the upper fortress at Krak des Chevaliers (below).

that only a few of them survived. These surrendered and the Franks took possession of the tower. They were staggered at the extent of the booty inside, but unfortunately this distracted them. The Crusade began to lose direction; the Frisians decided that they had done enough and wanted to return home, while others argued that the army should do no more until the main force, which had still not arrived from Italy, joined them.

As a result, Damietta was temporarily reprieved. An army was already on its way from Syria to remove the interlopers. However, in the interim the Muslim world had been dealt a shattering blow. Worn out by internal family plots and exhausted by a lifetime of intrigue, al-Adil expired. He lacked the chivalrous traits of his brother but he was, by any standard, a successful man and a capable leader. With him died the immediate chance of lasting Muslim unity. The news would give the Crusaders heart, as would confirmation that reinforcements from Europe were at last on their way.

It was the fate of this new expedition to be led by a vain, bombastic Spanish cardinal named Pelagius. Haughty to the point of arrogance and incapable of accepting anyone's opinion other than his own, his appointment was to prove disastrous. He had already caused difficulties when he had previously been tasked with bringing the Eastern and Western Churches closer together, his patronising attitudes widening rather than narrowing the gap. As soon as he arrived, he attempted to assert his authority over the effective secular leader of the Crusade, John of Brienne.

If he had shown some degree of skill and judgement, then this may have been acceptable. However, he did not. Legally, King John was in a weak constitutional position now that he was a widower, but he was an experienced and competent leader who knew the ways of the Levant. He should have been treated with diplomacy and tact but instead he was ignored. The Cardinal seriously underestimated the ability of the King. This was shown when John energetically responded to a Muslim counter-attack on the Christian's camp, which was consequently driven back.

Following this attack, in October 1218, the camp was assailed by a series of natural disasters that were far more effective than any assault by the Muslims. The death of al-Adil had postponed the arrival of the troops from Damascus but in truth they were not needed. In November, a ferocious gale whipped the waves of the sea over the low-lying lands and water flooded the Christian camp, drowning many horses. Several ships were wrecked. The troops were soaked and demoralised, and the camp was filled with the stench of rotting fish that the floodwaters had deposited. The floods were followed by an epidemic, the greatest enemy of the Franks in the East. Men's skin turned black and the troops began to drop by the score. Before it had run its course, disease would claim the lives of one in six of the besiegers.

Some at least saw a divine hand in all of this. James of Vitry wrote that:

> during that winter season . . . it did not please divine providence that we should cross the river without our souls profiting in many ways. For the Lord sent down a sickness that no doctor's skill could cure, a contagious disease with no

natural causes, divinely sent down on a great part of our army either to cleanse us from our sins or so that we should be more deserving of the crown.

Seeing that the army was demoralised by these setbacks, in a rare moment of perception Pelagius decided that the troops needed action to restore their flagging spirits. He directed the army to attack the suburbs of Damietta. Sadly for the Christians, God still did not appear to be on their side, and a torrential downpour forced them to retreat. But their disappointment was transformed to joy when news reached them that the Egyptians had abandoned the suburbs. A palace plot in Cairo had forced the leader of Egypt, al-Kamil, to withdraw all available troops to the capital. This effectively left Damietta completely surrounded and in real danger. When al-Kamil, having put down the plot, returned to eject the Franks, he could not budge them. But the garrison in the city had plenty of food and the defences were still strong. Stalemate ensued and after the horrors of the awful winter, a scorching summer of searing heat followed.

Nevertheless, the Muslims were greatly alarmed by the presence of the Franks. There was talk of surrendering Jerusalem to them, and work commenced on dismantling its walls, much to the consternation of the inhabitants. But such talk was premature. The Crusaders were demoralised. Exposed to climactic extremes, and afraid to attack, they became bored and morale plummeted. Leopold of Austria decided that he could take no more and resolved to leave. Devoid of any leadership, the troops took matters into their own hands and launched a heavy attack on the Muslims. The enemy retreated before them but, in time-honoured fashion, it was a trap and when the right moment arrived the Muslims turned on the Franks. Panic ensued and it was only through the discipline of King John and the Military Orders that catastrophe was averted.

A brief moment of relief occurred with the arrival in the Christian camp of St Francis of Assisi. Although the Church did not yet recognise him for the great man that he was to become, his arrival was nevertheless a point of note for some chroniclers. Born into a rich family, he rejected wealth and lived an ascetic life. He courted poverty and welcomed deprivation. He also had pacifist tendencies and, distressed by the constant warfare in the East, had journeyed to Egypt to seek to bring the fighting to an end. He was granted an audience with the Muslims but they could not understand him. Surrounded by luxury, they could not comprehend why this supposedly important man was dressed in rags and positively filthy. However, al-Kamil listened kindly to him; he desired peace himself anyway because there was a danger of famine in Egypt. Perhaps he also thought that this strange man was touched with madness, a perception not helped when he offered to prove his faith by the horrific ordeal of trial by fire. Not long after the meeting, a Christian prisoner was released and sent to offer the Franks a truce.

This the Franks accepted. They were further surprised when al-Kamil offered them an extraordinary deal. If the Franks would leave Egypt, they could have Jerusalem, Bethlehem and Nazareth in exchange. For a variety of reasons, most of the Crusaders would not agree. Pelagius simply thought it demeaning to bargain with the Infidel. The Military Orders did not approve because Jerusalem was indefensible without its now dismantled walls, and it would be impossible to hold without the buffer zone of Oultrejourdain. The Italian members of the Crusade would not agree because of the great wealth inside Damietta, from which they were hoping to profit. The Christians were completely disunited in their reasoning but the ultimate conclusion was the same from all angles – there would be no deal.

The Crusaders probably did not know how desperate Damietta now was. Without a realistic hope of relief, it could not hold out forever. On 4 November a small Frankish scouting party set out to inspect the perimeter of the city. They were startled to find the walls unmanned. The next day, the Christians gathered in force to attack. They were virtually unopposed. When they broke into the city, they discovered that almost the entire garrison was sick. Ironically, the city still had a large stock of food and water but had been overcome by disease. The Franks came across a scene direct from Dante. Most of the sick were too ill to bury those who had already died, and corpses lay rotting where they had expired. Some of the leading citizens were held as hostages and the rest of the inhabitants were taken away into slavery.

Now that this first objective had been taken, it was inevitable that the Franks would fall out among themselves. There was a predictable power struggle to decide who should rule the city. Pelagius, naturally, felt that it was his but King John disagreed. John was supported by the Military Orders in his claim and Pelagius backed down, agreeing that John should rule the city, at least until the arrival of Emperor Frederick of Germany, who was supposedly travelling to the East.

This squabbling was followed by a period of inaction. King John returned to Palestine to argue his case in a dynastic dispute involving the throne of Armenia. He had inherited the claim through his second marriage to an Armenian princess, Stephanie. On his return, she died in suspicious circumstances. There were rumours that John had beaten her violently when he found out that she had been ill-treating her stepdaughter. Her death was followed by that of her young son a few days later. This effectively deprived John of all claims to the throne of Armenia but he did not return to Egypt anyway.

For a whole year, the Franks stayed where they were. Dissension was rife and many deserted the army to return to Europe. Al-Kamil recovered his confidence but the spirits of Pelagius were boosted by good news. The Pope sent to tell him that the German Emperor, Frederick, had just been crowned by the Pope himself, and he was now definitely due to set out for Egypt within a few months. Several other German forces made their way east in advance of the Emperor. However, time passed and there was still no sign of Frederick's arrival. The Emperor was apparently a reluctant pilgrim. In his absence, Pelagius decided that he must advance against the Egyptian army.

However, the army was reluctant to go onto the offensive unless King John returned. Pelagius grudgingly acquiesced to these feelings. When he subsequently arrived, John was perturbed. An advance on Cairo had to be carefully timed to avoid the annual inundation, which was not far away. But John was a proud man, and he would not stand accused of cowardice. Therefore, he acceded to the persuasive powers of Pelagius. The Muslims came out to meet the advancing Christians but were alarmed at their number. The chroniclers assert that there were 630 ships as well as 50,000 fighting men. Even allowing for their inevitable hyperbole, this must have been a very large force indeed.

They set out in August 1220, advancing for 15 miles but John advised that they should stop. The inundation was now imminent and there were disturbing reports that an army was coming up from Syria, which could attack the Christians from the rear. Pelagius would not be diverted and insisted that the army should push on. The Crusaders marched past a ditch, not realising that when the flood came it would turn into a canal. To add to their predicament, a large Muslim force slipped behind them. And then the inundation finally arrived. The canal filled up, and an Egyptian fleet was able to move along it and cut off the Christian vessels down river. The awful reality of the situation was slow to dawn on Pelagius but it gradually became dreadfully apparent that he was surrounded. Suddenly, his sublime confidence changed to panic. The Duke of Bavaria urged retreat. Shocked, Pelagius realised that he had no alternative.

From here on, matters got progressively worse. The common soldiers could not bear to leave the stores abandoned so they consumed vast quantities of wine. Within a short space of time, a significant proportion of the army was so inebriated that they could not walk, let alone fight. Then a party of Teutonic Knights decided to burn their provisions rather than abandon them to the Muslims. It was a clear message to the enemy that a retreat was underway. They capitalised on their advantage by opening the sluice gates and flooding the land. A few ships managed to escape, including one with the shattered Cardinal on board. His escape did little to help his army, as his ship had all the medical supplies in its hold. For the rest, there was no escape and no option save surrender.

The Cardinal belatedly realised the hopelessness of his situation. Blinded by supreme self-belief, he had in fact been outwitted and outfought. To fight on would only lead to the loss of thousands of lives in a lost cause. Humiliated, he sued for peace. Although the Franks still held Damietta, the Muslims held the whip hand and al-Kamil knew it. He insisted on the surrender of Damietta and an eight-year truce. He would, in return, hand back the fragment of the True Cross that was in his possession. However, when the time came to do this, the piece could not be found. It was so unimportant to the Muslims that it had been mislaid. Nothing could be more symbolic or appropriate.

And so the Fifth Crusade ended in defeat and humiliation. At one stage close to success, the Franks had failed once again to achieve anything because of their disunity. If any Crusade were to succeed, it must have a strong and unified leadership. Pelagius was clearly not the man to provide this, lacking tactical awareness or the ability to motivate men. It was also essential that Crusaders who arrived from the West listened to those with local knowledge. If they had done so, then the disastrous march on Cairo when the flood was imminent might never have happened.

Despair and anxiety had replaced hope and expectation. And there was now great danger for the Franks. A new characteristic had infiltrated the psyche of the West, and it would find a permanent habitation there. Its name was apathy. Many

West European leaders were now asking if there was any point in committing resources to these expeditions when so little could be gained from them for so much effort. Besides the futility of it all, there were now easier pickings much closer to home.

An earlier Christian had written that the three greatest gifts were faith, hope and love. There had been precious little love lost between the varying different Christian factions involved in the Crusades since they started, so the dissension between the leaders of the Fifth Crusade could hardly be wondered at. Sadly, it now appeared that faith and hope had gone as well.

CHAPTER 23

The Heretic Emperor

Inevitably the drama of events in the Delta attracted attention away from what was happening in the northern Christian states in the Levant. However, it would be erroneous to think that little was changing there. Antioch especially went through a period of startling upheavals. There had been a vicious succession dispute between the Armenians and the Norman faction in the city. A bitter civil war ensued in which, eventually, the second son of Bohemond III defeated the Armenians and became Bohemond IV. The Armenian claimant to Antioch, Raymond Roupen, was captured and taken into custody where, predictably, he died a few months later, leaving Bohemond the undisputed ruler.

But the enmity created by the conflict left an indelible mark. The Templars had sided with Bohemond while the Hospitallers supported the Armenian cause. Bohemond ejected the Hospitallers forcibly from Antioch in revenge. Pelagius attempted to placate both factions; a dispute over the ownership of Jabala led to him suggesting that the Templars and Hospitallers should take half each. Bohemond would have none of this and Pelagius used his ultimate weapon, that of excommunication, against him. But Bohemond did not care. The Templars still supported him and he was, for the time being, secure. He further strengthened his position by arranging for his son Philip to marry the Queen of Armenia. As part of the arrangements, Philip was to accept the supremacy of the now restored Armenian Church, a suggestion that posed him no moral dilemmas.

However, the arrangement was not a success. Philip still lived like a Latin lord in his new realm and alienated many of the Armenians. They attempted to change his ways by persuasion but when this failed, they seized and imprisoned him. He was subsequently poisoned. Bohemond was powerless to avenge him, having lost the support of many of the Latins because of his excommunication. The Hospitallers sided with the Armenians, further limiting his ability to return the insult.

In the meantime, King John realised that he was living on borrowed time. He was in his seventies but his daughter, Yolande, was only eleven. He felt that it was high time to arrange a suitable husband for her and he travelled to Europe to find one, accompanied by Pelagius. He met the Pope, who agreed that all further conquests of any Crusade should be given to the Kingdom of Jerusalem. From here, he journeyed on to France, where he met King Philip. And then, the Master of the Teutonic Order, Hermann of Salza, made an intriguing suggestion. The wife of the Emperor Frederick had died a few months before, making him an eligible bachelor again. Why not marry him to Yolande?

It was a fascinating idea. Traditionally, consorts for the rulers of Outremer came from France but the proposed match offered many advantages. Frederick was already the nominal overlord of Cyprus and uniting the island with mainland Outremer would provide more stability. He was also one of the strongest men in Western Europe, with a huge pool of resources available to him, in terms of both men and money. King Philip was not happy with the suggestion and told John so, but this obstacle was conveniently eliminated when Philip died soon after. In his will, he left a large sum to John, which was gratefully accepted.

Without a doubt, Frederick was one of the most fascinating characters of his day. He was all-powerful within his Empire but he was certainly not unique among the rulers of Europe in this. What made him interesting were the idiosyncrasies of the way that he lived. He spoke six languages fluently and had studied most of the major religions of the world. Despite this, he was famed for his immorality. He could be cruel and ruthless; in summary a complex personality in the extreme. Even his pedigree was not straightforward. He was part German, part Norman but was brought up in the island of Sicily, which was part Greek, part Arab. Given the complications of his upbringing, he could have developed in one of two ways. He could either have become a man who understood all cultures, and was therefore able to make a positive impression on a vast array of men, or he could develop into someone who was uncertain of his roots, and consequently who found it difficult to communicate with others. Sadly, it appeared that Frederick belonged to the latter category.

The match was agreed to and eventually solemnised in Brindisi on 9 November 1225, after a previous ceremony when the marriage had taken place by proxy. Frederick was quick to display his true colours. He left the wedding banquet with his wife without telling his new father-in-law. When John of Brienne caught up with him next day, it was apparent that Yolande had been crying. The reason was quickly ascertained – Frederick had spent his wedding night seducing one of Yolande's maids. John berated the Emperor but was summarily dismissed. Frederick was in command now. The Master of the Teutonic Knights had promised John that he would remain as Regent but the Emperor was quick to repudiate this arrangement, saying that he had not been party to it. John was effectively dismissed from office, a disgraceful end to a career that had done much to stabilise the situation in Outremer. His grief must have been greatly increased when, within a few years, Yolande died at seventeen after giving birth to a son, Conrad. It was a tragic end to a young life but Frederick showed little in the way of grief.

It was important that he now made his way east. For years Frederick had been making empty promises about going on Crusade but these had not as yet been fulfilled. For the sake of his credibility, he could delay no longer. His marriage negotiations had spanned several years and this had given him a reason to stay in Europe. The situation changed in 1227 when Pope Honorius died. The new Pontiff, Gregory IX, came from an altogether different stock than his slightly timid predecessor. In many ways he was similar to Innocent III, a man convinced in the right of the Papacy to absolute power, demanding unquestioning allegiance from all men, be they king or commoner. He would tolerate no further delay from Frederick.

Frederick assembled an army and took it to Brindisi. His position had been undermined by the death of the poorly used Yolande, as he only had a claim to be King of Jerusalem through her. He now had to hope that the barons of Outremer would let him be Regent for his infant son. The fleet set sail but soon turned back when illness took hold of the ship on which the Emperor travelled. One of his closest friends was already dying and Frederick himself was ill. He therefore decided to return to the mainland to convalesce. Messengers were despatched to Rome to tell Gregory of this. He did not believe them. Frederick had procrastinated so much over the years – in fact, he had been talking of leading a Crusade for over a decade – that his illness at this time seemed slightly too convenient. Gregory's response to Frederick's request for time to recuperate was instant, decisive and blunt. He immediately excommunicated the Emperor.

Perhaps Gregory was sketching out the limits of his authority. The fact that several of Frederick's friends died suggests that, on this occasion at least, there was just cause for the Emperor's delay. However, Frederick's past record had caught up with him. He had been quick to see the potential kudos that a Crusade offered him but slow to provide concrete support to the movement. In any event, he responded in, for him, typical fashion by ignoring the excommunication. He claimed that Gregory had exceeded his powers and sent a circular around Europe justifying his actions. For his part, Gregory made clear that if Frederick were to go on Crusade without the excommunication being lifted then that would only make matters far worse than they already were. The two men were effectively locked in a power struggle, Gregory wanting to assert the supremacy of the Papacy over all men, and Frederick refusing to compromise his royal authority. Frederick would not acquiesce and set sail regardless on 28 June 1228.

He first stopped in Cyprus, where he was titular suzerain. It is probable that when the Cypriots first asked for support from Germany, they anticipated that it would be an arms-length experience. However, they were now about to experience the negative side of the arrangement. Frederick believed that he could merely land on the island, and instantly assume control. At that time, Cyprus had a child king, Henry I. A baron from Outremer, John of Ibelin, was acting as Regent until Henry was old enough to rule. He was a man of great determination, and was widely experienced. Unusually for the time, he was also highly principled. On the whole, his appointment had been a popular one.

Frederick landed on Cyprus on 21 July 1228. He was not without friends on the island, who advised him to depose John of Ibelin as soon as he could. Frederick accordingly set out to trap him by inviting him to a feast. John's friends, aware of the Emperor's cupidity, advised him not to go but John would not listen, feeling it discourteous to refuse. However, given his knowledge of the world, it is unlikely that he trusted the Emperor completely. The initial welcome he received on arrival was warm enough but surreptitiously Frederick's men locked the doors so that none could depart. Then, as innocuously as possible, armed men entered the hall and positioned themselves close to the guests.

At a given signal, the pretence was dropped. In an instant, the armed men confronted the guests. Frederick demanded of John that all the revenues of Cyprus should be given to him and also that John should hand over the city of

Beirut on the mainland, which was held by him. It was a dramatic moment, the bullying king, backed by the resources of an empire, dictating terms to the wise regent.

To be fair, Frederick had some talents. However, it seems that judgement of men was not one of them. If he expected John humbly to capitulate, he was seriously disappointed. Proudly and defiantly, oblivious to the sword-points so close to him, John faced the autocrat without fear. Cyprus already had a king, and John acted as regent for him. All the monies of the island could be accounted for. As for Beirut, it was John's by right. He had refortified the city, which had been undefended, at his own expense and he owed no allegiance to Frederick for it. With the death of Yolande, Frederick was no longer ruler of Outremer. Frederick's bluff had been called. He did not have enough men to take the island by force, and he therefore softened his tone. He demanded hostages of John and told him that he must accompany him to the mainland. John agreed to accept Frederick as Regent, but not King, of Jerusalem, and the rift was superficially healed. Few can have believed that this was the last of the matter.

Frederick summoned other barons from the mainland to join him. Balian of Sidon and Bohemond of Antioch responded to his call. Their forces gave Frederick the opportunity of taking the island by force, and he openly declared hostilities against John of Ibelin. Because of the size of Frederick's force, John backed down. It was agreed that Henry would pay homage to Frederick and in return the Emperor would release all the hostages that he held. However, the other barons were already seeing through Frederick's duplicity. Suspecting that he would be the next to lose his position, Bohemond feigned illness and returned to the mainland, narrowly escaping the fate he rightly feared.

Frederick followed close behind him. However, his high-handed behaviour with John of Ibelin had alienated many of the local barons. John had been active in protecting his rights, first of all making sure that the defences of Beirut were in order, then going to Acre to argue his case before the High Court of Outremer. News of the Emperor's excommunication had reached the kingdom and both the Hospitallers and the Templars would not help him. Frederick's army was not large, and only the Teutonic Knights, a relatively small order, would give him assistance. And worse news was to reach him from Italy. Gregory was no faint-hearted prelate who would stand meekly by while his authority was ignored. Even now, a large army was poised on the borders of Frederick's lands in Italy. At its head was the disenfranchised John of Brienne, for whom the prospect of revenge must have been sweet indeed.

Again, caveats need to be made about the documentary evidence that describes the situation in Outremer at this time. Many of the chroniclers were supporters of the Ibelins, and their objectivity must therefore be in question. However, Frederick's aggressive attitudes on the European mainland suggest that he was a man who liked to have his own way, and the events described in these chronicles do not, at least, appear to be out of character.

Short of military muscle, Frederick was forced to embrace diplomacy if he wished to be successful in Outremer. Even before he had left for the East, he had been in discussions with al-Kamil in Egypt. Al-Kamil's brothers, al-Mu'azzam in

Damascus and al-Ashraf in Mesopotamia, had been causing trouble. When al-Mu'azzam entered into discussions with the Khwarismians, a warlike Muslim people from the East who had been powerful enough to fight off the Mongols, he became very concerned indeed. He was therefore receptive to the approaches of Frederick, who had offered to help al-Kamil provided that in return he was given the city of Jerusalem – although, as it belonged to al-Mu'azzam, it was not really al-Kamil's to give.

Al-Kamil harangued Frederick persistently to set sail as much as a succession of Popes had. However, his views changed when al-Mu'azzam died, to be replaced by a young and untried ruler, an-Nasir. Al-Kamil no longer felt threatened and wished that Frederick had not come to the East. He had agreed to divide the lands of Damascus with al-Ashraf but it would be imprudent to leave the Christian army, small though it was, behind him at Acre. He therefore recommended discussions with Frederick. Both men appear to have been kindred spirits and developed a keen interest in each other and their respective cultures.

Despite the friendly discussions, no real progress was made until Frederick decided to force al-Kamil's hand. He led a military demonstration out of Acre. This initial bluff did not work very well, and some negotiations were needed to warm up rapidly chilling relationships. However, by February 1229 an-Nasir was still safely ensconced in Damascus and al-Kamil decided that real concessions to Frederick were now needed. By this time, al-Kamil owned much of Palestine. He had even taken Jerusalem from an-Nasir. It was agreed that the city, along with Bethlehem, Nazareth, Montfort and Toron, would be given to Frederick. However, this small territory would only have a narrow connecting strip to the sea, and would therefore be extremely vulnerable. Both parties agreed to a truce for ten years, and to the release of all prisoners.

Neither party would be commended for the deal. A Muslim chronicler, Ibn Al-Jawzi, tells us that 'when the master of Egypt decided to hand Jerusalem over to the Franj, a great storm of indignation swept all the lands of Islam'. The Franks considered that, without the strategic towns around it, Jerusalem would be indefensible. Further, the religious zealots among them were hardly enamoured of Frederick's initial moves. After his first night in the city, he was conscious that he could not hear the Muezzin calling the Muslims to prayer. He asked why, and was told that it was because the Muslims did not wish to offend him. Frederick insisted that the Muezzin be put back to work at once. He then proceeded to enter the al-Aqsa Mosque. Here, he berated a Christian priest who had followed him in for his impudence in entering a Muslim holy place. The priest was told to leave, and Frederick made clear that any other cleric who entered a mosque would be put to death.

Frederick divided up the city, allowing the Muslims to retain the al-Aqsa Mosque. This alienated the Templars, who traditionally had their base there. The Templars and Hospitallers had been prohibited from helping the heretic Emperor but had followed him at a safe distance. Any lingering, tacit thoughts they may have had of assisting him were gone now. Frederick also openly mocked the Christian religion. This angered the Christians, naturally enough, but did not endear him to the Muslims either, who did not like insincerity in matters of religion.

Frederick was crowned in the Holy Sepulchre on 18 March 1229, but it was an empty ceremony. Only the Teutonic Knights attended and no priest was present. The Master of the Teutonic Knights, in his speech during the ceremony, implied that it was time for the Christian world to forgive Frederick. If anyone believed that this would really happen, they were soon disabused of the idea. The Archbishop of Caesarea arrived outside the city and hurled insults at the Emperor, reaffirming his excommunication.

For Frederick, this was the last straw. He could not understand these people. He had regained the city of Jerusalem for them and yet they showed no gratitude. Just three days after entering Jerusalem, he abandoned his work on restoring the defences and led his army back to the coast to justify himself to the leaders of Outremer. His attempts to persuade them of his good intentions were met with anger. Faced with such opposition, he resorted to force. He talked of taking the Templar citadel of Athlit but his local supporters were horrified. They convinced him that its defences would take years to overcome. He then considered seizing the Master of the Templars and John of Ibelin but they were both too suspicious of him to be caught out. By now, Frederick had reached the end of his patience and resolved to stay in the East no longer. He would leave Balian of Sidon and Garnier, a local baron of German descent, as his representatives in the region.

Frederick wished to leave unobtrusively but he was not even successful in this. Word of his imminent departure on board ship from Acre leaked out. As he

The seal of Frederick II, king of Jerusalem and Sicily. (MS 16, f. 127r)

passed down the Street of Butchers in the city, he was pelted with offal. Dripping with intestines and excrement, he made his dejected way to his ships to leave far behind this strange land and its peculiar ways, which he had completely failed to understand. Within his empire he was the supreme autocrat and his word was law. Such a centralised system would not work in Outremer, where the Franks held only a few cities dispersed over a wide area. In such an environment, each town owed loyalty to its local lord. Neither did al-Kamil benefit from the affair. He had little use for Jerusalem strategically but had misread its religious significance. Many Muslims were horrified at its surrender, a reaction an-Nasir in Damascus was quick to exploit for his own advantage.

The departure of Frederick may have earned John of Ibelin some respite but the Emperor was still interested in the region. He would fight off the armies invading his lands in Italy easily enough, but his excommunication caused problems. Although he personally was not concerned at the Pope's actions, his people were and they eventually exerted enough influence to convince Frederick that he must rebuild his relationship with the Pontiff. For his part, Gregory was delighted to accept Frederick's repentance and an air of normality returned. Now that his Italian affairs were under control, the Emperor looked eastwards again. A civil war in Cyprus had ended with John of Ibelin restored as Regent. However, in 1231 Frederick despatched an army under his Marshal, Richard Filangieri, with the intention of installing the latter as governor. John would be hard to remove but Filangieri was under express instructions to ensure that he lost the Regency.

John of Ibelin knew that an army was on its way. He denuded his defences around Beirut and prepared to repulse Filangieri from Cyprus. The Marshal made contact directly with King Henry and tried to convince him that John must be replaced. However, the King would have none of this. The delegation went away disappointed, lucky to escape a lynching from the mob outside who remembered how badly they had suffered when Frederick's supporters had ruled the island for a short time during the recent civil war.

Filangieri made for Beirut, where he quickly took the city although the garrison held out. He then went on to Tyre, Sidon and finally Acre where, presenting the credentials given him by Frederick, he demanded to be made bailli in the country. To this the barons agreed. However, when he then demanded that John of Ibelin have all his lands confiscated, they refused. No case had been presented before the High Court, which was the only institution empowered to grant the Marshal's request. Filangieri was not impressed at such subtleties. He bluntly told them that the issue was not for debate; Frederick had decreed that John should lose his lands, and that was the end of the matter. Such tactics may have worked in Europe but they had no place here. Frederick had no real mandate in the country. He was no longer king and was only acting on behalf of his son. He could not enforce such unpopular decisions.

Opposition to Frederick and his representative hardened. Virtually the entire local leadership changed its stance and supported the Ibelin cause. In Acre, the merchants – who had benefited from John's sensible policies – openly declared for him. A commune was set up to rule the city, and they invited John to be their mayor. John had already set sail for the mainland to protect his interests. He had wisely insisted that Frederick's supporters in Cyprus accompany him. It was a prudent move; as soon as the army landed, one of Frederick's leading supporters, Almeric Barlais, made off to Filangieri with his men. If they had stayed on Cyprus while John was absent, they would have attempted to seize the island.

Other troops deserted too as John was en route to Beirut, and his army was therefore significantly depleted by the time that it arrived at the city. It nevertheless managed to fight its way through the streets and into the citadel. Some barons came to help him but more were interested in negotiating a compromise. The Military Orders were particularly prominent in discussions, as the lifting of the sentence of excommunication of Frederick meant that they could not actively oppose him. But Filangieri was stubborn and would not compromise, once again misreading the situation. More men supported John as a result and Tyre came over to his side. However, when he approached Bohemond of Antioch for help, he was received coldly, as Bohemond wished to see who was likely to win the confrontation before apportioning his support.

However, John was not to have things all his own way. While travelling to Acre in his absence, his poorly guarded camp was overrun by Filangieri's troops and King Henry himself barely escaped. Although there were many survivors, John's army was not large and he could ill afford to lose any men. Filangieri saw this success as a chance to launch an attack on an undefended Cyprus and he sailed his army over to the island. John reacted quickly, confiscating all the ships in Acre and setting sail with what appeared to be a hopelessly small force. By the time that his fleet arrived, Filangieri was safely installed in the town of Famagusta, with a ten-to-one numerical advantage. John landed his troops near the town at night. They made up in noise what they lacked in numbers. The din that they deliberately made led the defenders to believe that the force outside the town was much larger than it actually was. In panic, Filangieri's men set fire to their own ships in the port and deserted it. John's initiative had made up for his shortage of manpower.

Buoyed by this success, John's army then set off for Nicosia. The arrogance of Filangieri had already helped the Ibelin cause. The population, who had suffered from extortion, was ill disposed towards the German cause. Filangieri's Lombard army had tried to adopt a scorched earth policy, hoping to deprive John of provisions, but their measures were incomplete and John managed to obtain supplies in Nicosia, which he duly took. The Lombards retreated before him until they reached the hills near Kyrenia, overlooking a pass at Agridi. Here they decided to stand their ground.

John suspected that battle was imminent and had his army march in such a fashion that it would be able to prepare for it with minimum disruption. When they reached the plains beneath Agridi on 15 June 1232, the Lombards could see that they had overestimated the size of John's force. However, the new-found confidence generated by this discovery was quickly translated into complacency. Encouraged by the disparity in numbers, the first wave of Lombard cavalry charged downhill at John and his troops. But the Ibelin spearmen formed a wall in the face of the horsemen, who sped past the flank of their opponent's army and came to rest at the bottom of the hill. They then meekly deserted the field, having contributed virtually nothing. The next wave met with no more success. Many of the horses stumbled on the rocky ground, throwing their heavily armoured riders in the process.

Now, at the height of the battle, a small group of men under John's son, Balian of Ibelin, suddenly appeared next to Filangieri's camp, having made their way unseen up a narrow mountain track. This was the decisive moment of the contest. Faced by this unexpected development, the Lombard army wavered and then broke. Many Lombards escaped, including Filangieri, but it was the critical moment of the campaign. Men who had been neutral before the battle now threw themselves behind John, including the Templars. Within a few months, Filangieri had fled the island.

In a final attempt to restore his authority, Frederick sent news to Outremer that he had appointed a new bailli, Philip of Maugastel. This was accepted, until it was discovered that Tyre was to be left in the hands of Filangieri. Angrily, John of Ibelin organised opposition and much dissent followed. There were several attempts by delegations from the West to impose the changes on the kingdom but, even though Pope Gregory now sided with Frederick, they were unsuccessful. The realities of life in Outremer meant that these impractical ideas would never be implemented.

John of Ibelin died soon after. The wisdom of his counsel and his rational approach towards the problems of Outremer made his loss a heavy one to bear. His actions contrasted well with the inflated ego of Frederick. It was now forty years since the loss of Jerusalem and although it was once again in Christian hands its situation was precarious. In reality, the vulnerability of the city meant that the Muslims could retake it whenever they wanted to. It had been a period of some opportunity for the Franks. The Muslims had been divided and, if working together for a common cause, the Christians could have made much greater progress. It was not quite the last chance for recovery but it was not far from it. Once more, individual ambition had dominated the government of Outremer and the resources available had been frittered away for minimal result. Few such chances would come again.

CHAPTER 24

A Nation Divided

In 1167, in the far-distant lands of Mongolia, a baby boy entered the world. According to tradition, as he left his mother's womb he emerged clutching a blood clot. Thus he was born with blood on his hands. Before he died, on those same hands would be the blood of half of Asia. His name was Temujin but he would become better known as Genghis Khan. With his Mongol horsemen, he would forge the greatest empire the world had ever known. His renown would spread from Japan to England, and his name would inspire fear and panic universally. The shock waves that his actions generated would ripple across all civilisation. Some of those waves would break on the shores of Outremer, and would play a crucial part in finally bringing about the death and destruction of this fated Christian kingdom.

Although geographically removed from the West, the Far East exerted an influence on the consciousness of the Christian world, an ethereal power whose presence could not be seen but whose omnipotent strength could be sensed everywhere. That influence was distorted into a mutation of practical reality. The West never understood what was happening across Asia and did not comprehend the threat that the Mongols posed until huge raids had decimated enormous tracts of Poland and Hungary and even advanced to the shores of the Adriatic. It believed that there was a mighty monarch in the East who was a Christian. He was named Prester John. It was widely held that if only effective contact could be made with him, he would come to the aid of the Christian cause and would eradicate the Muslims from the face of the earth.

Such was the dream – the reality was somewhat different. The many Christians among the Mongols and their Turkish neighbours were Nestorians. Further, the concept of kingship espoused by Genghis Khan would brook no equal. In his eyes, everyone was subservient to him. His power was unchallenged and his word was death to any that offended him. His weapons were simple. Firstly, the manpower available to him was immense. Because so many tribes eventually recognised his sovereignty, the whole of Asia provided a source of men. When the Mongols fought, they were devastating. Seemingly at one with their horses, they were almost exclusively cavalry forces. This gave them enormous mobility, and meant that they could attack with virtually no warning. Further, Genghis imposed supreme discipline on his men. The combination was for decades an irresistible one.

One facet, however, underpinned all others. No man had ever used absolute terror as a weapon in the way that Genghis did. The greatest tyrants of history pale in comparison with the Khan of Khans, who regarded human life as the cheapest of all commodities. One example will illustrate the full extent of his barbarity. The city of Nishapur resisted the Mongols, and in the battle a son-in-law of Genghis died. When the city fell, Genghis ordered that every living creature within it should be put to the sword. A handful of artisans were sent eastwards into a life of perpetual slavery. The rest of the city were killed. Separate pyramids were formed of the men, women and children slain in the massacre. There were even pyramids for the cats and dogs. The completeness of the massacre served as a warning for others of what could be expected if absolute obedience was not forthcoming.

The upheaval caused by these rapacious tribesmen did not immediately impact on Outremer but set in train a sequence of events that was to have dire consequences. Vast empires were destroyed. The Christian kingdom of Georgia, a constant irritant to the Mongols, was conquered. Russia was raided, and major cities like Kiev obliterated along with minor towns such as a small trading post at a place called Moscow. However, the clash of greatest consequence for the Franks was that between the Mongols and the Khwarismians in Persia. The Khwarismians' ruler, Mohammed-Shah, had built a kingdom covering much of modern Iran and Iraq. A brutal and intolerant man, he antagonised many of his subjects. Therefore, Genghis was welcomed as a liberator. The size of the armies involved was immense, with Mohammed said to have had half a million men at his disposal while Genghis, heavily outnumbered, had two hundred thousand. But the

The supposed ferocity of the Mongols is shown in this thirteenth-century English print of them eating human flesh; stories of atrocities on both sides were common. (MS 16, f. 167r)

Mongols were irresistible. The great cities of Bokhara and Samarkand fell into their hands amid a sea of blood and slaughter. His armies crumbling around him, Mohammed fled to die a lonely death on a deserted island in the Caspian Sea.

His son, Jelal ad-Din, put up a stronger fight. He had the temerity to defeat the Mongols in battle but this was a dubious triumph. It only served to call down the wrath of Genghis on a greater scale. During the siege of Bamian, the favourite grandson of Genghis died. When the town fell, the whole population was massacred. So the Mongolian campaign progressed, with city after city falling into their hands and then being razed. Faced with defeat, Jelal ad-Din fled to India rather than face a horrendous death at the hands of Genghis. The army went on from here to advance into Russia and from there to the gates of Christian Europe itself.

However, Jelal ad-Din had not yet been destroyed. When the Mongols returned to their homes, he returned to Persia. By this time, the enslaved population had long been disabused of the notion that the Mongols were liberators. In a hugely successful campaign, Jelal ad-Din became lord of Persia, Azerbaijan and Baghdad. However, he did not ingratiate himself to his neighbours, antagonising Muslims and Georgians alike. The Mongols were currently engaged in putting down a revolt in China but, once they had done this, they set out to reconquer their lost territories. By the time they returned, Jelal ad-Din had ruled in Persia for six years but the memory of the previous Mongolian atrocities was still fresh in the minds of the people. Most cities meekly surrendered rather than face annihilation. Resistance was virtually non-existent and Jelal ad-Din quickly found himself without a kingdom once more. He fled to die an obscure death further west, but his demise meant that thousands of dispossessed and undisciplined Khwarismian warriors were, in effect, available for hire. They would soon find gainful employment.

Knowledge of these events was sketchy in Outremer. On its borders, in 1229, al-Kamil had succeeded in uniting the Muslim Empire. The young but resilient an-Nasir was ousted from Damascus and had been given land on the far side of the Jordan in compensation. Al-Kamil's brother, al-Ashraf, had been given Damascus but recognised the overlordship of al-Kamil, now indisputable *primus inter pares*. However, the Muslims faced immense external pressures. In 1230 the Khwarismians had challenged al-Ashraf and forced him into an alliance with the Seldjuk Turks of Anatolia. Their combined forces had subsequently inflicted a heavy defeat on the Khwarismian invaders. Meanwhile, the Franks had been at comparative peace. For a time, it appeared that they had weathered the storm, and they were further helped by the civil war that broke out among the Muslims when al-Kamil died in 1238. However, appearances were deceptive. The more ambitious elements in Frankish society had merely been waiting for the right moment to advance their personal ambitions at the expense of the state.

The last years of al-Kamil's reign were hard ones for the Muslim world. His hegemony turned out to be tenuous. Al-Ashraf did not enjoy being the junior partner, although at first his irritation was not openly displayed because he was too distracted by his constant battles with the Seldjuk Turks. Eventually, these two parties settled their differences, and even joined forces to plot against al-Kamil.

Before this could progress far, al-Ashraf died. His younger brother, as-Salih Ismail, took over in Damascus and tried to maintain the momentum of the plot. However, the plan was nipped in the bud when al-Kamil took Damascus with the help of an-Nasir. It was to be al-Kamil's last triumph, as two months later he died.

With al-Kamil's passing, all semblance of unity in the Muslim world dissolved. His eldest son, al-Salih Ayub, marched on Damascus and took it with the help of Khwarismian mercenaries. His younger brother, al-Adil, took over in Egypt. Ayub was not prepared to accept this situation without demur, but when he left Damascus to conquer Egypt he was removed from power by a coup and Ismail was restored. Ayub fled to an-Nasir, who supported him in his attempts to take Egypt. This proved not to be difficult as al-Adil was effeminate and weak. Ayub was given the country to rule. He was indeed fortunate as Syria and the surrounding lands were rent apart by the turmoil created by the Mongols. Thousands of migrant Khwarismians roamed the country looking for easy pickings. To add to this pressure the Seldjuks renewed their assaults. For a time, the northern part of the Muslim Empire disintegrated into a loosely knit province of isolated city-states, under a variety of rulers, none of whom was sure of his position.

It was in this environment, amid an atmosphere of chaos, upheaval and threat, that the truce made between Frederick and al-Kamil a decade previously came to an end. There had been some breaches of it, but until now it had held. The great external pressures on the Muslims seemed to offer opportunity to the Franks, though, and before the truce ended preparations had been made for another Crusade.

Pope Gregory IX was still alive. Unsurprisingly, he was once more at war with Frederick. The two men were too similar to be at peace for long. They both wished to be supreme, and there is never enough room in the world for two men with this same ambition. Gregory turned to traditional recruiting grounds for the Crusades, to England and France. Henry III of England was not secure and could not contemplate making the journey, and the King of France was no more willing to go. However, a suitable candidate was found to head an army in the form of Count Tibald of Champagne, the nephew of Henry of Champagne. He was King of Navarre. Other leading men joined him and the force that they assembled, although not enormous, appeared large enough to disquiet the Muslims.

Meanwhile, Frederick was totally opposed to the Crusade. He still felt that Outremer was his, and that the region was no business of anyone else. He had also been negotiating with

A crusader knight pays homage; this is possibly King Henry III of England. (Royal MS 2A XXII, f. 220)

the Muslims and an army arriving in Outremer would put paid to his plans there. His opposition meant that there was no possibility of the expedition passing through Italy, as had originally been hoped, and the Crusade was forced to take the longer sea passage from the south of France. The journey was rough and uncomfortable and many ships were driven off course. However, most of them found their way safely to Outremer, Count Tibald putting ashore there on 1 September 1239. His timing was immaculate, as the truce was due to expire only a month later.

The voyage was easy compared to the deliberations that followed. The army now had to decide who to fight. The surrounding Muslim lands had torn themselves apart and this presented a wonderful opportunity to the Franks, who could have exploited the situation by aligning themselves with one party or another, or indeed by playing the opposing factions off against each other. However, the hot-blooded new arrivals had no stomach for subtle games of politics or diplomacy. They had come to fight Muslims, and that was their sole objective. Yet again the educational value of history was ignored; failing to learn from past experience, the Crusaders refused the advice of the local Franks, and set themselves on a collision course with disaster.

In fairness, even the Franks of Outremer could not decide what the best course of action would be. Some felt that Egypt should be attacked, while others opted for Damascus. Faced with a plurality of options, Tibald quickly showed how unfitted he was for the command of the expedition. He resolved to attack Egypt first and then to turn on Damascus. As an example of strategic incompetence, it would be hard to better. The move was guaranteed to unite the Muslims in common cause against the Franks, and it vastly overstretched the limited resources available to them. The only hope of success would have been to concentrate attention on one primary target. As news of the decision leaked out, there was frantic activity in the Muslim lands as ambassadors rushed around making truces.

The Christian army duly set out for Egypt from Acre. They received news that a large caravan was in the area and determined to take it. The caravan was screened with a strong guard and there was a fierce fight before it was overwhelmed. Nevertheless, overwhelmed it was, and the Franks returned to camp well pleased with their success. They had enriched themselves considerably but in the process alienated an-Nasir, who might have been prepared to help them if courted properly.

The Egyptians sent out an army to intercept the Franks. It was under the command of a Mameluke. His name was Rukn ad-Din Baibars. In time, he would become the greatest enemy of the Franks. The Mamelukes were trained soldiers from foreign territories whom the Egyptians had welded into a strong fighting force. They were bought when very young from lands as far away as the Caucasus. They were not treated as slaves, and were often sold willingly by their families. They were adopted by the head of the household who purchased them, and who effectively became the equivalent of a godfather. They were treated well, and trained thoroughly in the military arts. If they performed well, honour, glory and wealth could be theirs.

The rumours that had reached the Franks suggested that the Egyptian army was small. The intelligence available to them must have been poor, because they seriously understated its size. The Franks were complacent. Henry of Bar, a noble in the Frankish army, decided to attack on his own, jealous of colleagues who had taken the caravan. Only a few other leaders were involved in the plan, which was kept secret.

At nightfall on 12 November 1239, a small force of 500 horsemen and 1,000 infantry set out for Gaza. However, it was impossible to maintain secrecy and the rest of the army quickly found out what had happened. The leaders of the Military Orders and Tibald himself raced after Henry, begging him to desist from his ill-advised scheme. But Henry was convinced that he knew better than all of them, and he would not be persuaded. No doubt angry and frustrated, Tibald moved his army to Ascalon where they would at least be on hand to help if needed.

Folly was now compounded by absolute incompetence. Henry nonchalantly told his men to rest among some sand-dunes near Gaza. He posted an inadequate guard and allowed the men to refresh themselves. To understand the full extent of his stupidity, it should be pointed out that the heavy Frankish cavalry was completely ineffective in sand, as they lost all mobility. While the Christians ate, drank and slept the Egyptian army crept up to them. It was at least six times as large as the Franks' spies had suggested. One of the Franks with Henry's force, Walter of Jaffa, became nervous, realising that things were not as they should be. Suspecting that a major attack was imminent he advised retreat, advice which was taken by many of the knights. To his credit, Henry of Bar may have lacked intelligence but he did not lack courage. Having led his infantry into a trap, he did not now desert them.

It would be inaccurate to describe the slaughter that followed the Egyptian attack as a battle. Resistance was gallant but completely futile. Among the many who died was Henry himself, paying the ultimate price for his lack of humility and judgement. The infantry were either killed or captured, and only the mounted men escaped to bring news of the disaster to the main camp.

It was a bitter blow for the Franks but worse was to follow. An-Nasir was smarting after the loss of the caravan. In revenge, he took his army to Jerusalem to punish the Franks for their temerity. It was an easy task. Most of the walls had not been re-erected since the city had come into the possession of the Franks again. An-Nasir's men merely had to walk in. The only focal point for any kind of defence was the Tower of David, which held out for twenty-seven days until, depleted of supplies and with no sign of any relieving force, those inside were forced to surrender. An-Nasir's revenge was complete. After a short occupation of the city, he demolished the already sparse fortifications and retired to his own territory.

Perhaps because of this abysmal start to the Franks' campaign, Ayub in Egypt no longer took the threat from them seriously, and the Muslims reverted to squabbling among themselves. However, concerned that Ayub would seek an alliance with an-Nasir, Ismail of Damascus sought the help of the Franks. The time for pretension had passed and, chastened by their disastrous campaign so far,

Tibald accepted the proposed alliance. He was offered good terms, with Ismail giving the castles of Beaufort and Safed to the Franks. Tibald, however, had misread the situation. The garrison in Beaufort refused to hand it over and Ismail had to take it by force. In Damascus, the people turned against Ismail because of his friendly overtures to the Franks, and several leading citizens went into voluntary exile in disgust.

For over a decade there had been an uneasy truce between the Hospitallers and the Templars. But now, the aggrandisement of the Templars became too much for the Hospitallers to bear. Infuriated by the success of their rivals, they resolved to seek a triumph of their own. Their chance was not long in coming. When the Crusaders joined forces with Ismail, Ayub brought his army up to face them. While the two armies cautiously awaited the next move, Ayub entered into secret negotiations with the Hospitallers. He offered the return of all those taken at Gaza in return for military assistance. It was a wonderful opportunity for the Hospitallers to advance their interests at the expense of the Templars and they were delighted to take advantage of the proposal. They were also offered the fortress of Ascalon, in itself a valuable prize. Given this chance to gain the release of many Christian troops, Tibald conveniently forgot his agreement with Ismail and agreed to the deal when he received word of it. Ayub was ecstatic at having broken the dangerous alliance between the Franks and the Damascenes, an agreement that had furthermore required much loss of face from the Emir of Damascus, who had made a great sacrifice for nothing.

Not all the Christians were happy with these developments. Many were shocked at the ease with which Tibald became a turncoat. Others remembered that Damascus had allied itself with Outremer in the past, and that there had been good trading links between the two. Much opposition was directed at Tibald. For his part, he could not understand the fuss. He saw nothing wrong in breaking his word to an Infidel and, dismayed at what he regarded as the ingratitude of the Franks, he resolved to return to the West, which he did after journeying to Jerusalem. His expedition was not a complete waste given the recovery of Ascalon, Beaufort and Safed but, with firmer leadership, it could have achieved much more.

When Tibald left in September 1240, his place was soon taken by an equally illustrious personality in the form of Richard of Cornwall. He was brother to Henry III of England and brother-in-law of the German Emperor. Because of their relationship, Frederick delegated full powers to him in Outremer. Richard was a capable man, who took stock of the situation as soon as he arrived. He was shocked beyond words by what he found. The Templars and Hospitallers were virtually at war with each other, and in the streets of Acre armed gangs roamed threateningly, often brawling with each other.

Ayub was quick to attempt to ensure that the peace made with Tibald still held. Richard reciprocated his overtures, but only on his terms – Ayub was to confirm the surrender of the lands handed over by Ismail, and he was further forced to agree to the surrender of the rest of Galilee. The terms were agreed and a handover of prisoners took place. By these moves the kingdom became almost as large as it was before Hattin, but was by no means as secure. Richard ruled well but had no ambition to stay long in the East, returning home within six months. The barons wanted Simon de Montfort, an ambitious young noble who had accompanied Richard, to take his place but Frederick would not sanction this move.

Frederick was soon to lose all vestige of influence in the region. In 1243 his son, Conrad, came of age and was entitled to claim the crown for himself. The barons requested that he come to Outremer as soon as possible to take up his position as king. Until he arrived, the next in line to the throne, Queen Alice of Cyprus, was made Regent. She was married to Ralph of Soissons, a man half her age (she was in her fifties) who had come to Outremer with Tibald's Crusade. Conrad in the meantime showed no urgency in making his way to the country.

The rapid decline of Frederick's influence was quickened by the final overthrow of the scurrilous Filangieri, who had stayed in Outremer for many years. This meant that the Hospitallers – traditionally associated with Frederick's supporters – had lost influence and the Templars had become more powerful as a result. Friendly moves were now made towards Ismail in Damascus rather than Ayub in Egypt. This alarmed the latter, who had recently fallen out with an-Nasir. The Templars made the most of their influence, even negotiating with the Muslims to desert the temple area of Jerusalem, allowing them to take up residence once more in the al-Aqsa Mosque.

However, any thoughts that this might herald the birth of a resurgent and vibrant Crusader state were misplaced. The Franks had only been able to take back territory because the Muslims were divided. Although the Crusaders had shown flashes of diplomatic aptitude in their dealings in the region, they had backed the wrong horse. In 1244 open war broke out between Ayub and Ismail. An-Nasir sided with Ismail but was lukewarm towards the Franks, who had also offered military support to the Emir of Damascus. The Franks agreed with Ismail that they should have a share in the division of Egypt once Ayub had been overthrown.

Superficially, the alliance looked powerful but beneath the surface relationships were strained. Further, Ayub had been negotiating with the dispossessed Khwarismian hordes. He obtained the support of 10,000 wild and aggressive warriors as a result. When these men launched their assault, it had devastating consequences. Like a whirlwind they tore through Syria, demolishing everything and everyone foolish enough to stand in their way. Only Damascus appeared too strong to take and was therefore avoided. They bypassed the city and burst into Palestine. In July the guards atop the newly re-erected walls of Jerusalem were disturbed by the sounds of hooves in the distance. As the dust settled, the hills surrounding the city seemed alive with wild cries and terrifying shouts. The Khwarismians had arrived. Some warning of their coming had been received but the real danger inherent in the situation was made apparent when the Grand Masters of the Military Orders saw fit to leave Jerusalem and fled to protect themselves.

The wisdom of their actions was soon shown. Although the fortifications of the city had only just been restored, they were too vast for the garrison to man adequately. The Khwarismians easily broke into the city. The citizens were put to

The Crusaders at war with the Khwarismians. (MS 16, f. 170v)

the sword in scenes of horrific destruction. The garrison made for the citadel, hoping to be relieved. An-Nasir sent troops to the city to intimidate the Khwarismians, and the garrison and many of the citizens were allowed to leave the city as a result. However, they fell into a Khwarismian trap, which lured thousands of the non-combatants back to the city walls where they were attacked and slaughtered. Those who carried on were subjected to constant attacks from Arab brigands and only 300 survivors finally arrived in Jaffa. On 23 August 1244 the Christian army was thrown out of Jerusalem, this time for good. There would not be another one in the city for 673 years.

Despite this terrible set-back, the Franks were still able to field a large army, which marched towards Gaza with their allies. There 5,000 Egyptians and the entire Khwarismian host faced them. The Muslims in the alliance argued for prudence. If the force put itself behind fortifications, the Khwarismians, who disliked this form of warfare, would soon lose interest. It was sound advice but anathema to the Franks. Walter of Jaffa pressed for an attack to be made, and was eventually successful in his arguments. In the subsequent confrontation on 17 October 1244, the Franks were on the right of the allied line. In the centre and on the left were the Muslim forces. The initial Frankish charge was held by the Egyptians while the Muslims of an-Nasir on the left were broken. The pressure on the centre was immense but it fought well and extracted itself with difficulty. However, the Khwarismians turned on the Franks, who were virtually surrounded. A small number escaped but the vast majority were either captured or died valiantly.

In this engagement, the losses of the Franks were enormous, only eclipsed by those at Hattin. Out of 300 Templars and 300 Hospitallers, a combined total of fifty-nine escaped. The kingdom could not afford losses of this magnitude from what was effectively its standing army. The allies lost 5,000 men overall. Ascalon was subsequently attacked by Ayub but survived, only to fall three years later.

The ongoing warfare between the Muslim factions meant that the Franks escaped complete destruction. However, the extent of the reverse could not be denied. The greatest blow was to the confidence of the Franks. When so much of Outremer had been recovered, their self-belief had soared but they had only managed to achieve this relative recovery through the sufferance of the Muslims. Now the delusion of that resurgent confidence was laid bare to be seen as the mirage that it was. It lacked substance and depth. The underlying problems of the kingdom were as real as ever and it was difficult to see how it could ever recover. Time was slipping by, and a new injection from the West was needed if there were to be any realistic chance of recovery. It was not at all clear from whence such help would come.

CHAPTER 25

The Last Hope

Given its loss of self-belief, Outremer now needed the impetus of someone who could quickly seize the initiative and give the Franks new momentum and hope. The man who believed that he was equipped to fill this role was Louis IX, King of France. He was devout to the point of fanaticism; whereas many contemporaries professed sanctity, he lived what he preached. His was a world of black and white. He would not contemplate compromise with those whom he believed to be the enemies of God. He was also a man of contradictions, rejecting frivolity but possessing great wealth. He married a young, fun-loving Queen, from whom he managed to squeeze the *joie de vivre*. Possessed of great self-belief, convinced that life was for him a divine mission, he was not a man who would be deterred easily.

In 1244 Louis was desperately ill with malaria. He took a vow that, if he recovered, he would launch a great Crusade in gratitude. A full recovery was granted and he began to make arrangements for such an expedition. His ministers tried to dissuade him. The Bishop of Paris expostulated with him, arguing that he could not be held responsible for fulfilling a pledge that he had made when he was semi-delirious. His mother supported the Bishop. Louis was not so easily dissuaded. In his frustration, he removed his Crusader's cross from his gown. Any sighs of relief from his ministers were premature. Louis conceded that he might have been deprived of his faculties when he first made the vow but no one could accuse him of not being *compos mentis* now. In complete control of himself and his actions, he took up the cross again and swore that he would fast, until death if necessary, until he had started to redeem his pledge. Seeing that all further dissent was useless, his advisers at last acquiesced.

At this time, Europe was at a critical stage in its development. For numerous reasons, its powerful men held different opinions about the merits of another Crusade. The King of England, an immensely wealthy man, had designs on France, and his schemes would be greatly assisted if Louis were to leave his kingdom for any length of time. Attempts to encourage Henry III of England to go on Crusade would, predictably enough, flounder. Equally predictably, greater concerns revolved around the Emperor Frederick. He was at odds with the Pope again and had, in fact, driven him out of Italy. In contrast to Henry III, the Pope would have preferred Louis to stay in Europe to act as a deterrent to any other plots that the Emperor hatched.

To Louis, however, all these considerations were secondary to his duty to God. His preparations were thorough in the extreme, and it took him three years to finalise the details of his mission. Nevertheless, when he finally set sail on 26 August 1248 it was at the head of a very large force. Most of the leading nobles of France accompanied him, and this at a time when the country was approaching the peak of the chivalric era. It is probable that notions of chivalry drove Louis almost as much as religious considerations. The glory of the mission attracted many others, and a large number of the leading men of England joined the force, despite the absence of their king. They were headed by William, Earl of Salisbury, grandson of Henry II. The Venetians, though, were hostile to the project and had refused to help with transportation, which was accordingly provided by the Genoese and Pisans.

The fleet was to rendezvous at Cyprus. On its arrival there, Louis met with the leading men of Outremer, including the Grand Masters of the Temple and the Hospital. Immediately, discussions turned to the objectives of the Crusade. There was little dissension this time that Egypt should be the target. However, the Franks, who knew well the vagaries of the East Mediterranean weather at this time of year, advised against a sea crossing until the spring. Louis accepted the advice, but this did pose some problems. Although the army was well provisioned, this delay had not been anticipated at the planning stage. Food ran low and the Cypriot merchants were able to charge extortionate prices for their produce.

In May 1249 the fleet set its course for Egypt. A severe storm scattered the ships at the outset but the fleet managed to regroup off Damietta. Sultan Ayub knew that the army was coming but had expected it to land in Syria and had to

Louis IX sets out for the Holy Land. (MS Plut. 61.10, c3356v)

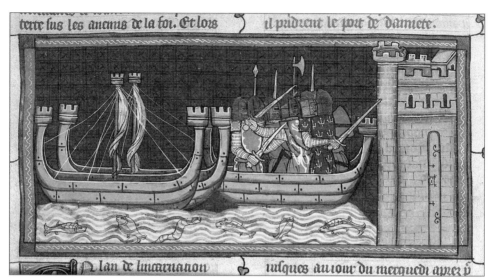

The siege of Damietta. (Roy 16 G VI f. 409v Attack on Damietta in Egypt during the Crusades, 1248, Chronicle of France or of St Denis *(14th century); British Library, London/ Bridgeman Art Library, London/New York)*

hurry back to Egypt when it landed there. He was a sick man, and his ill health had deprived him of some of his vitality. He therefore left the defence to his vizier, Fakhr ad-Din. Damietta itself was defended by a large garrison of Bedouins, renowned for their tenacity. Given the scale of the fortifications, a long siege could be anticipated. Attempts to repulse the Franks while they were landing – a vulnerable moment in any amphibious operation in any era – were not successful. The Muslims delayed their attack too long and when it came there were enough Franks ashore to form a shield wall and drive them back. Their security was assured when enough of the Frankish horsemen were landed to attack the lightly armed Bedouin. Many had not faced a heavy cavalry charge before and scattered.

The city sent word to Ayub, urging him to send help as quickly as possible. Then something inexplicable happened. In any age, one of the strangest of phenomena is that curse of self-doubt which transforms a strong position into a seemingly hopeless one, and makes the enemy appear invincible when in reality he is anything but. The defenders were safely ensconced behind walls that not too many years before had kept the Crusaders at bay for months. Now, for no apparent reason, they fled and surrendered the city without a fight. The Franks must have been extremely sceptical when a group of Coptic Christians came to their camp to tell them the news. However, a cursory inspection showed that indeed it was true. The city had been provisioned for a long siege and nothing had been destroyed. It was a fantastic windfall for the Christian army.

Now, however, the Franks did not know what to do. Having executed those who had given up the city so easily, Ayub offered Jerusalem to the Crusade if Damietta was returned. But Louis would not even think of negotiating with an Infidel. Ayub consequently sent guerrillas to the environs of the city to make life as difficult as possible for the Franks. Louis was content to bide his time. He knew that the annual flood was imminent and that the campaigning season was effectively over until the waters had receded. The army was too big for the city and most of the men were camped outside of the walls. It was soon ravaged by disease.

By October 1249, when the floods had abated, the Franks still had not agreed on their next objective. A strong argument was put forward that the Franks should attempt to take Alexandria, an idea with some merits as control of the city would enable the Franks to use their sea power to blockade the country and starve it into submission. However, King Louis' brother, Robert of Artois, cautioned against the scheme, arguing that the only proper objective for the Crusade was Cairo. The Count was persuasive and assertive; before the campaign was over he would also prove himself hot-headed, self-opinionated and very dangerous. His impassioned pleas were persuasive and Cairo was confirmed as the target for the army.

Tremendous news then reached the army. Ayub's health had at last completely given out and he had died. The most influential people in Egypt were now his elderly wife, the discredited Fakhr ad-Din and Ayub's son, Turanshah, who was hundreds of miles away in Syria. Ayub had not been loved but he had certainly inspired fear and respect. It was easy to believe that without his firm grip on the nation, order would dissolve. This inspired the Franks to push on quickly towards Cairo. However, there were serious obstacles to overcome; the road to Cairo was intersected by a number of deep canals and branches of the Nile, which could be easily defended and were difficult to traverse. There were a number of skirmishes as the Egyptians sought to obstruct the Franks' progress, but this only delayed the advance and could not prevent it altogether.

Eventually a canal wider than any other was reached, known as the Bahr as-Saghir. It was near the powerful Egyptian fortress of Mansourah. This was a new town, its existence due to a massive building programme initiated after the last Crusade against Egypt. Its role was to obstruct any advance towards Cairo. It took the Crusaders six weeks to develop a plan to cross the water and they only succeeded then because a group of Coptic sympathisers showed them where to cross. Progress was painfully slow. At the head of the army as it crossed were the Templars, the English and the rash Robert of Artois. Louis had given strict instructions that the vanguard was not to push on until the whole army was safely across.

What happened next is described primarily by John of Joinville. He was the leading chronicler of the Crusade, and he would have no wish to discredit Louis, who would later be canonised. Therefore, he may have overplayed the role of Robert of Artois in the events that followed. According to Joinville's account, once the vanguard had safely traversed the canal, Robert of Artois, intoxicated by the scent of glory, urged an immediate attack on the Muslims. In vain, the other leaders tried to dissuade him. He riposted that their hesitance must be because of their cowardice. This was the accusation that the Medieval knight disdained more than any other. Faced with this slur on their character, the knights determined to disprove Robert. They were well blessed with valour but not with intelligence. They charged headlong into the Muslim camp. In fact, their initial foray met with great success. The Egyptians were completely unprepared for the attack as the crossing had taken place at night 2 miles downstream from the Muslim camp. In minutes, the scene became one of chaos. Terrified Egyptian soldiers sought to flee the hacking blades and thrusting lances of the fearsome Frank warriors. Many died, among them Fakhr ad-Din. Those who survived rushed frantically towards the town of Mansourah.

So far, the alleged impetuosity of Robert of Artois had been greatly rewarded. However, now more than ever convinced of his invincibility he categorically refused to heed the advice of his fellow commanders once more. Joinville reports how they urged him to stay where they were, but he argued that one final push against Mansourah would cause the town to fall. His arguments again proved irresistible and the Frankish cavalry plunged headlong into the town itself. Cooler heads would have had their suspicions aroused by the fact that the gates had been left open, but such calm contemplation was presently in short supply.

Enthused by their imminent success, the horsemen charged through the streets of the town towards the citadel. As they were about to reach it, their way was blocked by Muslim cavalry. When they did not break through this human barrier, they turned about to be faced with an awful prospect. The whole episode had been a trap, improvised brilliantly by the Mameluke Baibars who had taken command when Fakhr ad-Din was struck down. Large numbers of Muslims blocked the Franks' retreat back through the streets. So narrow were these that few of them could even bring their weapons to bear on the enemy. To exacerbate their difficulties, eager hands were throwing heavy beams and stones down on them from the rooftops. The town quickly assumed the appearance of a charnel house. A few Franks escaped to the Nile, where they mostly drowned in futile attempts to swim away in their heavy armour. A few others, against all odds, hacked their way out and made their way back to Louis with the awful news. For the rest, only an inglorious death awaited. Robert of Artois paid for his folly with his life, after a vain attempt to barricade himself and a few followers in a house. William of Salisbury lay dead in the street. Among the Templars, the losses were truly catastrophic. Out of 295 only five survived, among them the Grand Master William de Sonnac, who had lost an eye, hacked out in the ferocious fighting.

Louis heard of the disaster while he was still crossing the Nile. He formed his men as quickly as he could to face the expected counter-attack. He managed to hold this off and then, when he believed the Muslims to be tiring, launched his own counter. The Muslims were driven back inside the town. Another Muslim attack focused on a bridge that the Franks were attempting to erect to cross the river but this was also repelled, allowing the Franks to take possession of the land before Mansourah. It could be argued that by securing their crossing, the Franks had technically won the day but if ever there was a Pyrrhic victory, then this was it. One more such triumph would be the death warrant of the army. Louis had shown courage and tenacity and some tactical awareness but only in what was effectively a damage limitation exercise. He had been poorly served by his commanders, primarily by his own brother, whose death was none the less a grievous personal blow to Louis.

The following days brought more sharp actions, including one in which de Sonnac lost his other eye; he died in agony a few days later. The losses among the Templars were particularly damaging. Effectively, they were the shock troops of

Outremer and they could not be replaced. Unsure of what to do, Louis decided to stay where he was, hoping that the accession of Turanshah might lead to internal divisions among the Muslims that he could exploit. Such hopes were in vain. The new Sultan threw himself energetically into the project to repel the Franks.

Turanshah's first move was to stop the Frankish supply ships making their way down the Nile. This policy was pursued with vigour and success, and severe deprivation was soon apparent in the Christian camp. Disease broke out among the troops, and scores of them were soon unfit for action. The intensity of Muslim raids on the supply lines also increased continually and it became apparent to Louis that, if he wished to have any kind of army left to command, his only option was retreat, however unpalatable that might be. He attempted to reopen negotiations with Turanshah with a view to trading Jerusalem for Damietta. Unfortunately, it was all too obvious that he was bargaining from a position of great weakness. Such approaches were too late. Turanshah would only contemplate a settlement on his terms.

On 5 April 1250 Mansourah was alive with excitement as news reached the town that the Christians had struck camp. The ferocious Mamelukes in the town rushed after them in pursuit. They were delighted to find that the Franks had made it easy for them. A pontoon bridge that had been built to let the Christian army cross the Bahr as-Saghir was thoughtfully left in situ so that the Mamelukes could also cross. They soon surrounded the Franks, who were demoralised, tired and weakened. When they attacked, Louis fought magnificently, but in a lost cause. Even he was eventually overtaken by fatigue and collapsed, and had to be taken to a place of relative safety to recuperate. Once he was off the field, the local barons sought terms with the enemy. Before these could be agreed, a message reached them that Louis had ordered immediate surrender. It was a lie, but it ensured the Franks' capitulation. The expedition, which had started with enormously high hopes, had ended in abject humiliation.

The Muslims took so many prisoners that they did not know what to do with them all. Several thousand of the common troops who had no value were beheaded. Those who would fetch a good ransom were kept, though their conditions were poor. The ransom agreed for them – and there were many – was huge. Louis had to pay a great sum for his own release. Damietta was to be given back to the Muslims and Louis was also asked to surrender the lands of the Franks in Outremer. He correctly replied that the lands

A depiction of Louis IX taken prisoner in Egypt.

there belonged to Conrad, and he held no jurisdiction over such matters. The Muslims did not press the argument.

Just as the negotiations were virtually concluded, Egypt was thrown into chaos by a palace coup. Turanshah had alienated the Mamelukes by not advancing their interests. This had been a very dangerous step. They resolved to overthrow him, the plotters being headed by Baibars. They burst in on Turanshah while he was eating. He managed to escape to a wooden tower, which was set ablaze. From here, he leapt into the Nile, where archers fired arrows at him from the banks. When Baibars saw that most had missed, he entered the water to finish Turanshah off. Though not intentionally, all this helped the Franks, as the ransom payments were reduced as a result of the new regime.

This small easing of the blow would have been scant compensation to Louis. Damietta was handed back to the Muslims on 6 May 1250. The city itself had only been saved from intense suffering by the actions of Louis' wife, Queen Margaret. She had paid for large amounts of supplies from her own treasury. Ironically, this left less money available within the city to pay the ransoms required. Louis' brother, Alfonse, was kept until the balance was cleared but Louis himself was released.

The Templars won themselves few friends when they proved reluctant to part with their funds for the ransom payments, and virtually had to be forced to do so. They were making too many enemies among their own kind. Perhaps Louis pondered this as he made his way back to Outremer upon a ship denuded of all basic requirements, with neither clothes nor bedding appropriate to his status. It was a filthy and degraded sovereign who arrived back in Acre, and to make matters worse the sea crossing had been stormy. His demoralisation was complete. Yet his actions since his defeat had endeared him to many, including the Muslims. He had shown great concern for his men and had refused to compromise his Christian principles. His deportment shows him to have been a far better man than he was a warrior or a monarch.

Many of Louis' troops now wanted him to return home but he was reluctant to do so before he had made amends. He offered to hire those men who wished to stay with him – only 1,500 accepted. Robbed of manpower, Louis turned to diplomacy. Gone was the earlier arrogance that had debarred him from negotiating with the Infidel. Fortunately for the Franks, the Muslim world was again divided. The Muslims in Syria were enraged at the murder of Turanshah and took up arms against his successor in Egypt, Aibek.

After an unsuccessful foray into Egypt, the new master of Damascus, an-Nasir Yusuf, asked for the help of the Franks. He offered Jerusalem as a reward. Louis told Aibek that an-Nasir was negotiating with him and warned that he would be forced to agree to his requests unless he was made a better offer from Egypt. He played the two men off so well that Aibek agreed to the return of all the old Frankish territories in Outremer (despite the fact that he did not currently hold them) as well as the release of all Christian prisoners. Just then, Louis received tidings that enraged him. The Templars had been holding separate discussions with Damascus and had made an offer of their own. Furious, Louis summoned the new Grand Master, Renaud de Vichiers, before him – despite the fact that he had no authority to do so – and made him withdraw from the proposed treaty.

However, his attempts at an alliance were stillborn. Before the Franks could combine with the Egyptians, an army from Damascus appeared. The stand-off that followed had lasted for nearly a year when depressing news reached Louis' ears. Under the auspices of the Caliph in Baghdad, the Muslims had reached a solution. There would be no need to use the Franks now, and the deal with Aibek was therefore cancelled. To add insult to injury, the army of an-Nasir raided heavily on its way back to Syria, and many prisoners were taken.

Equal disappointment came from the Christians' attempts to forge an alliance with the Mongols. The Franks did not understand that the Mongols did not regard them as equals, but merely as potential vassals. These failed attempts were to be Louis' last contributions to the affairs of Outremer. The death of his mother, who was governing France in his absence, made his return imperative. The Emperor Frederick had died in 1250 and Europe's stability had been compromised as a result. Even among the French, traditionally the strongest believers in the Crusading ideal, most people were now losing interest in the East.

Louis left Outremer for the last time on 24 April 1254. Devout and pure in spirit, he was undoubtedly a God-fearing man. His contemporaries must surely have wondered that, if a man such as him found nothing but heartbreak in Outremer, then the hand of God was no longer protecting the Crusaders. Although he was perhaps unlucky, no analysis could fail to conclude that Louis'

The coffin of Louis IX being taken on board ship at Tunis. With him effectively died the last hope of a successful crusade. (Snark M119 Crusade of Edward of England (1270–72), the crusaders loading St Louis' coffin on board at Tunis in 1270, Grandes Chroniques de France (1375–79); Chateau Roux, France/ Bridgeman Art Library, London/New York)

travails in Egypt were a disaster for the Franks. The blow to morale was, as ever, immense but the loss of already scarce manpower was even more so. It was a set-back that the Crusader territories in the Levant would never get over. Louis would personally never recover from the reverse and was determined to put matters right. He would eventually expire from disease on 25 August 1270, while besieging the Muslim city of Tunis. His last whispered words on this earth were simply 'Jerusalem! Jerusalem!'.

One of Louis' final acts before leaving Outremer had been to arrange a truce with the kingdom's Muslim neighbours. It held for a number of years and bought valuable time. However, the extinction of an immediate external threat merely caused the Franks to fight among themselves again. This conflict was particularly marked between the Genoese and the Venetians. What started out as something not much worse than petty brawling escalated to the point of all-out war. The catalyst came from Acre, where arguments broke out over the ownership of one strategic hill in the city that had been a bone of contention for some time. Discussions to resolve the dispute did not meet with success and the Genoese took the law into their own hands, storming the monastery that crowned the summit. When the Venetians tried to recover it, the battle spilled over into their sector of Acre, which was badly damaged in the looting that followed.

To add to their woes, Philip of Montfort, Lord of Tyre, evicted the Venetians from his city. They were powerless to respond immediately but it should have been obvious to most people that they would not meekly accept this situation. They had influential supporters in Outremer, in the shape, especially, of the Templars and the Teutonic Knights. The support of the Templars made it a guaranteed certainty that the Genoese would have the support of the Hospitallers. Many other men actively supported one side or another, and the kingdom braced itself for the Venetian response.

This response was not to disappoint expectations. A Venetian fleet arrived off Acre and broke through the chain that guarded the harbour. The Venetians stormed ashore and bitter hand-to-hand fighting followed. The Genoese were forced back to their own quarter that, for the time being, the Venetians could not take. The situation was not helped by the arrival of Plaisance, mother of Henry of Cyprus, in Outremer. Conrad was dead and she argued that his successor, Conradin, should not inherit the throne unless he actually came to the country. If he would not do so, then the next in line was her own son. He was too young to rule but Plaisance wished to act as Regent for him. Most of the important factions in the kingdom agreed with her, although the Hospitallers did not. However, the majority prevailed and her suggestions were accepted. All this merely inflamed an already delicate situation.

Matters came to a head when the Venetians arrived off Acre again. Great attempts had been made in Italy to find a negotiated solution to the problems but they were all in vain. The Venetians sent a fleet of twenty-eight ships to Palestine to enforce their supremacy over the Genoese. The Genoese despatched an even larger fleet but when the two met up the Venetian oarsmen were fresher, having had chance to rest. Given the labour-intensive method of propulsion that the galleys needed, physical tiredness was a key part of any sea battle. In the fierce fight that followed, half of the Genoese galleys were sent to the bottom of the Mediterranean along with nearly 2,000 men.

This effectively ended the internal confrontation within Outremer, at least for the time being. A compromise was agreed that allowed the Genoese to be based at Tyre while the Venetians and their Pisan allies were to have their headquarters in Acre. This reconciliation was, of course, never more than cosmetic. The Genoese longed for vengeance. And this they gained in the most spectacular way. The Byzantine Emperor in exile, Michael Paleologus, sought the help of the Genoese to recover Constantinople and they were glad to assist. On 25 July 1259 Michael entered his capital at the head of his victorious army. The Frankish interlude as the rulers of Constantinople was at an end, the Franks and their Venetian allies expelled. The Genoese were feted magnificently by the grateful Michael in recognition for their aid. It was a magnificent moment of revenge.

The Franks were devastated by their loss, and were unnerved by the renaissance of Byzantium, but the Greek revival was illusory. The empire that now existed was a pitiful and emaciated shadow of what it had once been. In reality, the Franks had governed so badly that they were easy prey for the Greeks. The restored empire was an irrelevance, acting out the last rites of a once-proud dynasty. With the pre-occupation of a self-interested West, far greater events in Syria passed virtually unnoticed. One of the greatest battles in history was to take place within a few miles of the Franks. Largely unknown in the West, it was to mark the beginning of the end for one great empire and the end of the beginning for another that was to last for several hundred years. It is one of history's great ironies that the time of the Crusades was witness to one of the most decisive battles in history and yet no Frankish soldier that we know of would be involved in it, even though it took place right on the frontier-lands around the small Christian enclave. And it meant much more, for the outcome of the battle effectively doomed Outremer to extinction.

CHAPTER 26

Twilight

The Muslim Levant was about to face its greatest crisis, which posed a far greater threat than any presented by the Crusades. Defeat would consign it to an era of servitude and subservience. The threat came from the East, from the numberless Mongol hordes, many of them Nestorian Christians. Since the death of the all-powerful Genghis, the Mongols had lost some of their unanimity of purpose. Nevertheless, they still presented a terrifying prospect. In 1251 a man named Mongka was elected supreme Khan. The Armenians tried to reach an understanding with the Mongols, hoping to obtain their help against the Seldjuk Turks in Asia Minor. Three years after the succession of Mongka, King Hethoum of Armenia journeyed to his court to renew his oath of allegiance to the Khan. The Mongol ruler, wishing to impress others who had not yet enthusiastically embraced him as overlord, made a huge fuss of Hethoum. The Armenian king was given a promise of everlasting protection from Mongka.

Other Christians were encouraged by this to view the Mongols as potential liberators of the Holy Land. However, it was a misguided notion. If the Mongols did invade the region, they would have no intention of meekly handing their gains back to the Franks. On the contrary, the Franks would be expected to become subjects of the Mongols. The West had singularly failed to grasp this truth, and had also misunderstood the importance of religion to the Mongols. The comfortable view of the Mongols as the rescuers of Outremer was held primarily by those installed in their pristine palaces, hundreds of miles away from the front line and its realities. The Franks of Outremer were far less willing to seek the help of the Mongols, having heard how terrifying they could be.

In January 1256 an enormous Mongol horde made its way west from its steppe homeland. It was commanded by Mongka's brother, Hulagu. Its first objective was the complete destruction of the Assassins. Some years before this group had been foolish enough to murder the son of Genghis. They never made a greater mistake. A terrible retribution was at hand, when the entire sect would be faced with genocide. It would provide an awful example to any others who might dare to defy the Mongols. The planning was meticulous. Roads were repaired in advance of the huge army, and flocks moved out of its path so that there would be sufficient pasture for the horses.

The Assassins, rightly alarmed at the nature of the punishment facing them, attempted to employ diplomacy to escape from their frightening predicament. But the insult they had offered was too great for retribution to be avoided. The

Assassins were prominent in two areas, in Persia and in Syria. Those in Persia were, by their location, doomed to suffer first. Their headquarters was at Alamut. The leader of the Assassins, Rukn ad-Din, begged permission of Hulagu to travel to Mongka to present his case personally. After Rukn ad-Din had travelled hundreds of miles, Mongka refused him an audience. The Assassin leader made his way wearily homewards. He would never see his land again – he was murdered on the way. It was as well, because by his death he was spared the sight of the destruction of his homeland.

Mongka now harangued Hulagu to persecute the Assassins aggressively. All prisoners were killed, regardless of age or sex. Many of the Assassins lived in rural areas; these were told to attend the nearest town for a census where, on their arrival, they were promptly killed. Only Rukn ad-Din's close family was spared, to be sent to the widow of the assassinated Mongol lord who would have them all put to death in revenge for his murder. After being robbed of its greatest treasures, the great Assassin library at Alamut was torched. It was a terrifying demonstration of the power of the Mongols, but it paled into insignificance in comparison with what was to come.

The greatest city in the Muslim world was Baghdad. Mecca held more religious importance and both Cairo and Damascus were at this time wealthier. However, Baghdad was the symbolic centre of Islam, the home of the Caliph, the head of the faith. Although more moral than practical, his influence was extremely important. And the city had also been at the centre of the arts for centuries. It was now made the subject of an ultimatum from the Mongols; either the Caliph must vow obedience to the Mongols or his territories would be ravaged. There was no possibility that the Caliph would respond to this suggestion and outright conflict was therefore an inevitability.

The Caliph now committed the most heinous of sins, that of underestimating one's enemy. He believed that the religious fanaticism of the Muslims would guarantee victory. The Caliph, al-Mustasim, had been blessed with a huge army when he came to power but it had been reduced over the years in the interests of economy. It had been a foolish policy, given the upheavals to which the area was then subject, and an appalling payback for it would accrue. Al-Mustasim had previously bought off the Mongols by paying tribute but now they wanted nothing less than complete subjugation.

The Caliph sent his armies out to block the Mongol advance, and they met about 30 miles from Baghdad. The tactics of the Mongols were simple and owed much to the Muslims. When the Muslims advanced, the Mongols retreated, luring their enemy into marshland. Then engineers broke the dykes that held back the waters of the Euphrates, flooding the lands to the Muslim rear and, in effect, cutting off any chance of retreat. The following day, the Mongols launched their assault. Their approach lacked subtlety but was mightily effective. They charged in a headlong mass, relying on their huge numbers for superiority. Inexorably the Muslims were forced back towards the floods at their rear, just as the Mongols had planned. Before the sun set on this catastrophic day, the field of battle was awash with the blood of Muslim martyrs. Baghdad was now naked before the Mongols.

The assault on the city began at the beginning of February 1258. The Mongols were equipped with vast siege engines that had been brought from China, and these soon made significant inroads into the walls of Baghdad. The end came on 10 February, when thousands of Mongols forced their way in. The Caliph surrendered in an attempt to save his life but the massacre that followed was horrendous even by Mongol standards. With the Mongols were a number of Georgian Christians, who were particularly ruthless. Men, women and children were put to the sword regardless of age or rank. In all, over 80,000 people died. The only ones to survive were either a few attractive youths who would make desirable slaves or the Christians who had sought sanctuary in their churches. For the Caliph, a special fate awaited. He was sewn up in a felt bag and then ridden over by hundreds of horses.

The sacking of Baghdad created shock waves that reverberated throughout Islam. It is not mere hyperbole to assert that it was the greatest disaster to strike the religion since its birth 700 years previously. It was also clear where the next assault would fall. Only Syria and Egypt stood between the Mongols and the complete extinction of the Muslim Empire. Syria was the first to be attacked. The Mongols' initial target was the town of Mayyafaraqin, in the north. After the city fell, the fate of its people was terrible, no doubt as an example to others that resisted this apocalyptic host. The ruler of the town had some time previously crucified a Christian priest who had been sent as an envoy by the Mongols. His fate was barbaric. The flesh was torn from his body and stuffed into his mouth before he died, choking on his own vomit.

City after city fell throughout Syria. The Mongol army, led by Hulagu, had the support of Hethoum of Armenia. He also received help from Bohemond VI in Antioch, the most direct co-operation yet between Frank and Mongol. The greatest prize of all in Syria would be Damascus. Aleppo had already gone, although its aged leader was spared because of his bravery. When news of Hulagu's coming reached Damascus, the Sultan, an-Nasir Yasuf, was so terrified that he offered to hand the city over to the Mamelukes if they would come to his aid. However, he was too late. The city fell after six days and the Muslim inhabitants were again slaughtered. It was another crushing blow, leaving the whole of Islam at the feet of the Mongols.

The seeming invincibility of the Mongols should have warned the pitiful number of Franks who had stayed in Outremer to take great care in their dealings. There still remained at least one hothead in their ranks, however, in the form of Julian of Sidon. He decided to raid Syria as he deemed it defenceless in the wake of the Mongol advance. However, he overlooked the rather significant detail that Syria was now in Mongol hands and he was therefore raiding Mongol, not Muslim, territory. In the raid, Julian compounded his folly by slaying the nephew of a great Mongol leader, Kitbuqa. The response from the Mongols was typically destructive. They rode to Sidon and destroyed it. It was only thanks to the presence of some Genoese ships in port that anyone escaped.

It was fortunate for the Franks that the Mongols did not naturally bear them animosity. Because of this, they did not provide an immediate threat, although the Mongols could have taken the Franks' tiny enclave with impunity if they so wished. The greatest danger by far was that faced by the Muslims. But now, when perhaps Islam itself stood on the edge of its own Dark Age, the fickle hand of fate intervened. Thousands of miles away in China, Mongka died on 11 August 1259. The succession was the subject of family intrigues, which dictated that Hulagu return to ensure that he was not disadvantaged as a result of them. Many of his troops went with him, depleting his army in Syria.

It was a supreme irony that the Mongols were now about to face their greatest challenge. Much of their success so far had come about because their opponents had been poorly trained, poorly led, and poorly motivated. Such criticisms did not hold true for the Mamelukes of Egypt. Disciplined and highly trained, taught to live for warfare from an early age, they formed a cohesive army. They were also formidably led, with Baibars prominent among the leaders.

In 1260, while sorting out his family affairs in China, Hulagu sent his envoys to demand the submission of the Sultan, Qutuz. The Sultan's reply was prompt and unambiguous; the two envoys were sliced in half. But the Mongols were already experiencing difficulties. The departure of Hulagu had encouraged rebellion in Damascus. Qutuz gathered together his forces and moved into Palestine. He also embarked on a bold diplomatic initiative. He sent to Acre, asking for permission to cross the lands held by the Franks, as well as for supplies. Even military assistance was discussed. In the end the Franks, showing unusual insight, hedged their bets, allowing the Muslims to pass through their lands but stopping short of outright military support. The Muslims were in fact encamped outside of Acre when news came that the Mongols had crossed the Jordan. The Muslims set out to meet them and set up camp at Ain Jalud in Palestine.

As the sun rose on 3 September 1260, it heralded the dawn of one of the most decisive days in Medieval history. The Muslims were roused by news that the Mongols, with their Georgian and Armenian allies, were advancing on the camp. However, the odds were very different now than they had been before Hulagu's return east. The Mamelukes had a bigger army and they knew the terrain well. Qutuz resolved to maximise these advantages by hiding the bulk of his force in the hills behind Ain Jalud. A small force under Baibars was left as bait. The move was a stunning success. The Mongols rushed headlong at Baibars' men, who retreated into the hills. As the Mongol leader, Kitbuqa, led his men on they became careless and failed to note that the ground favoured an ambush. It therefore came as a great shock when all of a sudden arrows rained down on them from the hills, and huge waves of cavalry descended upon them.

Though outnumbered and surprised, the Mongols fought magnificently. The Egyptians began to slacken and Qutuz had to enter the fray personally to inspire them. But in the slogging match that the battle became, it was inevitable that the numerically superior force would win, given equality of armament and spirit. The Mongols broke, and many desperately tried to fight their way to safety. Kitbuqa was not one of them. He fought on heroically until overpowered and captured. He was taken before Qutuz, who mocked him, but his spirit remained unbroken. He reminded Qutuz that the Mamelukes were renowned for disloyalty and would one day turn on him. The truth of the taunt infuriated Qutuz, who snatched a sword and cut off Kitbuqa's head.

Ain Jalud signified the high-water mark for the Mongols in Asia. Internal dissension would weaken their army and their threat would diminish. In contrast, their victory showed that the Mamelukes were now in the ascendancy. They were aggressive and confident and the Franks would be well advised to be on their guard against them. The Franks had been tolerated in the region in recent decades not because their power intimidated the Muslims but because they brought with them trading advantages. If ever a Muslim leader emerged who prized military domination ahead of commerce, then their days would be numbered.

For Qutuz, the taunts of Kitbuqa came home to roost much more quickly than he feared. On his return to Egypt, he lost the support of many of the Mamelukes. Given their involvement in past palace intrigues, these men were dangerous enemies. Even before the army arrived back in Cairo, Qutuz was deposed. He was lured into a trap while hunting and run through with a sword. The Egyptian leaders demanded to know who was responsible. A huge, towering figure of a man stepped forward and declaimed that it was him. His name was Baibars. He was proclaimed Sultan there and then. His enthronement was the start of a reign of terror for the Franks.

Baibars first consolidated his position in Egypt and then conquered much of Syria. He next sought to gain revenge on those who had helped the Mongols, especially the Armenians and the Franks of Antioch. The Franks of Outremer might have hoped to escape because of their neutral position in the conflict but they were to be undone by the greed of the Military Orders. Negotiations commenced to obtain the release of any Franks still held by the Muslims. However, the deal was undermined when the Hospitallers and the Templars refused to return in exchange the Muslim prisoners whom they held. Many of these captives were skilled artisans, who did useful work for the Orders. Baibars was incensed at their selfishness and arrogance and raided Galilee, seizing Nazareth and marching right up to the walls of Acre.

However, now the Mongols returned. Baibars raised a large army to turn them back but it was not needed, his forces already in Syria being adequate for the purpose. Baibars therefore decided to use the army he had just raised to raid Palestine. He attacked Caesarea, which fell easily, and then moved on to Haifa. The city was incapable of putting up a strong defence and those who could fled to safety in the ships in the harbour. Those not so fortunate were brutally massacred.

Soon after these events, Hulagu died in Central Asia. With him died the desire of the Mongols for vengeance. Freed of threat from this quarter, Baibars plotted his next step against the rapidly contracting Christian territories in the region. Galilee was watched over by the Templar fortress of Safed, a magnificent structure. Although well manned, many of the garrison were local troops without the desire or the accoutrements of the Franks. Nevertheless, determined attacks by the Muslims were repulsed, and Baibars resorted to trickery, offering safe conducts to the entire garrison if they would stop fighting. Many of the local troops took advantage of this offer and gave themselves up under cover of darkness. Now hopelessly short of men, the Templars sought terms. One of the Syrians who remained was sent to Baibars to arrange the details.

This man returned with a good offer. If the Templars gave themselves up, they could leave freely. They decided to take advantage of the terms, but they had been duped. Once disarmed, they were presented with a terrible ultimatum. The next morning, they had to choose between conversion to Islam or martyrdom. The Templars were often arrogant and self-important. Should anyone doubt that they had courage then the lessons of that morning serve as an object lesson. To a man, they chose decapitation rather than disgrace. Less than a century later, the Templars would collapse amid accusations of heresy. The actions of these brave men at Safed are perhaps the greatest proof of the falsehood of the stories that were told about them then.

All this was but a foretaste of things that were to come. A whirlwind was about to be unleashed on the Levant. Following the death of Hulagu, Hethoum of Armenia was well aware of his vulnerability. He hurried to the court of the Mongols, hoping to ensure support from the new regime. While he was there, a storm of frightening intensity ravaged his lands. The Mamelukes descended on Armenia in their thousands. The Armenians were ill prepared and outnumbered. Their capital, Sis, was ransacked and 40,000 prisoners taken away. The army then considered attacking Antioch but was bought off by Bohemond. The troops then returned to Baibars, who was not best pleased that Antioch had escaped.

Baibars' ambition was far from satiated. The next year, 1267, he raided Outremer again, riding right up to the walls of Acre with his forces disguised behind the captured banners of the Hospitallers. Only with difficulty was he

The arrest of the Knights Templar – the Knights were to return from Outremer to a future of uncertainty and ultimate destruction. (Roy 20 C VII f. 42v Arrest of the Templars, 1308, Chronicle of France or of St Denis *(14th century); British Library, London/ Bridgeman Art Library, London/New York)*

driven off. Incredibly, oblivious to the danger, the Genoese and Venetian factions continued to fight with each other. In the following year, Baibars returned and took Jaffa. What remained of Outremer now barely merited the status of a foothold.

Any misconception of the seriousness of the threat was about to be brutally banished. During 1268, Baibars captured the Templar castle of Beaufort and then marched north. His destination was soon made clear. On 14 May the citizens of Antioch, one of the oldest parts of the Crusader territories, woke to find themselves faced by the army of Baibars. Some of his force had been detached to prevent reinforcements from fighting their way through. Those who remained closely invested the city. Bohemond was absent and the defence was led by his Constable, Simon Mansel, a man of much courage but little judgement. Hopelessly outnumbered, he led most of his forces out in a futile and costly foray against the Muslims. He only succeeded in reducing the size of his already inadequate garrison. The walls of the city were in good repair but they were massive and there were simply not enough men to defend them.

The attempts of the Franks to negotiate with Baibars were unsuccessful and on 18 May a general assault was launched by the Muslims. Baibars was provided with excellent siege engines and, given his numerical advantage, the result was a foregone conclusion. A breach was quickly made, through which large numbers of Muslim warriors poured. What followed was an outrage that matched any crime committed by the Franks in their time in the East. Baibars was to prove himself to be a man devoid of honour, morals or pity every bit as much as Reynald of Chatillon. Now that the city was his, he determined that none would escape his vengeance. The gates were bolted to prevent anyone leaving and then thousands were put to the sword, and those who remained were dragged off into captivity. Baibars sent a mocking letter to Bohemond, who had indeed been fortunate to be absent.

Finally, Baibars now seems to have been satisfied with his gains. Rumours of a new Crusade from France were rife and there was also a resurgent Mongol power to contend with. Therefore, when the Franks sought a truce Baibars agreed to it. Hugh III of Cyprus, had succeeded officially to the crown of Jerusalem when Conradin was embroiled in a bitter war that he lost, along with his head. That war involved a brother of King Louis of France, a self-serving man named Charles of Anjou. He aspired to become Emperor of Constantinople and as part of his plan he was on good terms with Baibars. The Sultan, for his part, was still concerned that Louis would launch another Crusade but his death at Tunis removed that threat and he renewed his operations in Outremer in 1271, taking among other places the famous castle of the Hospitallers at Krak des Chevaliers.

The concept of the Crusade was now widely considered to be an anachronism. A few men still felt attachment to its precepts but they were in a minority. One of these was Prince Edward, son of Henry III. However, even he, an inspiring individual who epitomised chivalric and knightly virtues, could only raise an army of 1,000 men. Nevertheless, he determined to make a favourable impression. When he led his small force to Palestine, he was appalled at what he found on arrival. The Venetians had been supplying timber and metal to the Egyptians for years in the full knowledge that these would be used to make armaments for use against the Franks. The Genoese controlled the slave trade with Egypt, all with the approval of the authorities in Acre. Such materialism, blind to its terminal effect on Outremer, was alien to all that a man of honour like Edward believed in. After a few cursory raids into Muslim territory, it quickly became apparent that he was fighting for a lost cause. He decided to abandon his delusions of military grandeur and seek some diplomatic reward instead.

He therefore broached another truce. Baibars was amenable, deeming the Franks to be an insignificant threat against the might of the Mongols and also not wishing to call down a larger Crusade upon his kingdom. However, Edward appears to have disturbed him. Perhaps Baibars perceived his great fighting qualities which, if not treated with respect, might come back to haunt him in the future. He therefore enlisted the help of the Assassins. One of their number infiltrated the Prince's chamber and stabbed him with a poisoned dagger. Prompt action by his doctors (the prosaic version of the tale), or his wife (the more romantic alternative), saved his life and Edward eventually recovered after being seriously ill for some time. He returned home to England to inherit the throne as Edward I, and to devote his life to a great military career against the Welsh and the Scots.

The Archbishop of Liege had travelled with Edward. While he was at Acre he heard that he had been elected Pope. He took the name of Gregory X. He retained an intense interest in Outremer and commissioned a number of reports to try to identify what had gone wrong in the Frankish East. A number of surprisingly honest opinions were voiced. Many of them homed in on the view that the Papacy had lost credibility because of its vast wealth and widespread corruption. Others argued that there was little practical benefit in continuing to send expeditions to the Levant, while yet another faction argued that the West had become too decadent and worldly-wise to tolerate the hardships that a Crusade demanded. Gregory summoned a council to Tours to discuss the issues in depth. In a silent message that spoke volumes, none of the kings of Western Europe bothered to turn up. By the time that Gregory died in 1276, it was obvious to him that there was unlikely to be any other significant Crusading army heading east for some time, if indeed ever.

By this time, there was an aura of unreality abroad in Outremer. King Hugh was an honourable man but never won the support of the barons on the mainland and eventually retired in a huff to his other kingdom, Cyprus. Acre was taken over by the representative of Charles of Anjou and, because of his friendship with Baibars, a little more time was won. Baibars instead concentrated on Armenia and in 1275 launched another great raid into that country. A large Mongol army was making its way towards the region and he returned home. It was to be his last significant act. On 1 July 1277 he died, possibly of poisoning. A strong and capable ruler, he was a vicious and dishonourable man. In this respect, he fitted well with the needs of his time.

The Christians were ecstatic at the news but it was too late to matter. Baibars' life did not make the death of Outremer a formality – in reality it had been that for many years, possibly from the day that it was born – but he hastened its end. The kingdom was now in the twilight of its day. All that was left to the Franks were a few cities dotted along the coastline. The superstructure of the state still stood but the foundations that supported the edifice had been washed away.

CHAPTER 27

Armageddon

The death of Baibars gave the Franks some temporary respite. The Mongols were encouraged by his demise to try their luck against the Mamelukes again. For their part, the Muslims were still on good terms with Charles of Anjou and did not want to lose his friendship. And, not for the first time, the passing of a strong ruler left a vacuum that several candidates attempted to fill.

Baibars' son, Baraqa, was his heir. He inherited most of his father's negative attributes with few of the positive. He was cruel and spiteful but proved completely incapable of dealing with the political intrigues of his Emirs. In 1279, two years after Baibars died, the leader of the Syrian army, Qalawun, led his forces on Cairo. Such resistance as there was fell away quickly and Baraqa was fortunate to be allowed to abdicate rather than face execution. The new governor in Damascus, Sonqor al-Ashqar, refused to recognise the new regime in Egypt. However, a battle near Damascus in 1280 led to his defeat and he was forced to make peace with Qalawun.

But Qalawun was soon faced by an even greater threat. For some time now, the Mongols had been trying to induce the Franks to enter an alliance against the Muslims but the presence in the region of Roger of San Severino, the representative of Charles of Anjou, ensured that their advances were coldly received. A Mongol attack in northern Syria in September 1280 resulted in the sack of Aleppo, and large numbers of refugees fled south in abject terror. The Hospitallers seized on the opportunity to profit from their discomfort.

Another Mongol assault was planned for the following year, and the help of the Franks was sought once again. The Mongols promised to send 100,000 troops to Syria but even this generosity did not encourage the Franks to offer their assistance. Only the Hospitallers agreed to cooperate, thus marking themselves out for special attention from the Egyptians. However, the Armenians were longing to throw in their lot with the Mongols once more and the combined force that was raised, though smaller than originally anticipated, still created massive problems for the Mamelukes. The Mongol force was divided into two; the first was given the task of reducing the Muslim fortresses along the Euphrates, while the second, led by Mangu Timur, brother of the Mongol leader (known as the Ilkhan), would be the main assault force. This second force, accompanied by the Armenians, now marched into Syria where they were joined by a small group of Hospitallers. Qalawun came out to meet them. Another decisive battle was imminent.

This took place on 30 October 1281. The Mongols were arrayed with Mangu in the centre and other Mongols on the left flank. The right was made up of the Armenians and the Hospitallers, along with some Georgians. The charge of the right flank originally proved irresistible and the Muslim left streamed away in panic. At this, the Mongol cavalry, elated at their success, lost their always-suspect discipline and left the field to pursue the fleeing enemy. Then Timur was wounded and consequently lost his nerve, telling his forces to retreat. They were heavily cut up as they did so and the right wing, of a sudden dangerously isolated, only fought their way out with difficulty. Qalawun had achieved a famous victory.

The Franks seemed unaware that their position had deteriorated markedly as a result of Qalawun's triumph. The Mongols were their natural allies. Yet the Franks continued to carry on their constant internal wrangling oblivious to their precarious situation. In Tripoli, Guy of Jebail, with the support of the Templars, was at odds with Bohemond VII. There had been open warfare between the two for several years, with Bohemond generally getting the worst of it. Guy resolved to take Tripoli itself, Bohemond's capital now that Antioch was lost. He stole his way into the Templar headquarters in the city at dead of night. However, his planning was awry. The Templars who were due to support him were not present. Guy, deciding that discretion was definitely the better part of valour, tried to escape from the city. It was too late – the alarm had already been raised. Guy hurried to the nearest defensible position, a tower owned by the Hospitallers, and barricaded himself in.

The Hospitallers brokered a peaceful settlement, arranging that if the men in the tower gave themselves up, they would not be harmed. To these terms Guy readily agreed but he badly misread Bohemond; moral scruples counted for little with him. Guy's supporters were savagely blinded. An even worse fate awaited Guy and his brothers, who were captured with him. They were buried up to their neck in a ditch and left to die in the Levantine sun, a fate hastened by Bohemond's decree that passers-by could throw anything they liked at the men. Ironically, Bohemond did little to improve his own position by this cruel act as even his own supporters found it repugnant.

The situation in Outremer was about to change dramatically because of events hundreds of miles away. Charles of Anjou had taken control of Sicily after a bitter war. His rule of the island was tyrannical and the Sicilians eventually decided they could take no more. In a brilliantly co-ordinated uprising, every Frenchman in the island was killed overnight in an operation that would become known as the Sicilian Vespers. This shifted the attention of Charles away from the East and he would spend the next ten years trying unsuccessfully to recover the island from the native Sicilians. This dramatic turn of events forced Charles to recall Roger of San Severino; he was too valued an advisor to be left away from the heart of the action. His place was taken by Odo of Poilechien, who agreed a ten-year truce with the Muslims. Qalawun was happy to accept, still concerned at the Mongol menace. Following the truce, King Hugh of Cyprus crossed to Outremer to try to take control of the tiny kingdom but he was not universally welcomed by the population, and he died a year later in 1284, to be followed soon after by his son and heir John.

The castle at Marqab.

Qalawun had neither forgotten nor forgiven the Hospitallers for their part in the Mongol invasions. Ominously, they were specifically excluded from the truce. Their greatest remaining fortress was the castle at Marqab. It stood atop an isolated plateau, dominating the plains at its feet far below. Built of black basalt it epitomised strength and power. For years it had been used as a base to dominate the Muslims in the area. It had also been used as a point from which the Hospitallers could raid further afield.

When Qalawun attacked Marqab it proved a real challenge. Although the Muslims possessed many catapults, the angle of trajectory required for the projectiles to hit the walls proved impossible. The Hospitallers, on the other hand, had artillery of their own that they used to far greater effect. The siege lasted for a month, with Qalawun suffering the most. Finally, he resorted to his most lethal force, the humble miners within his army. They dug deep into the hillside, excavating vast caverns that they propped up with timbers. When they deemed the moment right, they set the logs ablaze. As the timber burned, the walls started to crumble. Although the Muslims who attempted to break into the castle were driven back, all the same they let the Hospitallers know that other mines went deep under the castle and that their position was therefore hopeless. In an attempt to prise the Franks out, Qalawun offered good terms, which were accepted. The knights could leave complete with their armour and the foot soldiers could also go, although they must leave their equipment behind. Unlike Baibars, Qalawun not only offered terms that were good, but he also saw that they were subsequently adhered to.

Two years later, in 1287, an earthquake allowed Qalawun to walk in and take possession of Lattakieh on 20 April. Only a few towns and cities now remained to the Franks: Acre, Tyre, Beirut, Tripoli and Sidon. It appeared that the situation was as parlous as it had been a century before when just Tyre had been left to the Franks but, in reality, it was much worse. Europe had lost interest in the Crusades, absorbed in its own dynastic struggles and disenchanted with a discredited ideal. The Franks of Outremer were exhausted and, worse still, divided, obsessed with their own factional intrigues. Their internecine hatred had prevented a Mongol alliance. They were secure in the knowledge of fools, believing that the trading advantages they offered the Muslims made them impervious to assault. Their analysis was wrong; they believed their arguments only because they wished to. They had completely misunderstood the situation.

Yet another dispute was to precipitate another crisis. The death of Bohemond VII in 1287 left the throne of Tripoli vacant. He had left the city to his sister, Lucia, but she had spent many years in Europe and therefore was unacceptable to the local leaders. They offered the city to Bohemond's mother, Sibylla of Armenia, but would not agree to her choice of bailli. They withdrew their offer and Sibylla returned to Armenia. Shortly afterwards, Sibylla arrived with her husband at Acre. However, the Commune in Tripoli refused to accept her as ruler and sought the help of the Genoese.

Another man desired Tripoli. He was Bartholomew Embriaco of Jebail, whose brother, Guy, had been executed by Bohemond a few years previously. He enlisted the aid of Qalawun for his schemes. The Sultan was delighted for the opportunity that this gave him to break the truce he had made with Odo of Poilechien, as he could legitimately argue that he was only responding to a request for help from the Franks themselves. Qalawun sent a large force to Syria, keeping their targeted destination secret. However, the Templars had many spies in his camp and one of them informed the Grand Master, William of Beaujeu, that an attack on the city was imminent. The Master was known to be a political intriguer and the inhabitants therefore disbelieved him. They carried on arguing against him in ignorant bliss, to be rudely awakened when a huge army materialised outside of the city walls.

Too late, the Franks were now aware of their predicament. They gave control of the city to Lucia, who must have pondered often why she had exchanged the relative security of Europe for this. The Christians kept the sea-routes open and defended their city bravely. However, they were hugely outnumbered by an enemy equipped with modern siege artillery. Eventually, one of the main towers protecting the city crumbled and the Venetians decided that it was high time that they made their escape. They were soon followed by the Genoese present. The people of Tripoli were now on their own. The fate of the city was sealed, and it was a terrible fate indeed. It fell on 26 April 1289. Lucia managed to escape but Bartholomew Embriaco died in the massacre that followed, a thoroughly merited end given his part in the loss of the city. All the men caught were killed, and the women and children taken away into captivity. Even a small group who managed to row across to a nearby island were relentlessly chased and slaughtered. Once this blood-bath had reached its inevitable conclusion,

The fall of Tripoli in 1289 – by this stage Outremer had little time to live. (Add. 27695 f. 5 Capture of Tripoli in Syria by the Sultan of Egypt in 1288 (Octavo), Tractatum de Septem Vitiis *(late 14th century); British Library, London / Bridgeman Art Library, London / New York)*

Qalawun demolished the city walls. The Franks would never be able to use the city again.

There were few vestiges of complacency among the Franks now. The temper of Qalawun was all too clear. Pleas for help born of desperation were sent to Europe but they fell on deaf ears. There was only weariness in response to the frantic requests, resulting from decades of unfulfilled promise and dashed hopes. Only one party responded and, in the final irony of the Crusades in the Levant, its involvement was directly responsible for the end of Outremer. Appeals for help now lacked credibility to such an extent that the sole response came from a group of unemployed and uneducated labourers in the north of Italy. The Franks could not afford to be selective and arrangements were made to transport this shambles of a force across the Mediterranean. The Venetians offered to help, aware that, although they could be ambivalent about the fall of Tripoli, which was in the Genoese sphere of influence, they could not afford to be complacent about Acre.

The rabble duly arrived in Outremer. They idly waited for an enemy to attack. Their wages quickly fell into arrears and they became restless. A dissatisfied army is a dangerous animal, and the soldiers quickly became unsettled. Around them in the markets of Acre they saw prosperous Muslim traders hawking their wares. It seemed to mock everything that the Crusades stood for. The undisciplined Italians quickly ran out of control. Inflamed by the Muslims, they started to taunt them. Harsh words led to jostling and then blows were openly traded. The Italians had killed many Muslims before the Military Orders arrived to restore order.

Once again, newcomers from the West who did not comprehend the politics of Outremer had struck out at those who were not the natural enemy. This time, their rashness would have devastating and irreversible consequences. The insulted merchants and their families sent representatives to the only place where they believed they could find justice – the court of Qalawun in Cairo. When he heard their pleas and saw the bloodstained robes of the murdered merchants his anger was roused. Although it suited him that he now had another excuse to break the truce, his anger was probably unfeigned. He sent word to the Christians of Acre that the perpetrators of this heinous crime should be sent to him for justice. This was a blatant challenge to the sovereignty of Acre and it is a measure of the deep concern felt by the city that it was not instantly rejected. However, the majority view was that the Franks could not comply with the request. They tried to muddy the issue by saying that the men were under the jurisdiction of the Venetians over whom the people of Acre held no authority. Predictably, these legal niceties were lost on Qalawun.

Qalawun took advice from his lawyers, who affirmed that he was within his rights to attack Acre. Word reached William of Beaujeu through his spies that the city was to be attacked but he cannot have been a convincing advocate as the inhabitants of Acre chose to disbelieve him. Frantic because of their incredulity, William sent his own mission to Cairo to forestall the attack. The Sultan agreed to halt the assault if the Franks would buy him off with a gold coin for each inhabitant. By the standards of the day this was a significant but not unobtainable ransom. However, when the Grand Master put this proposition to the leaders of the city he was shouted down and accused of cowardice. Qalawun made no secret of his intention now, openly announcing it to the world. However, he was suddenly struck down by illness and it became clear that he was dying. He would not, even now, reprieve the Franks and on his deathbed made his son and successor, al-Ashraf Khalil, swear to destroy them.

The Franks attempted to negotiate their salvation but al-Ashraf was no mild-mannered youth who would so easily ignore a solemn oath. He delivered an unmistakable message to the Franks. Without the formality of an audience the envoys of Acre were thrown into prison to die soon after. In March 1291 the Muslim army set out. With it were nearly 100 siege engines. Troops from Damascus and Egypt formed the army, which according to chroniclers totalled 60,000 cavalry and 160,000 infantry. Even allowing for exaggeration, it must be accepted that the force was massive. On 5 April it arrived before Acre. The sound of kettledrums and trumpets filled the skies around the city, which was tangibly tense with fear and trepidation. A few knights had arrived from Europe and King Henry II of Cyprus had also sent a force. But they were hugely outnumbered and even behind the towering walls of Acre, their prospects were bleak indeed.

The day after the Muslims arrived, they commenced their attack. Huge rocks were catapulted at the walls, dislodging masonry and crushing the defenders.

Flights of arrows rained down from the sky. The Christians still controlled the sea, so provisions continued to arrive, but the walls could not be manned adequately. The Military Orders launched several night-time raids but the first ended in chaos when the horses tripped over the tent-ropes of the Muslim camp and the second was beaten back when the Muslims lit torches to illuminate the darkness.

A month after the assault began, King Henry arrived in person with a few thousand troops. He at least provided a focal point for the defenders to rally round but the situation was now perilous in the extreme. A last attempt to negotiate was made but even as talks were in progress a missile fired from within the city missed al-Ashraf by a few feet. Any hope of a peaceful solution – which must have been remote anyway – disappeared at that moment. Once again the decisive moment was brought about by means of mines under the city walls. It was reported that there were 1,000 miners at work undermining each of twelve towers. On 8 May the Franks abandoned one tower that was now deemed to be indefensible and a week later another fell. Those defenders who could made their escape to the inner line of walls.

A full-blooded assault was launched on 18 May. It proved irresistible and the Muslims burst into the Accursed Tower, a key point in the defences. The defence put up by the doomed garrison was magnificent. Templars and Hospitallers, whose bickering had brought the kingdom to the edge of destruction, fought and died side by side. The fighting was intense and vicious, but the outcome certain. Although the Crusaders sold their lives dearly, this was no more than a brave valedictory gesture. The Hospitaller Master was badly wounded and had to be dragged on board ship. William of Beaujeu fought like a man possessed but was eventually struck down by a freak arrow that hit an unprotected part of his body under his armpit. Aware that nothing more could be done, and conscious of his duty to survive, King Henry also escaped. It was not, as some suggested, the act of a coward but of a wise and prudent man.

Although there were a number of ships in the harbour, their capacity was pathetically inadequate to cope with those who now frantically sought to escape from Acre. There was pandemonium as the Muslims, fired by blood-lust, slew everyone that they came across. Even at this stage, unscrupulous merchants made a profit by selling berths on their ships to the highest bidder. Of those that did not find passage, few survived and even they would live out their lives as slaves.

There was one last drama of note to be enacted. The Templars had their headquarters at the south-west corner of the city and this became a place of last refuge. Once again, miners were called in. After five days, al-Ashraf became inpatient. He offered the defenders freedom if they would surrender. There seemed little point in refusing the terms, especially as so many non-combatants were inside. However, when the Mamelukes arrived to take possession they started to sexually abuse many of the women and boys in the building. Furious, the Templars snatched up their weapons, slew the insolent Muslims and raised their banners over the building once again.

Al-Ashraf apologised to the Templars and discussions were reopened. When Templar envoys arrived at his camp, however, he had them beheaded. Aware that there was no possibility of escape, the defenders steeled themselves to die. The mines were now doing their work, and the walls were visibly moving. Exulted by their imminent success, thousands of Muslims poured into the building. Their weight was too much for the sagging structure, which collapsed in a heap, burying Christian and Muslim alike. Nothing could better serve as a symbol of the destruction of the Christian Kingdom of Outremer, which disappeared in a cloud of dust. The vision and the state of the Christians were now nothing more than rubble.

The other Christian cities of Outremer died meekly. Tyre, the scene of Conrad of Montferrat's heroic defence, was governed by a weak man with little stomach for a fight, who sailed away as soon as the Muslims came into view. Sidon followed suit and then Beirut. The last to fall was the port of Haifa. Deprived of hope, it surrendered without a fight.

One hundred and ninety-five years after the First Crusade set out, the dream of a Christian kingdom in the East had evaporated. The Templars held two fortresses on the mainland, but that of Tortosa was evacuated on 3 August, and the massive citadel at Athlit was abandoned eleven days later, still untaken by siege. There was only the tiniest remnant left, the minuscule isle of Ruad 2 miles offshore. It lacked fresh water supplies, which had to be brought in by sea. The Templars who inhabited this God-forsaken rock hung on to it for twelve years before voluntarily leaving. They sailed back to France, to the destruction of their Order by an avaricious King of France, the country that more than any other had given birth to the Templars. It was the final contradiction of an era of contradictions.

As these last weary survivors sailed towards the setting sun, they must surely have reflected on the brief and ultimately tragic history of the Kingdom of Outremer. The great hopes that Christendom had once held were long gone, replaced by scenes of terror and despair. The last Templars, returning to an uncertain future, must have felt that the shedding of so much blood and the sacrifice of so many lives had been a pointless gesture. Euphoria and ecstasy had been transformed into disillusionment. The land of Christ was stained red with the blood of humanity. If they truly believed that God would reward the righteous in their endeavours, then surely they must be sinners indeed. The Muslims' perspective was clear and is best summed up in the simple words of one of their chroniclers: 'God grant that they never set foot here again'.

Scholars have argued for centuries over the merits of the Crusades, and indeed continue to do so – it sometimes seems that the Crusades are still being fought on academic battlefields. While some Western academics declare that they played little part in the attitudes of the modern Muslim world, there are Muslim writers who take an opposing view. For example, Amin Madlouf asserts that 'it is often surprising to discover the extent to which the attitude of the Arabs (and of the Muslims in general) towards the West is still influenced, even today, by events that supposedly ended seven centuries ago'.

Some scholars have seen the movement as an integral part in the development of the West, even suggesting that it helped give momentum to that rebirth of Western civilisation known as the Renaissance. Others have argued that the

Crusades were a complete failure, and are of no consequence to the history of the world. Whatever one's perspective it is difficult not to conclude that, despite the good intentions of some of the men involved, the results of the Crusades were mostly negative.

The First Crusade was launched ostensibly to help Eastern Christendom. The Crusades ended with the Byzantine Empire teetering on the brink of ruin. The Crusades cannot be held completely, or even mainly, responsible for that. The disaster of Manzikert, one of an incredible sequence of events that gave life to the Crusades, shows well enough that matters were badly amiss within Byzantium. However, the Western warriors were at fault in their vision. Their best chance of a strong Christian power in the East lay with Byzantium. If the Franks had supported the Eastern Emperor, and helped him to recover the heart of his empire in Anatolia, then the Muslim threat might have been held off. As it was, the end of the Crusades saw Byzantium as the most pitiful shadow of what it had once been. Later Crusades, particularly the misguided Fourth Crusade, had helped to decimate the empire. The Byzantines exhausted themselves in winning back the lands that they lost to the Franks.

The Crusades also did little to discourage the growth of Muslim fundamentalism. Although they were not the main reason for the rebirth of Muslim fundamentalism – and it must be emphasised that the Muslims were by no means unused to such fundamentalism at times in their past – they were part of a process that hardened Muslim attitudes. After a period when their conquests had been based on terror, Islam had developed into a tolerant and civilised culture. It must be allowed that other events led to the growth of intolerance, of which the clashes with the Mongols were perhaps the most significant, but the Crusades did nothing to discourage this trend. The fanaticism of the Franks spawned violent hatred among the Muslims of Palestine and its surrounding territories. The horrific blood-letting after the capture of Jerusalem genuinely shocked Islam. Of course, Muslims had committed, and would commit, equally savage atrocities but perhaps the greatest lesson of the Crusades is that intolerance breeds intolerance.

The enormous effort required to destroy the Franks when taken together with the almost genocidal assault of the Mongols weakened the Muslims. Much of their vitality went and their lands fell victim to the Ottoman Turks. Perhaps if the Islamic world had been more robust then the Ottomans could have been assimilated and their more excessive attitudes controlled. As it was, they came to dominate the Muslim world and treated their Christian subjects on many occasions with great cruelty. This was the direct result of the debilitation of the Muslim world that occurred when they had to repel the Mongol threat while watching their backs at the same time. Some might argue that by the time the Mongols arrived the Franks were already a spent force. The actions of successive Sultans argue against this. Men such as Baibars and Qalawun were no longer prepared to tolerate the Franks, despite the commercial potential they brought to the region, and therefore saw them as a threat.

Perhaps the Crusades had lasted for too long. The dream should have ended with the capture of Tyre after Hattin. If this had happened, then the Muslims would have been spared a century more of conflict and toil. It would also have saved an ocean of Christian blood. An end at this time may have avoided the abuse by the Church of the Crusading ideal. By channelling the aggression of the barbarian warlords of Western Europe into 'acceptable' objectives Urban II had unleashed a demon. However unpalatable it may be to moralists, there was a certain logic in defending Christians against those whom the Church argued were natural enemies. Although the propagandists were wrong in assigning so much blame to the Muslims, the Crusades nevertheless captured the spirit of very violent times.

But when later Popes chose to use the Crusading ideal as a means of persecuting other Christians, much credibility was lost. Other Crusades would be launched, against the Ottoman Turks, the pagan tribes around the Baltic, the Moors in Spain. However, no more would the Holy Land be held by Christians. It had become increasingly difficult to raise sufficient numbers to launch a credible bid to recover it. After all, why should men travel so far when the benefits of the Crusade could be gained so much closer to home? Europe would anyway be forced onto the defensive by the expansion of the Turks into the Balkans and beyond.

There were great men involved in the Crusades but they were without exception flawed. Courage took precedence over wisdom and prudence, and honour was too often overshadowed by savagery and selfishness. Few, if any, benefited from the Crusades. The merchant cities of Italy exploited the situation to their best advantage but it is probable that even without the Crusades they would have found another way of trading with the East – as indeed they had been doing long before the first Western knight set foot in the Levant.

It had been a bitter experience for all those involved. No happiness came from them, only misery, for Christian, Muslim, Jew, Frank, Slav and Arab. As human drama the Crusades are unrivalled in Western history but their colour cannot obscure the fact that, as an illustration of the way to live, their example is best forgotten.

Bibliography

There is a wealth of material available covering the Crusades. In this bibliography, I have attempted to highlight the information that has been particularly valuable in my research for *God Wills It!*. As such, this list of titles is a very personal selection of those that I have found to be interesting and thought-provoking. Many of them are eminently approachable for the general reader.

My intention in this bibliography is to suggest works to which readers might turn if they wish to investigate further this fascinating period of history. The books listed provide a cross-section covering many aspects of the Crusades, from their inception to their end. It is not my aim to provide comprehensive details of all the works available, but merely to point readers in the direction of publications that are likely to stimulate their interest.

I have analysed the books in two sections; the first deals with primary sources. Some are complete translations and others are modern books that contain selected excerpts translated from original chroniclers. Most of the quotations in *God Wills It!* draw on sources in this bibliography. The accounts given in these primary sources add considerable colour to the story of the Crusades but, when reading them, their lack of objectivity needs to be borne in mind.

The second section deals with more modern works. Those listed have been extensively used in research for this book. All of them provide very accessible accounts of various aspects of the Crusades. The intention within this section is to provide enough information on books covering a range of topics to allow the general readers to search for more detail on a subject which is of particular interest to them.

These form just a small selection from the large range available. Many of the titles suggested include comprehensive bibliographies that give details of publications on more specific aspects of the Crusading movement.

1. Primary Sources

Ambroise. *Crusade of Richard the Lionheart*, tr. M.J. Hubert, New York, 1976

Anon. *Gesta Francorum*, ed. R. Hill, London, 1962

Brundage, J. *The Crusades: a documentary survey*, Milwaukee, 1976 edn

Fulcher of Chartres. *A History of the Expedition to Jerusalem*, ed. H.S. Fink, tr. F.R. Ryan, New York, 1973

Hallam, E. (gen. ed.). *Chronicles of the Crusades*, Guildford, 1996

Krey, C. *The First Crusade – Accounts of Eyewitnesses and Participants*, Gloucester, Mass., 1958 edn

Marzals, Sir F. *Memoirs of the Crusades – Villehardouin and de Joinville*, Herts., repr 1957

Odo of Deuil. *The Journey of Louis VII to the East*, ed. V.G. Berry, New York, 1948

Peters, E. *Christian Society and the Crusades*, Philadelphia, 1971

———. *The First Crusade – The Chronicles of Fulcher of Chartres and Other Source Materials*, Philadelphia, 1971

Raymond d'Aguilers. *Historia Francorum Qui Ceperunt Iherusalem*, tr. J.H. and L.L. Hill, Philadelphia, 1968

Riley-Smith, J. and L. (eds). *The Crusades: Idea and Reality*, London, 1981

Robert of Clari. *The Conquest of Constantinople*, tr. E.H. McNeal, New York, 1976

William of Tyre. *A History of Deeds done beyond the Sea*, ed. E.A. Babcock and A.C. Kray, Columbia Records of Civilization 35, 2 vols, New York, 1943

2. Modern Works

I have sub-divided this section into several categories. First, a number of works that help to set the context of the world in which the Crusading movement was born:

Barber, R. *The Knight & Chivalry*, London, 1974
Fossier, R. (ed.). *The Cambridge Illustrated History of the Middle Ages*, vols 1 and 2, tr. Cambridge, 1997
Holmes, G. *The Oxford Illustrated History of Medieval Europe*, Oxford, 1988
Norwich, J.J. *A Short History of Byzantium*, London, 1997

The social and religious factors that led to the development of the Crusades are complex, and cannot be adequately covered in a book the size of *God Wills It!*. For a greater understanding of these ideas, readers are pointed towards the following:

Bull, M. *Knightly Piety and the Lay Response to the First Crusade*, Oxford, 1993
Cowdrey, H. 'Pope Urban II's Preaching of the First Crusade' in *History*, Vol. 55, 1970
Erdmann, C. *The Origin of the Idea of Crusade*, tr. M.W. Baldwin and W. Goffart, Princeton, NJ, 1977
Riley-Smith, J. *The First Crusade and the Idea of Crusading*, London, 1986
——. *What were the Crusades?*, Basingstoke, 1992

There are many general histories of the Crusades available, and also a number of books that cover a wide range of topics over the entire period of the Crusades. These include:

Erbstosser, M. *The Crusades*, translated, Newton Abbot, 1978
Kedar, B. (ed.). *Outremer – Studies in the History of the Crusading Kingdom of Jerusalem*, Jerusalem, 1982
Maalouf, A. *The Crusades through Arab Eyes*, London, 1984
Mayer, H. *The Crusades*, translated, Oxford, 1978
Murphy, T. *The Holy War*, Ohio, 1976
Pernoud, R. *The Crusaders*, translated, London, 1963
Phillips, J. *Defenders of the Holy Land*, Oxford, 1996
Powell, J.M. (ed.). *Muslims under Latin Rule, 1100–1300*, Princeton, NJ, 1991
Prawer, J. *Crusader Institutions*, Oxford, 1980
Riley-Smith, J. *The Crusades*, London, 1978
—— (ed.). *The Oxford Illustrated History of the Crusades*, Oxford, 1995
Robinson, J. *Dungeon, Fire & Sword*, London, 1991
Runciman, S. *A History of the Crusades*, 3 vols, reissued by Penguin, Harmondsworth, 1971
Setton, K. *A History of the Crusades*, Madison, WI, 1975
Siberry, E. *Criticism of Crusading, 1095–1274*, Oxford, 1985
Smail, R. *The Crusaders*, London, 1973
Tyerman, C.J. *England and the Crusades, 1095–1588*, Chicago & London, 1988

Maalouf's work is very useful as it gives a Muslim perspective to the Crusades, while Runciman's volumes, although nearly half a century old, still offer a comprehensive and eminently readable narrative.

For military aspects of the Crusades, the reader is recommended to look at some of the publications listed below:

Hooper, N. and Bennett, M. *Cambridge Illustrated Atlas of Warfare in the Middle Ages 768–1487*, Cambridge, 1996
Kennedy, H. *Crusader Castles*, Cambridge, 1994
Koch, W.H. *Medieval Warfare*, London, 1978
Marshal, C. *Warfare in the Latin East*, Cambridge, 1992
Nicolle, D. *Arms and Armour of the Crusading Era, 1050–1350*, 2 vols, White Plains, NY 1988
——. *Medieval Warfare Source Book*, vol. 2, London, 1996
Oman, C. *The Art of War in the Middle Ages*, vol. 1, London, 1991 edn
Rogers, R. *Latin Siege Warfare in the Twelfth Century*, Oxford, 1992

Much has also been written on specific Crusades, and concerning individuals who were prominent in the Crusading movement. These works include:

France, J. *Victory in the East: A Military History of the First Crusade*, Cambridge, 1994, which provides a history of the First Crusade
Gervers, M. (ed.). *The Second Crusade and the Cistercians*, New York, 1992

There are several works available covering the Third Crusade and the key protagonists in it, including:

Ehrenkreutz, A. *Saladin*, Albany, 1972
Gillingham, J. *Richard the Lionheart*, London, 1976
Kedar, B. (ed.). *The Horns of Hattin*, Jerusalem, 1992
Lyons, M.C. and Jackson, D.E.P. *Saladin; The Politics of Holy War*, Cambridge, 1982
Nicolle, D. *Saladin and the Saracens*, London, 1986

For the complex details of the Fourth Crusade, the reader should refer to:

Godfrey, J. *1204 – The Unholy Crusade*, Oxford, 1980
Queller, D. *The Latin Conquest of Constantinople*, USA, 1971

Finally, for the later Crusading period, readers are recommended to refer to the following:

Abulafia, D. *Frederick II: A Medieval Emperor*, Cambridge, 1983
Powell, T.M. *Anatomy of a Crusade 1213–21*, Philadelphia, 1986
Richard, J. *Saint Louis, Crusader King of France*, ed. S.D. Lloyd, tr. J Birrell, Cambridge, 1992

Index